Recent archaeological excavations in Europe

Contributors

Josef Poulík   Czechoslovakia

Wolfgang Kimmig   German Federal Republic

Asbjørn E. Herteig   Norway

Olaf Olsen   Denmark

Wilhelm Holmqvist   Sweden

M. U. and W. T. Jones   England

A. A. Formazov, E. N. Chernykh,
D. B. Shelov, R. L. Rozenfeldt
and B. A. Rybakov   USSR

Fernand Benoît   France

Pieter Modderman   Netherlands

Laszlo Vértes   Hungary

Konrad Jażdżewski   Poland

Recent archaeological excavations in Europe

edited by

Rupert Bruce-Mitford MA, D.Litt., V-PSA

*Keeper of Medieval and Later Antiquities
in the British Museum*

Routledge & Kegan Paul
London and Boston

First published in 1975
by Routledge & Kegan Paul Ltd
Broadway House, 68–74 Carter Lane,
London EC4V 5EL and
9 Park Street,
Boston, Mass. 02108, USA
Set in Lumitype Imprint
and printed in Great Britain by
Butler & Tanner Ltd
Frome and London
© Routledge & Kegan Paul Ltd 1975

ISBN 0 7100 7963 X

Contents

Plates

Figures

Notes on the contributors

Josef Poulík, D.Phil., Vice-President of the Czechoslovak Academy of Sciences, Professor at the University of Brno, Czechoslovakia, and Director of the Institute of Archaeology (The Czechoslovak Academy of Sciences).

Wolfgang Kimmig, Professor of Prehistory at the University of Tübingen (German Federal Republic) and Director of the University's Institute for Pre- and Proto-History. Born 1910 at Constance, studied at the Universities of Berlin, Marburg and Freiburg (Ph.D. 1935). Member of the Deutsches Archäologisches Institut, Honorary Corresponding Member of the Prehistoric Society of Great Britain, Foreign Member of the Istituto di Studi Etruschi ed Italici and of the Istituto Italiano di Pre- e Protostoria and Corresponding Member of the Schweizerische Gesellschaft für Urgeschichte.

Publications include *Die Urnenfelderkultur in Baden* (1940), *Vorzeit an Rhein und Donau* (1958), *Die Heuneburg an der oberen Donau* (1968). Author of many papers on the Early Iron Age in Europe.

Asbjorn E. Herteig, Mag. Art., Keeper at the University Museum, Bergen, Norway. Directed excavations at the medieval sites of Kaupangs Veoy (Romsdal) and Borgund (Sunnmore) and the Hanseatic traders' site, Bryggen, in Bergen. Author of many papers on Medieval Archaeology in Norway.

Olaf Olsen, Professor of Medieval Archaeology at Aarhus, Denmark, 1971. Born 1928. Graduated from Copenhagen University in 1953 and took his Doctorate in history and archaeology in 1966, with a thesis on pagan cult sites in Scandinavia. On the staff of the National Museum, Copenhagen, from 1950 to 1971. Excavator of numerous Danish Churches, including wooden churches of the Viking period and, with Øle Crumlin-Pedersen, of the Viking ships at Skuldelev in Roskilde Fjord. Took over the excavation of the Viking fortress at Fyrkat in 1958 on the death of C. G. Schultz, whose assistant he was from 1949 to 1954. Fellow of the Society of Antiquaries of London, 1961.

Wilhelm Holmqvist, Professor, Stockholm, archaeologist and art-historian. Born 1905. Doctor of Philosophy, 1940. Assistant Professor in Northern and Related Archaeology, Stockholm University, 1940–56. Keeper of the Iron Age Department, National Historical Museum from 1953. Author of *Kunstprobleme der Merowingerzeit* (*Art Problems of the Merovingian Era*) (Stockholm, 1939) and many other books. Director of the Helgö excavations since 1954. Hon. Fellow of the Society of Antiquaries of London, 1968.

M. U. Jones (Mrs), Fellow of the Society of Antiquaries of London, Archaeological Consultant to the Department of the Environment since 1956. Born 1916. Began field archaeology when an undergraduate in the School of Geography, University of Liverpool. Has directed the excavation at Mucking since 1965.

W. T. Jones, ARPS. Fellow of the Society of Antiquaries of London. Born 1912. Photographic specialist. Has taken part in archaeological excavations since 1933 and is now Archaeological Consultant to the Department of the Environment. Has been responsible for the excavation of more than a thousand graves at Mucking since 1965.

A. A. Formazov, MA (Historical Science), Senior Scientific Worker at the Institute of Archaeology, Moscow.

E. N. Chernykh, MA (Historical Science), Senior Scientific Worker at the Institute of Archaeology, Moscow.

D. B. Shelov, MA (Historical Science), Senior Scientific Worker at the Institute of Archaeology, Moscow.

R. A. Rozenfeldt, MA (Historical Science), Scientific Worker at the Institute of Archaeology, Moscow.

Boris Aleksandrovich Rybakov, historian and archaeologist. Born 1908, graduate of Moscow University. Academician, Professor at Moscow University since 1943; Director of the Institute of the History of Material Culture, now the Institute of Archaeology. Foreign member of the Czechoslovak Academy of Sciences. Co-author and editor of vols 1–6 of the *History of the USSR*. Other published works include *Handicrafts of Ancient Russia* (1949); (co-author) *The Cultural History of Ancient Russia* (1948–51); (ed.) *An Outline History of the Russian Village in the 10th–13th Centuries* (1956); (ed.) *Chernyakhov Culture* (1960); *Ancient Russia, Legends and Chronicles* (1963); *The First Centuries of Russian History* (1964); *History of the USSR*, vol. 12 (1961), etc. Badge of Honour, Stalin prize winner, 1949 and 1952.

Director of excavations in Vshchizh, Vyshgorod, Moscow, Zvenigorod, Chernigov, etc.

Fernand Benoît, Director of Antiquities in Provence and Corsica. Member of the Institute. Born at Avignon, 1892. Educated at the University of Paris where he obtained a diploma in archives and palaeography; and at the French School at Rome. Senior official dealing with Press and publicity for the Resident General in Tunis and Rabat. Director of the Library and Museums at Arles and of the Borely Museum at Marseille.

Pieter Modderman, Professor of Prehistory in the University of Leiden, Netherlands. Formerly Inspector for Prehistoric Archaeology in the State Service for Archaeological Investigation, Amersfoort. Born 1919, studied in the Universities of Utrecht and Groningen. Publications include many papers on the Neolithic, Bronze and Iron Ages and the Roman period.

Laszlo Vértes. Dr Vértes died prematurely and as his career does not figure adequately in reference books I include a brief obituary, for which I am indebted to my colleague Mr Gale de G. Sieveking, FSA. *(Ed.)*

Dr Laszlo Vértes spent his professional career at the Hungarian National Museum at Budapest, with the exception of a period after 1956, when with many other intellectual men with liberal views, he was constrained to spend some years in a manual occupation. He made many outstanding contributions to European palaeolithic archaeology both before and after this period and was responsible for a number of successful excavations, brilliantly chosen to throw light on particular problems and published with expedition. Dr Vertes first came to the notice of west European scholars in connection with his Aurignacian excavations at Istallosko, radio carbon samples from which were submitted to Groningen for dating in the early days of isotopic enrichment. The early dates obtained for the Hungarian Aurignacian caused much controversy but have since been vindicated. Other excavations carried out by Vértes include those at the only upper palaeolithic paint mine and a Mousterian site at Tata, related to the so-called Micro-Mousterian and distinguished by its extremely small tools, made mostly of quartz. Vértes always said that without the experience of Tata he would never have recognised that the implements at Vértesszöllös were not natural. Besides excavation, Vértes carried out some extremely enlightening research into some tool-flaking processes and into the statistical analysis of stone industries. He was a man of varied talents including music, poetry and sculpture. Palaeontologists will remember his model of the head of Vértesszöllös man.

Vértes was always worried that foreign archaeologists would think that he had named the site of Vértesszöllös after himself and would explain that it was a place name, and that Vértes, in Hungary, was a name as common as Smith in England.

The imaginatively designed and organised open-air museum which Vértes himself conceived and brought into being on the site of his discoveries is one of the most exciting places to visit in Hungary and is a fitting memorial to a great European archaeologist.

Konrad Jażdżewski, Professor of Archaeology at the University of Lódź and Director of the Museum of Archaeology and Ethnography at Lódź (Poland); formerly Director of the State Archaeological Museum at Warsaw. Born in 1908. Studied at the University of Poznań. Member and Vice-President (until 1971) of the Polish Archaeological Society. Honorary Fellow of the Society of Antiquaries of Scotland. Member of the Jutland Archaeological Society. Counsellor of the Palaeological Association of Japan. Author of numerous books and articles, including *Poland* in the *Ancient Peoples and Places* series. Polish editor of *Inventaria Archaeologica, Acta Archaeologica Lodziensia* and *Prace i Materialy Muzeum Archeologicznego i Etnograficznego w Lodzi.* Director of great excavations at Brześć Kujawski and Gdańsk. Particularly interested in the neolithic, migration and early medieval periods.

Introduction

The task of selecting eleven excavations to represent contemporary archaeological fieldwork in Europe is invidious and difficult. Well over a thousand excavations are either in progress or recently concluded. Some countries must go unrepresented, and many sites of notable importance and technical achievement be omitted. I have tried to ensure that the east European countries are adequately represented and the balance not unduly weighted towards the west, and also that the book reflects, in some degree, the vast span of archaeology, from the Palaeolithic to the Middle Ages. In scope the book is essentially north and east European, since it does not cover the classical civilisations. Their inclusion would so widen the scope as to make it impossible to achieve any sort of unity or balance. Several of the chosen sites, such as the Heuneburg (W. Germany), Entremont (France) and Mucking (Britain) do nevertheless have Roman episodes or connections with the classical world. East European representation would have been stronger had a chapter projected from East Germany, on the sacred site at Oberdorla, in Thuringia, been forthcoming. This would have made an interesting comparison with the Celtic oppidum and sanctuary at Entremont, in Provence, the subject of Dr Benoît's chapter. Some outstanding sites have been omitted because they are accessibly published elsewhere. This was the case with the unique Danubian settlement of Lepenski Vir (Yugoslavia), which has revealed Europe's earliest monumental sculpture. Srejovic's well-illustrated book on these excavations, in English, appeared in 1972.

We are extremely fortunate in obtaining from the Soviet Union a broad survey of recent fieldwork under the headings *Palaeolithic, Neolithic and Bronze Age, Scythians, Sarmatians and Greeks,* and *Mediaeval.* Work in the Soviet Union has been proceeding on an immense scale, and with few exceptions is unknown in the west. A notable Soviet parallel with England has been in the study of the development of towns in the early mediaeval period. Intensive work at York, Southampton, Norwich, Winchester, Oxford, King's Lynn and elsewhere in this country is matched by a similar intensive study of the origins and growth of Moscow, Kiev, Galich, Lyubech, Polotsk, Minsk, Novgorod (especially) and many other sites.

Many of the excavations that are described in this book have been prolonged campaigns leaving a formidable task of publication yet to be accomplished. Herteig's work at the mediaeval Hanseatic port at Bryggen, Bergen (Norway), has been in progress for eighteen years. Holmqvist's work at the settlement of the fifth to eighth century A.D. on Helgö, in Lake Malar, near Stockholm (Sweden), began in 1954. At both places the finds, which have run into tens of thousands of items, and the structures uncovered give a new complexion to the archaeology not only of their countries but of northern Europe in their periods. Helgö, a place of many workshops and startling imports (including an enamelled crozier from Ireland and a bronze Buddha from India), has already given rise to a series of international conferences. Poulík's work at the remarkable site of Mikulčice, Czechoslovakia (chapter I), has been in progress since 1954; yet less than 3 per cent of its whole area has so far been explored. The ten very early churches so far found suggest, in their architecture, influences both from Byzantium and the British Isles. By contrast, in discussing four astonishing Viking camps, Olaf Olsen has dealt with a class of monument rather than a single site; a class first revealed by Nörlund's work at Trelleborg in 1937–9, and now given a sound historical explanation. A neolithic chapter envisaged for Switzerland, a nodal area of European movements, could not, unfortunately, be completed.

Finally, Britain is represented by perhaps the most remarkable of recent Anglo-Saxon excavations, the settlement-sites and cemeteries at Mucking, near East Tilbury, in Essex, revealed by crop-marks on a gravel spur dominating the lower reaches of the Thames estuary. This site does much to illuminate the lives and origins of the first Germanic settlers to come to Britain. It also illustrates, although a 'rescue dig', the advantages of the comprehensive exploration over sampling. Cemetery Two has been excavated in its entirety.

None of the great continental excavations described have been rescue digs. They are often massive undertakings backed by the state, which have yielded enough in depth and proportion to enable the true nature of the sites to emerge. In this country we owe a great debt to the Department of the Environment and its Inspectorate of Ancient Monuments for their support of rescue work. Government expenditure in Britain on rescue digs alone is now approaching £1,500,000 annually. Occasionally a site, initially investigated under threat of destruction, can, thanks to the Department, still be the object of thorough, even complete, exploration. We cannot, however, compete with some of the major field projects of our east European colleagues, let alone the gigantic three hundred volume corpus of finds under way in Russia, involving every archaeologist in the Soviet Union.

Translation has been a major problem in the production of this book. I have been fortunate in securing as translators a number of well-known archaeologists who are also linguists and in obtaining archaeological specialists to revise texts submitted in English.

I would like, finally, to pay a special tribute to the work of Miss Marilyn Luscombe in preparing this book for the press, after its delay through a series of near-fatal accidents. If, in certain cases, the chapters, in spite of revisions in proof, are not as up to the minute as their authors might wish, the blame for this is not to be laid upon them.

London, 1975   Rupert Bruce-Mitford

Acknowledgments

I am grateful for the assistance, in the translation and revision of English texts of foreign language chapters, to the following: chapter I: English text extensively revised, Miss Marilyn Luscombe; chapter II: translation from German, Peter S. Wells, Cambridge, USA; chapter III: translation from Norwegian, Mrs Toni Ramholt, Bergen; chapter IV: translation from Danish, Mrs J. C. D. Olsen; chapter V: translation from Swedish, Dr Helen Clarke, FSA; chapter VII: translation from Russian, Dr Michael Thompson, FSA; chapter VIII: translation from French, Miss Marilyn Luscombe; chapter IX: English text extensively revised, Miss Marilyn Luscombe; chapter X: English text extensively revised, after the death of Dr Laszlo Vértes, by Gale de G. Sieveking, FSA; chapter XI: translation from German, Professor Anthony Birley, FSA.

The following pictures have been kindly lent by Walter de Gruyter, Berlin, and the Directors of the Römisch-Germanische Kommission in Frankfurt: Plates VIIIa; IXb: Figures 19 (a, b), 20 (a), 22, 24, 26, 27, 28.

Chapter I

Mikulčice:[1] capital of the lords of Great Moravia

Josef Poulík

At the beginning of the ninth century a new state began to form in the territory inhabited by the Western Slavs, between the Empire of the Eastern Franks (that is, the Eastern part of the Carolingian Empire) and Byzantium. Its centre lay north of the Danube in the middle of present-day Czechoslovakia. This state (Fig. 1) was referred to by the Byzantine Emperor Constantine Porphyrogenetos, in his book *De administrando imperii*, as 'Great Moravia'. It was ruled by the Princess Mojmír, Rastislav and Svatopluk of the Mojmír dynasty. In the second half of the century the rulers of Great Moravia extended their power east, west, north and south (Fig. 1). The boundaries of Great Moravia, however, were never firmly established and historians are still guessing its exact limits. The history and fate of this state, its military and diplomatic conflicts and its clashes with the Frankish Empire, with the Bavarian ecclesiastical hierarchy and with the Roman Curia, are referred to to some extent in Latin written sources of western origin, such as the *Annales Fuldenses*, *Annales regni Francorum, De conversione Baoariorum et Carantanorum,* papa letters, etc. Records also exist written in Glagolitic, which is a Slavonic script ingeniously constructed by the brothers Cyril and Methodius, missionaries from Thessalonica, who were sent to Great Moravia in 863 by the Byzantine Emperor Michael III, at the request of Prince Rastislav, to explain the gospel to his people in their own Slavonic language. The two teachers, of whom Cyril died in a monastery in Rome, while Methodius became Archbishop of Moravia, laid the foundations of a national Slav literature and culture by translating the Bible into Slavonic and introducing (in Moravia) the local Slavonic language into the liturgy. These were events of great significance in Central Europe in the second half of the ninth century,

[1] Phonetic pronunciation, 'Mĭkŭlcheatzer' – Ed.

for services prescribed for public worship were at that time conducted in the west in Latin and in the Byzantine regions in Greek.

Czechoslovak and non-Czechoslovak historians alike, using some hundred written records, have failed in their efforts to give a clear picture of the political history and life of Great Moravia. Czechoslovak archaeologists, however, trying to solve these problems in the course of the past three decades, have concentrated on its central region (Fig. 2), which was characterized by a series of fortified settlements, strongholds and large administrative and industrial centres, and have been more successful. Their efforts have yielded valuable and surprising new results, which throw new light not only upon the history of the Great Moravian State but also on the history of east-central Europe. It would be a matter of great interest to review

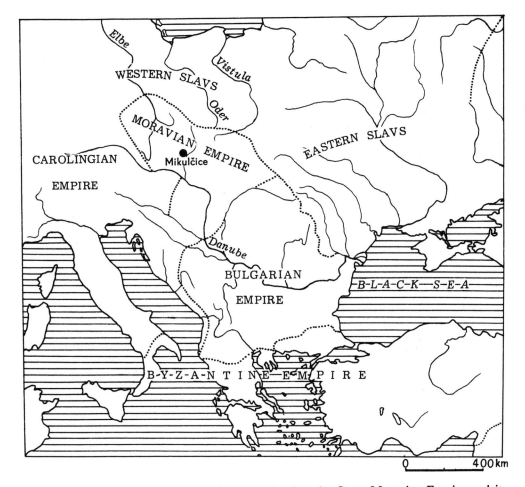

Figure 1   Mikulčice, Czechoslovakia: Map showing the Great Moravian Empire and its neighbours

all the new archaeological discoveries that bear on Great Moravia but, as the scope of this chapter is limited, we shall have to confine ourselves to an account of one of the most important and interesting of the Great Moravian fortified settlements, Mikulčice, which lies in the south of Moravia, about 120 km north of the Danube (Figs 1–2).

Approximately 5 km south-east of the modern village of Mikulčice on the right bank of the river Morava, there is a site which, from time immemorial, has been called *Valy* (ramparts) by the local people. The ruins of the ramparts – *valy* – are still quite clear on the ground (Fig. 3). Czechoslovak archaeologists already knew of this site in the last century and concluded, from fragments of pottery found on the surface inside the fortified area, that it was a Slav stronghold dating back to the eleventh to twelfth centuries of our era. For years, however, the *Valy* of Mikulčice remained archaeologically unexplored. Excavation was not begun until 1954 and is not yet complete. Although excavation is still in progress, we shall endeavour to

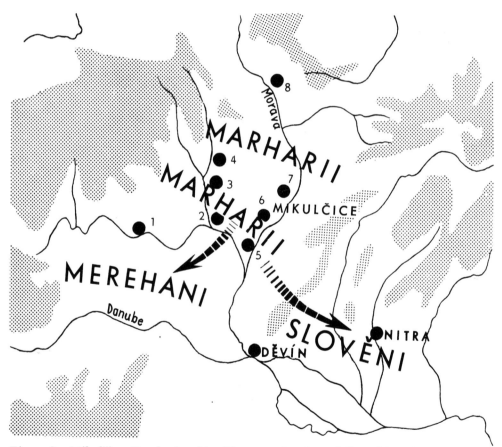

Figure 2   Mikulčice, Czechoslovakia: The central region of Great Moravia and its strongholds

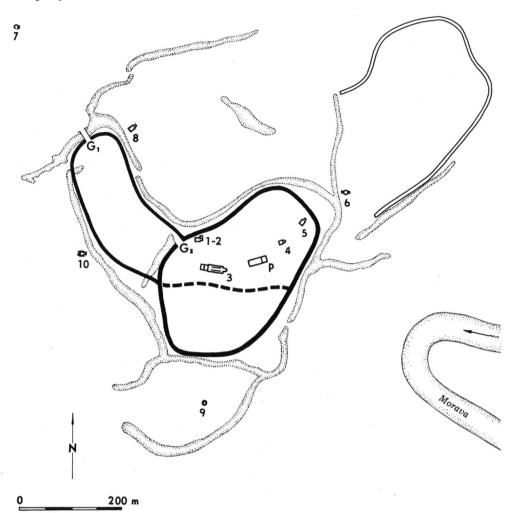

Figure 3   Mikulčice, Czechoslovakia: The ducal stronghold and its sub-burgium
(1–10 – churches, P – palace, G₁–G₂ – gates)

present a brief account at least of the results so far, and to explain their contribution to the history of Great Moravia, as well as to that of central Europe of the ninth century. At the outset, it should be said that the situation is not so clear and simple as it seemed to earlier archaeologists who knew of the site but did not suspect that finds would date back to periods earlier than the eleventh and twelfth centuries.

The excavations at Mikulčice, which cover a large area, have demonstrated that in the seventh to eighth centuries a large Slav settlement, extending over 40 to 50 hectares, existed on the site of the Mikulčice *Valy.* In its middle there was a stronghold, covering about four hectares, fortified by sizable oaken palisades arranged in four to five rows (Fig. 3). The approach to these defences, which were about 25 m in depth, was protected by the bed of the river Morava. The entrance to the fortified area lay to the north-west. At this point, a settlement nearly 3 hectares in extent (Fig. 3) protected by a simple palisade of oak stakes more than 5 m in height, lay closely connected with the fortified enclosure. The settlement, too, was difficult of access, because of the river flowing round it. Today, the river bed is dry and about 6 m below the surface but in those days it was in full flood. This situation is advantageous to archaeologists, for the muddy and sandy deposits of the river bed yield wooden objects and other organic matter not preserved in the soil of the settlement itself.

In the alluvial deposits of the river bed, palaeobotanists have found trees, bushes and plants, the identification of which makes it possible to reconstruct the flora of the Morava basin more than a thousand years ago. It is an interesting fact that cucumber seeds datable to the Great Moravian period have been found in this alluvium, although botanists believed that cucumbers were not cultivated in central Europe until the late Middle Ages. Grape pips have also been found, which would suggest that vines grew in the neighbourhood of Mikulčice in the ninth century, perhaps earlier. Such facts are of great interest, but archaeologists could not establish them without the co-operation of other scientists, especially natural historians. We also worked closely with hydrologists and engineers, without whose help we could not get along at all, since the water table is less than 1 m below the present surface and our trenches began to fill with water at this depth. The water could only be removed by a system of wells and highly efficient drainage pumps. Without them, we could not have discovered certain parts of the fortification, nor the timber supporting piers of a 5 m wide bridge in the north-westernmost tip of the settlement (Fig. 3). This settlement was in existence in the seventh to eighth centuries but did not lose its importance in the late Great Moravian period. We will return to it later.

The whole residential complex, outlined above, lost its rural character and became what may be described as a stronghold. This conclusion from the excavations does not contradict the evidence of the written sources. The Frankish chronicler Fredegar tells us, in a passage important for the history of east-central Europe, that 'in the 40th year of Chlotochar's reign, a man named Samo, of Frankish nationality, from the region of Senon, gathered around himself a number of merchants and set out with them into the country of Slavs called Vinedi.' From Fredegar we further learn that Samo led the revolt of the Slavs (Vinedi) against the Avars and became king of the Slavs (until 658–9). Mention is made in connection with Samo of *Wogastisburg*, a stronghold which some historians think lay at the westernmost tip of Czechoslovak territory. However, no one has so far located this stronghold, where the armies of the Frankish King Dagobert were defeated by the Slavs in 631. The name *Wogastisburg* seems to imply the existence of fortified strongholds — centres of power, industry and trade — in Slav territory as early as the first half of the seventh century. At Mikulčice, we have succeeded in discovering just such a fortified settlement from Samo's time. This does not, however, mean that we have discovered here, on the lower course of the river Morava, the historical *Wogastisburg*.

The importance of the latest archaeological discoveries at Mikulčice, which help us to a better understanding of the economic and social developments in these parts of central Europe in the seventh to eighth centuries, is underlined by the fact that production of cast metal was concentrated in the settlement in this period (Plate I, nos 2–6). This is shown by the discovery of small furnaces and metal-casting work-shops, where gold, bronze and iron were smelted (Fig. 4). This industry derives from long established tradition in this region, for south Moravia had been in direct contact with the Roman provinces of Pannonia and Noricum. It is especially note-worthy that these workshops were producing cast mountings and fastenings that, in archaeological literature, used to be called Avar, that is, made by the Avar ethnic group. Workshops resembling those unearthed at Mikulčice have never been dis-covered in the Carpathian basin where the Avars were settled. These cast mountings and fastenings, whose ornaments contain antique Byzantine as well as east Mediterranean elements, are at present not known in central Asia either, in the region from which Avar horsemen came to settle in the territory of present-day Hungary, in the middle of the sixth century of our era. It seems to have been the fashion of the Slavs to combine Avar garments with richly mounted leather belts.

In the Mikulčice settlement of the pre-Great Moravian period, that is, during the seventh to eighth centuries, there occurred, in addition to the finds that demonstrate the existence of a local metal-working industry, a characteristic group of iron and bronze spurs with hooks. Spurs of this shape are known from Poland and the western Ukraine, where they occur up to the ninth century. They may, there-fore, be regarded as characteristic of the territories inhabited by the Slavs. More of these spurs have been found at Mikulčice than anywhere else and they consequently would seem to furnish evidence for the existence of a significant and privileged class of horsemen and warriors. We will probably not be wrong if we consider these spurs as an essential element in the equipment of warriors, that is to say, of the members of the military retinue of the tribal prince and of the holder of the stronghold of Mikulčice.

The end of the eighth century saw the climax of the struggle between the various Slav tribes inhabiting the regions north of the middle Danube. It was the Moravians with their central stronghold at Mikulčice who emerged victorious from the struggle. Their victory resulted initially in the establishment of a rather small Moravian state; but in the course of the ninth century they extended their power and influence into neighbouring territories. According to the *Annales regni Francorum*, the assembly at Frankfurt on Main, convened by the Frankish king Louis the Pious, was attended, amongst other delegates, by *legati Marvanorum* – ambassadors (delegates) of the Moravians. The strengthening and further fortification of the Moravian strongholds and consequently of Mikulčice, too, must have been associated with changes and political events taking place in Europe at that time. The threat

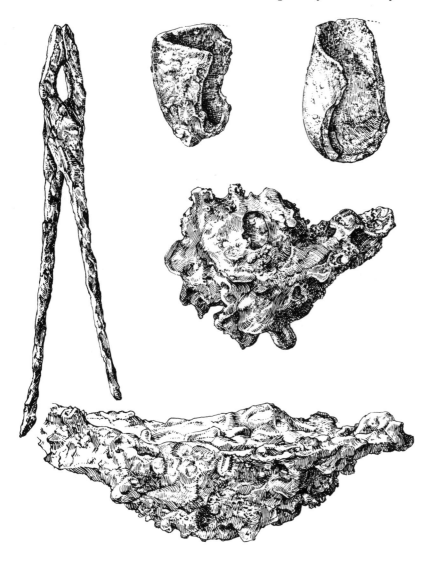

Figure 4   Mikulčice, Czechoslovakia: Iron tongs, crucibles, and a mass of melted bronze and iron, found in the ruins of a metal-worker's workshop on the site of a pre-Great Moravian settlement (seventh to eighth centuries) (Scales: 2:3)

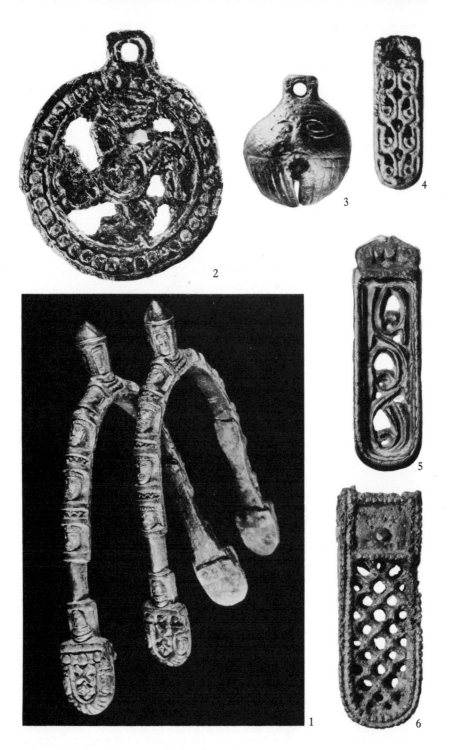

Plate I *Mikulčice, Czechoslovakia:* Gilt spurs, first half of the ninth century (1), bronze bell (3) and cast bronze strap-ends (2, 4, 5, 6) (Scales: 1, approx. 4:5; 2–6, 1:1)

of possible invasion by the armies of the Frankish Empire was probably behind it.

On the site of the stronghold of Mikulčice, which had been fortified by timber palisades, a new stronghold, about 3 hectares larger, was erected. The timber palisades were replaced by an outer stone-faced wall, about 3 m thick, built up of timber boxes or compartments filled with earth and stone. The wall was about 8 m high. The settlement to the north, associated with the stronghold, was also fortified in the same way.

The site of the Great Moravian stronghold covered an area of 7 hectares. About one-fifth has been explored. The foundations of five churches have been uncovered and the remains of an oblong building, apparently a palace (Fig. 3). The foundations of these buildings were sunk into the seventh to ninth century stratum. On the western side of the stronghold near the entrance gate we discovered, in 1956, the remains of the foundations of a smaller church (designated as the second church) with oblong nave and rectangular presbytery, the outer length of the building being 12·60 m. The northern side of the presbytery was connected with an almost square annexe (Fig. 5). This annexe was built of rough sandstone laid on mortar. The outer and inner walls of the church were plastered. In the nave and presbytery were the remains of the original floor, a paving of sandstone slabs. At first it appeared that the terrain below the sandstone paving and in its vicinity was sterile, but subsequent excavations proved this to be wrong. At a depth of about 1 m inside the nave and the presbytery we discovered a rather buckled cast mortar floor, with two transverse grooves, which no doubt belonged to the first construction stage of the church.

Following the gently sloping terrain north-west of the presbytery of the second church, we unearthed the foundations and the destroyed masonry of another building of rough sandstone laid on mortar. The ground plan of this building is not preserved. It is designated as the first Mikulčice church and must have been built at the beginning of the ninth century. In dating the second Mikulčice church we base our evidence on the total stratigraphy of the site and naturally on the finds discovered in the graves in its vicinity. More than two hundred graves have so far been unearthed. Approximately half the graves contained rich finds, such as silver and gilt ear-rings enriched with granular filigree work, silver- and bronze-gilt buttons (Plate III, nos 5–6) (typically Great Moravian jewels) with ornamental foliate designs (Fig. 7); iron spurs, some of which are inlaid with copper and silver; iron daggers; knives, etc. Two graves contained an unusual wealth of ornament. In one of them we found two heavily gilded bronze spurs richly decorated with human masks. In this grave there were also two gilt buttons with an ornamental foliate design all over the surface. The gilded spurs, which are of Carolingian shape, must have been made at the beginning of the ninth century.

On the western side of the second Mikulčice church we discovered the grave of a five-year-old boy buried with a leather belt with silver-gilt fastenings. The tongue-shaped metal belt-end is particularly interesting. Its outer face is decorated with very coarse filigree. The inner face is the more remarkable, bearing engraved on its smooth surface the figure of a saint, priest or bishop, *orans* (i.e., with hands raised in the gesture of prayer) (Plate II, nos 1, 1a). The shape of the end-piece is Carolingian, while the engraved figure of the *orans* appears Byzantine.

Two noblemen's graves containing swords are particularly important in dating the débris of the first building stage of the second church. The first was discovered under the cast mortar floor of its nave. Along the left side of the skeleton of a man

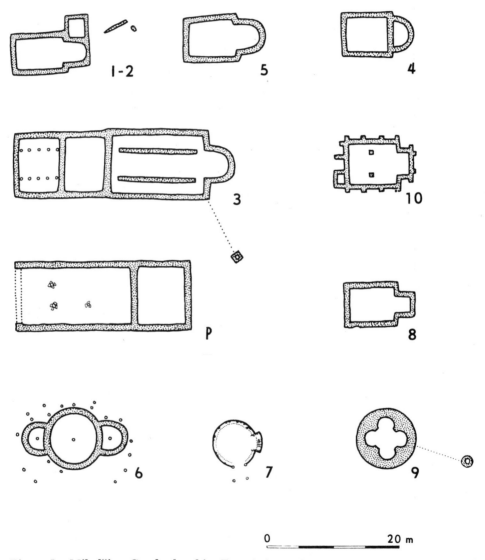

Figure 5   Mikulčice, Czechoslovakia: Foundations of ten churches (all ninth century)

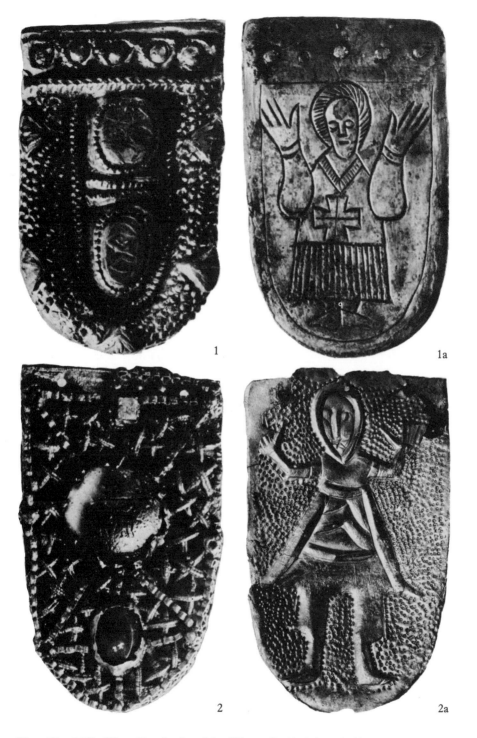

Plate II *Mikulčice, Czechoslovakia:* Silver-gilt (1–1a) and silver (2–2a) strap-ends with engraved figures in the gesture of prayer (*orantes*); ninth century (Scales: approx. 3:2)

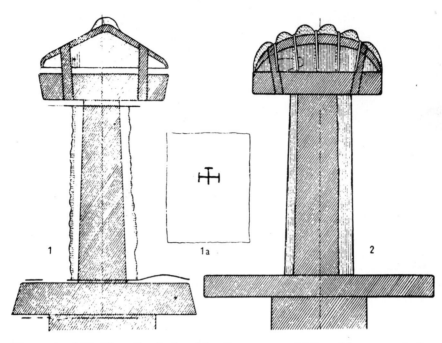

Figure 6 Mikulčice, Czechoslovakia: Reconstructed hilts of iron swords found in Great Moravian graves. Note the inlaid gold cross on the blade of the sword No. 1 (1a) (early ninth century) (Scale: 2 : 3)

of about nineteen years of age lay a heavy double-edged iron sword; a pair of iron spurs lay beside the feet. From the shape of the pommel it may be concluded that the sword dates back to the first quarter of the ninth century at the latest. Radiographs revealed an inlaid gold cross on the blade (Fig. 6, nos 1, 1a). A cross of this kind is referred to in an interesting entry written by an unknown monk at the monastery of St Gall in Switzerland. The entry reads:

> The sword was encased first with a (wooden) sheath, then with leather and third in very white linen reinforced with light wax, so that, with its glittering cross for destroying the heathen, it might be long preserved . . . (cited in H. Reinerth (ed.), *Vorgeschichte der deutschen Stämme*, I, Berlin, 1941, chapter 'Die Franken' by R. Stampfuss, p. 223).

All these features were present on the sword found at Mikulčice. This text tells us that the unknown monk of St Gall was well acquainted with swords and their manufacture and suggests that these weapons were made in monastic workshops. It is further known that Frankish swords were exported to and sold in the east, that is, in the regions inhabited by the Slavs, and interdicts also survive forbidding this export and sale. In the so-called interdict of Thionville of A.D. 805, it is explicitly

Plate III *Mikulčice, Czechoslovakia:* Lead (1), silver (2), and gilt bronze (3) crosses, gold pendant (4) and gold buttons (5–6), eighth century (Scales: 1, 2, 1 : 1; 3–6, slightly enlarged)

Figure 7   Mikulčice, Czechoslovakia: Ornamental design from typical Great Moravian buttons of the late ninth century (Scale: slightly enlarged)

stated that 'arms', meaning swords, 'must not be exported and sold to Slavs and Avars'. Worth mentioning is another interdict, that of the Bonn Capitulary of 811, according to which, 'bishops, abbots, priests and church custodians are forbidden to sell or give weapons to a foreigner'.

The second grave, dating from the first construction phase of the second church, contained the skeleton of a nobleman with a sword lying along the right-hand side. The shape of the pommel shows that it is a so-called 'type K' sword (Fig. 6, no. 2). The late Professor Holger Arbman, an outstanding Swedish archaeologist, studied and analysed these heavy weapons. On the basis of his study of swords found in noblemen's graves near the Church of the Virgin Mary at Biskupije, near Knin in Dalmatia, he concluded that the swords, and consequently the graves in which they were found, dated back to about the year 800. In a new study of the finds at Biskupije Dr Zd. Vinski, an archaeologist from Zagreb, suggests that these sword types belong to the end of the eighth or the beginning of the ninth century, confirming Arbman's opinion.

On the basis of the grave finds, then, it may be presumed that the second Mikulčice church, which had two construction stages, already existed in the years 840 to 860, before the arrival of the two missionaries, Cyril and Methodius, in Moravia. The ground plan of the second Mikulčice church (Fig. 5, nos 1–2) resembles that of the church unearthed near the village of Modrá (not far from Staré Město) about 50 km north of the Mikulčice stronghold. Archaeologists believe that the church near Modrá dates from about A.D. 850 or even from the first half of the ninth century. The late Professor J. Cibulka, a Czech historian who specialised in art history, dated it to the year 800 on the basis of sporadic finds of belt fastenings and fittings and associated its foundation with the Insular missionaries who played a great role in Christianising the Frankish world. Foreign scholars do not seem to think it likely that the Insular missions influenced Moravia directly. Most of the parallels for church ground plans with rectangular presbyteries are known from Carolingian areas, where the Insular arts and crafts of the eighth century certainly left deep marks, but the direct influence of Insular arts and crafts in Great Moravia appears to have been small.

Following the uncovering of the foundations of these two churches (the first and second Mikulčice churches) at the north-western side of the stronghold *Na valech*, investigations were continued eastwards almost as far as its centre, where traces of destroyed masonry with fragments of mortar and plaster appeared immediately below the surface. Among this débris, as amongst the ruins of the first and second churches already described, we discovered numerous pits. Their shapes vary and apart from the occasional semi-dugouts (*Grubenhäuser*) they cannot be regarded as dwellings. They are mostly associated with the pre-Great Moravian, that is, seventh- to eighth-century, settlement. One of the striking features of our excavation was that as it progressed eastwards, towards the extensive building débris in the centre of the stronghold, so the number of graves sunk into the structures of lowest layer increased. This in turn focused attention on the building débris, amongst which we hoped to find the foundations of some ecclesiastical building. We did indeed unearth the foundations of a three-nave church (35 m in length and 9 m in width) oriented from west to east (Fig. 5, no. 3). West of the three-nave eastern part, with its slightly elongated semi-circular apse, is a *narthex* (vestibule); and further west is another room, most probably the atrium (forecourt) in which parts of wooden posts supporting the roofings were found.

About 15 m south of the apse of the three-nave church, the ruins of another smaller building were found. Its ground plan was not preserved but in its middle there were the remains of a square well-like cistern, into which ground water penetrated. These structures, taken together, seem to have formed a complex that must have been connected with a baptistery. It seems probable that the three-nave church (basilica), so far the largest ecclesiastical building of the Great Moravian period known (there are sixteen in all, ten at Mikulčice, five at Staré Město, and one at Pohansko, near Břeclav), may have had the function of an episcopal church. In the three-nave church we found burial chambers in the walls. The walls of the chambers themselves were damaged. It may be presumed that at the beginning of the tenth century, when the state of Great Moravia was destroyed by the Magyar invasion, the graves were plundered and anything valuable, especially the gold objects, removed. Single gold jewels found in the graves seem to have been part of sets of jewellery which were buried with the bodies. Two graves were discovered in the north aisle. One had been completely plundered. The second had apparently contained the interment of a woman furnished with gold jewellery. These seem to have been ducal graves. In the nave proper was a burial-chamber containing the skeleton of a nobleman. A heavy iron sword lay at his left side, a scramasax (a one-edged sword) and a pair of iron spurs were at his feet. Three robbed graves, containing only vestiges of once rich grave-goods, were unearthed in the *narthex*.

More than four hundred graves, mostly orientated west–east, were excavated around the three-nave church. Near the foundation walls they were sometimes superimposed in several layers. The graves were reinforced with timber or sandstone slabs but some resembled the walled burial chambers found inside. Some graves were more deeply sunk than others into the seventh- to eighth-century structures of the older pre-Great Moravian settlement. About half the graves so far explored contained no finds at all, but some were extremely rich. Six graves, presumably of noblemen, contained swords and spurs. Other male graves contained iron axes (Fig. 10) and spears, as well as bronze and iron spurs, some inlaid with silver. Iron spurs, some of them silver-plated, were found in the graves of boys of three to five years old. The presence of spurs in their graves suggests that the boys belonged to the ruling class. In some of the male graves that contained spurs the remains of leather belts with silver and gilt fittings and fastenings were also found. Particularly characteristic of these belt-fittings were showy, tongue-shaped belt-ends, richly decorated on the side that showed when worn. The inner side of one of them bears the engraved figure of a man with the attributes of a prince (Fig. 8, no. 1a). This particular strap-end is heavily gilt; the corresponding loop, through which it was drawn, is gilt-bronze. On another strap-end there is a repoussé figure of a man shown in the attitude of prayer (Plate II, nos 2, 2a). It is interesting to note that although these silver tongue-shaped belt-ends and also buckles executed in repoussé work belong to the Carolingian sphere, the clothes of the man on one of them and particularly the knee-length soft boots he wears are unlike the dress worn in the west at that time. The only element, on the other hand, derived from the Byzantine or eastern Mediterranean sphere is the *orans* or praying attitude. The craftsman who produced this piece must have worked in one of the local workshops of the Great Moravian stronghold at Mikulčice and portrayed the nobleman as he saw and knew him in his domestic setting.

Female graves, both of adults and children, found near the three-nave basilica, contained many items of gold and silver jewellery, often embellished with filigree work and granulation, typical Moravian gold and silver buttons, often decorated with inlays of coloured glass, gilded and silver rings, etc. In one of the graves was found a gilded bronze reliquary in the shape of a miniature book (Plate IV, no. 2). This seems to suggest that books of this kind, bibles and missals, must have existed

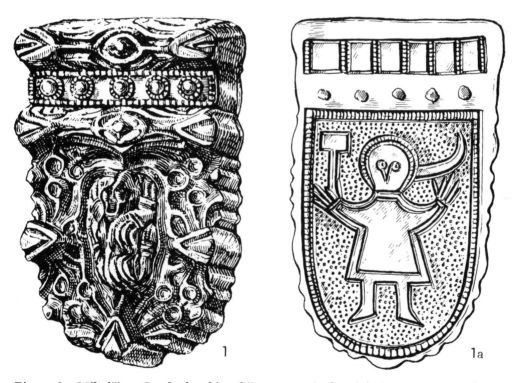

Figure 8   Mikulčice, Czechoslovakia: Gilt strap-ends found in graves, excavated near the three-nave basilica (late ninth century) (Scale: 3 : 2)

in Great Moravia. Another jewel, made of gold and granulated, is inlaid with garnets and enriched with two rows of genuine pearls, loosely mounted on gold wires. There is no doubt that this piece is of Great Moravian origin but the artist must have been influenced by Byzantine jewellery. Byzantine influences are also reflected on a silver and a leaden crucifix showing Christ (Plate III, nos 1, 2). In a child's grave, a round bone disc was found showing a four-legged animal and a crocodile on one side and an archer on the other (Fig. 9, nos 1–1a). This find appears to indicate some contacts between the Great Moravian workshops and the Coptic sphere.

Figure 9   Mikulčice, Czechoslovakia: Horn disc with crocodile and four-legged animal, and archer on reverse (1–1a) (Scale: 5 : 4; ornamented horn object (2) (Scale: 2 : 3) and (3) part of a cast-bronze strap-end (Scale: 2 : 1)

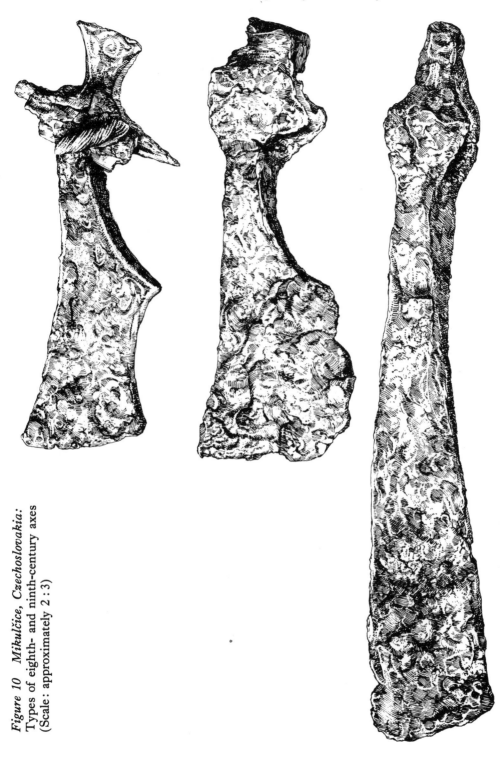

Figure 10   Mikulčice, Czechoslovakia:
Types of eighth- and ninth-century axes
(Scale: approximately 2 : 3)

Plate IV *Mikulčice, Czechoslovakia:* Gold button (1), gilt bronze reliquary (2), gold ear-rings (3–5) and gilt ring (6), found in graves excavated near the three-nave basilica. Second half of the ninth century (Scales: all 2:1)

Typical Slav pottery ornamented with wavy lines, produced on hand-turned potters' wheels, occurred only in a few of the graves, but some small amphorae with two handles, made of fine washed yellow clay, were found, as well as wooden buckets with iron hoops and handles which testify to the very high-class workmanship of the local coopers and smiths. Among the finds there is a glass goblet, which seems to imply commercial contacts between Great Moravia and the factories of the Rhineland during the ninth century. It has already been mentioned that the foundations of the three-nave basilica, its *narthex* and *atrium*, were sunk into the structures of the layer dating from the seventh to eighth centuries. The graves discovered in the three-nave church were also dug into this layer. This stratigraphy, together with the finds from the graves, is of great significance for dating the large ecclesiastical building. Its three-nave part appears to belong to the first half of the ninth century, while the *narthex* and *atrium* may be considered to be additional annexes erected at the time of Cyril and Methodius. The richest graves, containing gold and silver jewels, belong to the first half of the ninth century but the site around the church continued in use as a burial place until the middle of the tenth century.

Of significance for the dating of the church is a gold coin, a *solidus*, of the Byzantine Emperor Michael III, struck in the year 865–6, which was found inside a human skull. It is, however, not conclusive evidence. The coin is the first of its kind to be found in the Great Moravian sphere, indicating close contacts between Great Moravia and the Byzantine Empire. This gold coin, as well as the small pieces of gold found inside some human skulls unearthed in the vicinity of the three-nave church at Mikulčice, should be interpreted as the *obol* of the dead souls ferried by Charon—Charon's coin. Coins placed in the hand or mouth of the corpse have been found in several instances in Slav graves of the eleventh to twelfth centuries excavated within the boundaries of present-day Czechoslovakia.

The interest of archaeologists and historians is focused not only on the question of dating the three-nave church of Mikulčice but also on the problem of its origin. Professor Cibulka believed that the nave and aisles were separated by walls with smaller openings, and that it may have been a church with partitions (*église cloisonnée*) and a straight timber ceiling. Similar structures were associated with elements of late Roman architecture in the vicinity of the Patriarchate of Aquileia in Dalmatia and in Bosnia. Other Czechoslovak experts assume that the aisles of the basilica of Mikulčice were separated from one another by openwork walls with wide pillars, connected by means of archivolts carrying the cupola. This reconstruction, which seeks to substantiate the Byzantine origin of the church, is not very probable.

The foundations of an oblong building (25 m long and $8\frac{1}{2}$ m wide: Fig. 5, P) were unearthed at the highest point of the Mikulčice stronghold (Fig. 3). The interior of building was divided by a partition into a larger western room and a smaller eastern room. The building has no ecclesiastical character and appears to have been a secular building, probably the palace of an important leader, perhaps even the Prince. North-east of this building, further débris was unearthed. Excavation revealed the foundations of a smaller church (the fourth to be discovered at Mikulčice). This church, whose walls were plastered inside and outside, had an almost square nave and a semi-circular apse (total inside length 9·6 m: Fig. 5, no. 4). The plaster fragments retained traces of the original wall painting. Two badly damaged burial vaults or graves, which had been completely plundered, were discovered in the eastern part of the nave. One of the graves contained the scattered bones of a man whose age must have been about forty at the time of his interment. It is supposed that this small church served as a kind of mausoleum, destined for the interment of the members of the ruler's family or perhaps of high church dignitaries.

Approximately a hundred graves were unearthed in its vicinity. Grave-goods in them appear to show that the church must have been erected in the second half of the ninth century at the latest.

Czechoslovak art historians and architects have been trying to find the model that served for the ground plan of the fourth Mikulčice church. Professor Cibulka compared its architecture with that of the Great Moravian churches unearthed on the site *Na valách* and *Špitálky* at Staré Město in Moravia. He saw some connection between this church at Mikulčice with its elongated apse and those found in the area of the Patriarchate of Aquileia (Velschland on the northern coast of the Adriatic Sea) whence Italian priests came to Moravia before the arrival of the Byzantine missionaries, to which reference is made in the legend *The Life of St Methodius*. Archaeologists favour this view and do not share the view of other historians who seek for the prototype of this church in Byzantine architecture.

Excavations continued in a north-westerly direction from the so-called ruler's palace and uncovered a further group of graves, three of which contained skeletons of noblemen with swords. Thus the number of graves containing swords found at Mikulčice is thirteen, the greatest number of heavy weapons of this kind to have been found at a single Slav site of the Great Moravian period.

In the north-eastern part of the stronghold near the ramparts, where destroyed masonry was detected, the matrix, as well as some original parts of the foundations, of a fifth small church were unearthed. It had an oblong nave with a presbytery narrowing to the east (the length of the church inside was 10·8 m: Fig. 5, no. 5). Inside the nave were the remains of the original paving of flat sandstone slabs. A grave appears to have existed in its western part, to judge from some destroyed remains. Scattered human bones occurred on the site, apparently derived from the destroyed graves in the church nave. There was no burial area outside the church, which had been erected on the site of the old settlement from the seventh and eighth centuries. In the vicinity of the church, we found the remains of a workshop for the working of bronze, gold and iron. The workshop, unparalleled in Moravia and the Slav territories of central Europe, has no connection with the fifth church, built in the ninth century. Judging from its ground plan, this church belongs to the same type as the second Mikulčice church.

Excavation proceeded for several years on the site of the stronghold proper. Since

1960, however, more attention has been focused on the so-called sub-burgium (suburbs or areas immediately outside the fortified stronghold) and particularly on the masonry ruins running about 50 m north-east of the stronghold (Fig. 3). Excavations have yielded the matrix and, in part, the original foundations of a two-apse rotunda, the circular nave of which has an inner diameter of 7·3 m, while the total inner length from the western to the eastern apse is 14·75 m (Fig. 5, no. 6). The architecture is perfect, the ground plan being accurately based on circles. The rotunda must have been built by highly skilled masters of their trade. The building material used was rough sandstone. The walls of this magnificent church were plastered both inside and outside, while the inner spaces of the apse and the central rotunda were richly decorated with figured and geometrical designs, the colours used being white, dark red, yellow, black, metallic grey and dark blue.

The rotunda must have been very high, because large fallen pieces of masonry were found at distances up to 15 m from the central point of its floor. We can rightly infer that the nave was covered by a cupola. For this purpose the builders must have erected an ingenious system of scaffolding. This is evidenced by numerous post-holes found both inside and outside the church. Some historians believe that the outside poles supported the roof of a covered ambulatory.

One hundred and ninety graves have been excavated in the vicinity of the rotunda. Among them there is a nobleman's grave containing gilt spurs decorated with foliate palmette designs. About 25 per cent of all interred men and young boys have iron spurs, in some cases inlaid with silver and copper. The graves of women and girls contained gold and gilt jewels. A combination of the evidence of the grave-goods and of stratigraphy allows us to conclude that the rotunda was built as early as the beginning of the ninth century. Its origins are to be associated with the Adriatic regions, where the western Roman and the Byzantine worlds met. In the course of the exploration of the two-apse rotunda, we discovered the traces of a strong fortification with stone wall and timber structures. Behind this ran the old river-bed of the Morava, which in the ninth century separated the ruler's stronghold proper from a manorial estate, in the southern part of which this ostentatious church had been erected.

The two-apse rotunda of Mikulčice, built with great accuracy and perfect accomplishment by Great Moravian architects and masons, was not the only ecclesiastical building unearthed in the sub-burgium of the ruined stronghold. About 500 m north-west of the stronghold (Fig. 3), the ruins of another church with a circular nave (inner diameter about 6 m) and with an apse on its eastern side have been unearthed (Fig. 5, no. 7), on a gently rising elevation standing only a little higher than the surrounding flood plain. On the western side of this church, which was built for the greater part of timber, we discovered four holes used for posts that must have originally supported a projecting roof. This building was much simpler and far less exacting for the builders than the two-apse rotunda. The spurs and silver jewels found in sixteen graves unearthed around the simple church, which can be associated with similar churches in the Adriatic area, appear to indicate that it was built in the second half of the ninth century.

The remains of the foundations of yet another church, the eighth, were discovered about half-way between the seventh church and the ducal stronghold (Fig. 5, no. 8). The church, oriented approximately from west to east, was built on the site of a pre-Great Moravian settlement. On the eastern side of the oblong nave was a rectangular presbytery, in the southern part of which we discovered a millstone and beneath it ninety-five fragments of iron tools and farming implements (Fig. 11), one of the largest iron hoards so far unearthed in Moravia. It is assumed that these iron articles were hidden in the presbytery of the eighth church at the time of the Magyar incursions into Moravia at the beginning of the tenth century. A small churchyard was attached to this church but the finds from the graves, dating back to the second half of the ninth and the first half of the tenth centuries, are not so rich as those found in the graves associated with the other churches at Mikulčice.

The ground-plan of the eighth Mikulčice church greatly resembles that of the second, and it too is considered to have been associated with the western cultural current so strongly influenced by the heritage of the Insular missionaries.

South of the ducal stronghold, on a site called *Kostelisko*, we succeeded in establishing that three buildings had been successively erected on the same spot (Fig. 5, no. 9). In the construction of the latest, that is, the uppermost, both rough stones and fire-hardened stakes were utilised, which appears to indicate that it was built in the fifteenth to sixteenth centuries. It cannot be said with certainty to have been a church. This uppermost building, which was associated with some timber structures, was destroyed by fire. During its erection a defensive ditch, which had restricted access to the building that preceded it, was filled up. The latter had a cast mortar floor and its ground plan respected the foundations of the oldest and the lowest of the three buildings, which was also partly destroyed by local people extracting stone, although some original parts of its foundation walls still remained. It was a rotunda (outer diameter 9·6–9·7 m) with four circular *conchae* (recesses). For the time being, we shall call it the ninth church. In the vicinity of the three structures excavated on the Kostelisko site at Mikulčice, 144 graves were investigated, 81 of which could be associated with the rotunda with the four *conchae*. These contained iron knives, axes, spurs, jewels and pottery, indicating that the rotunda, erected in the first half of the ninth century, had been built on the ruins of the pre-Great Moravian settlement, which dates from the seventh to eight centuries. Excavation in an easterly direction from this perfect rotunda revealed a strip of rubble running to a distance of 14 m where it formed a circle. This was another circular building containing a well-shaped cistern built of rough sandstone. The cistern must have collected underground water. It appears that the rotunda proper was most probably a baptistery in the first half of the ninth century, while the circular building with the cistern may have been similar to that of the three-nave church. This theory will

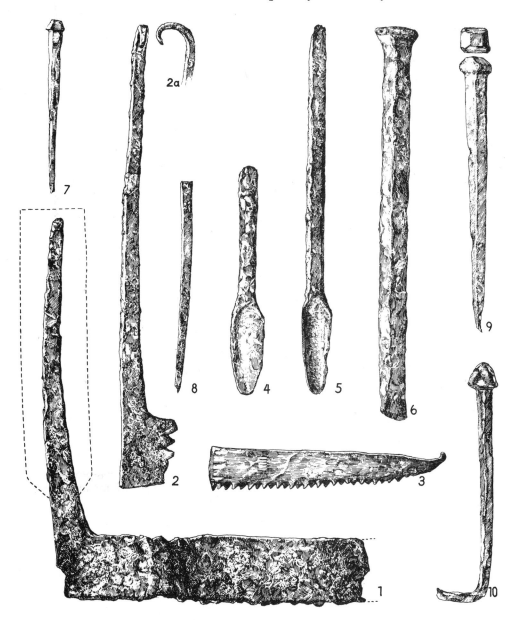

Figure 11   Mikulčice, Czechoslovakia: Iron saws (1–3), boring tools (4–5), a chisel (6) and nails (7–10) (eighth to ninth centuries) (Scales: approx. 2 : 3)

certainly need further expert consideration. There is no doubt that this early rotunda-baptistery complex is a discovery of great importance for the solution of the question of the beginnings of Christianity and of the nature of the ecclesiastical organisation that existed in Great Moravia as early as the first half of the ninth century.

As in the case of the two-apse rotunda, art historians have considered the origin of the rotunda at the Kostelisko site. Professor Cibulka believed that its model should be looked for in late Roman concentric architectural designs, giving as examples the Baths of Constantine in Rome and the church of St George at Thessalonica. In his view rotunda-shaped buildings with inner recesses, such as the rotunda at Marienburg, near Würzburg in Germany, and several others in the west, followed these models. Other experts think that the Mikulčice rotunda, the 'ninth church', was constructed after Italian and Byzantine models.

In 1963, we began the exploration of a mound-shaped heap of destroyed masonry located to the west of the ducal stronghold (Fig. 5, no. 10). Though stone had been extracted here on a large scale by the local inhabitants in the past, we succeeded in uncovering the foundations of another church, the tenth. This has an oblong nave and rectangular presbytery (inner length of the building 9 m) in the eastern wall. On the south-western outer side of the nave there was an oblong annexe, to the north of which remains of a stone pier were unearthed. On the outer side of the nave and the presbytery there are piers, while the foundations of further pillars that apparently once supported the tribune were revealed in the western part of the nave.

This tenth Mikulčice church was erected on the ruins of an earlier stone structure but no traces of mortar have been found and the original ground plan of this building, which rested on the layer of a pre-Great Moravian settlement from the seventh to eighth centuries, has not been established. There is no direct evidence for dating the construction of this church, because the stone-built graves uncovered here contained no finds and the destroyed stone tomb on the south side of the presbytery was also empty. However, the discovery on the site of an oven and several pottery fragments datable to the second half of the tenth century suggest that this ecclesiastical building was by then probably in ruins. It was perhaps built during the ninth century.

The ground plan, with piers on the exterior of nave and presbytery, is the first find of its kind in the Great Moravian region. No wonder that different theories have been expressed and written about its origin. It seems that it was built under influence from Dalmatia and the Adriatic area, where similar churches were constructed in the course of the ninth century. Contacts between Moravia and those regions, as well as with the Patriarchate of Aquileia, are attested by written sources.

Excavations have been in progress for several years on the site of a hillock directly connected with the north-western part of the Mikulčice stronghold (Fig. 3). Scores of houses with a square or oblong ground plan and 16 to 17 m² in area have so far been unearthed. They were originally built as timber structures with firmly beaten clay floors and oval ovens built of clay. These houses form irregular rows oriented from north to south and are separated one from another by narrow lanes (in many cases no more than 1 m wide) which are practically covered with animal bones and pottery fragments. It appears that the place must have been used as a rubbish-dump for the garbage from a once rich kitchen, in which young pigs in particular (accounting for about 60 per cent of the bone remains) were cooked or roasted.

Excavations have shown that the palisades round this settlement, which covered an area of about 3 hectares, were replaced during the Great Moravian period by a stone-faced wall with timber compartments, this fortification resembling that of the stronghold. It was assumed that there had been a ditch on the outer side of this fortification, but excavations carried out in 1964 have shown that in the Great Moravian period the access to the settlement was guarded by a 25 m wide arm of the river Morava, over which a timber bridge had been erected. The timber piers supporting this bridge have been unearthed in the river-bed. Two boats cut from oak stocks, approximately 10 m long, were found in the muddy deposits caught on the piers, together with small wooden objects. Twenty-four battle-axes with well-preserved wooden handles may provide evidence for struggles taking place at this strategic point, protecting the entrance to the stronghold. From the excavations carried out so far it can be calculated that this fortified settlement may have been inhabited by about 1,000 persons. They were probably not craftsmen because no traces of workshops have been discovered so far. Numerous finds of spurs and gilded bronze fittings and belt-fastenings suggest that the occupants of the large wooden houses must have been members of a well-to-do privileged class, most probably warriors and horsemen belonging to the retinue of an important leader, perhaps even the Prince.

The fact that this fortified complex of houses is directly connected with the ducal stronghold appears to indicate its special status. The building material used in the construction of the churches and other stone edifices of the Mikulčice stronghold and its suburbs was chiefly rough sandstone, brought from the western slopes of the White Carpathians. This stone was also used for building the fortifications of the stronghold and of the settlements connected with it. Immeasurable quantities of this sandstone were used and its transport from a distance of more than 15 km must have required resourceful organisation. Peasants forced into bondage, and apparently slaves too, must have played an important role in this work. Among the ruins and débris of the foundation masonry of both the ecclesiastical and secular buildings at Mikulčice there were also paving bricks and brick fragments, one of them with the stamp of the XIVth Roman legion, which was stationed at Carnuntum (near Vienna). It does not seem likely that Roman building material was transported along the river Morava all the way from the Roman military camp to Mikulčice. It is more probable that between the first and fourth centuries A.D. there existed somewhere on the river Morava a small Roman camp and that the builders of

Mikulčice used its material for their own purposes in the ninth century. In the rectangular annexe built on the northern side of the second Mikulčice church we discovered among the mortar and plaster débris three fragments of polished slabs of dark-green rock showing some kind of light flower-work.

A similar fragment was also found in the presbytery of the seventh Mikulčice church. Mineralogists have identified it as labradoritic porphyrite. The fragments found at Mikulčice can be best compared with porphyrite quarried in the south of the Peloponnese in Greece. This rock does not occur in Moravia at all, and it is not very probable that porphyrite slabs were imported to Great Moravia all the way from Greece. It is a well-known fact that this decorative stone was used by the Romans. Consequently, it is quite possible that the fragments found in the débris of the second and the seventh churches at Mikulčice came from the camp of the Roman garrison we have postulated as stationed somewhere on the river Morava.

As yet, scarcely 2 per cent of the total area that comprises the Great Moravian stronghold of Mikulčice and its sub-burgium has been archaeologically explored. This is naturally not sufficient to allow us to draw far-reaching conclusions. On the other hand, even the relatively little that has been achieved so far at Mikulčice should be valued as a positive contribution, throwing new light on the Great Moravian period and on the society and life of the people. In the light of the latest archaeological discoveries made at Mikulčice and elsewhere, the gaps left by scanty historical records are being gradually filled.

Excavations have revealed that the churches unearthed at Mikulčice had their foundations sunk in the earlier pre-Great Moravian horizon dating from the seventh to eighth centuries. Archaeological evidence clearly shows that, in the course of that period, there existed all over the site of Mikulčice, which had gradually lost its purely agrarian character, several workshops with small furnaces made of stone, where non-ferrous metals, used for making ornaments, were melted in earthen crucibles. This old local craft and its traditions, which had been influenced by antique stimuli surviving in the Danubian Basin, were passed on and continued up to the first half of the ninth century. At that time, the craftsmen of Mikulčice, metal-founders and silversmiths, influenced by Carolingian workshops, created a new style which can be compared and synchronised with the well-known Blatnice group of relics from western Slovakia, associated with the workshops of the Principality of Nitra, its centre being the stronghold of Nitra on the site of the present town of the same name (Fig. 2). The most significant artistic finds of this archaeological horizon of Mikulčice from the ninth century are the gilded spurs already mentioned and sets of metal mounts belonging to them.

The development of the material culture of Mikulčice continued until the second half of the ninth century, when artistic crafts, particularly jewellery, began to be influenced by practices and ideas introduced into Moravia from the regions of Byzantium and the western Mediterranean. Refined techniques in treating metals, such as granulation and filigree work, were used by local jewellers, who at that time produced items of jewellery that were unequalled in contemporary central and eastern Europe. Among the typical Great Moravian jewels there are gold, gilded and silver buttons (*gombíky*), often decorated with finely wrought foliate and geometrical designs (Plate III, nos 5, 6, Fig. 7). As typical of this period, we have mentioned richly mounted leather belts with gilded and silver buckles, clasps and belt end-pieces, some of them decorated with secular and ecclesiastical figures in the gesture of prayer (so called *orantes*) (Plate II, Fig. 8). These as well as other finds in graves furnish evidence for the existence of a differentiated society in Great Moravia, where Christianity undoubtedly played an important and at times also a progressive role.

It was not only the manufacture of jewellery and ornaments that flourished at Mikulčice at this time. Rich finds of farming implements, craftsmen's tools and weapons testify to the highly developed state of Great Moravian industry. Craftsmen also worked lead, manufactured wooden buckets with metal hoops and handles, wove linen cloth, produced decorative articles of horn (Fig. 9), knife handles, combs and objects of every kind (Fig. 12). Numerous finds of bone tools and instruments, particularly awls, suggest that the skins and hides of animals were scraped, cleaned, prepared, further treated and worked.

The Great Moravian centre at Mikulčice, where specialised crafts flourished and cattle were raised on a large scale, is characterised not only by its strong fortifications but also by the spurs and heavy iron swords so frequently found in the Great Moravian horizon proper as well as in the earlier graves. So far, thirteen of these heavy iron swords have been found at Mikulčice, the highest number of weapons of this kind ever found at any Great Moravian archaeological site. Naturally these significant discoveries and finds, including the strong fortifications, lead us to hard thinking about the true role of Mikulčice in the economic, political and religious organisation of Great Moravia. According to the *Annales Fuldenses*, in the year 869 the Frankish king Charles, who was at the head of the Frankish army, marched into Moravia and came to one of Rastislav's 'unspeakable fortresses' (*ineffabilis munitio Rastizi*), which was quite different from all then known fortresses. This reference in the *Annales Fuldenses* may well be to the Mikulčice region, whose strongholds and fortified settlements must have impressed and greatly astonished the Frankish army approaching from the west. With recent discoveries at Mikulčice in mind we should also cite another reference in the *Annales Fuldenses* (ca. A.D. 871), that to Rastislav's 'ancient city' (*urbs antiqua Rastizi*).

The archaeological evidence which we have discussed indicates that the stronghold of Mikulčice reached the peak of its growth as a military, cultural and industrial centre in the ninth century, that is, when southern Moravia was the political, ecclesiastical and administrative centre of the Great Moravian Empire, a powerful, progressive, pre-feudal state formed in central Europe. Written records tell us that this organisation, the Great Moravian state, was destroyed at the beginning of the tenth century by the Magyars, who swept into Moravia through the Carpathian passes.

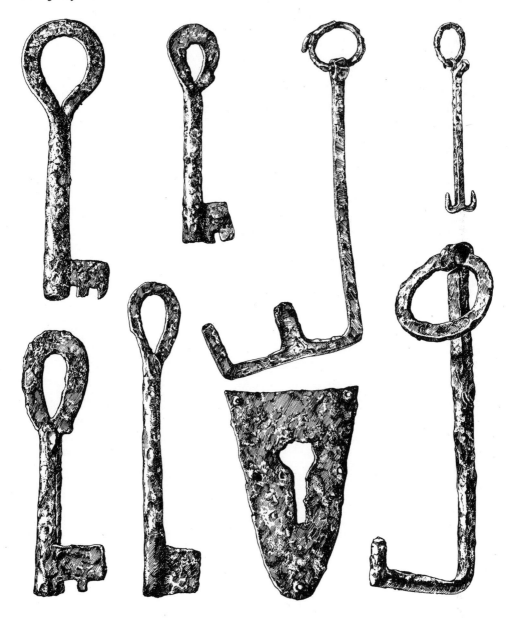

Figure 12 Mikulčice, Czechoslovakia: Ninth century types of iron keys and an iron lock fitting (Scale: approx. 2:3)

Our excavations have shown that in the tenth century the stone buildings and fortifications of Mikulčice were more or less left to their fate and gradually fell into decay. Bodies were buried around the churches only until the middle of the tenth century, at the latest. Over the débris and ruins of the once powerful stronghold, its fortifications and churches, a large settlement subsequently grew up, whose detailed structure is not yet fully known. The Great Moravian industrial tradition continued but the original core of the earlier municipal formation did not develop into a medieval town, as was the case in the eastern Slav territories.

So far only about 2 per cent of a site covering 200 hectares has been explored at Mikulčice and consequently definite answers to many problems must await the results of further archaeological field-work. Archaeologists will continue to work at Mikulčice for many more years, perhaps even decades, to fill the gaps left by scanty written records and to throw more light on the history of this once proud stronghold, which in the ninth century A.D. must have played an important role in the economic, social and cultural life of Great Moravia and of the eastern part of central Europe.

Bibliography

Poulík, J., 'Výsledky výzkumu na velkomoravském hradišti "Valy" u Mikulčic' ('Results of the excavation of the Great Moravian fortress "Valy" near Mikulčice'), *Památky archeologické* XLVIII, Prague, 1957.

Poulík, J., 'The latest archaeological discoveries from the Great Moravian Empire', *Historica* I, Prague, 1959.

Poulík, J., 'Dvě velkomoravské rotundy v Mikulčicích' ('Two Great Moravian rotunda in Mikulčice'), *Monumenta Archaeologica* XII, Prague, 1965.

Poulík, J., 'Archäologische Entdeckungen und Grossmähren', *Das grossmährische Reich*, Prague, 1966.

Poulík, J., 'Beziehungen Grossmährens zu den europäischen Kulturgebieten', in *Festschrift zum 70. Geburtstag von Adalbert Klaar und Herbert Mitscha-Märheim*, Jahrbuch für Landeskunde von Niederösterreich, vol. 38, Vienna, 1968–70.

Chapter II

Early Celts on the upper Danube: the excavations at the Heuneburg

Wolfgang Kimmig

On the edge of upper Swabia, where the Swabian Alb, sloping towards the south-east, meets the hilly moraine landscape of the northern Lake Constance region, the Heuneberg is situated, high above the small stream of the upper Danube (Plate V). The citadel, crowning one of the many spurs jutting out from the steep slopes on the western side of the Danube, dominates the landscape from a distance. North of the site rises the 800 m high hill, the Bussen. The horizon to the north-west is defined by the dark wooded hills of the Alb. To the south, in clear weather, the Bavarian, Austrian and Swiss Alps can be seen, forming a row of jagged peaks.

The Heuneburg is located in an area unequalled in its archaeological importance (Fig. 13). At conspicuous points around the fortress lie the immense burial mounds of the former lords of the site. The most outstanding of these is the 13 m high *Hohmichele* (Plate VIa). Groups of smaller burial mounds and half a dozen *Viereckschanzen*, Celtic religious sanctuaries, are located in wooded areas west of the site. Just 15 km to the east is Bad Buchau on the Federsee, well-known for its marsh-villages of the Stone and late Bronze Ages. Up on to the limestone plateaux of the Alb leads a series of strong fortified sites, from *Alt-Hayingen* at Zwiefalten to the *Grosse Heuneburg* at Upflamör, to the *Alte Burg* at Fridingen. All of these date to the earlier Iron Age of the eighth to sixth centuries B.C.; all were rebuilt and re-used in later periods as well.

During earliest historical times, the region around the Heuneburg was of major tactical importance. In the year A.D. 40, under the emperor Claudius, the northern boundary of the Roman Empire lay just to the east of our site, near the hills forming the eastern edge of the Danube valley. This boundary was defined by occasional forts and by an outer frontier path controlled by the Roman troops – the *limes*. As

Plate V   *The Heuneburg on the upper Danube:* In the woods above the citadel can be seen the rebuilt warrior's burial mound 4, of the 'Talhau-Group'. On the horizon are the foot-hills of the Swabian Alps

succeeding Roman emperors pushed the imperial borders further into Germany, first to the Swabian Alb, then to the Neckar, the Heuneburg fell into the Roman hinterland. Roman estates were built in the vicinity of the citadel, which by this time had already been in ruins for five hundred years. Along the lowlands of the Danube valley led the important 'south Danube route', still recognisable today as a perfectly straight way through the landscape, at that time a road of considerable economic significance as well as of military supply. In the year A.D. 260 the attacks of the Alemanni drove the Romans back behind the line formed by Lake Constance and the upper Rhine. As a result, the land around the Heuneburg became available for settlement to the Germanic peasant groups. It was these farming communities

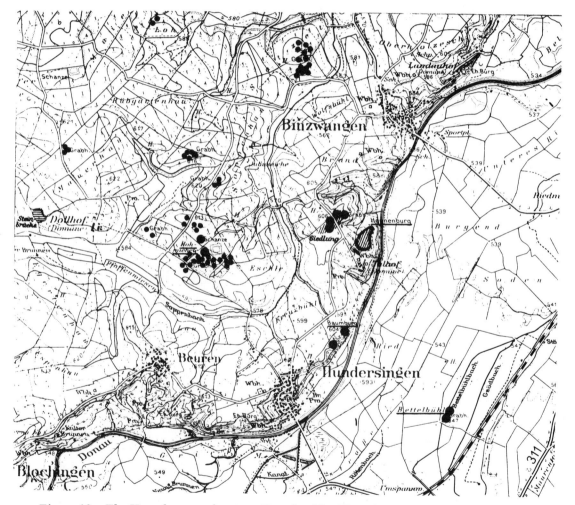

Figure 13 The Heuneburg on the upper Danube: The Heuneburg and the surrounding area

Plate VI   (a) (above) *The Heuneburg on the upper Danube:* The *Hohmichele* nearby on
the upper Danube. The mound covered a *Fürstengrab*, which was excavated in 1938.
The mound was rebuilt in 1951 to its original height of 13 m
(b) (below) *The Heuneburg on the upper Danube:* Model of the clay-brick wall
superimposed on a photograph of the Heuneburg

who left the large *Reihengräber* cemeteries dating from the sixth to eighth centuries A.D., found today in the vicinity of nearly all villages whose names end in *-ingen* or *-heim*.

This archaeologically rich area on the upper Danube attracted the attention of investigators at an early date. In 1876, the *Landeskonservator* Paulus of the *Staatssammlung vaterländischer Kunst- und Altertumsdenkmale*, in Stuttgart, now the *Württembergisches Landesmuseum*, carried out excavations at three large burial mounds in the immediate vicinity of the Heuneburg. In these mounds he found gold jewellery and a considerable number of bronze vessels. Influenced by the discoveries in the same year by Heinrich Schliemann of rich graves at Mycenae, Paulus named the graves in the Heuneburg area *Fürstengräber*, a designation which has remained in general use in pre- and protohistoric studies to the present day. Paulus had recognised the importance of the Heuneburg, yet it was not until seventy-five years later in 1950 that Kurt Bittel, then Professor of Prehistory at the University of Tübingen, began with his students the first systematic excavations at the site. Supported primarily by the *Deutsche Forschungsgemeinschaft* and also aided by public and private sources, the investigations have been carried out continuously since then.

It was several years before the unusually complex stratigraphic sequence at the site could be established with relative certainty (Fig. 14). During the centuries of the site's occupation, generations of inhabitants had been building upon the débris left by preceding generations. In places, the cultural levels are as thick as 5 m, containing

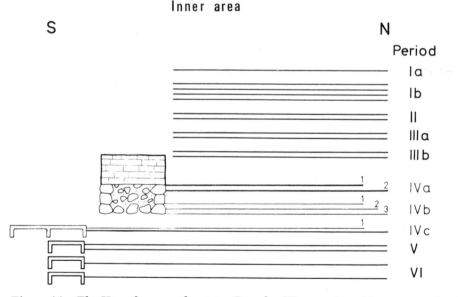

Figure 14   The Heuneburg on the upper Danube: The stratigraphic sequence in the south-east corner

the remains of foundations and finds from a number of different periods of occupation. The finds indicate that three periods were of particular significance in the history of the Heuneburg. The first is the middle and late Bronze Age. Finds from this period occur at the base of the stratigraphic sequence. They suggest that as early as the fifteenth to thirteenth centuries B.C. a small village was situated on this spur above the Danube. Traces of the settlement itself have almost completely disappeared as a result of intensive building activities during the following centuries.

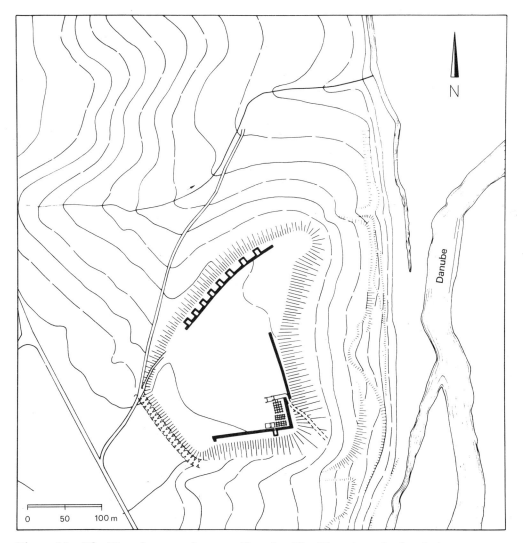

Figure 15   The Heuneburg on the upper Danube: The Heuneburg in the sixth century B.C. (Hallstatt D 1). The plan shows the clay-brick wall and the structure of Period IV a/2 in the south-east corner of the citadel

At the time when the fortress sites of Tiryns and Mycenae in Greece were at the peak of their power, this village settlement occupied the Heuneburg. Following the abandonment of the Bronze Age village the site lay unoccupied for seven hundred and fifty years.

In the late Hallstatt period, during the sixth and fifth centuries B.C., the Heuneburg witnessed a phase of very intense activity (Fig. 15). About a dozen walls around the citadel, frequently destroyed and rebuilt (Fig. 16), as well as a series of settlements within the defended area, characterise this period as the most important for the site in the course of its long history. Some time during the fifth century B.C. the latest wall was destroyed by fire. Another period of inactivity began for the site, this one lasting for nearly a millennium.

The final phase of major activity here was during the early Middle Ages, the 'dark' centuries between the time of the departure of the Romans from central Europe and that of the full development of the Carolingian Empire. From this period we possess a certain number of historical documents but comparatively few archaeological monuments. It was at this time that the Heuneburg acquired the features visible today – the sharp contours and the deep double ditches, still distinct on the west side of the hill (Fig. 17). The details of the events which led to the expansion and rebuilding of the site at this time are unknown. In this process the earlier cultural levels and defensive systems were buried under the new settlement or disappeared altogether.

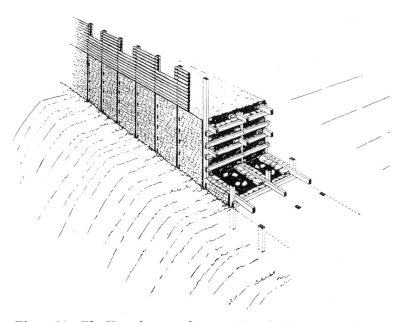

Figure 16   The Heuneburg on the upper Danube: Reconstruction on one of the many citadel walls of wood and stone construction

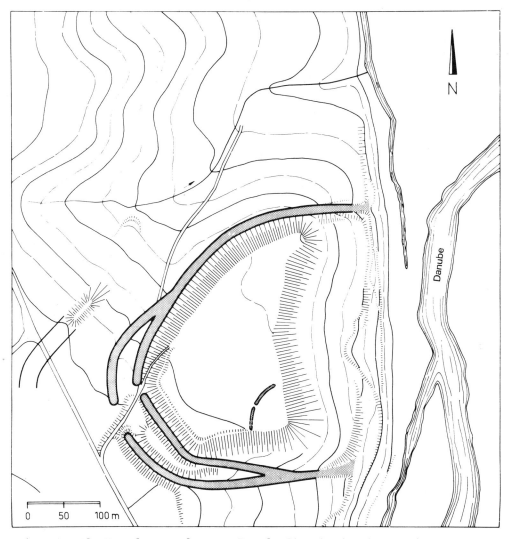

Figure 17   The Heuneburg on the upper Danube: Plan showing the deep fortress ditches and the small fortification in the south-east corner as they were in the seventh to tenth centuries A.D.

As we have suggested, the most important and best documented period of the occupation of the Heuneburg was the late Hallstatt. During this period the site served as the residence of a local nobility. Such local seats of power seem to have dominated the cultural and social developments of the broad zone north-west of the Alps at that time. The precise areas of control of the individual 'principalities' are extremely difficult to determine. The political situation most likely resembled that suggested by a political map of the same area during the seventeenth and eighteenth

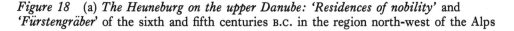

■ 'Residence of nobility'. Established
□ 'Residence of nobility'. Probable
● 'Fürstengrab'. Established
○ 'Fürstengrab'. Probable

Figure 18   (a) *The Heuneburg on the upper Danube: 'Residences of nobility'* and
'Fürstengräber' of the sixth and fifth centuries B.C. in the region north-west of the Alps

centuries A.D. According to the testimony of Herodotus and of Hecataeus of Miletus powerful individuals, probably Celts, established their sites of residence and their styles of life in ways contrasting markedly with those of the other settlements of the time.

Especially characteristic of these residences of the late Hallstatt aristocracy are the imposing burial mounds associated with them (Fig. 18a). The size of these mounds suggests that they were often erected for purposes of display. Around the Heuneburg are nine such mounds, of which the 13 m high *Hohmichele* has already been mentioned (Plate VIa). Another residence of the nobility of this period closely related to the Heuneburg in its topographical situation is the Hohenasperg near Stuttgart, with the associated tombs of *Kleinaspergle*, the *Römerhügel*, and the

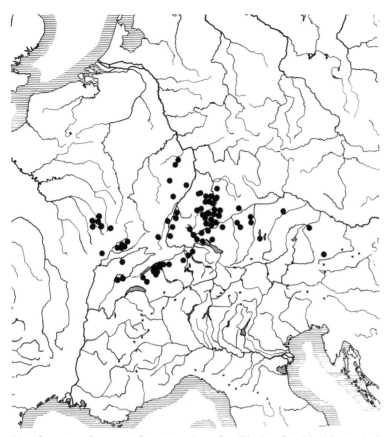

(b) *The Heuneburg on the upper Danube:* Finds of gold objects dating from the sixth and fifth centuries B.C., in the region north-east of the Alps

Grafenbühl. Also similar is the Mont Lassois near Châtillon-sur-Seine in eastern France, with the richest and best-known *Fürstengrab* of this type, the grave of Vix. The numerous *Fürstengräber* known to us, characterised particularly by rich finds of gold, suggest that many such residences must have existed throughout the country-side during the late Hallstatt (Fig. 19a,b). In this connection, the gold finds of this period from the area between the upper Seine and the upper Danube (Fig. 18b) make it clear that this region was a distinct 'culture-province', owing its development to a very specific political–historical situation.

The Heuneburg excavations have contributed considerably to our understanding of this situation. In 1950 Kurt Bittel uncovered a wall of prefabricated, sun-dried clay bricks (Plate VIIa), built to a height of about 4 m, on top of a 3 m wide foundation of limestone blocks. Never before in central Europe had a wall of this type been encountered. This wall had at least nine towers (Plate VIIb) and probably two gates and most likely enclosed the entire land surface on top of the plateau

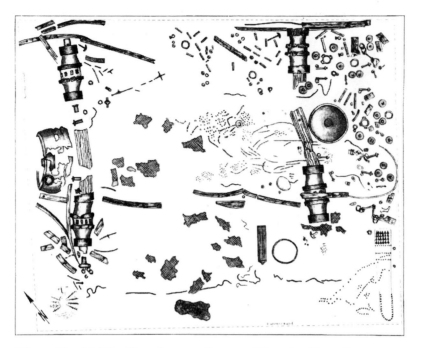

Figure 19   (a) *The Heuneburg on the upper Danube:* Plan of wagon-grave VI, in a side-chamber of the 'Hohmichele' *Fürstengrab* near the Heuneburg

(b) *The Heuneburg on the upper Danube:* Reconstruction of wagon-grave VI

Plate VII (a) (above) *The Heuneburg on the upper Danube:* The outer surface of the clay-brick wall with stone base and ten layers of brick *in situ*. In front of this, on the berm, the burned wooden parts of the walkway (b) (left) *The Heuneburg on the upper Danube:* The foundations of a bastion. The brick structure above them has been removed. Note the precision of the architecture

(Plate VIb). Prototypes for this defence system are to be found throughout the Mediterranean area from Asia Minor to Spain. We may assume that Celtic architects learned the techniques of constructing such a wall in the south, perhaps in the area around Massalia, the present-day Marseille. They built the wall at the Heuneburg using what they had learned, even if some details of the technique were not thoroughly understood. In spite of the moist central European climate, the clay-brick wall has survived surprisingly well, probably because it was frequently replastered. Since the wall possessed a wooden walkway as part of the defensive system, it was susceptible to destruction by fire. The conflagration that finally destroyed it can only have been the result of an attack.

In order to determine the routes by which familiarity with this Mediterranean type of defence system and perhaps also familiarity with urban living in general, may have reached the Celtic regions on the upper Danube, we must turn our attention to the finds. During the past twenty years, the excavations at the Heuneburg have recovered a body of fine material whose quantity, quality and evidential value far surpass that of similar material from other hill settlements of the period. Although the cultural materials recovered represent only a small fraction of those present at the site during the late Hallstatt, nevertheless they indicate beyond doubt that the Heuneburg must have occupied a special position in the political and social spheres of the time. It is of major importance to our consideration of the precise sources of the Mediterranean architectural features at our site that the lords of the citadel seem to have maintained active contacts with the south. These contacts extended over a considerable area, from the *caput Adriae* in the east to the eastern coast of Spain in the west. From this extensive area imported goods as well as less tangible cultural influences were constantly arriving at the region north-west of the Alps and in particular at the Heuneburg. Able craftsmen in central European workshops assimilated the southern fashions, producing work whose character indicates influences from both areas. We may cite several examples here, without discussing the chronological problems at this point.

Wine apparently played a significant role in the lives of the lords of the Heuneburg. Since vines were not yet cultivated north-west of the Alps, it had to be imported. The southern exporters seem to have made good use of the opportunity to supply their northern customers with the necessary tableware at the same time. At the Heuneburg we find in ever-increasing numbers sherds of black-figure Greek vases (Plate VIIIc) and also fragments of Graeco-Massaliote amphorae for transport (Plate VIIIa). As the distribution map indicates (Fig. 20a), the wine trade evidently emanated from Provence, where Massalia, founded about 600 B.C. by Phocaean Greeks, had been cultivating the grape. The precious liquid must have been transported up the Rhône, Saône and Doubs rivers to Mont Lassois and to the Heuneburg. The accompanying black-figure tableware presumably travelled the same route. At the same time the Graeco-Etruscan 'trading posts' of Spina and

Plate VIII   (a) (above left) *The Heuneburg on the upper Danube:* A Graeco-Massaliote wine amphora with fragments of others (Scale: approx. 1 : 8)
(b) (above right) *The Heuneburg on the upper Danube:* Sherds of wheel-made chamfered pottery (Scale: approx. 1 : 3)
(c) (below) *The Heuneburg on the upper Danube:* 'Warrior's farewell'. Fragment of a *columen*, or volute krater, about 500 B.C. (Scale 1 : 1)

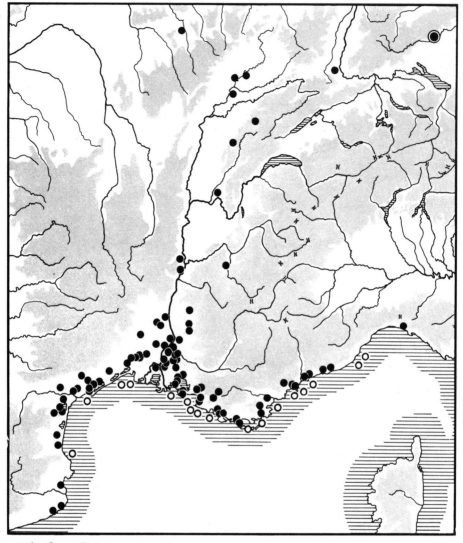

○ *Amphorae* finds in sunken ships

Figure 20   (a) *The Heuneburg on the upper Danube:* Distribution map of Graeco-Massaliote *amphorae,* on the Gulf of Lyon and in the north-west Alpine foreland

Adria in the Po delta may also have been taking part in this profitable commerce. Their participation would of course presuppose the existence of a route over the Alps (Fig. 20b).

Long before the route up the Rhône valley was of commercial importance, an Alpine route between north and south must have been in use. As a dissertation written at the University of Tübingen shows, a high-quality wheel-made chamfered

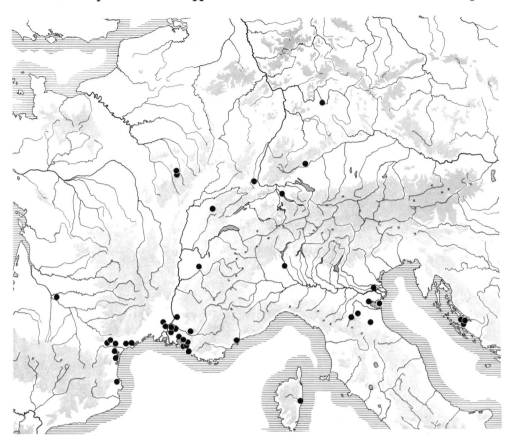

(b) *The Heuneburg on the upper Danube:* Distribution map of Greek black-figure vases, in the area of the Gulf of Lyon, the *caput Adriae* and the north-west Alpine foreland

pottery occurs at the Heuneburg (Plate VIIIb). The precursors of this type are to be found in central Italy. The knowledge of such wheel-made pottery must have arrived at the Heuneburg from over the central Alpine passes, with the Golasecca culture acting as intermediary, probably as early as the first part of the fifth century B.C. At the Heuneburg wheel-made ceramics were developed into a variety of forms. The Golasecca culture apparently played a major role in the north–south trade in general. We might briefly mention a few of the many objects which found their way from central and northern Italy into rich graves of the north-west Alpine foreland through the agency of this group. They include the pyxis from Kastenwald near Colmar, ribbed bowls and beaded-edged basins of bronze, Etruscan gold jewellery from Jegensdorf and Ins, the bronze hydria from Grächwil and finally, the latest example of this imported material and already dating to the early La Tène period, the bronze beaked flagons. In addition to such spectacular items, many objects of everyday use also arrived via this route at the north Alpine settlements and again

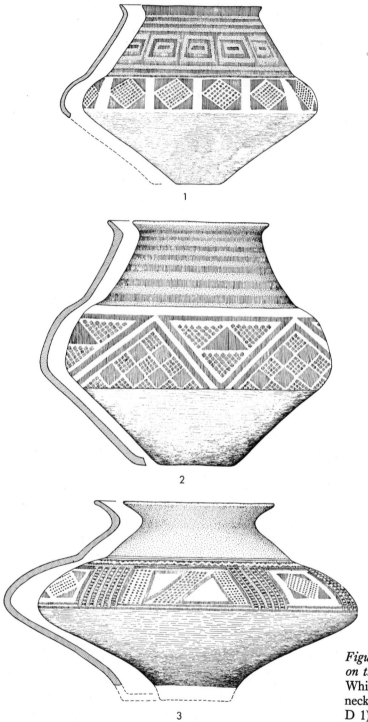

Figure 21   The Heuneburg on the upper Danube: White-red painted high-necked vessels (Hallstatt D 1) (Scale 1 : 4)

particularly at the Heuneburg. Of these we might mention fragments of ceramic beaked flagons and a particularly interesting find from excavations in 1971, the fragment of a black-and-red banded urn of Este-type.

The readiness on the part of the Heuneburg residents to accept southern influences and to imitate southern products is evident not only in the realm of architecture, as the case of the clay-brick wall has shown, but also, and to an even greater extent, in the small finds. For example, the introduction of the technique of making pottery on the wheel around the middle of the fifth century B.C. seems to have had a particularly strong influence on the Heuneburg artisans. Numerous vessels at the site, though hand-made themselves, demonstrate in their form the influence of the introduction of wheel-made forms. In this context we can understand the development of the high-necked vessels of the late Hallstatt from the plump-bellied middle Hallstatt forms and, from the former, the development of the elegant flasks, often in fact wheel-made.

A special development at this time is that of painting (Fig. 21). There is little doubt that the various painting techniques in use in the mid-sixth century B.C. at the Heuneburg (and to some extent only here) are to be seen as developments of painting styles known from numerous Provençal manufactures from the hinterland of Massalia. These have been designated *pseudo-Ionnienne* by the French investigators. All probably developed after the founding of Massalia in 600 B.C. We should also mention that the Heuneburg potters made attempts to imitate the Etruscan *Bucchero nero*. An extremely thin, highly burnished, glazed black ware, without precursors in central Europe, can only thus be explained. Whether this particular influence arrived over the Alpine routes or from Provence and the Rhône valley is not at present clear. Influences of direct importance to the work of the

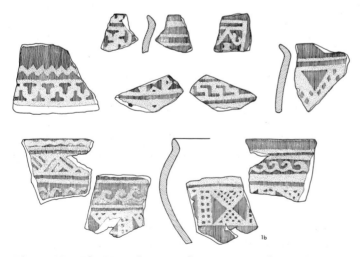

Figure 22   The Heuneburg on the upper Danube: Red burnished and dark painted pottery (Hallstatt D 2–3) (Scale: 1 : 2)

Heuneburg potters originated from areas even as far distant as northern Iberia. A series of painted sherds bearing concentric semicircles as a decorative pattern seem most likely to represent an imitation of a design in use in that area (Fig. 22).

It was assuredly only a small number of selected forms from the total repertoire of southern material available that the late Hallstatt inhabitants of the Heuneburg chose to develop further. The manifold nature of their contacts with the Mediterranean world is indicated perhaps by the increasing use of west Mediterranean coral at the site, prized particularly as inlay for fibulae. Finally, another demonstration of this diversity of cultural influences from the south is the importation of chickens, bones of which have been identified among the animal remains recovered during excavation. It can be no accident that the cock suddenly now appears in the plastic arts of the late Hallstatt and early La Tène.

All of this evidence provides us with a remarkably full picture of activity at the site. Much of this striking activity can be explained in terms of the wide-ranging political changes taking place in the Mediterranean area at this time. In the eighth century B.C., Greek colonists began moving westward from their homeland. This emigration led to the founding of numerous Greek cities in southern Italy and Sicily, later to become Magna Graecia. Greek activity reached the upper Adriatic, the Rhône delta and the eastern coast of Spain. Around the middle of the last millennium B.C. a new Greek cultural community existed in the western Mediterranean, rivalling the mother country in activity. In time, other peoples joined this Greek culture-province, contributing their own shares to the development of the region. The principal rivals of the Greeks were the Carthaginians, who united with the Etruscans in an attempt to defeat the Greeks. Also entering into the struggle was the young city-state of Rome. This new force began to apply pressure against the Etruscans. The result of this intricate political situation which was decisive for central Europe was the agreement, during the sixth and fifth centuries, between the Greeks and the Etruscans to open up new markets in the northern hinterlands of their areas of control. In the north, the indigenous peoples eagerly accepted the new influences coming in their direction. When Hecataeus of Miletus, around 500 B.C., speaks of 'Κελτική' in the hinterland of Massalia and fifty years later Herodotus mentions Celts on tne upper Danube, the two historians can only have been referring to the Hallstatt 'culture-province' in the north-western Alpine foreland opened to southern commerce by the Greeks and the Etruscans. It seems clear that, around the middle of the last millennium before Christ, early Celts were residing at the Heuneburg whose relations with the south have been demonstrated.

Since 1963 the Heuneburg excavations have been conducted under the direction of Egon Gersbach. His investigations have been concerned with the inner area of the citadel as well as with the defences and aim to investigate, if not the entire surface area, at least a substantial part of it (Fig. 24). The first direct result of this study of the inner area was the establishment of the complicated stratigraphic sequence (Fig. 14). From this sequence it became evident that associated with the dozen or so walls of the Hallstatt citadel are over twice as many habitation levels. Either one or two habitation levels are associated with each of the walls, with the exception of the brick wall. This one, the most substantial of all the defence systems, has five distinct habitation levels associated with it (Fig. 14; Plate VIII). Building activity in the inner area thus occurred at much more frequent intervals than it did at the walls. Whereas the walls were rebuilt only after destruction or after natural deterioration, the habitation sites were apparently re-established more than twice as often. This was very frequently, as we note when we consider that the cidatel was in use for only some two hundred years during its late Hallstatt period of occupation.

The reasons for this rapid succession of newly laid out habitation areas are not known at present. This feature of the site surely indicates that the Heuneburg was a focal point of political activity. Another unexpected discovery has been that before each new building phase the settlement area was intentionally levelled. The layers representing these grading operations, although containing finds, must nevertheless be regarded as 'sterile' for purposes of establishing the chronological sequence. These levels permit an exact separation of the individual building phases and make clear the fact that the character of the citadel's settlement must have changed rapidly. These artificial alterations in the site's surface are recognisable today, particularly in aerial photographs.

To date only the south-eastern corner of the citadel has been fully excavated (but see p. 63). The results here indicate that each new habitation level (thus each new settlement phase) possessed its own individual external aspects. No structural features were precisely like those of the previous phase (Plate XIa). It is clear that along with this constant change in settlement structure, economic functions of the phases must also have changed. For example, during the early phase of the Hallstatt period occupation, before the construction of the brick wall, individual 'farmsteads', built of heavy wooden beams, and the storage structures associated with them, were located in the south-eastern corner of the site. These farmsteads were separated from one another by fences. During the time of the existence of the brick wall, a 'workshop quarter' was situated at this part of the citadel, consisting of groups of buildings lined up along narrow lanes, surrounded by drainage ditches for rainwater (Fig. 23). We know this to have been a workshop quarter not only because the individual structures possessed special technical features such as smoke outlets and smelting furnaces but also because of the discovery within them of thousands of tiny globules of bronze, indicating the working of this metal. From the relatively small part of the inner area already excavated it is clear that, at the time of the brick wall, the site was divided into workshop and dwelling areas. This also would seem to represent a feature adopted from the south, one that survives today in the bazaars (*souks*) of Oriental cities.

The houses excavated reveal a high standard of carpentry. In addition to simple 'post-built' houses there are large 'pillar-buildings', with ground-sills of strong beams up to 40 cm thick, carefully hewn with an axe. The ground plans of the

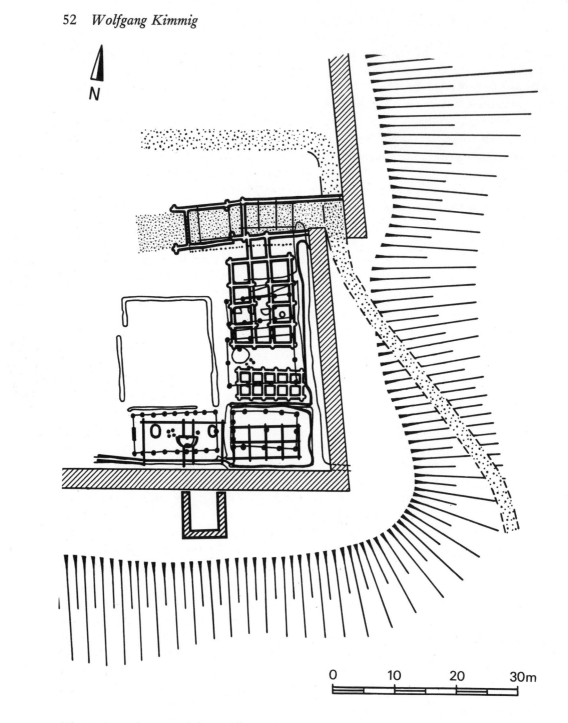

Figure 23 The Heuneburg on the upper Danube: The south-east corner, with two overlapping building phases of Period IV, demonstrating the difficulties of excavation, involving a total of twenty-two levels

Plate IX   (a) (above) *The Heuneburg on the upper Danube:* Gold straining-spoon
(length 10 cm)
(b) (below) *The Heuneburg on the upper Danube:* Pottery from the period of the clay-
brick wall (Heuneburg IV = Hallstatt D1)

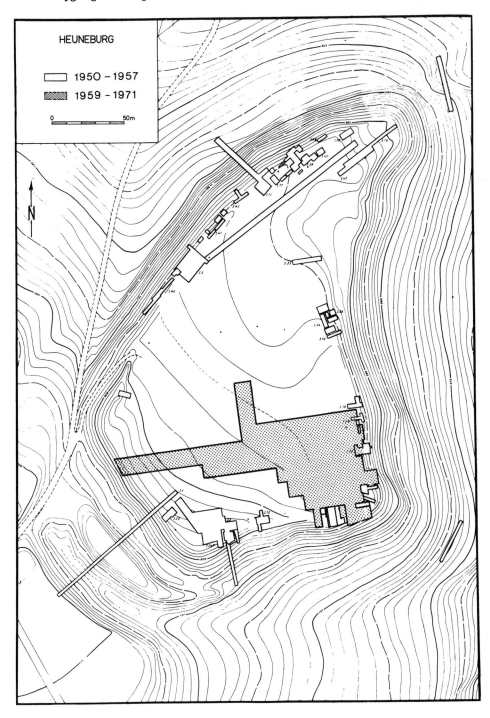

Figure 24   The Heuneburg on the upper Danube: Excavated areas, including 1973

buildings are neither simple nor standardized, as they were during the Neolithic and Bronze Ages. Buildings seem to have been constructed solely on the basis of immediate needs. Especially striking is a structure at least 30 m long, divided into three 'naves', the middle one having a width of 9 m (Fig. 25). The construction of such buildings presupposes a knowledge of statics, particularly in the roof construction.

With this information about the nature of their settlements we may conclude that citadels such as the Heuneburg and certainly also those on Mont Lassois and Hohen-Asperg were of an essentially different type from other settlements. The quality and the individuality of the find material, the richly furnished graves of the lords of the sites and other observations surely imply some special organisation or planning of the inner areas of these sites. With such strong Mediterranean influence as we have seen in the case of the brick wall, we must also consider the effects of such influence on the internal structure of the citadel's settlement. The existence of a workshop quarter already demonstrates the presence of southern influence. If we may speculate about the future, further excavations may be concerned with a sanctuary, a market and dwellings for the *nobilitas* and the 'lords of the citadel'. Whether all these structures were in fact located within the citadel itself, or whether some were situated in the outer precincts of the site (the *suburbium*), we cannot at present say.

We may add a few words about the finds themselves. Predictably, the bulk consists of broken pottery. This pottery is of considerable significance, because with this

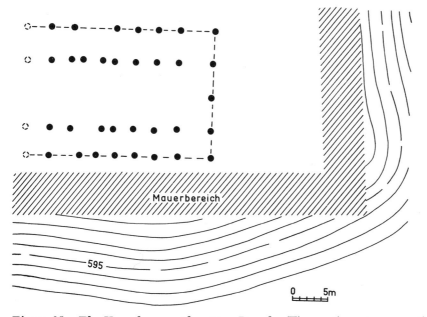

Figure 25   The Heuneburg on the upper Danube: The south-east corner: three-naved 'pillar' structure (*Ständerbau*) of Period III

assemblage we have the first opportunity to study the pottery manufacture of the late Hallstatt in detail. Until now, information on this subject has been derived almost exclusively from pottery in graves. The Heuneburg has provided the first possibility of studying the ceramic remains of a large settlement (Plate IXb). It is noteworthy that the forms are totally different from those found in graves. Numerous new forms – some of them already being mass-produced – new firing techniques and new decoration seem to suggest that pottery was being manufactured not merely for use on the site but also for a larger circle of customers. The fast wheel, also from the south, must have been in use at the Heuneburg by the end of the sixth century. Along with large storage vessels and the highly valued flasks, bowls and basins, the most unexpected find has been that of an extremely high-quality painted pottery, also derived from the south. The strong influence of imported southern ceramics, such as Greek vases, Provençal wine amphorae, and Phocaean *poterie grise*, on the Heuneburg potters is demonstrated by their active imitation of many of the Mediterranean forms.

Of the numerous small bronze finds at the site, the fibulae are of particular importance. Over two hundred specimens have already been recovered (Plate Xa, b). There is little doubt that fibulae were manufactured in workshops at the Heuneburg. These shops must have played a significant role in the development of the custom of wearing fibulae in the west Hallstatt region. The series of types extends from the older snake fibula (*Schlangenfibel*), to the boat and kettle-drum forms (*Kahn* and *Paukenfibel*), to the fibula with ornamented foot (*Fusszierfibel*), often richly trimmed with coral. La Tène fibulae are absent, though some forms indicate the influence of La Tène traditions in the construction of the foot. From the fibula series it can be said that the Hallstatt citadel must have existed during all of the late Hallstatt phases (D1–D3 of Zürn's chronology). To what extent Hallstatt D3 is contemporary with La Tène A is not yet clear.

Finds of other types of jewellery (Plate IXa) are also numerous. In addition to plain arm and neck rings of bronze, of special interest is the variety of forms in which rings of sapropelite (lignite) occur. These include thin, streamlined arm bands as well as large, heavy 'barrel' forms. Since numerous scraps of sapropelite have also been found, we may assume that these rings, made of fossilised wood, were produced in local workshops. The number of small bronze pins is also considerable. As the contemporary grave finds show, these were worn on the head and probably held the coiffure or a hair net in place. At this time – the beginning of the 'age of the fibula' – garment pins disappear almost completely. Still, there are a few specimens with large heads of glass or of skilfully drilled amber. Analyses have shown this to be Baltic amber, northern amber, and not that from the Mediterranean, as one might suppose in the light of the active relations between our site and the south. It is likely that the raw amber was imported from the eastern Alpine area, through which the great amber route, originating at the mouth of the Weichsel and continuing over the Slovakian passes, led into Picenum in Italy. On the other hand the coral (Plate

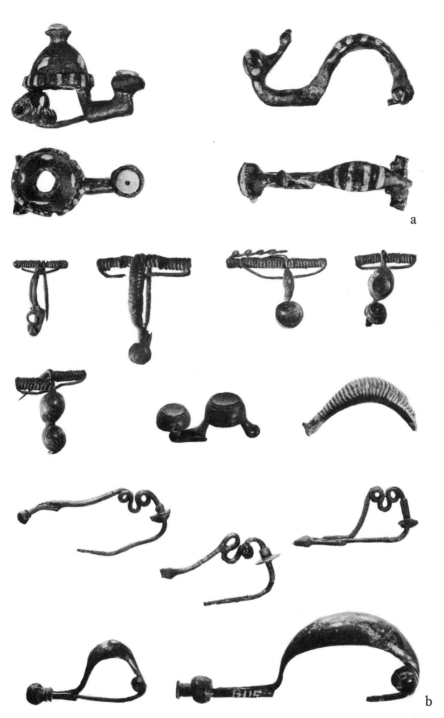

Plate X   (a) *The Heuneburg on the upper Danube:* 'Kettle-drum' and bird-head fibulae
with rich coral inlay (Scale: 1 : 1)
(b) *The Heuneburg on the upper Danube:* Late Hallstatt fibulae (Hallstatt D1–3)
(Scale: 1 : 1)

Xa), used chiefly for inlay, certainly came from the western Mediterranean area. A small 'branch' of coral indicates that this material was probably imported in its native state and worked into usable form at the site.

Sheet-bronze was apparently also worked here. A large number of fragments of sheet-bronze have been found. These are often folded together, suggesting that they represent raw material to be remelted. Many pieces are decorated with finely punched bosses, indicating that in addition to sheet-bronze waistbands, various forms of vessels of this material were produced. Also present is a fragment of a repeatedly mended kettle of sheet-iron with ring handles.

Iron as well as bronze was worked to a considerable extent at the Heuneburg. A large number of iron implements, particularly knives, have been recovered. It is not always easy to distinguish certain Hallstatt tool forms from those of the early Middle Ages. Of importance is a large four-sided iron bar, with ends drawn out to a point, found on the latest habitation surface of the last Heuneburg period, I (Plate XIb). This is one of the very few well-dated specimens of this type of bar, which belongs to the phase of transition to early La Tène (Fig. 26). It consists of iron of a high purity and indicates, along with several smaller fragments of others, that iron was worked at the site. If there is still any doubt about the existence of metalworking shops in the citadel area, then the discovery of numerous fragments of casting-moulds, pieces of crucibles of fireclay and slag from bronze and iron processing, all found particularly within the 'workshop area', should dispel any such uncertainty.

We have not yet mentioned the numerous finds of antler and horn. Antler was a particularly favoured material, used for a variety of purposes. Of specially skilful workmanship are a number of 'spacer beads' of thinly worked slabs of horn. These objects, serving as links in large pendants similar to the well-known amber 'spacers' of the Bronze Age, were perforated with the use of extremely fine boring tools. In all probability, mechanical tools such as drills and lathes were in use during the late Hallstatt. Familiarity with such devices would also have come from the south. The small finds from the Heuneburg, in spite of their fragmentary condition, provide a profound insight into the handicraft skills of the late Hallstatt. Until now this information was available only in small assemblages, primarily from grave goods.

An insight into the dietary habits of the Heuneburg residents is provided by the immense quantity of animal bones recovered, already amounting to over 5,000 kg. These are being analysed by the Institute of Animal Medicine of the University of Munich. The studies have demonstrated that domestic animals were of far greater importance to the inhabitants than wild animals. Over half the bones recovered are those of a small breed of cattle. Many others of the total number represent the domestic pig, which presumably subsisted on acorns in the nearby forests. Sheep, goats and horses played only a subordinate role. The small percentage of wild animal bones present is striking, particularly since the forests at that time supported a wild life incomparably richer than that of today. In several cases aurochs, bison, brown bear, wolf, lynx, fox, badger and beaver have been identified among the

Plate XI   (a) (above) *The Heuneburg on the upper Danube:* Excavated surface in the interior, with settlement remains from different periods of occupation
(b) (below left) *The Heuneburg on the upper Danube:* Iron bars of 'double pyramidal' form, from a living floor of Period I (Scale: approx. 1:6)
(c) (below right) *The Heuneburg on the upper Danube:* Impression from a mould for the handle of an Etruscan bronze ewer (Scale: 1:1)

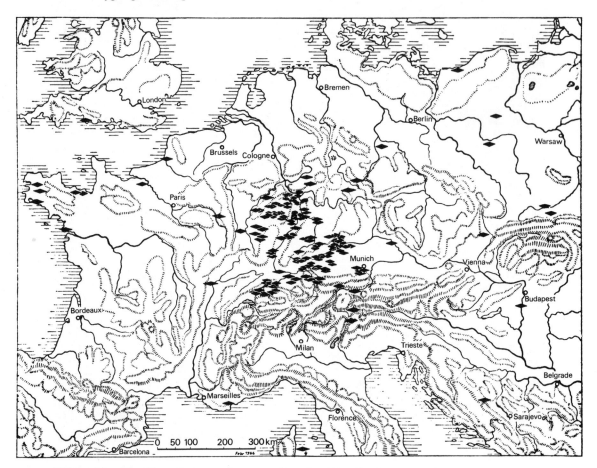

Figure 26   The Heuneburg on the upper Danube: Distribution map of 'double pyramidal' iron bars

bones analysed. The animal most hunted was the red deer, whose antlers were prized for the manufacture of various items. The wild boar was also hunted to some extent. Among the numerous birds represented were hawk, eagle, moor-hen and wild goose, whose habitat was most likely the marshy and wooded *'Donaumoos'* – the boggy areas of the Danube valley.

Some time during the fifth century B.C. the Hallstatt citadel suffered its final destruction in a conflagration. Its abandonment can perhaps be connected with the great wanderings of the Celts which began in this century and had major effects upon the Old World of the time. Besides the Heuneburg, the other 'seats of the nobility' known to us, such as the Hohenasperg near Ludwigsburg and Mont Lassois near Châtillon-sur-Seine, were also abandoned at that time. The culture-province north-west of the Alps, which once flourished so actively, suddenly faded from the lime-light of central European development.

Not until the seventh century A.D. did the Heuneburg again attract substantial settlement. The excavations have unexpectedly brought to light iron spurs, keys, and various iron tools (Fig. 27), as well as characteristic pottery types, all found in small rectangular house pits typical of this period (Fig. 28). For the first time, in the eighth century, literary sources become available. For example, the Old High German word *huntari* lies behind the name of the village of Hundersingen, just 2 km

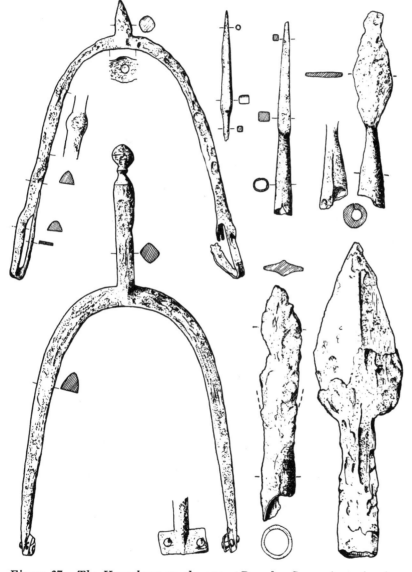

Figure 27   The Heuneburg on the upper Danube: Spurs, lance heads and crossbow bolts from the Carolingian–Ottonian Period (Scale: 1 : 1)

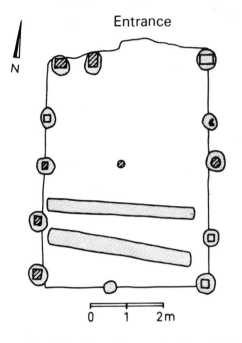

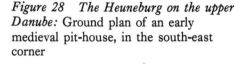

Figure 28 The Heuneburg on the upper Danube: Ground plan of an early medieval pit-house, in the south-east corner

west of the Heuneburg, cited in old charters as *Huntari-singen*. The *huntari*, Latin *centenarius*, was a leader of a body of one hundred men, in this case a leader of garrison units such as those the Frank, Chlodwig, sent into the upper Danube area following his victory over the Alemanni in A.D. 496. As representatives of the Frankish imperial power, the *huntari* naturally had their strongholds and it seems obvious to see in the Heuneburg such a stronghold. The rebuilding of the ruins on the Heuneburg, quite possibly accomplished by the *huntari* and his men, is not mentioned in any documents. The only evidence for this event is the preservation of the word in the name of the village of Hundersingen. Presumably the *huntari* who established his residence here eventually found entry into the important families of the region and he may himself have finally become the progenitor of a noble line which had its residence in the territory beneath the Bussen hill.

The new lords of the Heuneburg completely rebuilt the site, changing its form and enlarging it (Fig. 17). The huge ditches which girded the entire citadel belong to this latest major building phase. The double ditches at the west side of the site, nearly 20 m deep, were probably dug during the ninth or tenth centuries, when rider-bands of Hungarians plundered the land north of the Alps and forced the populace to take major defensive measures. Probably it was also at this time that an extensive outer fort was added on to the Heuneburg, of which one last wall fragment outside of the main citadel has survived. In any case, the tenth-century Heuneburg seems to have had a significance hardly less than that of the Hallstatt fortress, though the political situations were totally different.

As the danger of the Hungarian raids passed, the Heuneburg gradually lost its importance. At the very last phase of its occupation, only the outermost part of the south-east corner of the site was still occupied and this was blocked off from the rest by a ditch and a wall. The remaining land of the old citadel was left empty. We do not know who lived here at that time, but it was still a man living with his band of followers, one who did not withdraw to the seclusion of a knight's castle, as was the custom then. This last archaeologically recognisable period in the history of the citadel was an episode of short duration. Soon afterwards the plough obliterated inside the ramparts all the traces of a splendid past.

Acknowledgments

Plans and sketches were made available by the Tübingen Heuneburg Project, under the direction of Dr Egon Gersbach. Photographers not connected with the Institute in Tübingen are cited in the text; Mrs Heidi Rein, the Institute photographer, arranged the entire photographic section of the chapter. Drawings of finds and excavation plans were done by the Institute draftsmen, Mr Rolf Wagner and Miss Kathrin Rosskoth. I am very grateful to Peter Wells of the Peabody Museum, Boston, for his excellent translation of this chapter.

Addendum

Between 1970 and 1973 three additional excavation campaigns have been carried out. The plan shown in Fig. 24 reflects results through 1973. The south-east corner has been almost completely excavated. During the 1971–2 field seasons the east–west axis was completed; in the course of this work remains of a large timber-framed wall (*Holzkastenmauer*) of Middle Bronze Age date were found in the western area above the big ditches. This wall, the first of its type in central Europe, belongs to the settlement of Middle and Late Bronze Age date mentioned in the text. During the 1972–3 excavation campaigns the 'Danube Gate' on the eastern side of the site was fully exposed. In addition, evidence came to light of intensive building activity in the centre of the inner area. In the coming years the north–south axis of the grid system is to be completed, the entire southern half of the site excavated, and the main gate in the north-west investigated, along with the still unexposed part of the clay brick wall.

Among the rich finds of the last three years, especially noteworthy is the fragment of a casting mould for an Etruscan bronze flagon (*Germania* 51, 1973, 72ff. with Fig. 1 and Plates 5 and 6; here, Plate XI(c)). O. von Vacano suggests that the still recognisable Silenus mask of the handle attachment can be dated roughly to the period 480–460 B.C. Thus the find provides a substantially later absolute dating point for the Heuneburg than that indicated by the Attic black-figure pottery. Since all dates derived from southern imports are *termini post quem*, the end of the Heuneburg can well have been as late as the second half of the fifth century. This evidence provides a new point for discussion of the problem of the end of Hallstatt D and the beginning of La Tène A.

Bibliography (1974)

Gersbach, E., 'Heuneburg – Aussensiedlung – Jüngere Adelsnekropole. Eine historische Studie', *Marburger Beiträge zur Archäologie der Kelten. Festschrift Wolfgang Dehn* (report of excavations), No. 1, 1969, 29ff.

Gersbach, E., 'Die mittelbronzezeitlichen Wehranlagen der Heuneburg bei Hundersingen a.d. Donau', *Archäologisches Korrespondenzblatt* 3, 1973, 417ff.

Kimmig, W., *Die Heuneburg an der oberen Donau* (guide to prehistoric and early historical monuments in Württemberg and Hohenzollern, with complete bibliography up to 1968), No. 1, 1968.

Kimmig, W., 'Frühe Kelten an der oberen Donau', *Bild der Wissenschaft* 1971, 1132ff.

Kimmig, W., 'Zum Fragment eines Este III – Gefässes von der Heuneburg an der oberen Donau', *Hamburger Beiträge zur Archäologie* III, 2, 1973.

Kimmig, W. and Gersbach, E., 'Die Grabungen auf der Heuneburg 1966–1969', *Germania* 49, 1971, 21ff.

Kimmig, W. and Vacano, O. v., 'Zu einem Gussform-Fragment einer etruskischen Bronzekanne von der Heuneburg an der oberen Donau', *Germania* 51, 1973, 72ff.

Lang, Amei, 'Die geriefte Drehscheibenkeramik der Heuneburg', *Römisch-Germanische Forschungen* 34, 1973 (Heuneburgstudien III).

Mansfeld, G., 'Die Fibeln der Heuneburg. Ein Beitrag zur Geschichte der Späthallstattfibel', *Römisch-Germanische Forschungen* 33, 1973 (Heuneburgstudien II).

Chapter III

The excavation of Bryggen, Bergen, Norway

Asbjørn E. Herteig

Bergen is situated on the west coast of Norway midway between Oslo and Trondheim. It is often called 'the town of the seven mountains'. This gives rather an inexact picture of the topographical situation, for although surrounded by high, fairly steep mountains, the town lies almost open to the North Sea.

To the north, low, green islands give lee to the town and sheltered waters for shipping. The coastal passage between these islands was the country's main traffic artery from north to south. Bergen's position on this artery and consequent ease of access has been of fundamental importance for its development through the centuries. The town offers little in the way of hinterland and the many fjords and mountains of western Norway may appear forbidding to a modern observer. But to Norwegians the fjords — like the ocean itself — have rarely been a hindrance and even a thousand years ago, when Bergen was still in an embryonic stage, the deep fjords served as a connecting link. This is why, in spite of its relatively barren hinterland, Bergen could take root precisely where it did, by a sheltered harbour behind the skerries.

Literary sources tell us very little about the town during its first century of existence but we may conclude that it must have developed very rapidly, even by modern standards. As the capital of the ancient Kingdom of Norway, it enjoyed a flourishing and rapid expansion; this was followed by a long period of foreign dominations and ultimately by an arduous recovery of lost status.

When Bergen was little more than a century old, in 1191, Danish crusaders described it in these words:

Its great power (*eminentiori potentia*) makes it the most important town (*civitas*) in the land. It is rich and has abundant resources of many kinds. Of the large fish called 'skrei' there are such quantities that weight and number fail to describe them. There one can, if one will, see a gathering of ships and people from all quarters – Icelanders, Greenlanders, Englishmen, Germans, Danes, Swedes and Gotlanders, and still more that would be too lengthy to list. There are also large quantities of honey, grain, fine garments, silver and other merchandise, and one may purchase all of these things.

Until the middle of the thirteenth century foreigners were only permitted to stay in Bergen between the two Holy Rood Days – 3 May and 14 September. But from about 1260 there are definite indications of 'winter dwellers', some of them Germans. Apart from the Germans, the strongest influx was of Dutch and English merchants, of whom we have lasting evidence in place and street names.

Towards the middle of the fourteenth century the German Office was established in Bergen, and, with the support of the Hanseatic League, rapidly gained more and more power. It obtained a dominating position and its members were under an obligation to obey the special laws laid down by 'the Office'. This extraordinary state of affairs led to many difficulties and conflicts, both local and national, but economic and political conditions at the time made it impossible to alter the situation.

The German Office became so deeply and strongly rooted in the commercial life of Bergen that it continued to exist for over a century after the dissolution of the Hanseatic League in 1630. It was not until 1764 that the last German property passed into Norwegian ownership. This interim period was characterised by the acquisition of Norwegian citizenship by many of the remaining German merchants.

When we speak of *Bryggen* (the Wharf) in Bergen, we mean the characteristic row of old timber buildings along the eastern shore of the inner harbour – *Vågen* – stretching from the former Royal Castle southwards. In the main, this quarter has retained the distinctive features of the early Middle Ages to the present day (Plate XIIa, Fig. 29).

Here, in the heart of the town, is also the Mariakirken, Bergen's oldest building (Fig. 29). This church of St Mary, the Castle and Bryggen form a venerable triad of historical significance, representing royal might, ecclesiastical power and the commercial strength of the townsmen.

Ships anchored at Bryggen for loading and unloading and a considerable trade, both wholesale and retail, was carried out here. Along the 'Street' (the present *Övregaten*) (Fig. 29), which bordered the rear of Bryggen, lay the workshops of the artisans.

The buildings today consist of parallel rows of houses, 80–90 m long, their gables facing seawards (Plate XIIb). The rows are mainly grouped two by two, with a passage between. In medieval times, several merchants and journeymen lived together in a *gård* such as this and when the gates at each end of the common

Plate XII (a) (above) *Bryggen, Norway:* The seaward façade as it looked at the turn of the century. Only the central part now remains. The northern end burnt down in 1955 and the near section was rebuilt about 1900

(b) (below) *Bryggen, Norway:* Only a small quarter of Bryggen now exists but the old wooden buildings with pointed gables facing seawards still give the harbour its distinctive character. The architecture is a fragment of medieval life preserved into modern times. The ground floors are narrow and the upper storeys wide, with a gallery overlooking the passage. Each unit of houses (*gård*) still has its original name: for example, *Bugården, Bredsgården, Enhjörningen* (the Unicorn), *Svensgården*

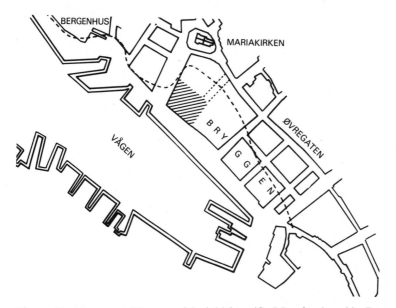

Figure 29 Bryggen, Norway: Mariakirken (St Mary's church), *Bergenhus* (the fortress) and *Vågen* (the inner harbour). The area hatched with diagonal lines was burned to the ground on 4 July 1955. It is in this area that the archaeological excavations have since taken place. The dotted line indicates the apparent course of the waterline at the time of the foundation of the township, nine hundred years ago. As time passed, building encroached more and more on the inner harbour. The houses which are still intact are situated about 100 yd beyond the old waterfront. The modern quays of the city lie 140 yd farther out in the original harbour and indicate a vigorous growth which took place mainly during the Middle Ages

passage were closed, it constituted an enclosed community. The system which developed from this special kind of fellowship and communal life had great significance as a stabilising and conserving factor. Together with the complicated conditions of ownership, this social order was one of the most important causes of the preservation of Bryggen in its original form right up to our times. The very earliest stages of this development were unknown to us, or at the best a matter of guesswork. Now, archaeological investigation has brought to light material which provides new sources of knowledge and, above all, has brought us into close and living contact with the people of the times and given us a better understanding of their daily life, and cultural and economic relations, in a hitherto obscure period. It is particularly important that the Bryggen excavations have uncovered a wealth of finds from the pre-Hanseatic period, for which documentary evidence was sparse. Such material has come to light under the 'German Wharf', as Bryggen was once called (Fig. 29).

In the course of the years, many theories have been put forward concerning the foundation of the city. Superficial enquiry might suggest that the matter is simple, for the Norse sagas are unanimous in recounting how this took place. King

Olav Kyrre – Olav the Peaceful – founded a market town in *Biorgyn*, they say, and this seems to tell us that the town was established, by royal order, in about A.D. 1070. However, we do not know what really lies behind the words of the sagas, whether they mean that King Olav really laid out completely, or almost completely, a new settlement, or whether he simply set his seal on an earlier settlement or market place, giving it rights and privileges.

The excavations that were begun after half Bryggen was laid in ashes in the great fire of 1955 brought these problems to the fore.

After the fire of 1955, an area measuring about 70 m square was available for archaeological excavations (cf. the cross-hatched area on Fig. 29), the aim of which was defined by the State Antiquary, whose office is responsible for such excavations, as 'to ascertain the character and development of the buildings through the centuries'.

This objective, and the period of approximately six months which was originally considered sufficient to attain it, reflects the general concept of an urban excavation at that time. The excavations very soon took on a wider perspective and work actually took thirteen years and forty-five days, with 110 months in the field.

When starting, we had almost no idea of what the excavations would bring to light. We knew that there were no cellars in the area concerned, only horizontal timberwork. The excavations soon showed that not only foundations dating from the many building phases but also floors and passages were often intact, although the houses had been ravaged by fire (Plate XIIIa). After each conflagration – and there were many of them – the débris was simply levelled and new foundations built on top.

The richly structured sub-stratum made it natural to dig stratigraphically, a main principle that was followed throughout the whole excavation.

In places where the structures found were more than approximately 15 cm thick, excavation was carried out in even layers but with the localisation of the layer structure as its object. In both cases the data concerned were interrelated by a system of permanent profiles and of temporary profiles established as work proceeded.

Recording of finds

According to tradition, the original breadth of the buildings was preserved best in Bugården, in the row of houses furthest to the south. As we originally did not know whether the excavations would cover more than this one building, we started furthest back in the southernmost section and we considered it would be an advantage, within the framework of a traditional grid system of measurement, to choose a square size that would embrace the full width of the row of houses. This was possible with an 8 m square.

The square was always the recording or localisation unit. In later phases, when we were using a more flexible system of sections – relatively low sections removed as work advanced – the work was carried on independently of the square boundaries. The finds were at first recorded in the traditional manner within squares, and in relation to archaeological elements in the square, such as building features, floors, walls, hearths, streets, wells, privies, wharves and so on, and to the stratigraphical layers, often with a detailed verbal description. To ensure uniformity in these descriptions in spite of a rapidly changing and often poorly qualified body of excavators, the archaeologist in charge had to carry out recording himself, a task which a constantly changing stratigraphical situation made extensive and difficult. The need to rationalise and simplify the procedure soon became clear.

To solve this problem, verbal descriptions which, with very large numbers of finds in very complex situations, proved to be of doubtful value, were abandoned and standardised forms were prepared, in which columns were completed with simple, easily comprehensible symbols. The system we evolved functioned well. The recorded data are commensurable from object to object, and can be readily transferred to forms suitable for electronic data processing. Finally, with this system, reliable localisation of finds could be carried out by untrained, or only partially trained, excavators, a factor of no small importance in major excavations.

Chronology

During its history the buildings of Bryggen are supposed to have been ravaged by seven fires. These conflagrations are recorded in annals, sagas and official documents and we know not only the year but sometimes even the day or the night that they raged.

The burnt strata that came to light in the field were therefore invaluable chronological clues. With their help we established a detailed relative dating system. In a few cases we have even been able to link the burnt layers to historically known conflagrations and thus firmly 'anchor' our relative dating. The best known of these 'anchor finds' is a runic inscription written by Sigurd Lavard, eldest son of King Sverre Sigurdsson. This inscription, which our established chronology had already dated at about 1200, was subsequently and independently connected by the runic specialist Aslak Liestöl with a historical event that took place on the eve of the battle of Florvåg, near Bergen, between King Sverre and a band of rebels, 'the Bearded Islanders', on 2 April 1194.

The importance of this relatively exact chronology will perhaps be better understood if I mention that the excavations at Bryggen have brought to light materials from many different parts of northern and western Europe.

The dating system built up on the basis of stratigraphy will in due course be supplemented and controlled by a tree-ring chronology. About 1,200 dendro-

Plate XIII (a) *Bryggen, Norway:* Part of the excavation showing foundations for quays and buildings dating from the twelfth and thirteenth centuries

(b) (left) *Bryggen, Norway:* Wicker fishpot made from young willow shoots, found just above the sea-bed some 8 m below the present street level; thirteenth century

(c) (right) *Bryggen, Norway:* Numerous leather objects have been found, for instance more than four thousand shoes. The shoe illustrated is of thirteenth century date, a very fine specimen for the right foot, and is richly decorated with a stamped design

chronological specimens have been taken. On the basis of these it may well be possible to establish a continuous annual-ring sequence right back to the early eleventh century.

For various reasons we began, as already mentioned, in the back right-hand corner of the area, in Bugården, 60–70 m behind the present Bryggen façade. According to the theory held by local historians, we should then have been at least 35–40 m inside the shore line at the time of the founding of the city. If so, the excavation should sooner or later have reached bedrock, the natural undisturbed subsoil. However, this did not happen, for the theory on which we based our assumption was not correct. Instead of working slowly down to bedrock, we fairly quickly struck wharf timbers, in what must once have been the harbour of the town. A total of four wharves were found, one in front of the other, as we dug our way forwards in Bugården (Plate XIIIa).

After the finding of these wharves we could draw the provisional conclusion that not only the front section of the wharf, but almost the whole of the burnt-out area must originally have been part of the actual harbour basin. This was an interesting observation, as it meant a considerable reduction of the narrow strip of *terra firma* between the foot of the mountains and the sea, and as this zone was the original building area it was important to determine its extent. This necessitated further digging, backwards from the original starting point.

The shore line at the time of the foundation of the town became our immediate aim. Only by establishing it could we get a yardstick for the subsequent architectural development and a means of reconstructing the topographical situation in the pre-urban period. We feel that we have succeeded in this object unexpectedly well, for the following reasons.

1 After having cleaned away the different layers down to the sandy subsoil we observed that at the point where the gentle-shelving foreshore met *terra firma* there was a well-defined terrace-like ledge.

2 A particularly fortunate architectural find, combined with certain other observations, made it possible for us to assess the degree of isostatic movement during the historical, or Christian, era.

This building was a wharfside shed built in the middle of the twelfth century and placed directly on the beach (Fig. 30). We could therefore draw the conclusion that in the twelfth century, at least, the rear half of the beach, where the shed was placed, had been dry in normal tide conditions. A certain number of mussels, spread over the beach in front of the shed, added confusion to our puzzle because they left a clear belt of only about 4 m in front of the shed.

If the distribution of the mussels expressed the range of the twelfth century high tide line, the area in front of the shed would in fact only have been passable at ebb-tide, a quite unsatisfactory explanation.

To our delight, marine biologists have stated that the range of mussels does not coincide with the normal high tide line. Under conditions such as those in the inner

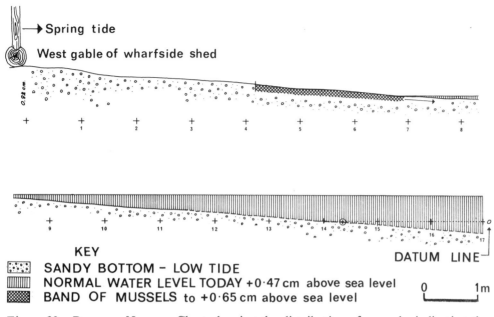

KEY

SANDY BOTTOM – LOW TIDE

NORMAL WATER LEVEL TODAY +0·47 cm above sea level

BAND OF MUSSELS to +0·65 cm above sea level

DATUM LINE

0   1m

Figure 30   Bryggen, Norway: Chart showing the distribution of mussels, indicating the high water mark

harbour of Bergen, the mussels normally occupy the 'splash zone', in this area about 20 cm above sea level at normal high tide (Fig. 30).

The maximum range of our mussels from the twelfth century corresponds to a height of 15–17 cm above present normal high tide level. It coincides perfectly well with the situation which would have occurred if the water had been allowed to run freely into our excavation ditches. In other words, if the relation between high and low tide is the same today as in the twelfth century, which is believed to be the case, and if mussels still behave as in the days of yore, we must assume that the relation between sea and land has been almost static in this area throughout the historical era.

This rather unexpected observation gives us exceptionally good possibilities of reconstructing the topographical point of departure for the foundation of the city, for the terrace-like shelf that terminated the foreshore was marked enough to stop even the highest of spring tides and thus marks the outermost point for natural building land in this area. This was a zone covering a total length of about 500 m, with an average breadth of about 120–130 m between the sea on one side and the 15 m line at the foot of the rather steep mountainous hillside on the other. So this confirmed that the first inhabitants of the area had only a narrow belt of land at their disposal, its total area comprising not more than approximately 60,000–65,000 m².

For comparison it can be mentioned that Birka in Sweden covers an area of about 90,000 m²; Hedeby, in Schleswig, about 240,000 m²; the deserted market centre

Veöy in Romsdal 35,000 m²; and Borgund in Sunmore about 40,000 m². The comparatively modest building area in Bergen must have been exceeded at a rather early date. According to our observations the first moves towards drawing the beach into the building area were made not later than sixty to seventy years after the official foundation of the city. The wharfside shed represents this second phase. Here it must be added that even this early phase was characterised by planned building, with the same ground plan as that we can see at Bryggen today, the so-called 'double building'. In the course of the next phase, in the second half of the twelfth century, the buildings spread over the whole beach, on posts or on timberwork foundations, right down to where the foreshore slopes steeply to deep water. The general appearance of the shore area, would, we think, have been approximately as shown in Fig. 31, with rows of cottages or houses on both sides of a narrow passage, each unit-house and passage on its own foundations. In the subsequent phase, the units of the double building were built on common foundations, the fronts of the passageways running together in front of the gables to form one long more or less continuous line of quays. At that time, shortly after the year 1200, Bryggen had taken on the aspect it has today (Plate XIIb).

As far as topography and the structure of building are concerned, the archaeological material provides a completely new background for an understanding of the earliest phases of local architectural development. The absolute regularity found in the pattern of the double buildings in a zone approximately 30 m along the shore, must surely indicate a considerable degree of regularity along much of the original shore from the middle of the twelfth century at the latest. But does this tell us any-

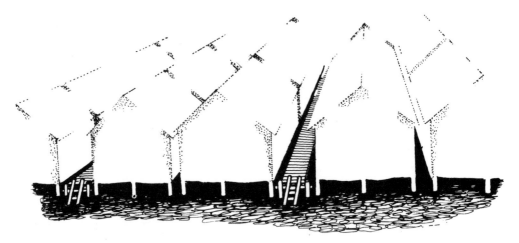

Figure 31   Bryggen, Norway: Diagram to show the appearance of the buildings along the sea-front in A.D. 1200, with rows of small buildings, most of them one storey high, built in the 'double-building' pattern. At this time each unit, consisting of building and passage, was built on a separate foundation, but as early as the next building phase the various elements of the 'double-building', were constructed on a joint foundation

thing about the actual foundation of the city? Does it tell us whether the city just grew up naturally, or whether it was founded by a deliberate act? Personally I should say yes, although it must be admitted that there is still a gap of sixty to seventy years between our excavated material and the supposed time of the foundation of the city. A review of our results in the light of the written sources opens up certain possibilities for a closer pinpointing of the foundation problem. I feel it my duty and my privilege to indicate the direction in which the archaeological evidence now available, as I see it, points.

My point of departure is our demonstration of a phase of planned construction sixty to seventy years after the supposed foundation of the city, or forty to fifty years after the death of its supposed founder. I have come to the conclusion, partly on the basis of the documented rapid growth of the city during its first half-century and partly by a combination of the written and archaeological data, details of which I shall not go into here, that the planning demonstrated can hardly be the work of anyone but the person unanimously acclaimed by the sagas as the founder of the city, King Olav Kyrre.

A previous phase as a seaside village or market place would have necessitated

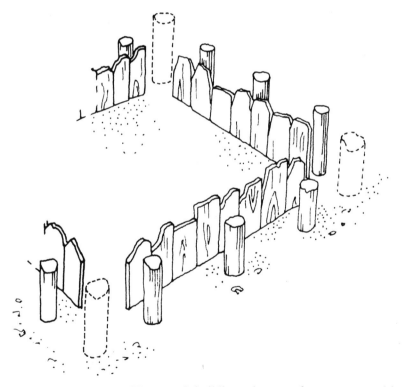

Figure 32   Bryggen, Norway: A building whose roof was supported by posts outside the walls

a relatively extensive expropriation process and the clearing away of existing build-ings, but no historian has wished to go as far as this. On the other hand, it is diffi-cult to get the historians to accept that the responsibility for this early planning really must be ascribed to Olav Kyrre, for in that case the theories concerning an earlier phase as a seaside village or market place must be dropped or considerably modified, and most historians are not yet willing to do this. That is the situation today. Only further excavation can settle the controversy.

Before the thirteenth century most of the buildings along the shore were appar-ently warehouses (Plate XIIIa). This is at any rate what is indicated by the archaeo-logical finds. The constructions sometimes appear to have been rather simple and primitive.

From the middle and later part of the twelfth century, we have wooden buildings carried on poles with a cellar-like construction under the floor (Fig. 32).

Two buildings from the latter half of the twelfth century, with open corners on the ground floor (Fig. 33) are of uncertain use. They have wooden floors and hori-zontal sills in which the vertical boards of the walls were placed.

What really lies behind this peculiar method of construction is not quite clear but it is no doubt carefully calculated, perhaps because such houses were destined for the storage of goods which needed a strong current of air.

Figure 33   Bryggen, Norway: A building with open corners on the ground plan and sills in which the vertical boards of the walls were placed

Plate XIV   (a) (above) *Bryggen, Norway:* Parts of a long building erected after the fire of 1248. The house had two doors on the ground floor and a gallery on the first floor. From this find it has been possible to determine the measurements of the storeys and the width of the gallery

(b) (below) *Bryggen, Norway:* Reconstruction of the house seen above in course of excavation. The type of house is familiar from Norwegian rural building methods. Many similar buildings are still extant in country districts and in folk museums, and indeed can still be found in Bryggen today

Besides these types it has been possible, by a happy chance, to establish that the type of building seen today at Bryggen had already been employed in the rebuilding of the Wharf after the fire of 1248. Characteristic of this type of house is a narrow ground floor and a broader first storey with projecting galleries running the length of the house (Plate XIV).

This is an extremely interesting observation, against the background of our discussions on the origin of Bryggen — whether the types of building that we know in Bryggen today were introduced by the Hanseatic merchants or descend from older Norwegian types. Our discoveries establish that the buildings had already attained their form, both as regards ground plan and individual house types, by the mid-thirteenth century at the latest. So far as I can judge, this was long before foreign elements were in a position to exert any influence in this aspect of local evolution. The landlords and builders were Norwegian; but it cannot on this account be claimed that Bryggen represents a specifically Norwegian style. More probably it is a part of our common European cultural heritage. Houses with balconies, or rows of balconies, facing the street were to be found even at the time of the Caesars in Italy, for example at Ostia; and in the Middle Ages they were known not only in Scandinavia but also on the continent. Contrary to continental practice, timber building was continued in Bergen beyond this period. This is one of the reasons why immediate architectural parallels to Bryggen no longer exist today.

The style of building is in itself interesting inasmuch as we find it repeated in our country outhouses and storage lofts (*stabbur*) (Plate XIVb). It has long been contended that these *stabbur* were typical of west European rural culture. Nevertheless, there is reason to believe that this special house type belongs in an urban milieu, where rigid conditions of property prevailed, such as those found in nearly all the towns of northern and central Europe in which archaeological investigations have been carried out.

Because of fixed property regulations, it was usual to rebuild on the previous site after a fire. There was in fact no possibility for lateral expansion, and in waterside towns the harbour set natural limits for building (like the central market-place in inland towns). Moreover, local regulations as a rule prohibited the building of taller houses.

It was natural to make use of the air above street level with the aid of galleries built onto the upper storey (Plate XIVa). This was the principle followed in densely populated Ostia, in contrast for instance to Pompeii, and it is this same principle which has been used in the closely packed quarters of Bryggen, in Visby and other towns. Our Italian colleagues, it is gratifying to learn, have found their explanation of this fact in full accordance with our own. I am therefore convinced that this type of house-building, in common with our so-called 'rose-painting', found its way to the rural districts, particularly in the mountain villages, but was originally a product of common European urban culture, possibly with its roots even farther afield, beyond the borders of our continent.

Since the thirteenth century — that is, as far back as documentary evidence goes — it seems that at least the ground floors of the Bryggen buildings were used as warehouses, whereas the upper floors, when they existed, may have been used for other purposes, for instance as dwellings for the journeymen.

Considering these rather undifferentiated functions, it seems curious that the building remains are so rich in detail. First, it has been established that framework houses exist side by side with rafted houses.

Next there is a continual change in the treatment of details, seen notably in the cutting of the log heads. Two quite different influences seem apparent in the development of the building technique. One derives from the style of the building itself, a style whose roots may be sought widely abroad. The other is the taste and fashions of succeeding generations, expressed in many details, in which can be traced the building and working methods of the various districts of western Norway.

The latter influence is inferred mainly from information from documentary sources about owners of buildings at Bryggen from the earlier period (thirteenth and fourteenth centuries). The buildings were then to a large extent owned by governors and landowners, abbots and bishops, and it is reasonable to assume that these men to some extent brought their own local building traditions to Bryggen, thereby giving it the wealth of colourful and varied detail witnessed by our finds.

There is also a considerable development from the rather simple buildings of the twelfth century, often with the wall-planks sunk into the earth, to the highly developed technique and fine treatment of detail of the thirteenth and fourteenth centuries.

In addition to rich finds of a topographical and architectural nature, the excavations have brought to light an extensive material of pottery, leather, bone, horn, wood, textiles, remains of ships and large quantities of food remains consisting of fish and animal bones, berries, nuts, grapes, and shellfish (Plates XIIIb,c; XVa–c; XVIa, b).

The objects of wood, bone and horn and the majority of the leather work and textile fragments most probably derive from local sources. On the other hand, a number of decorated sheaths for knives and swords have apparently been imported from England, where there are parallels for almost all the motifs and patterns found on ours.

The majority of the finds belong to the twelfth and thirteenth centuries. Of the many thousands of earthenware pots, we have not been able to establish Norwegian provenance for a single one.

The abundant production of pottery which was such a striking feature of the Migration Period declined during the Merovingian and Viking times, and when the establishment of towns and other population centres towards the end of the Viking period and in the early Middle Ages provided a basis for indigenous production, the local market seems to have been completely swamped by cheap pottery from England and the continent (Plate XVa,b). Against this flood of mass-produced goods, rural craftsmanship, which might have survived, had no chance. This must be the main reason why it has not been possible to find remains of Norwegian pottery in the archaeological material at Bryggen.

A superficial study of the ceramic finds leaves us with the impression that the period from the middle of the twelfth to the eighteenth century can, broadly speaking, be divided into three distinct phases.

In the earliest phase, from the middle of the twelfth century to the first half of the thirteenth, most of the pottery, cooking pots, wine jars and beakers seem to have come from the continental North Sea district, with a lesser amount from south-east England (Plate XVa,b).

Continental imports continued in the next phase (the thirteenth and fourteenth centuries) but during this period the English material is wholly predominant. Then, in the third phase – from about 1400 – came a change, in that English pottery disappeared and the continental, mostly represented by goods of high quality, completely dominated the local market.

If a graph were drawn to illustrate the respective occurrence of English and continental pottery in Norway, it would coincide most strikingly with the fluctuations of our trade with these regions, in accordance with accepted deductions from written sources.

In addition to Rhenish, Dutch and Belgian goods in the earliest phase, mineralogical tests have shown that a certain variant of the Pingsdorf type of pottery was imported from the Duinge district of Hanover, and it is reasonable to suppose that this was shipped via Bremen (Plate XVa).

In the English material a number of export centres are represented, ranging from Dover and the London–Winchester area in the south, up the east coast to King's Lynn, Boston and Scarborough (Plate XVb). If marked on a map these British localities would faithfully reflect the regions which, according to the written sources, were most frequently visited by Norwegian seamen and merchants during the periods in question, the thirteenth and fourteenth centuries. It is not surprising that the archaeological material confirms these trade connections with the British Isles, already so well documented through literary sources. Of greater interest is the fact that the material indicates a lively commerce with countries south of the North Sea and throws light on important aspects of a period very poorly served by documentary evidence. The rich material of ceramic imports from the fifteenth and sixteenth centuries points exclusively in the direction of the Rhineland and the types from this period are often of such unmistakable individual and local design that it is as a rule not difficult to point to the actual place of production.

It is a curious fact that imported pottery is never mentioned in Scandinavian medieval literature. There has been a tendency to regard these vessels as no more than containers for other commodities, not as independent merchandise. To a certain degree this was probably the case, but it cannot be considered an acceptable explanation for the great mass of pottery and the widespread use to which it was put, as

Plate XV   (a) (above left) *Bryggen, Norway:* Containers and beakers, most of them with painted decoration of the Pingsdorf type. Mineralogical tests show that they come from the area around Hanover

(b) (above right) *Bryggen, Norway:* Face-jug with short pointed beard, probably made in East Anglia

(c) (below) *Bryggen, Norway:* When the excavations of Bryggen began, in the autumn of 1955, only six or seven runic inscriptions originating from Bergen were known. By October 1967, five hundred and thirty-seven inscriptions had been found from Bryggen alone. For the most part they are carved on wooden pegs, which may be anything from one to twelve inches long. The peg illustrated, inscribed on all four sides, accommodates a complete letter, the content of which is quoted on page 84

Plate XVI   (a) (above) *Bryggen, Norway:* A small knotted stick, portraying a fleet of thirteenth-century ships, arranged in battle order. There are no less than forty-eight 'Viking' ships depicted, with dragon's heads and golden vanes on the bows. On the back of the stick is carved a 'Viking' ship with dragon heads at bow and stern and a runic inscription which reads: 'Here sails the valiant seafarer'
(b) (below) *Bryggen, Norway:* Miniature boat, the stems or sternposts of others, miniature weapons, pottery figures, etc., which show that children lived and played at Bryggen

far as we can judge. Pottery has been used for toys and for decoration, for lamps, containers, beakers, and cooking-pots. It is possible that this group of goods is concealed behind the term *merceria*, which apparently included everything that could be called merchandise of minor importance.

Apart from imports from England, Germany, Holland and Belgium, the Bryggen finds bear witness to relations with a number of other countries. Whereas polychrome pottery came from south-west France, a mortar of special type points to north-east France. Grapes of different kinds came from the Rhineland and grain reveals trading contacts with Eastern Europe. Decorated walrus skulls and chessmen carved from walrus tusks point to connections with Iceland and Greenland. Italian leaden seals and combs of boxwood all tell their tale of long-distance trade in all directions.

The character of domestic trade is more difficult to ascertain, since many goods were of a perishable nature. Research in recent years lends support to the assumption that merchandise such as pottery and textiles has in any case been distributed to smaller trading and marketing places along the coast, but it is not known if they ever found their way to farmers and fishers of western and northern Norway.

The finds on which we have commented are all objects (artefacts) but the excavations have also enriched us with written records, dealing for the most part with other aspects of life. These are runic inscriptions on pieces of bone or stone, sometimes as decoration on shoes but mostly carved on small wooden pegs of anything from an inch to a foot in length (Plate XVc).

The content covers many subjects, from childbirth to life in the next world, from magic charms to ensure safe confinements to erotic poems and lays, curses, pious prayers and confidential reports.

Approximately a third of the runic material of 551 inscriptions is made up of labels with a man's or woman's name carved on a wooden peg, which is either pointed at one end or supplied with a hole (to fasten to a bale of goods or something similar). Several of the inscriptions illustrate the commercial life of the day: 'Ragnar owns this yarn', 'Solveig owns these threads'. On the back is given the weight of the threads in question: $4\frac{1}{2}$ marks (a little more than two pounds).

One inscription shows the settlement of three bills. We can imagine that the creditor has sent his collector to the debtors and that this man has received the monies owing and inscribed on a wooden peg the amount paid by each debtor. The peg has been delivered together with the cash to the creditor, with the following inscription: 'Baard has paid $1\frac{1}{2}$ öre but with short weight'; 'Henrik has paid 2 ertogs but with bad silver'; 'Ingemund has paid $2\frac{1}{2}$ ertogs'. The creditor has then given his acquittance by writing *uihi* next to each of the amounts, probably a corruption of the Latin *vidi* – 'I have seen'. We can perhaps claim that not only is this the very first receipt known in Norway but that *vidi* is an anticipation of the accountant's well known tick, shaped like a V.

The following must be regarded as a confidential business letter:

To Havgrim, his friend Tore the Fair sends greeting in the name of God and himself, true fellowship and friendship. I have failed sorely in our pact. Neither beer nor fish has been forthcoming. This I would have thee know but make no demands on me. Bid the husbandman journey south and see how we fare.
Urge him to this and make no demands on me. Do not suffer Long Torstein to know of this. Send me gloves. Should Sigrid want for aught, bid her come to thee . . .

(Plate XVc). The rest of the letter is obscure.

One of the most significant inscriptions, from an archaeologist's point of view, is the letter from Sigurd Lavard referred to above; but there also exist others referring to known historical personages. A letter related in style to the sagas of the time of the civil wars in Norway contains this passage:

I would bid thee hie from this creek and cut a letter to Olav Hettusvein's sister. She is in the nunnery in Bergen. Ask her and thy friends for counsel if it be thy wish to come to terms. Thy feeling for justice is not as that of the Earl . . .

The rest of the letter is missing; it was probably continued on another tablet. The nun here mentioned must have been the sister of one of the rebels in the service of Olav Ugjaeva, who were known by the name of *hettusveiner*. It should also be mentioned that this inscription was probably of a secret nature, as it was cut into the base of a typical wax tablet. It had most likely been covered with wax on which a letter of a more innocuous character had been inscribed – a procedure not unknown at the time. A number of inscriptions in various types of cryptic runes have also been uncovered.

Most of the runic inscriptions throw light on the people of those times far more clearly than purely material remains could ever do: 'Torkel the coinmaker sends thee pepper'; 'The Fana belt enhanced thy beauty'; 'Ingebjorg loved me when I was in Stavanger' . . .

The linguistic and literary value of the runic inscriptions is a study in itself. Lines in the verse-forms of the skalds and inscriptions connected with the poetic Edda represent a valuable addition to the few such Norwegian inscriptions that were known before the Bryggen material came to light. The runic scholar Aslak Liestøl, who is engaged in continuous research in connection with these finds and upon whose translations and conclusions I rely, maintains that the study of the Bryggen runic material has shown results that will influence our interpretation of the history of literature at the height of the Middle Ages in Norway.

The precondition for the extensive commercial relations to which the Bryggen finds bear witness is, in my opinion, the century-old voyaging across the North Sea, westwards and southwards. These connections cannot, as was earlier assumed, have been broken off with the advent of Christianity but seem to have gradually taken on a more peaceable, more mercantile character.

Another factor that furthered trade was Norwegian shipping and shipbuilding, which had reached such remarkable heights in the Viking era. Recent finds at Bryggen have aroused fresh discussion on these points and I shall make a few brief comments on the matter.

It has been maintained that the shipbuilding technique developed by the Nordic peoples almost to a fine art, as demonstrated in such splendid ships as those of Gokstad and Oseberg, was incapable of renewal or further progress (Fig. 34). With the largest ocean-going longships such as Håkon Håkonsson's *Kristsuden* which boasted thirty-seven benches (seventy-four oarsmen), a zenith was reached that must have been difficult to surpass. Other technical solutions had to be found if progress were to be made in this field and many contend that we were not capable of it in the northern countries. On the other hand, we know that not only the Dutch but also the Germans developed new types of ships with a larger cargo capacity and the hegemony of the North Sea trade and all that followed in its wake was lost to the Norwegians.

In opposition to this theory, it has been claimed that the old sagas often mention various types of vessels. We know their names: *dreki, knǫrr, skeið, snekkja, karfi, buza* and it seems highly unlikely that these terms refer merely to the various purposes for which the ships were used. They must designate ships of different constructions or types.

English customs rolls from the early fourteenth century have documented not only the ship's name and that of the owner and the skipper but also the size and type of cargo. Ships such as *Olavsbussen* (Olavesbusce), *Biskopsbussen, Norgesbussen* (Buska Norvagie), *Gullskobussen* (Goldscobusce) and others were Norwegian vessels and several of them have carried cargoes that must have been considerably larger than those the Viking ships usually transported.

From one of the oldest customs rolls extant – that of King's Lynn, dealing with the period from 5 February 1303 to 19 May 1304 – we learn that of 235 foreign ships calling, thirty were Norwegian – that is, about one eighth of the total number. Nevertheless, the value of the goods imported in the Norwegian ships represented more than half of the total import. This testifies in the first place to the importance, demand for and value of the Norwegian goods, but it also leaves one with a clear impression that it was not only small ships that the Norwegians used to ply the trade-routes of the North Sea and for voyages to Iceland and Greenland. In the case of these two countries there is clear evidence in the sagas that stoutly built ships of a specially broad type were employed by the Norwegians.

Previous archaeological investigations have, with only a few exceptions, brought to light only the traditional types of ship. In the course of recent years, ship finds have altered the picture completely. We shall here draw especial attention to the finds excavated some years ago at Kalmar in Sweden (Fig. 34). In all, four ships were

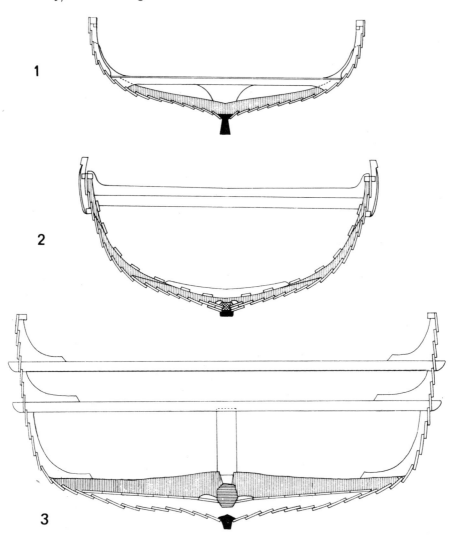

Figure 34   Bryggen, Norway: Cross-sections showing the comparative size and type of midships construction of the largest Bryggen ship (3), the largest of the Kalmar ships (2) and the Gokstad ship (1)

found, of a construction distinguished by its solid shoring, with massive square timbers of which the bulkheads protruded beyond the planking. These ships were equipped with stern rudders and capstans. There can be no doubt that we are here confronted with a specialized type of vessel — a trading-ship or freighter most likely utilized for the Baltic traffic.

Until the Kalmar ships came to light, this type of ship was almost unknown, but now it has been documented archaeologically not only in Sweden and Norway but also in England, Denmark and Germany. The characteristic bulkheads, which protrude beyond the outer planking, can be recognised on a number of medieval seals from the whole North Sea area. They can be seen for instance on the seals of Sandwich and Winchelsea in the thirteenth century, Harderwijk in 1280, Kiel in 1365 and Amsterdam in 1418.

It seems reasonable to conclude that we have here some basic elements in a very common type of ship, probably well known in all the ports bordering the North Sea. There are good grounds for the theory that the vessels that crossed the great open seas – the North Sea and the North Atlantic to England, Iceland and Greenland – must have been considerably larger and sturdier than the ships found at Kalmar. This has been shown to be the case by Norwegian material.

The special method of construction entails not just shoring up against pressure from without but also bracing against pressure from within. It must have been considered of vital importance to guard against pressures from within, to warrant the equipment of ships with apparently such impractical beam heads protruding through the planking even partly below the water-line. It is only possible to understand the purposes of this construction when one considers the special harbour conditions of medieval times. Many of the oldest towns and trading-ports along the coast had beaches that were dry at low tide. Here the ships lay to (Plate XVIa), so that both loading and unloading could take place conveniently at ebb-tide. Such were the conditions in many of the oldest seaports on the North Sea and, surprisingly enough, also in Bergen.

Our excavations have revealed the sloping beaches of which the sagas give confirmation in their picturesque description of how *The Guest Wing*, one of King Magnus Erlingsson's ships, was left on the beach once when he was forced to flee from King Sverre. *The Guest Wing* was, characteristically enough, his supply ship.

The special shipbuilding technique here described seems to have been characteristic of trading vessels and may have evolved from the necessity to strengthen the ships against pressure from within when lying fully loaded, high and dry on the beaches, prior to unloading.

Whereas the Kalmar ships were relatively small, varying between 53 and 60 ft in length, the ship finds at Bryggen, of corresponding construction, show considerably larger dimensions (Fig. 34). In addition to frames, knees, masts, sheathing planks, oars, etc., the Bryggen finds include square timbers and beams of the characteristic Kalmar type and other important parts of at least three large ships. The first two are made of pine, the third of oak, and two of these ships must have been nearly double the size of the Kalmar ships.

A series of discoveries which has enabled us to reconstruct the largest of the Bryggen ships was made in the spring of 1962. Various timbers from the vessel had been used to shore up wharves and house foundations. Further pieces were excavated during the 1965 season, so that we now have between fifty and sixty parts of the same ship, most of them showing important structural details. This ship had a maximum width of nearly 30 ft and a maximum length of between 87 and 90 ft.

The length is calculated from the proportions of the Kalmar ships. The windlass is 18 ft long and has a diameter of about 20 in.; the keelson is approximately 40 ft in length.

The ship remains at Bryggen (Plate XVIb) have special significance since we can infer that in all probability two of them, including the largest of the three, were of Norwegian origin. They were built of pine, which in those days pointed to the west and north of Norway as the place of origin. The case for indigenous origin is strengthened by two finds, one apparently the raw material for a large stern rudder, the other for a stout frame. The relatively narrow outer planking of the vessels also differs from continental shipbuilding traditions. Both finds seem to confirm the saga records of the building of large ships in Bergen. Håkon Håkonsson, for instance, had his large *Kristsuden* built here about the middle of the thirteenth century, slightly earlier than the presumed date of our vessel.

On the basis of the Bryggen material so far uncovered one may deduce that here in the north during the eleventh, twelfth and thirteenth centuries types of vessel other than the usual Viking longships existed, as the sagas in fact indicate. The local coastal war-fleet – the *Leidangen*, as it was called – continued, however, to make use of the Viking type of ship until far into the fourteenth century. Pictorial evidence of this has been found at Bryggen (Plate XVI).

The Bryggen finds, seen as a whole, give an impression of intense economic activity and this harmonises perfectly with the well-nigh unbelievable technical and topographical development of the town. The excavations have uncovered one town after another, with wharves and harbour constructions pushed steadily further out into the sea, until the present waterfront lies some 140 m beyond the original beach.

This striking expansion, which for the most part took place in the Middle Ages, must reflect a steadily rising demand as the result of increasing economic resources. It was this economic background that created the right conditions for a growth of national power around A.D. 1200 and for the cultural advances that followed in its wake. Strong west European influences can be traced in our architecture, sculpture and pictorial arts, not least in Bergen, where a school of painting developed that produced works of art which still give constant pleasure. Foreign influences were also felt in literature, music, costume and way of life. It can be claimed with good reason that in the latter half of the thirteenth century west European culture had truly taken root in Norway.

The enormous number and variety of finds from the Bryggen excavations have created special problems of conservation and storage. Thanks to the moistness of the earth, organic material such as food remains, building material, objects of wood (Plate XVIa, b), leather (Plate XIIIc), bones and textiles were well preserved at the moment of excavation, but far more objects were brought to light (Plate XIIIb) than we were able to conserve or even to store in a proper way; and methods for conserving organic material were far from satisfactory at the beginning. During the 1950s, however, encouraging developments in this field, from which we have greatly benefited, took place in different countries. Responsibility for conservation has now been taken over by the Technical Section of the Historical Museum and storage, as well as technical standards, have improved. While waiting for conservation facilities, we had to find temporary solutions to prevent deterioration and deformation of the material. Our find material has been exposed artificially to about the same conditions as the now famous Russian finds from the frozen Ural kurgans. The objects of wood, leather and textiles were deep frozen, a method which has proved extremely useful. The objects are frozen to about $-25°C$ in a slightly moist condition, and even after two or three years in the deep freeze no shrinkage or deformation has been observed but only a very slow drying process. This method is particularly suitable for the storage of our extensive wooden finds, which will take a long time to classify and which it would neither be economically nor scientifically justifiable to conserve in their entirety.

Since the excavation ended, in 1968, work has been concentrated on the correlation of chronological data, so that an absolute dating framework for the whole range of material can be established. In addition, outside specialists are engaged in the study of special subjects, as for instance the runic material, skeletal and food remains, dendrochronology and zoological and botanical analysis of ropes and textiles. While all this research work is progressing, plans have been drawn up for the construction of a museum on the site to house the Bryggen finds. This is making rapid progress, thanks to the benefaction of a Norwegian ship-owner residing in Bermuda, and the new Bryggen Museum has been opened in 1975.

Chapter IV

Viking fortresses in Denmark

Olaf Olsen

The Viking period spans a quarter of a millennium, from about A.D. 800 until about A.D. 1050, during which time the Scandinavian peoples influenced the course of European history to a greater extent than at any subsequent time. Tens of thousands of Danes, Norwegians and Swedes left their native soil for the uncertainties of a difficult existence both at sea and abroad. In large and small groups, they sailed away in slender craft – some in search of farmland, some to harry and loot, and others to trade peacefully. It was during this period that the colonisation of Iceland and Greenland took place and Viking domination was established in England, Ireland and Normandy. Eastwards too, along the great rivers of Russia, enterprising Viking merchants found the trade routes to the Byzantine Empire and the Near East.

These dramatic aspects of Viking history are fairly well documented. We can follow the expeditions of the Vikings in contemporary chronicles and letters and also to some degree their trade. But these are foreign sources with little to say about conditions in the homelands of the Vikings, for the traveller from abroad seldom came closer to the vast, heathen hinterland of Scandinavia than the trading centres of Hedeby, Ribe and Birka. Contemporary native sources are far more limited and consist only of a few short epitaphs carved on rune-stones and some complicated heroic verse. Only scattered glimpses can be caught of what was happening inside Scandinavia at this period.

The archaeologist, however, may succeed where the historian is forced to give up and sometimes a discovery falls to his lot which entirely disrupts established concepts, giving a fresh and surprising perspective to historical questions under discussion. Such was the case when in 1934 Poul Nørlund, the Danish archaeologist, began the excavation of an earthwork in Zealand known as *Trelleborg*. A circular

Plate XVII   (a) (above)
*Viking fortresses in
Denmark:* Trelleborg.
Air photograph
(b) (left) *Viking fortresses
in Denmark:* Fyrkat. Air
photograph

rampart was all that remained, but below the turf were traces of a settlement unlike anything previously seen. After excavating for ten years, Dr Norlund was able to reconstruct the ground plan of a large fortified barracks of the Viking period, set out on the ground with geometrical precision and striking technical skill to equal that of the Roman *castra* (Plate XVIIa). Trelleborg bore witness to an organisation and highly developed technical culture not hitherto expected of the barbaric Viking armies.

The discoveries .made at Trelleborg caused a quickening of interest among archaeologists regarding other circular earthenworks in Denmark, as it seemed unlikely that Trelleborg represented an isolated phenomenon. This assumption proved correct and, between 1945 and 1952, C. G. Schultz, Poul Nørlund's close

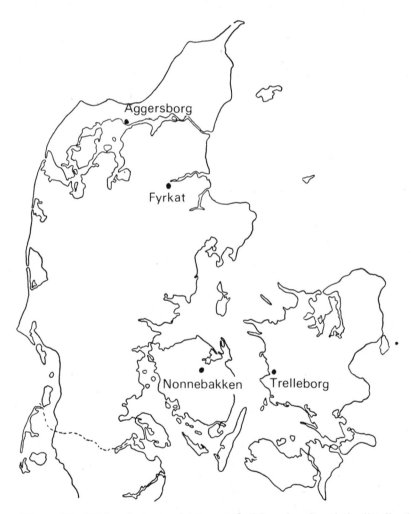

Figure 35   Viking fortresses in Denmark: Map showing their distribution

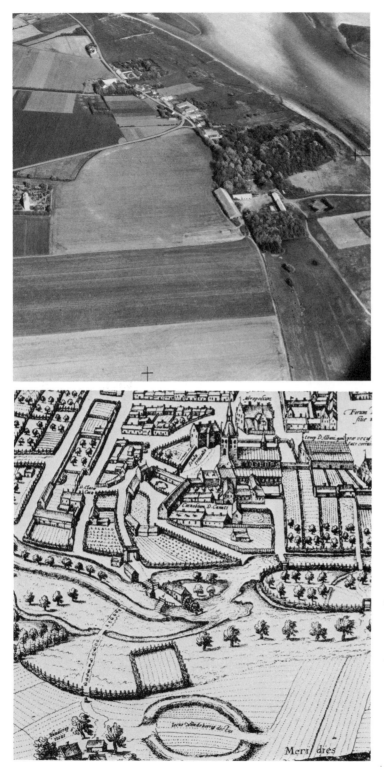

Plate XVIII (a) (above) *Viking fortresses in Denmark:* Aggersborg. Air photograph
(b) (left) *Viking fortresses in Denmark:* Nonnebakken. Detail from a picture-map of Odense dated 1593, published in Braun and Hogenberg's *Civitates Orbis Terrarum*

colleague, identified three more sites of the Trelleborg type in Denmark: *Aggersborg* on the shores of the Lim Fjord in North Jutland (Plate XVIIIa), *Fyrkat* near Hobro in East Jutland (Plate XVIIb) and *Nonnebakken* near Odense on the island of Funen (Plate XVIIIb). More may yet be discovered. It will be seen from the map in Fig. 35 that no fortress has been found in South Jutland, yet if the fortresses were distributed more or less evenly throughout the country, there should be at least one in this area. Similarly, we would expect to find a fortress in Scania (now part of Sweden) which was one of Denmark's most important provinces until 1658. But this the future alone can decide. Meanwhile, the four known sites provide enough for historians and archaeologists to ponder.

The ground plans of the four fortresses are shown in Figs 36 and 37. They are by no means identical in size or in every detail, yet their similarity of layout is such that they represent a special Trelleborg type. Common to all is the circular rampart with gateways at the four points of the compass, the road system dividing the fortress into four equal sections and the arrangement of houses in squares within each of the four sections. The houses in the fortresses are identical in type, consisting of a large long-house with curved longitudinal walls partitioned into three rooms. To complete the system is a narrow dry ditch, concentric with the rampart, although only where the rampart is not otherwise protected by marsh or water.

In only two of the camps is there any major deviation from the standard plan. Trelleborg has an outer ward to the south-east, protected by a ditch and rampart, which contains fifteen long-houses of the same type as those in the inner ward. The axes of these houses are radially orientated in relation to the centre of the fortress.

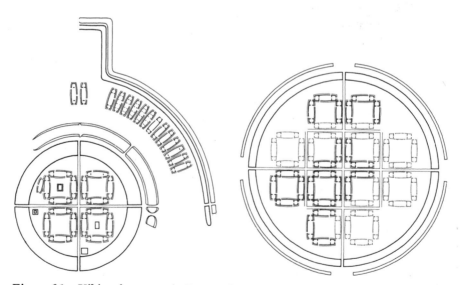

Figure 36   Viking fortresses in Denmark: General plans of fortresses at Trelleborg (left) and Aggersborg (right) (Scale: 1 : 5000)

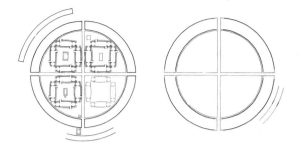

Figure 37   Viking fortresses in Denmark: General plans of fortresses at Fyrkat (left) and Nonnebakken (right) (Scale: 1:5000)

No outer defence-work has been located at the other camps and Aggersborg and Fyrkat (Plates XVIIb) almost certainly did not have one. The second notable deviation is at Aggersborg, by far the largest camp of the four, where the interior diameter of the rampart is exactly twice that of Fyrkat and Nonnebakken. Here, the long-houses are arranged in three blocks of four in each quarter of the interior, whereas the other fortresses have only a single block of four houses per quarter.

It should be remembered, when studying the ground plans, that Trelleborg alone is fully excavated (Plate XVIIa). At Fyrkat, the south-westerly sector has been intentionally left, in order that future archaeologists may check our results. At the great Aggersborg fortress, only twenty-three of the forty-eight houses have been examined and the rampart and ditch are only partially excavated. Nonnebakken is the fortress about which least is known, as the site is almost totally levelled and in a built-up area. Until now, the excavation of Nonnebakken has only established the construction and dimensions of the rampart and ditch. So far, nothing is known about the houses and there is nothing to disprove the possibility that the arrangement of these differs from the system adopted in the other fortresses. In spite of this, the similarity between Nonnebakken and the rest is striking. For example, the interior diameter of the rampart corresponds exactly to that of Fyrkat, and there can be little doubt as to its kinship with the Trelleborg group.

The weakest link in the defence-works of the fortresses is the ditch, which is in each case dry, V-shaped and of negligible depth. Only at Trelleborg has it the character of a fortification, with a width of 17–18 m and traces of an obstruction of posts or palisades at the bottom, that was once an additional hindrance. At the rest of the fortresses the ditch is almost symbolic. It is 8 m wide and barely 2 m deep at Nonnebakken and Fyrkat, while at Aggersborg it resembles a trench, 4–5 m wide and not more than 1·3 m deep. These ditches were never intended as serious obstacles and clearly little importance was attached to them. The ditch at Fyrkat was not even finished, for over a considerable distance in the south-west those digging it had stopped work halfway through the job.

The circular rampart forms a sharp contrast with the ineffectual ditch. It is everywhere constructed with great care, displaying a high degree of fortificational skill and using large quantities of building materials. The dimensions of the ramparts vary. At Trelleborg and Nonnebakken (Plates XVIIa and XVIIIb) they are at their most forbidding with a breadth of 17 m and 15 m respectively and a height of not less than 6 m. The Aggersborg and Fyrkat ramparts are of more modest proportions, being respectively 10 m and 12 m in breadth and not much more than 3 m in height. The complicated construction of the rampart is a common feature shared by all the camps, for although they stand today as simple earthen defence-works, they were originally faced on both sides with planks and must have resembled vast, earth-filled crates. The wooden façades were kept in position and strengthened by a solid framework of struts and beams which, in the Jutland fortresses, traversed the entire body of the ramparts (Fig. 38). The exterior face had a double casing of planks, the outer wall of which sloped slightly inwards, whereas the one behind was vertical. The earth core of the rampart was largely made up of carefully stacked grass turves. All these features were precautionary measures for stabilising the rampart and preventing subsidence. What the top of the rampart was like remains a matter of conjecture. It was probably crowned by a breastwork and there is reason to believe that the massive ramparts at Trelleborg and Nonnebakken had an additional breastwork halfway up their outer face.

Access to the fortresses was by four gateways at the four compass points. These were narrow tunnels through the rampart with a wooden gate at the outer opening. Consequently, the rampart formed an unbroken circle and the four sections could be defended as one.

The interior diameter of the rampart at Trelleborg is 137 m, at Nonnebakken and Fyrkat it is 120 m and at Aggersborg 240 m. Thus in the smaller fortresses the area

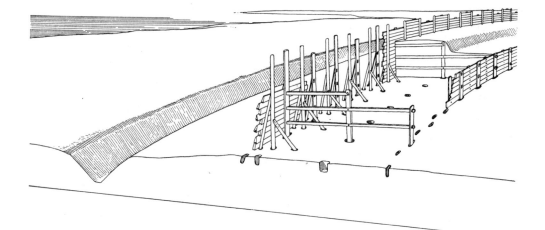

Figure 38   Viking fortresses in Denmark: The timber skeleton of the Aggersborg rampart, as reconstructed by C. G. Schultz

within the rampart is approximately 3 acres, while that of Aggersborg is as much as 11 acres. The enclosed area is always perfectly flat.

The main thoroughfares within the fortresses were the straight axial roads linking the north gate to the south gate and the east gate to the west gate. They were 3 m wide and paved with wooden planks resting on longitudinal joists. Four large, deep post-holes at the geometric centre of the fortress indicated some kind of structure at the junction of the axial roads. This may have been a watch-tower, or possibly a platform, raised sufficiently above the crossroads to allow for the unobstructed passage of traffic beneath.

The characteristic long-houses (Plate XIXa, Fig. 40) arranged in squares of four are undoubtedly the most interesting feature. Because they were built of wood, all that remained were the post-holes, yet the outline of the houses and important constructional details were revealed by the pattern of these post-holes in the soil (Plate XXa). Altogether there are 96 houses in blocks of four in the fortresses, plus the 15 houses in the outer ward at Trelleborg: in all, 111 houses of the same special type. The houses differ in certain minor details (chiefly measurements) from fortress to fortress, but in principle their construction is identical and they may therefore be judged as a whole.

Four different sizes occur. In each case the unit of measurement employed appears to have been the Roman foot (29·5 cm or approximately $11\frac{1}{2}$ in.). The largest houses are at Aggersborg with a length of 110 Roman ft. The houses within the circular rampart at Trelleborg are exactly 100 ft, at Fyrkat they are 96 ft, while the houses in the outer ward at Trelleborg are 90 ft.

A conspicuous feature of the houses (Fig. 39), which gives them greater breadth at the middle than at the gable-ends, is the slight curve of the longitudinal walls. The interior is divided into three, consisting of a large hall occupying three-fifths of the total length and a smaller room at each gable. In many cases a rectangular hearth has been found in the centre of the hall and traces of a broad bench along the side-walls. In the partition walls between the hall and the gable-rooms is a doorway, flanked by a strong post on each side dug deep into the ground – presumably for supporting the roof. Each house has no fewer than four outside doors. There is one in each gable-end and one in each long wall leading into the hall. The latter are always diagonally opposite each other near the partition walls. These entrances have small porches at Fyrkat but as yet none have been established with complete certainty in the other fortresses, although the renewed excavations at Trelleborg in 1966 and 1967 provided some indication of their presence.

The outer walls of the houses at Trelleborg were stave-built – that is, upright planks fitted together in the tongue-and-groove technique. Judging by the traces left by these in the soil, it would appear that thick grooved planks alternated with thin tongued planks. The house walls at Aggersborg and Fyrkat are slightly different, perhaps because timber with the necessary dimensions for a proper stave construction was difficult to find locally. Instead of planks with tongues and grooves,

Plate XIX   (a) (above) *Viking fortresses in Denmark:* Trelleborg. The reconstructed house
(b) (below) *Viking fortresses in Denmark:* Hog-backs in Brompton Church, Yorkshire

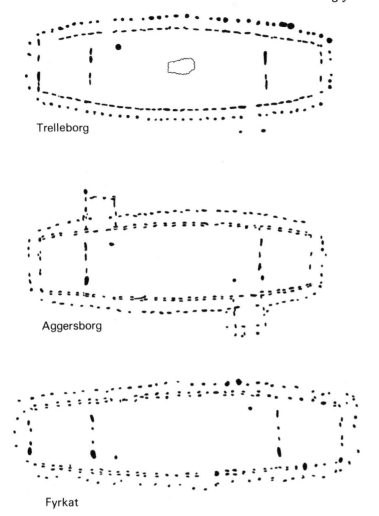

Trelleborg

Aggersborg

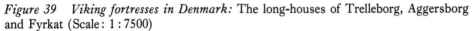

Fyrkat

Figure 39 Viking fortresses in Denmark: The long-houses of Trelleborg, Aggersborg and Fyrkat (Scale: 1 : 7500)

double rows of close-set uprights were used with vertical boards in the space between, perhaps supplemented here and there by wattle and daub. The different walling techniques may seem very marked when the ground plans of the houses are studied, yet they in no way influence the basic structural principles of the houses, for these are virtually identical in all the houses excavated.

It will be seen from the ground plans in Fig. 39 that each house is surrounded by an outer row of posts which follows the walls at a distance of approximately 3 ft. The purpose of these posts has been the subject of much discussion, particularly after C. G. Schultz had a full-scale reconstruction made at Trelleborg of one of the houses in the outer ward in 1943 (Plate XIXa, Fig. 40). This reconstruction proved

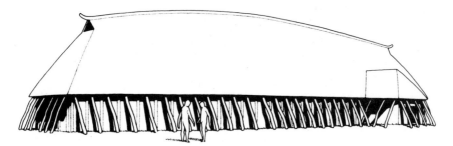

Figure 40 Viking fortresses in Denmark: An alternative reconstruction of the Trelleborg house

an exceedingly useful experiment, although to build a house about which nothing is known, apart from post-hole traces in the ground, is obviously an accomplishment of some daring. However, the number of identical houses provided a unique opportunity, because what was missing in one house could be found in others and a more or less complete impression of the structural elements below the soil-line could be pieced together. This, with the help of contemporary representations in pictures and carvings, made it possible to create a reconstruction whose fundamental characteristics are within the bounds of possibility.

There is little doubt as to the shape of the roof. The slight curve of the long walls means that the ridge of the roof was convex, giving the roof greater depth at the centre than at the gables. Perhaps the best known long-houses of this type are those represented by the so-called 'hog-backs', the house-shaped tombstones found in considerable numbers in the north of England and attributed to the Viking element of the population in this area (Plate XIXb). Many of the hog-backs depict houses with shingle roofs and this is the material used in the reconstruction at Trelleborg.

The outside walls alone are not strong enough to support a roof of such size, and large long-houses of this period usually had two rows of strong posts inside to carry the weight of the roof. This construction occurs in five of the houses in the outer ward at Trelleborg, where four pairs of uprights support the purlins for the roof. On the other hand, the characteristic partition walls found in all the other long-houses in the fortresses are absent. The standard Trelleborg type has only two pairs of roof-bearing posts and these are incorporated in the partition walls – clearly for the purpose of avoiding free, upright posts in the interior of the great hall. The wide span of the roof made heavy demands on the roof-bearing posts in the partition walls and it is scarcely a coincidence that their post-holes are larger and deeper than any of the others in the house. How the roof was supported across the middle of the hall is not entirely clear. In the Trelleborg reconstruction, the problem was solved by side purlins over the uprights.

Poul Nørlund and C. G. Schultz interpreted the outer row of post-holes around the house as evidence of an open gallery like that found in twelfth and thirteenth century

stave-churches in Norway. The purpose of the gallery was considered twofold –
partly to protect the house walls from driving rain and partly to provide a covered
shelter round the houses for the occupants. This interpretation has been subject to
much criticism and is considered implausible today.

The most important argument in favour of the gallery was that the posts appeared
to be uprights. At Trelleborg, the post-holes were emptied from the top, but later, at
Fyrkat, corresponding post-holes were excavated from the side and the sections
showed that the posts sloped slightly towards the walls of the house (about 70°).
The more time-consuming method of excavating post-holes in section was then
adopted during renewed excavations at Trelleborg between 1963–7 and here, too, it
was established that the outer row of posts did in fact incline towards the house.
Consequently, the theory of an open gallery had to be abandoned, for the function of
the posts must have been to strengthen the walls and to support the roof. At Fyrkat
and presumably also at Trelleborg, the slanting posts were fashioned as planks – not
a suitable shape if their sole purpose were to act as struts. Mr Holger Schmidt, who
has assisted me during the recent excavations at Trelleborg, suggests that they may
have been the rafters of the roof itself, which continue into the ground, and that these
plank-shaped rafters were bent from the ridge into the soil in a curve. A house built
in this manner is illustrated in Fig. 40.

Large elliptical houses have been found in settlement sites of the Viking period
and we know that they could be built without any form of strut outside the walls.
The reason why, in spite of this, the houses in the Viking fortresses had outer posts
is presumably that it enabled thinner timber to be used. It was obviously an advantage in large-scale fortress building to make rational use of the available timber.
Indeed, with its strict geometric shape, the boldness of its construction and the
matchless precision with which this is carried out, the Trelleborg house is a refined
version of the long-house of the period.

The house-type is Nordic and undoubtedly based on Scandinavian building traditions. But does this apply to the fortresses as a whole? It is a question which has
been answered variously. Poul Nørlund rightly put forward his opinion on the subject tentatively, yet he favoured the idea that the ancient Roman engineering
techniques had served as inspiration. Trelleborg was laid out according to a Roman
measure and Dr Nørlund assumed that the Vikings could well have encountered the
remains of Roman camps in England. However, a typical Roman camp is not round
but rectangular and the buildings within it are arranged on other principles. Knowledge of the achievements of the Romans is not, then, a fully satisfactory explanation.

A significant step forward in the discussion occurred in 1951, when Professor
H. P. L'Orange demonstrated striking parallels between Viking camps and the
fortified circular towns of Arabia – Baghdad, for example, founded in A.D. 762. To
the Vikings, the Arabian Empire was far distant but not inaccessible, as testified by
the large hoards of Arabian silver coins from this period recovered in southern
Scandinavia. Traders from the North acted as intermediaries through whom the flow

of silver from Arab mines in central Asia reached western Europe. Their route was along the rivers of Russia and although it may be supposed that they were generally met half-way, or availed themselves of middlemen, Viking traders and seafarers must also have occasionally come into direct contact with the highly developed civilisation and culture of Arabia.

Not all scholars have accepted the idea of Arab influence. Professor Johannes Brøndsted considered that the forerunner of Trelleborg was more likely to be found in Byzantium, where Roman culture and scholarship lived on after the collapse of the Roman Empire in the West and where the Vikings indisputably journeyed. Another prominent Danish archaeologist, Dr Vilhelm la Cour, maintains that the fortress building traditions of north-western Europe could have inspired the Trelleborg type. Only the geometrical precision in the layout of the latter is something new, but this, writes Dr la Cour, does not justify searching for its archetype at sites remote both in distance and time.

It has always to be borne in mind, when discussing these questions, that very little is known about the castles and earthworks of Europe of this period. New excavations anywhere may, at any time, open up fresh perspectives causing a reassessment of earlier theories. To date, only a few circular earthworks of the Viking period have been examined in detail and the revolution in our knowledge brought about by the discovery of Trelleborg may well be repeated elsewhere.

Recent excavations of the earthwork of Souburg in Zeeland, Netherlands, carried out by Mr J. A. Trimpe Burger, have established that the circular camp of Souburg possesses the geometrical perfection of Trelleborg, including the cross-road system with gateways at the four points of the compass. Only the houses are different. They represent a local tradition of house-building and they are not arranged in blocks. Souburg seems to be more or less contemporary with the Trelleborg-type camps. But the question of an accurate dating is vexed and so far it is not certain whether the Souburg type might have provided inspiration for the Viking builders in Denmark, or whether Souburg in fact itself copies prominent features from the Viking camps.

The number of single finds recovered during the painstaking excavation of the fortresses is comparatively small and it is difficult to date the sites with complete accuracy. The Trelleborg finds belong primarily to the late Viking period. Only one coin was found in the entire area and this had been struck in Denmark between about A.D. 975 and 980. One ornament was clearly a copy of an Anglo-Saxon coin (of Aethelred) and can therefore be dated to about A.D. 1000. A considerably wider margin must be allowed for the rest of the Trelleborg finds, although they give the general impression that the fortress was built during one of the last decades of the tenth century and fell into disuse soon after the beginning of the eleventh century.

The finds recovered at Fyrkat present much the same picture. Here, too, only one coin was found and in such a bad state of preservation that it cannot be dated more closely than to the period between about A.D. 930 and 985. A number of ornaments were found – some within the fortress but the greater part in the fortress burial-ground – which clearly belong to the last half of the tenth century. It is unlikely, then, that the fortress existed before about A.D. 970 and, like Trelleborg, it did not survive for very many years beyond the turn of the century.

The dating of Aggersborg is difficult to establish because it was built on the site of a village. The village itself appeared to have been pulled down to make way for the fortress and it was often impossible to differentiate between the finds from the village and those from the camp. The most important finds are two coins minted by Emperor Otto II (996–1002), because both were found in pit-houses which, judging from their position and character, must have belonged to the village period. This indicates that the fortress was not built much before the year 1000 at the earliest. C. G. Schultz was inclined to believe after the first series of excavations that Aggersborg was built towards the middle of the eleventh century. However, because the number of eleventh century finds from the site is extremely small, this late dating is no longer considered feasible. Furthermore, the close kinship between Aggersborg and Fyrkat, apparent not only in the ratio of their size but also in structural details, makes it inconceivable that Aggersborg should be so much later. The fortress must be from the beginning of the eleventh century, and to judge from the collection of finds the duration of its occupation appears to have been short-lived.

A reliable historical account from about 1100 relates how Aggersborg was stormed and destroyed during a revolt against the Danish king in 1086, but it is very unlikely that the Aggersborg mentioned here is identical with the Viking fortress, which must have been abandoned and allowed to go to ruin far earlier. The revolt could well have struck a later fortification that was situated, like the existing manor-farm Aggersborggård, south of the site of the Viking fortress.

At present, only small-scale excavations have been undertaken at Nonnebakken and the finds recovered cannot be used as a basis for dating. Nevertheless, certain conclusions may be reached, albeit with reservations, as to the age of the fortress, due to three (possibly four) Viking hoards found here during the course of ploughing and building, long before it was realised that Nonnebakken was the site of a Viking fortress. The hoards include three circular brooches of silver filigree and a silver armlet, all types common to hoards from the last decades of the tenth and the beginning of the eleventh centuries. The coins in the hoards amount to thirty-three in all, of which twenty-three are Arab (Cufic), the latest being about 950, one is German, struck in the reign of king Otto I (936–62), and nine are Danish and appear to have been struck in Hedeby (Schleswig) near the Danish frontier in the south. Thanks to the Swedish numismatist Brita Malmer, it is now possible to date the Hedeby coins with a considerable degree of accuracy and the dating of the latest coins can be narrowed down to between about 975 and 980. On the other hand, it is difficult to judge how long the coins circulated before being buried at Nonnebakken. As no regulated monetary system existed at this time in Denmark coins were generally in circulation for a considerable period. However, the combination of Arab and

Danish coins and the presence of only one German coin indicates that the hoards were deposited before the year 1000.

It should of course be added that we have no conclusive proof as to whether the hoards are from the fortress. It is not yet known if there was a settlement on the site before the fortress, as at Aggersborg and Trelleborg. Should this be the case, the finds might be of an earlier date than the fortress. It is wiser for the present to bracket Nonnebakken with the other sites when discussing the dating of the fortresses and sufficient to say that its resemblance to Trelleborg and Fyrkat is close enough for us to assume that it dates to the same decades. A collective dating of the four fortresses based on the finds – and one which allows a reasonable margin – falls within the period between about 970 and 1020. Only in the case of Aggersborg may we venture to date more closely and conclude that this was built very shortly after the year 1000.

With these datings in mind, an attempt can be made to explain the fortresses and their function in a historical context. As not one of these mighty fortresses is mentioned in historical records, this attempt must be based essentially on the archaeological evidence.

Historians provided a variety of answers to the questions of who built the fortress, when Trelleborg was discovered. Attention was drawn to the fluctuating power of the Crown in Denmark during the Viking period. No hereditary right of succession existed. Indeed, the country was hardly a unified kingdom, and the periods between dominant rulers were times when several aspirants to the Crown fought for power, but none succeeded in establishing his supremacy throughout the entire country. Under these circumstances, it was the local chieftains who formed the ruling class. Two extremely powerful land-owning families are known to have possessed large estates in West Zealand. Leading historians considered it likely that Trelleborg was built by a Viking chieftain, perhaps in direct opposition to the king.

The subsequent discovery of three additional fortresses in Jutland and Funen has made this explanation less credible, for the power of the chieftains rarely extended beyond their own region. The completion of such a large-scale project as the building of four practically identical fortresses in different parts of the country could only be accomplished by a central power – a strong king. Denmark was ruled by two powerful kings during the period in question: Harald (ca. 940–85) and his son Svend (ca. 985–1014). Harald, who has gone down to posterity with the curious nickname of 'Bluetooth', raised a large runestone in Jelling on which he acclaims himself 'the conqueror of all Denmark'. King Svend, called Svend Forkbeard, was also the undisputed ruler of Denmark and won particular renown as a Viking king – the scourge of the Baltic and the North Sea – and the year before his death he succeeded in winning the throne of England.

It is, then, in the light of these achievements that the four fortresses must be considered. Were they built to strengthen the position of the king in his native land, or did they serve as bases from which to mount attacks abroad? Was their purpose perhaps a combination of the two? In any event, the fortresses should be regarded as purely military sites. Although fortified towns are known to have existed in the Viking period, the strict layout of the fortresses indicates that they were intended as barracks for a detachment of soldiers under stern military discipline. The normal life of a town with its trades and crafts would never have developed and flourished here. There is evidence that various craftsmen plied their trade within the ramparts of Trelleborg and Fyrkat, particularly blacksmiths, but this is to be expected in military establishments of such size. At Fyrkat it is amusing to note how the resident craftsmen were forced to submit to military perfectionism, in that some small workshops were arranged in close harmony with the axes and general layout of the fortress. Nothing was permitted to disturb its symmetry.

The military character of the camps is also reflected by the finds. At Fyrkat, for example, whetstones and not pottery make up the largest group of finds – almost two hundred and fifty were recovered, largely from the forge sites, although a fair scattering was found throughout the fortress as well as in the houses (Plate XXb). The large quantity of whetstones suggests that the Viking warriors spent a great deal of time keeping their weapons in trim, very much as the modern soldier is expected to polish and oil his rifle conscientiously.

To this day, the cleaning of roads and enclosures plays an important part in the occupational therapy of barrack life. That this was almost certainly the case among the Vikings, too, is indicated by the striking scarcity of refuse in the fortresses. Whereas the excavation of town settlements and farmsteads of this period almost always produces large quantities of small finds, especially potsherds, bones and tools, little has been recovered from the Viking fortresses. The wood-paved roads were presumably swept each day and instead of allowing refuse to collect between the houses, it was carted away.

The four fortresses appear to have functioned as fortified barracks for quartering a large military force. The exact number of men cannot be calculated, although it is possible to make a rough estimate of the size of the garrisons from the wide sleeping-benches in the central room of the houses. Each house at Trelleborg had 35 m of benching with room enough for about fifty men lying side by side, consequently the sixteen houses of the inner ward could accommodate a garrison of about eight hundred, if all used for habitation. This figure may well have been greater if some of the fifteen houses in the outer ward were also used as living-quarters, which is not certain. Fyrkat has no outer ward and its capacity cannot be compared with that of Trelleborg because as many as half of the buildings within the rampart evidently served as workshops and storehouses. It seems likely that in the region of four hundred men could be garrisoned at Fyrkat. The ratio between living-quarters and outbuildings at Aggersborg is not known but the maximum capacity of this, the largest of the fortresses, must have been not less than two thousand men. Thus, the Danish king possessed an army of several thousand men, if all four camps were occupied at the same time.

An army of this size had obviously to be organised in smaller detachments. Statutes drawn up for the royal housecarls and recorded in about 1180 contain a reliable reference to the effect that Canute the Great (ruler of England from 1016 until 1035 and of Denmark between 1018 and 1035) divided his men into four units. The clear division of the Viking fortresses into four quarters, each containing houses in blocks of four, suggests that this ratio of military subdivision is of an earlier date than the reign of Canute.

A complement of fifty men per house represents the smallest unit in each fortress. This number corresponds approximately to the crew of a long-ship and it seems possible that each house accommodated one crew. In any event, there is little doubt that the occupants of the four fortresses were sailor warriors. Denmark was a highly developed seafaring nation in the Viking period and the very nature of the country, with its numerous islands and inlets, made it easier to journey by water than by foot or on horseback. For this reason, the call to arms was concentrated on maritime strength in Denmark well into the Middle Ages. Infantry as such did not exist.

All the Viking fortresses are situated near water: Trelleborg, Nonnebakken and Fyrkat by small rivers a few miles from the open sea and Aggersborg by one of the principal fairways for shipping, the Lim Fjord — a factor which in itself illustrates the close maritime links shared by the fortresses. None the less, no special arrangement for the protection of ships has been found in the vicinity of the fortresses. At Trelleborg, they could have been drawn up inside the shelter of the outer ward, but this was ineffectually fortified. No ship could be brought into the stronghold of the fortresses themselves as the gateways were too narrow and the area within the rampart too constricted. Any large-scale attack that compelled the defenders to retreat into the fortress would result in the loss of the ships. The question is, then, whether the fortresses were built as a protection against massive attacks, or whether they fulfilled an entirely different purpose.

Danish coastal waters were very troubled during the time of the Vikings. Piracy flourished and Norwegian Vikings carried out repeated raids along the Danish coast. Seafarers from the Slavic areas south of the Baltic may have also made their presence felt. Last but not least, the unity of the Danish nation was not yet strong enough to prevent the inhabitants of one part of the country from raiding the villages in another. However, it is unlikely that these motley bands of marauders descended in numbers large enough, at the close of the tenth century, to cause great fortresses to be built and maintained as defensive measures against them.

The position of the fortresses at a considerable distance from the open sea shows that they were clearly not intended to serve as a defence against attacks by sea. Even the position of Aggersborg was evidently not dictated by any desire to control the passage of ships through the Lim Fjord, because at this point the fjord is about one and a half miles wide. Yet the distance between each shore narrows to five hundred yards two miles further east, thus providing a far better strategic position for the protection of the waterway.

Plate XX (a) (above) *Viking fortresses in Denmark:* Fyrkat. The post-holes are filled with concrete to show the contours of the houses (b) (left) *Viking fortresses in Denmark:* Fyrkat. Whetstones

On the other hand, all the fortresses were strategically situated in relation to major overland routes. Aggersborg stands at what was once an important fording place across the fjord for traffic from central Jutland *en route* for the north coast, where the passage by sea to southern Norway was shortest. Fyrkat is situated close to where the main eastern highway up through Jutland crossed the marshy valley drained by the river Onsild. The fortress at Nonnebakken was in the immediate vicinity of the main route across Funen as it passed over the river Odense, and Trelleborg was close to the highway across Zealand.

In theory, the primary purpose for their situation near important overland routes could well have been to ensure an adequate flow of supplies to the fortresses and also perhaps to serve as toll points for travellers. The skill with which they were fortified and the immense effort in manpower and material that went into the construction of the defence-works must mean that there was an important military reason for their position, not as a defence against foreign invaders but directed against the population of Denmark itself.

Our thoughts turn in this context to Harald Bluetooth as 'the conqueror of all Denmark', for the union he implemented may have required a nucleus of regional strongholds from which to quell any separatist tendencies among his subjects. There is great doubt as to whether king Harald possessed sufficient resources to accomplish a task of such dimensions, which entailed the additional financial burden of maintaining a standing army large enough to man the fortresses. As far as can be judged today, it appears that Viking kings received only limited revenues from their possessions. Proper tax levies apparently did not exist. The king had to pay his personal bodyguard, the housecarls, out of incomes accrued from the royal estates and boroughs, supplemented by *servitium noctium*, the provision for himself and his retinue that was his right when journeying through his realm. Therefore, the opportunity of building up a large private army was severely limited and it is estimated that only about fifty housecarls served under Canute the Holy (1080–6). The great Viking fleet commanded by chieftains and manned by peasants could be gathered by the Danish king when the country was attacked and he was also allowed to deploy the fleet for offensive measures when empowered to do so by the *Landsthings*. It was clearly not in his power to compel the male populations to serve in barracks on its native soil.

These are all factors which argue against the theory linking the fortresses with the reign of Harald Bluetooth. If, however, we turn our attention to his son, Svend Forkbeard, we find a historical situation that would justify the presence of four mighty fortresses in Denmark.

Throughout his entire life, king Svend was above all a warrior. He started his military career by raising arms against his father and ousting him from the Danish throne in ca. 985. He then carried out raids with varying degrees of success in the Baltic and found the chance of a lifetime across the North Sea in king Aethelred's disrupted realm, England. Here his name occurs in records for the first time in

A.D. 994, when he joined the Viking fleet outside London under the command of the Norwegian king Olaf Tryggvasson and received a share in the tribute of sixteen thousand pounds in silver with which king Aethelred attempted to buy peace. This price was respected by king Olaf, who never came back, but it served to whet Svend Forkbeard's appetite and for two successive decades he returned almost every summer, plundering and extorting ransom throughout an ever-increasing area and leaving again only after receiving still larger payments of tribute.

Through the short entries in Anglo-Saxon chronicles, we can follow the raids and see how the Viking army steadily increased in power and strength during those twenty dark years. Bands of Vikings who had earlier operated independently, or in a casual alliance with others, were now an integrated army under the firm leadership of a determined king. The Vikings, although often outnumbered, were evidently more hardened and disciplined soldiers than their English counterparts. Hence England, impoverished and battle-worn, had to concede in 1013 and proclaim Svend Forkbeard king.

Twenty profitable years of warfare provided king Svend with riches in a quantity never before experienced by a Danish king and the impact was felt not only in Denmark but throughout Scandinavia. Bands of adventurers from all over the north flocked to his banner, lured by the prospect of the rich spoils to be won across the North Sea. These years must have produced a large force of professional warriors, men to whom war was a way of life. There are grounds for believing that king Svend built the great circular fortresses as barracks for his mercenaries. The resources needed for building the fortresses and the upkeep of the Viking army would have stemmed from the flow of silver from England. We can assume that soldiers were garrisoned and trained at the fortresses between expeditions. It is hardly a coincidence that the site chosen for Aggersborg, the largest fortress, was on the shores of the Lim Fjord, the gateway to England. At the same time, the position of the fortresses at key points across the country suggests that king Svend also used them as a means of keeping his own perennially unsettled country under control.

The four fortresses stand as a monument to a great warlord's dream of endless strife, but their heyday was short-lived. A large force of warriors was no longer needed after the conquest of England. In 1018, Svend Forkbeard's son, Canute the Great, disbanded the greater part of the Viking army that had helped his father win the English throne. For the Danes, everyday routine had returned. There were no more soldiers to garrison the fortresses, nor was there any reason to maintain them. They fell into decay so rapidly that by the time the history of the Danes was chronicled one hundred years later, they were already obliterated from living memory.

Bibliography

Christiansen, Tage E., 'Traeningslejr eller tvangsborg', *Kuml*, 1970 (interprets the camps as garrison-forts, erected by the Danish throne to strengthen its control over the surrounding areas).

Klindt-Jensen, Ole, 'La possibilité d'utiliser des sources archaeologiques dans les historiques', *VIIIe Congrès International des Sciences Préhistoriques et Proto-historiques 1971*. Belgrade, 1974.

la Cour, Vilh., 'Trelleborg-typen', Exursus in *Danske Voldsteder. Hjorring amt*. Copenhagen, 1963. With an English summary.

Norlund, Poul, 'Trelleborg', *Nordiske Fortidsminder* vol. iv, 1. Copenhagen, 1948. With an English summary.

Nørlund, Poul, 'Trelleborg' (English edition), *Nationalmuseets blå bøger*. 4th revised edition. Copenhagen, 1968.

L'Orange, H. P., 'The illustrious ancestry of the newly excavated Viking castles Trelleborg and Aggersborg', *Studies Presented to David Moore Robinson*. St Louis, 1951.

Olsen, Olaf, *Fyrkat. The Viking camp near Hobro*, Copenhagen, 1959 (guide book).

Olsen, Olaf, 'Trelleborg-problemer. De danske vikingeborge og deres historiske baggrund', *Scandia* vol. xxviii, Lund, 1962. With an English summary.

Roesdahl, Else, 'The Viking fortress of Fyrkat in the light of the objects found', *Château Gaillard* vol. vi, 1973, pp. 195–202 (suggests that the camps might have been built as centres of production of goods for the king, storage places for valuables and centres of royal administration).

Schmidt, Holger, 'The Trelleborg house reconsidered', *Medieval Archaeology*, vol. xvii, 1973, pp. 52–77.

Schultz, C. G., 'Aggersborg, Vikingelejren ved Limfjorden', *Fra Nationalmuseets Arbejdsmark*. Copenhagen, 1949.

Chapter V

Helgö, an early trading settlement in central Sweden

Wilhelm Holmqvist

Until twenty years ago, the Lake Mälar island of Helgö in the centre of Sweden, scarcely 30 km from Stockholm (Fig. 41), had no place in the archaeology and history of Sweden. Its former importance was never suspected. No significant antiquity was known from Helgö, not so much as a runic inscription, although the island lies in the part of Sweden which is richest in runestones. About twenty years ago, however, a building development of summer cottages was begun on Helgö and, as a result, its thousand-year-old peace came to an abrupt end. A fortunate landowner came across a pair of spiral gold rings while he was digging on his building plot and a few years later, when he was putting up a flag-pole in front of his little summer cottage, he found a bronze ladle of unusual shape (Plate XXIIa). It was certainly not modern, probably quite old, but he had no idea how old it really was.

The ladle had been found about 30 cm below the ground surface and an exploratory trench around the hole for the flag-pole unearthed other interesting objects such as a fragment of a silver bowl, potsherds, a piece from a glass beaker and so on. After this cursory investigation in 1950, I was convinced that we were dealing with a prehistoric settlement and accordingly wrote to the relevant authorities for permission to investigate the area. My hope was to conduct a trial excavation which would substantiate my convictions, but official sources remained sceptical, partly because the bronze ladle was of an unknown type and also because the remarkable silver bowl, the fragment of glass and the sherds were, to say the least, unusual.

Work finally began because of the interest of the king himself. With characteristic archaeological insight he himself initiated an excavation to establish whether Helgö was a significant site. An investigation thus began in 1954, which has since grown

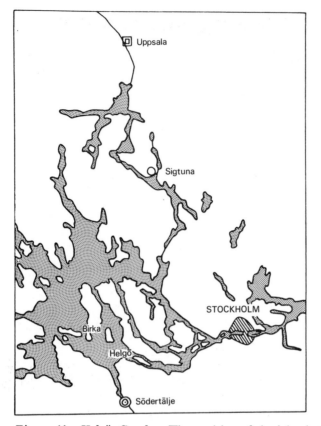

Figure 41   Helgö, Sweden: The position of the island of Helgö in Lake Mälar

into an excavation financed by the Swedish government, entailing total exploration of the site and scientific treatment of the finds.

State financial support has been forthcoming largely because of the sensational finds which have turned up time and again, but it is not only because of such finds that Helgö became and remains so important.

After eighteen seasons of excavation (1971), on a very modest scale, we can now build up a fairly complete picture of early Helgö. Although we cannot reconstruct all the houses in detail, nor discover all the activities carried on at the site, we know enough to prove that Helgö is a valuable link in the early history of Sweden.

As already mentioned, the first finds from Helgö were made because of the building of summer cottages. Building has progressed all over the little island, so it is almost impossible to make a complete archaeological survey of the area, but during the early days of the excavations we were lucky enough to expose many building remains and since then the pattern of the settlement has gradually emerged.

We have not exposed anything like the whole settlement. Hints dropped by

Plate XXI (a, b) *Helgö, Sweden:* Part of the stone foundations for a timber-framed building of Group I

summer visitors about building remains, occupation material and so on to be found on their neighbours' properties have led us to believe that the area of occupation is much more extensive than we had anticipated. It is impossible at present to try to verify these hints, so we must limit ourselves to the results from the excavations themselves.

The early settlement on Helgö occupies an area of about a third of a mile (500–600 m) from east to west by some 300 yd (about 250 m) (Fig. 42). If the numerous small associated cemeteries are included, the area is much greater. It is strategically placed on the eastern promontory of a little island in Lake Mälar, which here narrows down to two strips of water running to the north and south between the island and the mainland. Helgö lies in the middle of the channel connecting the inland parts of the Lake Mälar system with the sea to the east.

The settlement stands beside the northern channel – *Norrsund* (North Sound) – and stretches along the northern slope of a low ridge. The house remains consist of tight-knit groups of buildings separated by areas of sparser settlements, but further excavation may produce a more uniform pattern. So far, we know of one doubtful and five certain groups of buildings, of which only one group has been completely investigated. Archaeological work has begun on three others.

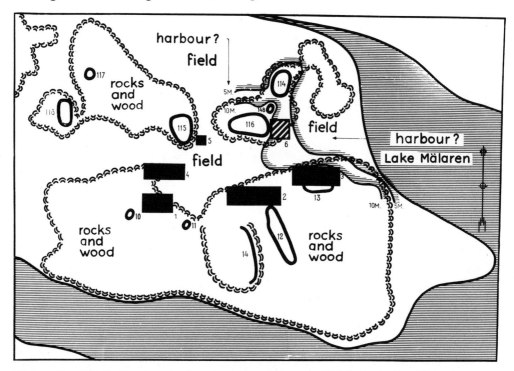

Figure 42   Helgö, Sweden: Ancient monuments on east Helgö; 1–6: Dwelling sites; 10–13, 114–118, 148: Cemeteries; 14: Hillfort; 5M: Sea-level *c.* A.D. 1000; 10M: Sea-level at the beginning of the first century A.D.

The work has been beset by great technical difficulties, since the occupation layer is generally no more than 25–30 cm thick, often thinner although occasionally slightly thicker. The buildings also lie on an extremely stony hillside which has been forest-crowned for the past thousand years. Thus, during the course of time, nature itself has wrought much destruction both in the occupation layer and in the foundations of the buildings.

At this point the chronology of the site must be mentioned. The earliest finds include a very worn *denarius* and a fragment of a Roman bronze cauldron, both probably first century A.D., and bread, hearth stones and ashes dated by carbon 14 to the second and third centuries. A Germanic silver coin from the first half of the eleventh century and a bronze buckle decorated with a face-mask from the latter part of the same century are the most recent finds. The settlement thus extends over a thousand years, that is, throughout the first millennium of our era.

In many cases, only the foundations of the buildings remain. This is both the result of the natural conditions and also because the same spot had been settled for so long that many buildings had been superimposed. As a result, the occupation layer is too thin to provide any definite stratification and the remains of buildings from different periods are found at the same level. The study of building types is therefore quite an intricate puzzle.

The information from the completely excavated building complex (Group 2) and from the incomplete investigations of Groups 1 and 3 suggests that the houses were of many different types. Post-built houses are common and are rectangular in shape with an internal arrangement of two rows of posts running longitudinally. This type may be either short or long, in one case as long as 43 m. The construction of the walls is not known but often the southern long wall, that which lies up the hillside, is defined by a ditch or foundation trench slightly curving in towards the gable ends. The houses are usually orientated from east to west (Plate XXIa, b).

Another type of house is the sunken hut, which is similar in all essentials to those found in England and on the continent. Their floors lie 0·5 m or a little more beneath the ground surface and their length varies from 3 m to 5 m. Many such huts contain primitive ovens built of stones set on edge. In Group 1 there were no less than three huts with ovens, but we cannot say whether these were all for baking or whether some had served another function, such as ovens in bath houses.

All that remains of the third type of house is its stone foundation. This presumably supported a timber-framed structure, but no organic remains were preserved, so the reconstruction of the buildings can only be based on the rows of stones and an occasional post-hole. The houses seem to have had drainage channels around their gables and some possessed extensions which were possible entrance ramps, porches or the like.

The layout of Group 1 was particularly well organised (Fig. 43). Its principal building, with an entrance ramp, lay on the southern edge of the group and higher up the hillside. To the north and further down the slope lay an open area or yard

Plate XXII   (a) (above) *Helgö, Sweden:* Bronze ladle with stamped decoration
(b) (below) *Helgö, Sweden:* Hoard of forty-seven gold coins and a gold bracelet

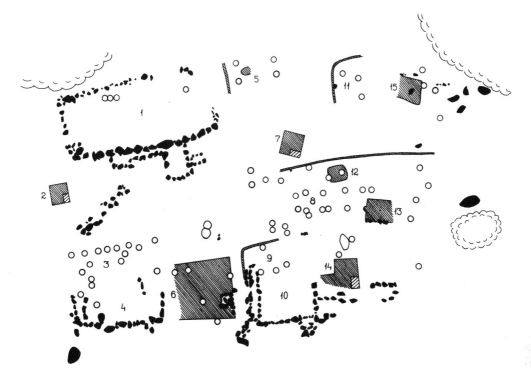

Figure 43   Helgö, Sweden: Group 1 buildings: 1, 4, 10, Stone foundations for timber-framed buildings; 3, 5, 8, 9, 11, Post-built houses; 2, 6, 7, 12, 13, 14, 15, Sunken huts

containing a hearth. On the far side of this open space, two smaller buildings lay more or less symmetrically in front of the principal house and formed the northern boundary to the yard.

Some buildings did not fall into any of the three categories mentioned above. A circular, flat, stone paving in Group 2 (IIIE) was probably the floor in a conical hut and the same may have been true of a paving of IA in the same group, although its disturbed condition makes interpretation uncertain.

It is difficult to deduce the function of sites 37 and 39 in Group 2. They may have been timber buildings, possibly with a hearth in the middle.

It is still too soon to draw firm conclusions about the building history of Helgö. As the evidence has not yet been fully examined, we must confine ourselves to a general survey.

The arrangement of the settlement is of great interest and is shown particularly clearly in Group 2 (Fig. 44) where post-built houses with their long sides lying along the slope are the most common. They were built on obvious terraces formed by digging into the slope where the houses were to stand and depositing the spoil as a platform along the lower side. These houses were thus arranged as on a flight of steps up the hillside.

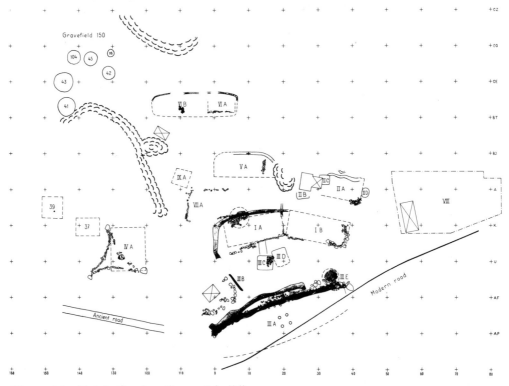

Figure 44   Helgö, Sweden: Group 2 buildings

This has led to the suggestion that these so-called terrace houses were typical of the later Iron Age in Sweden, but only further excavation can decide this. On Helgö the terrace house developed as a response to the type of terrain and might not be suitable in other situations.

It is noteworthy that Groups 1 and 2 were both arranged in the same way, so may have been two parts of a single settlement pattern, but it is impossible at present to be more definite.

Interpretation of this site has been made particularly difficult due to the scarcity of comparable Swedish data. The settlement at Helgö was a surprising and unprecedented discovery, with the result that researches have had to begin from first principles. We may confidently expect that similar sites will one day be discovered and will help to elucidate the history of Sweden before the time of written records.

Let us for the moment postpone discussion of house types and the associated question of the end of Helgö as a settlement and instead move on to the finds. On this score, Helgö truly has been an enthralling venture and a memorable experience, so far unique in Sweden.

The first sensation occurred during the first summer's excavations with the find of the crook of a late Celtic bronze crozier highly decorated with glass, enamel and

Plate XXIII   (a) (left) *Helgö, Sweden:* Bronze statuette of Buddha, made in North India. The lips and eyebrows are painted and the caste mark is of gold
(b) (right) *Helgö, Sweden:* The crook of an Irish crozier and some smaller enamelled objects

millefiori inlay (Plate XXIIIb). I have already stated in the *Antiquaries Journal* that I believe it to have been made during the eighth century. It is therefore an unusually early example of the use of such an object in the west European church. The crook of the crozier is formed by the curving neck of a dragon whose gaping jaws hold a human face-mask between the fangs. On one side the dragon's eye is inlaid with a blue stone and the tip of each jaw is embellished with an enamelled boss. On the other side – which is of higher artistic quality – the eye is inlaid with silver. A bird's head projects like a horn from the dragon's forehead and a wolf's head protrudes from the neck. The original colours have probably changed because of the conditions to which the object has been subjected over the centuries and the light-coloured enamel may once have been red. The shaft of the crozier head is entirely inlaid with enamel interspersed with blue stones and millefiori.

The total height of the crozier head including the knop – the attachment ring at the base of the shaft – is only 11·3 cm. This has led to some doubt about its having been a bishop's or abbot's crozier but size alone is not a decisive criterion. There are no strictly contemporary parallels but we can compare it with late Celtic croziers of a slightly more recent date. In these examples it is the crozier case (or reliquary) rather than the crozier itself which has been preserved, so it is hardly surprising that such cases should be larger than the Helgö crozier.

It is highly likely that this object is a genuine late Celtic crozier head of the eighth century A.D. As its origin and date are not in doubt, the only question is how it came to Helgö. Contemporary material from the British Isles has been found in great quantity in Norway and to a lesser degree in Denmark and was probably connected with the early Viking expeditions 'west-over-sea'. Churches and monasteries in England and Ireland were plundered and their treasures brought home as loot by the Norsemen, avid for luxuries. Although there is much less of this material in Sweden because of its geographical position, a certain amount has been found at Helgö and at nearby Birka. The crozier appears to be clear evidence for external contacts and some other objects have been found to lend support to this view.

The first year's field-work also produced, among other things, many fragments of imported glass beakers and bowls. Although these fragments are mainly small and insignificant, many different types of vessel can be reconstructed from them and they represent sixty to seventy different glass vessels. This is an astonishingly large number for a Swedish context. It has been suggested that the glass at Helgö was imported as scrap for bead-making but this theory is quite untenable, as not a single kiln for the melting down of all these beakers and bowls has been found, either on Helgö or in its neighbourhood. The glass vessels are of many different types dating from the fourth to the ninth century A.D. and without supporting evidence it is difficult to believe that scrap would have been imported over such a length of time. It may seem to be more likely that we had our own indigenous glass industry, but as we know that glass-making was introduced into Sweden only in the seventeenth century it is not really credible that such a tradition had existed in prehistoric times.

Fragments of late Roman cut-glass scalloped cups, those decorated with large medallions and those with marvered trails as ornament (of the so-called Snartemo type) are particularly noteworthy. The cut-glass beakers date from the fourth or fifth centuries and the Snartemo glass belongs to the period between A.D. 450 and A.D. 550. Their source has not yet been established and the origin of the latter type is particularly obscure. As a significant number of glass vessels of the Snartemo type has been found in Scandinavia – Helgö alone produced a dozen different forms – while few are known from the continent, one may well wonder whether they could possibly have been made by a Nordic glass industry.

Sixth- and seventh-century claw beakers are also represented in the Helgö material and there is also an astonishing quantity of filigree glass. Only five different vessels can be reconstructed but the material contains fragments of at least three more. Such glass is probably even more rare than the Snartemo beakers and so far has been discovered on only a few sites. Birka and Valsgärde have produced it in Sweden. One filigree beaker was found at Hopperstad in Norway and in England there are some fragments from Southampton. On the continent it is totally absent except for the beaker of unknown provenance in the Vatican Museum.

I prefer to think that the glass at Helgö came from regular trading contacts between Helgö and the continent during the first millennium of our era.

A remarkable number of fragments of glass from Helgö belong to funnel beakers of the type illustrated in Carolingian manuscripts of the eighth and ninth centuries. Many of these beakers are of colourless glass with their rims picked out in blue or green.

The glass from Helgö forms an important group whose significance is not purely local. The majority of the fragments date from the late Roman and Carolingian periods and help to illuminate these darkest centuries of European history.

During the third summer of the excavations an event occurred which brought a reminder of far distant lands. A colleague, who was busily working on an area quite close to the place where the crozier had been discovered earlier, came across a small bronze figurine, only about 30 cm beneath the ground surface. This was a statuette of a north Indian Buddha (Plate XXIIIa), authoritatively dated to the sixth or seventh centuries A.D. The bronze sculpture depicts Buddha sitting on his lotus throne. He is dressed in a finely-embroidered cloak and has a gold caste mark on his forehead. His lips and eyebrows are painted. Traces of fastenings on the back of the figure show that it had once been attached to a decorative base, now lost.

The figure of Buddha belongs to an extremely rare group of bronzes which is very little known even in its homeland and it is therefore a unique and spectacular find in a European context. It has its closest parallel in a private collection in Kashmir which contains its twin. This is so similar to the Helgö Buddha that it must have been made in the same workshop and by the same craftsman.

It is difficult to explain how the beautiful Buddha could have come to Sweden. Did it come through trade? Was it booty from a piratical journey? Why would a plunderer have chosen such an object? One must remember that a great distance separates northern India from Sweden. Written records do not suggest that the Scandinavians ventured further south than Baghdad and even from there it is a very long way to India. What is more, the extensive Islamic world lay between northern India and the part of the Near East visited by the Nordic peoples. Orthodox Muslims would certainly not have been inclined to trade such a heathen article as a statue of a Buddha, so the Scandinavians can hardly have acquired it through an Islamic contact. It may have been acquired from one of the Jewish merchants who at this time were travelling throughout Europe and Asia on their trading journeys. If a Norseman himself found the figurine at the place where it was made, it would be the result of the longest journey undertaken by any Scandinavian of the period.

Whatever the means by which the statuette reached Sweden, they can hardly have been as spectacular as its sensational discovery during the archaeological work at Helgö. Many people hinted that it was found there in suspicious circumstances and that at all events it was archaeologically unique and certainly could not be compared with any other finds. This has led to the object being played down, so that until very recently the many archaeological questions which arise from it have scarcely been discussed.

Each year the excavations have produced the most outstanding finds and Helgö stands with Birka as one of the two richest archaeological sites in Sweden. I shall now try to give the reader a brief glimpse of what has so far been found. The best way will be to describe the various groups of finds and as the late Celtic crozier (Plate XXIIIb) and the Indian Buddha (Plate XXIIIa) have headed the list, I shall continue with some of the other imports.

Helgö's contacts with the outside world began as early as the Roman Iron Age — the first building period on the site. The Roman *denarius* has already been mentioned. It is too badly worn for precise identification but it probably dates from the first century A.D. There is also a fragment of a Roman bronze cauldron of about the same date, decorated with bands of interlace accentuated by silver inlay. This had belonged to the rim of a ceremonial cauldron of the same type as those found, among other places, at Hagenow in Germany and Hoby in Denmark.

Other Roman imports include one white and one black playing piece of glass and two fragments of two bronze discs, probably phalerae, each decorated with a rosette. Their backs are completely without ornament and they are unfortunately so fragmentary that there are no traces of attachment loops, but there is no doubt that they are of Roman date.

The great gold hoard which was discovered several years after the beginning of the excavations at Helgö also belongs to the Roman period (Plate XXIIb). It was not found on the excavation site itself but some 100 m to the west. It consists of forty-seven gold coins in mint condition and a massive gold bracelet. Thirty-seven coins are from the Eastern Empire, four from the Western Empire and six from the Ostrogothic Empire. The earliest was struck in the reign of Valentinian III (425–55), the latest under Anastasius (491–518) and no less than six of the coins were struck for Theodoric the Great (493–526). The mints of Milan, Rome, Ravenna and Constantinople are represented.

Another hoard of twenty-one gold coins from the latest of these periods was found in the eighteenth century. Together with a single coin which was discovered near the excavation and one from a metalworking site on the excavation, they comprise the impressive total of seventy gold coins found on Helgö. This total is particularly remarkable in view of the fact that no more than fifty gold coins of similar date have been recovered from the whole of mainland Sweden.

I shall not discuss the coins further but continue with the description of the other imported goods. Many of the fragments of glass come from cut-glass beakers manufactured in Roman glassworks during the fourth and fifth centuries and confirm Helgö's foreign contacts at an early period. I shall now turn to some of the other objects.

The bronze ladle (Plate XXIIa) which was the first (or some say the second) find, is very puzzling. Its punched decoration, handle and profile place it in the group of Coptic bronzes which spread throughout western Europe from the sixth century onwards in connection with the ever-increasing influence of the Christian church. A sixth century date is thus not improbable. What it was used for and where it was kept before it was hidden 25 cm deep in Swedish soil is another and more difficult question. We can only be certain that it was not made in Sweden.

The rim of a small, undecorated, bronze bowl with a simple profile was found at the same depth and in the same layer as the ladle. It is difficult to be precise about the origin and type of such an object through lack of evidence and I am afraid that I can say no more than that it has many continental parallels and may be ascribed to the same date as the bronze ladle.

During the course of the excavations on Helgö we have, of course, found many other fragments of bronze vessels – too many to discuss in a summary such as this.

As mentioned in the introduction, I made another find, just as mysterious as the bronze ladle, on my first trip to Helgö. In the hole for the flag-pole (which must surely have been sited there by Providence) lay a fragment of a shallow silver dish decorated with a simple engraved design. It can be difficult to give a date to such a piece which displays no very characteristic details but in this case it seems reasonable to draw some conclusions from all the other objects which were found at the same time as, and close to, the silver bowl. But the ladle and the fragments of seventh or eighth century glass and pottery which were found with the bowl cannot be used for precise dating. Rather, one must look to comparative material from elsewhere.

The Helgö silver bowl is shallow and simple in shape, about 20 cm in diameter and decorated with a simple, punched ornament forming an equal-armed cross. In form and decoration, it is reminiscent of a silver bowl found in a hoard from Hostentorp in Denmark. This is more elegant than the Helgö bowl and displays more obvious late Roman and Byzantine influences but both indicate provincial workmanship which had a very long life. For instance, the earliest in this series are the well-known silver bowls of about A.D. 300 from the Leuna grave, now in the British Museum. The next stage is represented by the bowls in the hoards from Montcornet and Notre Dame d'Alençon in France and by the one from the fifth century Coleraine hoard (British Museum). It appears that this type of silver work was particularly attractive to the Anglo-Saxons and is represented, among other places, in the grave goods from Sutton Hoo where there were ten engraved bowls. The silver bowls in the rich treasure from St Ninian's Isle, Shetland (National Museum of Antiquities of Scotland), are particularly interesting and very close in type to the Helgö bowl. They belong to the eighth century, the Hostentorp hoard to the sixth century. The Helgö bowl falls in date somewhere between the two and is therefore more or less contemporaneous with the bronze ladle.

One must not forget that Baltic objects were also imported into Helgö (Plate XXIVb). They are less exotic than the Buddha and the crozier but nevertheless very important. They bear witness to contacts with the eastern shores of the Baltic Sea and confirm that water transport was the best method of communication in early periods. The finds may be counted on the fingers of two hands but even so this is the largest concentration of pre-ninth century Baltic objects from Sweden, consisting of four bronze fibulae, two neck rings, a dress pin and a bronze pendant. They date from the second or third century to the eighth century A.D.

Other imports, such as wheel-turned pottery, a Merovingian gold bracteate and so on, should also be mentioned.

The great majority of the material from Helgö is local and mostly unpublished. The three volumes of excavation reports which have so far appeared deal only with objects found before 1964, and about the same amount remains unpublished.

So many different types of finds have been discovered that I cannot discuss them all, but I must say a few words about the twenty-six small gold figures found on the excavation (Plate XXV). Each is made of thin gold foil and is only about 1 cm high. They all depict love scenes – a man and a woman standing face to face, hugging and kissing each other. The designs vary greatly in detail and only two of the small gold plaques display identical groups of figures. All the others show different scenes: a nobleman and his lady, a worthy citizen with his wife, a male and a female slave. The figures look rather more like clothed animals than human beings but the motif is always the same.

One can imagine them as a procession of people from long ago who have come to life again through their different faces and figures. But who can these two lovers be? They are not the first to be found in Scandinavia. Both Norway and Denmark have examples and three were known from Sweden before the Helgö finds. Their dating is vague but they seem to belong to the eighth and ninth centuries and may even stretch back into the seventh century.

Much may be said for and against the interpretation of the gold foil plaques as a

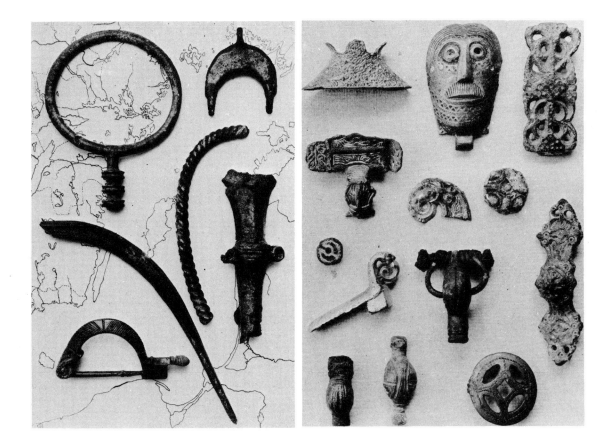

Plate XXIV (a) (left) *Helgö, Sweden:* Bronze objects found at Helgö and probably manufactured there
(b) (right) *Helgö, Sweden:* Objects from the eastern Baltic

Plate XXV   (a) (above) *Helgö, Sweden:* Nine of twenty-six gold foil plaques
(b) (below) *Helgö, Sweden:* Three spade-shaped iron ingots and smaller fragments of iron

form of fertility symbol, perhaps showing the ceremonial wedding of the god Frey, perhaps a cult dance. At any rate, it is not improbable that the figural scenes are concerned with the fertility of man and the land.

One cannot, of course, draw very many conclusions about the former importance and wealth of Helgö on the basis of the gold figures alone. They are very small and thin and were possibly buried for religious reasons.

The other gold objects, which had been lost when in use and subsequently found through excavation, tell us much more about Helgö's wealth. The two spiral gold rings were the first finds from Helgö and since then many other objects have appeared. These include two more rings, small lumps of gold, a rolled-up gold wire, part of a large Scandinavian bracteate of sixth century type and a fragment of a continental, Merovingiàn or Carolingian bracteate. It is difficult to imagine that they would have found their way to Helgö had it not been a wealthy settlement.

Silver is considerably less common than gold on the site. The fragmentary Arabic silver coins date from about A.D. 800 and one of the Omayyad dynasty from 669. Other silver objects include the bowl fragment mentioned earlier, a lunulate pendant, some pins and unrecognisable fragments.

The time-span of the settlement can be estimated by a hundred or so bronze brooches and pins of well-known types. Keys and padlocks, of bronze and iron, are also numerous and, at the time of writing, we have eighty whole or fragmentary examples of the latter. The occupation layer contained very many implements, spearheads and knives. More knives have so far been found at Helgö than in the whole of Uppland, even more than in Viking Birka where one thousand graves and a significant percentage of the so-called 'black earth' (the area of the Viking town) have been investigated.

The most common finds of all are indeterminate pieces of bronze, scrap iron of various sorts and potsherds, all of which showed both that the site had been intensively occupied for a considerable length of time and that it had extended over a large area.

The evidence for early metalworking is another interesting feature of the site. Both the working areas and their material are so important that they deserve a section to themselves. Traces of metalworking have so far been found in Groups 2, 3, 4 and 5 and everything points to the likelihood of Group 6 producing similar results. Objects from Group 2 are the only ones which have already been studied thoroughly. The metalworking sites in Groups 3, 4 and 5 have only been partially excavated but Group 3 has already proved to be far and away the richest.

Many different places on the excavation show the remains of iron-smithing or bronze (Plate XXIVa), gold or silver casting. Group 2 included an area 40–50 m long which was scattered with hearths and smelting pits. The latter were frequently very shallow but sometimes up to 60 cm deep, their diameters varying between 30 and 100 cm. The stone infilling was also very variable, with some smelting pits almost completely filled but others containing only a few stones. The pits lay in and around a thick layer of red-burnt clay which covered the central part of the working area.

Although it is difficult to prove how temperatures sufficiently high for smelting of iron and bronze were obtained, it is significant both that the smelting pits were dug into the hill slope in such a position as to take advantage of the prevailing wind and that a large number of tuyères were found, indicating that artificial means were used to raise the temperatures.

The large amount of iron slag and the number of ingots for use as raw material demonstrate that there was an ironworking site on Helgö. Three long, spade-shaped ingots are of the type found in great numbers in northern Sweden whence they were probably imported into Helgö (Plate XXVb). Other small pieces of iron, rectangular or square in section, seem also to have been ingots. Scrap iron was found in great quantities and there were also some finished products.

Scientific investigation and analysis of the iron have already begun. This ought to establish its sources, the methods used in its manufacture and its distribution and help to solve the problems which surround the early iron industry in Sweden.

Thousands of moulds – decisive proof of bronze smelting – have been found on Helgö and, as the centre of bronze working has not yet been discovered, it is possible that future excavations will produce even richer material. Hundreds of the moulds show traces of decoration which in many cases can be directly parallelled and dated by actual bronze objects.

We have also found many thousand fragments of the type of crucible which consists of a bowl and lid of baked clay. In use, the raw metal was placed in the crucible, the lid put on and sealed with clay. It was then placed in a smelting pit. Most bronze objects were cast and scrap bronze was probably used as the raw material, although long rods of bronze, of which many have been found, were also used by being chopped up into suitable pieces before smelting. It seems likely that the amount of metal to be used for each object was selected by weight. Cylindrical and disc-shaped bronze weights of Migration period date have been found on the site. They vary from 1·140 to 46·690 g, the smaller being used for precious metals. Traces of gold and silver from crucibles indicate that jewellery was also made in these materials.

The moulds are by far the most interesting objects. The *cire perdue* (lost wax) method was not the only process used for casting, for the discovery of a large number of the upper and lower casings of moulds implies that a method employing moulds of two or more pieces had also been practised. Such moulds were used several times over and many of the shapes are almost identical. This suggests that casts were made in clay from wooden or wax models on which all the decorations were carved, down to the finest detail which was to adorn the finished product. Small pieces of the wax which was used in making the moulds have been found in the occupation débris. Such organisation suggests some sort of industry.

The great majority of moulds are for dress ornaments of the fifth and sixth centuries – square-headed brooches, equal-armed brooches and buckles. The fact that there are about 170 for buckles alone gives some idea of the vast numbers of moulds which we are dealing with at Helgö.

Objects from a date later than A.D. 600 have not yet been mentioned. The seventh and later centuries are less well represented at Helgö and it is clear that bronze working was at its height during the fifth and sixth centuries. The few later moulds show that production continued but one can say no more than that. It may well be that we have not yet discovered the material from these later centuries and future excavation may fill in the gap.

I have already mentioned the large number of moulds of the most common fifth and sixth century Scandinavian jewellery. Most of the buckle types are already known from Swedish finds — from the simple undecorated forms to large ones embellished with animal ornament. Their distribution has previously been thought to be concentrated in northern Sweden, with a comparatively light scatter around Lake Mälar, and the new finds have put quite a new complexion on the contacts between north and central Sweden. Some other buckle types have hitherto been found only in Finland.

A great many moulds of square-headed brooches display a style of ornament characteristic of northern Sweden, Finland and Gotland but previously unknown in the Mälar region. There were also very many moulds of small, simple, equal-armed brooches, including quite a number of hitherto unknown types. Up to a couple of decades ago they were very rare in the Mälar region but common in Finland, particularly in their more developed form.

The moulds are invaluable both for comparative analysis and for the interpretation of the archaeological and cultural history of the period. The fact that so many moulds were found on the site means that the objects themselves must have been cast at Helgö and this is most important for our knowledge of the influence of central Sweden in the fifth and sixth centuries.

Up to now, it has seemed that the area immediately around Lake Mälar, the heartland of Sweden, had only a small part to play at this period and it was thought that the area was an archaeological vacuum, difficult to fill or explain away. In contrast, the richness of the finds from north Sweden suggests that the area enjoyed a flourishing culture at the same period, probably as a result of its westerly connections with Norway and the lands around the North Sea. Reflections of the same culture may even be seen on the east side of the Gulf of Bothnia, in the rich contemporaneous material from Österbotten in Finland.

While northern Scandinavia flourished, it appeared that the Mälar region was less advanced and only began to move forward at the end of the period, that is, about A.D. 600. From then on, the wealth of the area increased enormously and the necessary political contacts were established and the foundations laid for the future Swedish kingdom.

This hypothesis has been in the forefront of our thoughts throughout the excavations. It now appears that the Mälar region was far more important in the fifth and sixth centuries than we had previously suspected.

Another anomaly which has been resolved through our investigations is the lack of objects from the Mälar region, a lack which has puzzled the experts for so long. In order to fill in the blank period from A.D. 400 to 600, one school of thought has attempted to put back as early as possible the beginning of the Vendel period which marks the start of cultural advancement in the area. A date of A.D. 500, or even earlier, was suggested on scant evidence. Other explanations for the lack of finds were also put forward. For instance, that in the fifth and sixth centuries, the Mälar region was the scene of radical disturbances, such as slave rebellions and wholesale grave robbing, which led to the almost complete destruction of archaeological material. The beginning of a new era has been inferred from the abandonment and re-siting of settlements, the change in burial customs and so on. In extreme cases, the situation has been dramatised into one of general destruction. I cannot judge to what degree the contemporary disturbances on the continent have influenced thinking, but I believe that the situation in the Mälar region in the fifth and sixth centuries has been greatly exaggerated. Although disturbances may have occurred on certain individual sites, it would be wrong to generalise from these, and recent finds from the area, particularly from Helgö, have shown the falseness of such conclusions.

Exciting fifth and sixth century finds have been made in the Mälar basin during the last two decades. Most objects have come from graves but there is also the amazing wealth of Helgö. As a result, the Mälar region is now archaeologically one of the richest areas in Sweden. The vacuum has been filled and all earlier theories invalidated. It is no longer necessary to pad out the fifth and sixth centuries with objects which clearly and incontrovertibly belong to a later period.

The finds from Helgö can tell us many things. A study of the material immediately reveals that Helgö was in active contact with northern Sweden. For instance, iron from Norrland is found at Helgö and Helgö-type jewellery in Norrland. Waterborne contacts are indicated by the parallels between the moulds from Helgö and jewellery found in Finland. Similarities between the Helgö material and contemporary Gotland types imply lively contacts between these two places. Numerous and richly varied imports illustrate connections with the lands of the eastern Baltic, the continent and the British Isles, let alone the even more far-flung contacts represented by the Arabic coins, the Buddha and the bronze ladle.

Despite all this, it is extremely difficult to give a clear picture of the society and settlement of Helgö. There have been many theories but caution should be observed.

It is obvious that the site does not consist of a single farmstead, nor yet is it a village. Two of the latter have recently been excavated in Sweden, Vallhagar on Gotland and Halleby in Östergötland. The material from these sites is so completely different from that from Helgö that there is no possible comparison. Helgö is clearly quite a different type of site.

During the early years of the excavation we believed that Helgö was a chieftain's dwelling but as field-work continued and the size of the settlement became clear, this idea was abandoned. Helgö could not be a lordly establishment, nor yet a group of them. The site may possibly have been part farm, part trading-post (*farmanne-gård*), perhaps with dependent dwellings. The Scandinavian *farmännen*, known particularly from Gotland, were peasants who indulged in a little trade at the same time as practising mixed farming. This might explain the many imports on Helgö but it does not account for the size of the settlement, the metalworking sites, nor for the long period of time during which Helgö existed as an independent power, even though it lies only a few hours' travelling time from Uppsala, the home of the Svea kings. It must be inferred from this that Helgö could scarcely have been a trading farmstead, however large.

It has also been suggested that Helgö was a large, seasonally occupied market centre, rather than a permanent settlement. I find this impossible to reconcile with the evidence as seen in depth, as I do also another theory, that Birka, only a few kilometres distant, existed concurrently with Helgö in the Viking period and took over international commerce, leaving Helgö with internal trade.

My own interpretation of the site, in brief and with the reservation, naturally, that future field-work may modify my views, is as follows. Helgö was the focal point for trade and manufacture in central Sweden. No other site in the whole of Scandinavia was anything like as important for metalworking. There is nowhere else, except Birka, in the whole of Scandinavia with so many objects imported from distant countries. Up to the present, the Helgö material has given us information about trade and handicrafts while other aspects of economy, for example, crop-raising and cattle-breeding, remain ill-represented. Helgö, in fact, has an urban aspect without being a town in the strict sense of the word. It does not have the organised character of a medieval town, nor has it a defensive wall or fortress against possible enemies. The settlement on Helgö seems rather to be composed of a number of units with a common function and, perhaps, a common origin. It is significant, for instance, that many of the units possessed metalworking sites. It is not possible to say any more about the type of settlement. The difficulty arises mostly from the fact that one has to look so far back in time for comparable sites. Helgö's main period of importance was indisputably during the fifth and sixth centuries and as the settlement was fully developed at this time, prototypes might be expected from the late Roman period; but there are no similar settlements at that period either.

It is hardly surprising in itself that a centre for trade and handicrafts should develop in the centre of the Mälar region. According to our most recent inventory of archaeological finds, this area is the richest in Sweden and therefore likely to have been well-populated. The function of the site would have been to provide the population with goods which were otherwise difficult to obtain, objects such as fine metal-work, art products and imported luxuries. Local products were brought to the site for exchange and probably mainly exported. In the light of this, the similarities between the Helgö material and the jewellery types in Norrland, Finland and Gotland are perfectly understandable as the result of extensive and lively trading connections. Then, as later, Norrland and Finland were producers of raw materials and

Gotland's position in the Baltic Sea made the island a natural focus for commercial contacts between the various countries.

I believe that Helgö played a dominant role in both the local and foreign trade of central Sweden. This began early, in the late Roman period, and continued for a long time. Whatever type of community it was, it is hardly likely that it was independent of the central royal power. The Ansgar chronicle records that the Svea king had a governor or overseer in Birka to look after the interests of the king and country. Helgö lies only a few kilometres away and it flourished at the same time as Birka. Conditions must have been more or less the same in both places, particularly in the Viking period, and the kings of the Svea are unlikely to have been interested in Birka alone. Helgö was founded many centuries before Birka and one may well wonder where Birka was when Helgö first began. We know next to nothing about this but we are certainly on the way to accumulating sufficient archaeological evidence for future conclusions.

It is unlikely that Helgö will turn out to be unique. Other similar places will probably be found in Sweden. Only 1 or 2 per cent of our land's antiquities have been excavated so far, so we have much to hope for from future discoveries. It is also very likely that foreign parallels and prototypes will emerge to help us to fill in the picture of Helgö's foreign contacts and understand the real significance of Helgö as a flourishing Scandinavian oasis in a chaotic Dark Age Europe.

Bibliography

Holmqvist, W., Arrhenius, B. and Lundström, P., *Excavations at Helgö, I*; Report for 1954–6, Uppsala, 1961.

Holmqvist, W. and Arrhenius, B., *Excavations at Helgö, II*; Report for 1957–9, Uppsala, 1964.

Holmqvist, W., 'Die Metallwerkstätten auf Helgö', *Kölner Jahrbuch* vol. 9, 1968.

Holmqvist, W., Lamm, K. and Lundström, A., *Excavations at Helgö, III*; Report for 1960–4, Uppsala, 1970.

Holmqvist, W., Lamm, K., Lundström, A. and Waller, J., *Excavations at Helgö, IV*; Workshop, Part 1, Uppsala, 1972.

Holmqvist, W., 'Helgö als Zentralort im Ostseeraum in der jüngeren Eisenzeit', *Berichte über den II internationalen Kongress für Slavische Archaeologie*, vol. II, Berlin, 1973.

Holmqvist, W., 'Rapport från Helgö. 20 års arkeologiska undersökningar', *Jernkontorets Annaler* 157, 1973.

Lamm, K., 'The manufacture of jewellery during the Migration Period at Helgö in Sweden', *Bulletin of the Historical Metallurgy Group*, vol. 7, no. 2, 1973.

Chapter VI

The crop-mark sites at Mucking, Essex, England

M. U. and W. T. Jones

'air reconnaissance . . . perhaps the most sensational and revolutionary single factor in the post-war phase . . .' (Rupert Bruce-Mitford in his preface to *Recent Archaeological Excavations in Britain*, 1956)

Quarrying and rescue excavation have long been major sources of new archaeological material. Few British museums or archaeological journals do not acknowledge gravel pits for a large part of their collections and contributions. Since the war this long pre-eminence of gravel archaeology has been accentuated by the greatly increased rate of gravel working, by the growing, yet still quite inadequate, resources in finance and personnel now available for rescue excavation and, above all, by the accelerating knowledge of new sites through crop-marks recorded from the air.

The investigation of the Mucking crop-mark sites, which began in 1965, can be seen as a logical step. Yet, in spite of an official report published in 1960 on the growing loss of sites through gravel quarrying, Mucking is still the only gravel pit rescue where a deliberate attempt is being made to record the entire palimpsest of ancient landscapes, rather than specific features. Its significance therefore derives not only from its discovery of new material. It is also a type site for method, based on the positive attitude that quarrying provides unique opportunities. Few would dispute that the use of many hectares of land solely for archaeological study is an impracticable dream.

A project of this size could, of course, develop only from a sound blueprint. This was provided by a remarkable photograph which Professor J. K. St Joseph (Director of Aerial Photography, University of Cambridge), published in 1964. Nearby, two earlier state-financed rescue excavations had established a local Iron Age to pagan Saxon occupation range. So, although there was never much doubt that 'excavation would prove to be especially rewarding', those rewards contained several surprises.

A henge-like double ditched earthwork, for instance, proved to be a hillfort, ring ditches proved not to be barrows but (with one exception) penannular hut gullies. Most astonishing of all, discrete crop-marks within one enclosure turned out to be the graves of a Romano-British cemetery, while elsewhere (Plate XXVIa) they proved to be a veritable rash of Saxon sunken huts in a quantity and extent quite unknown in England. Then, without any clues from crop-marks, as a direct outcome of the policy of attempting 100 per cent rescue, came the discovery of two separate pagan Saxon cemeteries, of which one promises to be the first of any size in England to have been excavated in its entirety.

Although British excavation attitudes are moving away from sections and stratigraphy to area stripping, landscape rescue is sufficiently rare to justify a note on method. Its results cannot be appreciated without awareness of its practice, its advantages and its limitations. Basically, work at Mucking is a simple affair of removing topsoil and subsoil, to enable first the planning and then the excavation of soil-marks in the gravel, already known broadly from crop-marks. These are usually quite shallow, rarely deeper than $1\frac{1}{2}$ m. Geophysical surveys are superfluous and there is no dilemma in deciding where to site trenches. It is difficult only because of many imponderables. The rate of quarrying cannot be foreseen, as it responds immediately to varying demand, which might include new roads. The available finance, the vagaries of weather and the supply of labour are rarely in harmony.

Optimum information from soil excavation comes from fine hand work in diffused light in a drying breeze on saturated ground. These are most often winter conditions, yet labour for most British excavations is provided by students on summer vacation. Over two thousand students have now worked on the Mucking excavation, many from abroad, in particular the Netherlands, USA and Poland. Because of the thin (30–45 cm) soil covering, the heavy machinery now commonly employed can be damaging. Yet the need to strip and remove topsoil from two hectares annually renders tracked vehicles pulling box scrapers the only economic solution. Ideally, the last few cm should be dug by hand but for practical considerations this stage must usually be mechanised.

Ground planning, a more demanding task than most of the digging, could theoretically be mechanised by photogrammetry. Low-level air photography is a most useful aid but not yet a substitute for hand drawing and help has come from individuals, private firms and public bodies. A mosaic of ground-level photographs proved to be impracticable over such large areas.

Although finance and personnel will always restrict the number of excavations on a scale comparable to those at Mucking, a strong case can be made for landscape investigations in key areas, as Mucking is to the lower Thames.

The Mucking crop-mark sites lie within the 100 ft contour in the centre of an out-

Plate XXVI (a) (above) *Mucking, Essex:* Ancient landscapes seen from the air. A panoramic view looking south across the Thames of the western end of the crop-mark sites, now mostly destroyed by quarrying. Saxon huts extend right across the picture, and the two Saxon cemeteries are arrowed

(b) (left) *Mucking, Essex:* The 1971 excavation area, located by the half-circular Belgic ditch 50 m across

lying remnant, barely 3×1 km in extent, at the east end of the highest and oldest of the Thames gravel terraces. This is called variously the 100 ft, 30 m or Boyn hill terrace. At this point the Thames meanders, so creating a double vantage point, affording extensive views over the river marshes south to the Kent bank, as well as east down the widening estuary. The impression of height, which air photographs fail to register, is best realised at night when one looks down onto the moving lights of road and river traffic.

Only a third of this terrace remnant now survives unquarried and it is on this central part that the crop-marks lie (Fig. 49a). Luckily most of this has, since the war, been cultivated almost without hedges and mostly for cereals. Between 1959 and 1970, both years of exceptional early summer drought, almost complete air cover over some 20 hectares has been recorded. Excellent detail of buried pits and ditches has resulted from barley and wheat, with less sensitive crop-marks from a long ley of lucerne.

Ploughing has long removed any surface traces of ancient habitation and little besides infrequent flints can be picked up from field surveys. Such large machinery is now used for quarrying that it is barely possible to see, let alone interpret, disconnected settlement traces, or rescue more than occasional finds, while quarrying is in progress. Without crop-marks recorded by air photography, such settlement areas as this, which must still cover thousands of acres throughout Britain, would never be known.

It is from underground traces such as these, which crop-marks reflect in dramatic fashion, that archaeologists must try to picture not just ancient landscapes but the people who created them.

The jigsaw of prehistoric, Roman and Saxon Mucking will always defy completion. Not only is so much adjacent land already destroyed but it is evident from incomplete enclosures, recorded by crop-marks only on the thin soil covering the terrace top, that settlement traces continue down the slope. There, crop-marks are never likely to develop, because of the deep soils formed from the brick earths which flank the terrace like silted valleys flowing down to the marsh. How then can we catch a glimpse of the ancient landscapes below the terrace?

Obviously we must begin by stripping off the paraphernalia of the modern landscape – electricity pylons, power stations, oil refineries, roads, railways, farms, houses, even hedges and trees. But this is not nearly enough – the sea wall must go too.

The flood disasters of 1953 and now the Thames barrage provide reminders that south-eastern England is still sinking, and sites in Essex have yielded essential evidence of once habitable coastlands that are now drowned. Hazzledine Warren's researches on the Lyonesse surface developed from his Essex discoveries of Neolithic and Beaker occupation near Clacton. Quite close to Mucking are the huts of the Roman period found on the shore at East Tilbury in 1920. It is still possible to pick up from the beaches outside the sea wall near Mucking creek sherds eroded by the sea from Roman and medieval sites and deposited by the tides among such other jetsam as the plastic containers of our own age. Indeed, comparable submergence of the North Sea coastlands is now thought to have been a significant factor, forcing people to leave their homes on the Dutch *terpen* and German *wurten* during the Migration period.

So, if we lower the Thames by several metres we shall see dramatically how the river changes from the barrier it is today to an easily crossed thoroughfare in an inhabited coastal fringe. Extensive marshlands probably dictated a few main crossing places. Tilbury, still marked out by Henry VIII's fort and the ferry, is an obvious candidate. There is also a hard way right to the water's edge further east, at East Tilbury. Arriving here from Kent, a traveller could easily make his way towards the crop-mark sites, conspicuous not only because of their height but also because of the light vegetation of their thin soil covering. The modern road from East Tilbury may perpetuate such an ancient route.

In a sense this area, cut off from its hinterland by London clay, can be regarded as geographically linked with Kent rather than Essex. The mapping of some finds such as potin coins and garnet-inlaid Saxon jewellery shows this clearly.

It is always exciting to join the wagtails and seagulls in the wake of the box scraper, stripping yet more hectares of topsoil from the windswept gravel terrace. The first noticeable soil change is the sharp boundary between the dark plough soil and the pebbly subsoil. Here lie many of the flints of Mucking's earlier prehistory. So far (surprisingly, since ninety-nine hand axes have come from the terrace at Chadwell St Mary, two miles to the south-west) no Palaeolithic artefacts have been found either on or in the gravels. Mesolithic core rejuvenators have been recognised but the relatively small total of a few thousand flints seems to derive mainly from Neolithic and Bronze Age occupation. There are several fragments of polished flint axes and bifacial tools such as knives and arrowheads but most pieces are waste flakes and blades, cores, cricket ball-like hammer stones and many scrapers. Both nodular flint (the chalk outcrops only a few miles to the west) and pebble flint, from the gravel itself, were used.

As well as these stray finds, a few flint groups have come from pits and hollows. The hollows seem to have been natural puddle-like depressions in the gravel bed laid down by the proto-Thames. In periglacial conditions of frost and thaw they must have filled with finer silts. Consequently they produce crop-marks. Even as soil-marks they are often difficult to distinguish from pits dug by man. Flint groups from hollows include cores, flakes and blades and some may be Mesolithic but flint groups from pits, in association with Beaker and later pottery, burnt pebbles and charcoal, are more decisive, though still scanty evidence for the first inhabitants of Mucking. Beaker pits provide the first of several outstanding settlement-with-burial associations, part of the bonus of landscape excavation.

Burials provide the more spectacular finds and the scraps of pottery, including two possible all-over corded sherds, cannot compare with the contents of grave 137

(Fig. 45b). This just missed inclusion in Clarke's second corpus of British Beakers (the first being Abercromby's in 1912) as the forty-second intact European bell Beaker. Figure 46 shows this all-over combed pot, assigned to the most numerous, East Anglian, group. Clarke suggests their main settlement period as 1900–1800 B.C. and sees the people behind the pots as simple peasant agriculturalists, seamen and traders, migrating to Britain in 'their sea-going canoes pushed out from the sand islands of the Rhine delta and the Drenthe peninsula . . . carrying their livestock, cereal seed and equipment'. This first clear statement of the role of Mucking as a landfall within the North Sea littoral is echoed almost exactly two and a half millennia later by the Saxon immigrants.

Beside the pot was the second largest quiverful of barbed and tanged arrowheads yet found in a British Beaker grave (Fig. 47). Of a total of eleven, five were still lying undisturbed, behind the body and pointing towards the feet of the corpse. This fine

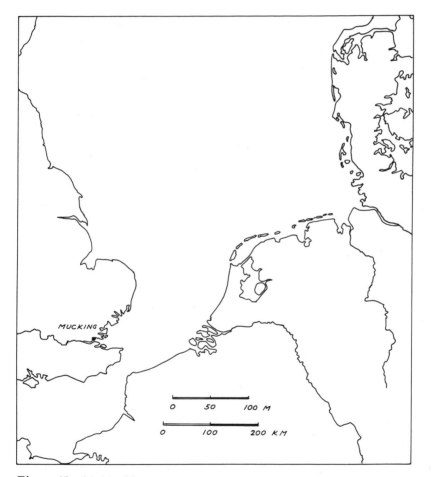

Figure 45   (a) *Mucking, Essex:* Position of Mucking on North Sea littoral

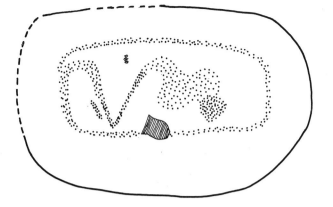

(b) *Mucking, Essex:* Plan of Beaker grave 137, showing the pot and arrow-heads to either side of the silhouette. Only the head and flexed legs are recognisable. The faint surrounding stain may have been a coffin (Scale: 1:24)

group of weapons is an early illustration of technological inspiration coming from the European community, since Clarke regards the Beaker Folk as probably responsible for introducing barbed and tanged arrowheads into Britain.

The body was represented only by a silhouette of which only the head (at the north) and the flexed legs were clear. Grave 137 introduces one of the more interesting aspects of the necrology of Mucking (over one thousand graves in all have now been excavated) – that of body silhouettes.

Only burnt bone (as in cremations), survives intact. Raw bone, especially when found in soil rich in humus, sometimes retains part of its shape. In the majority of inhumation burials, the only trace of a body is a stain, described as an iron manganese stain replacement. This, of course, means the loss of skeletal information. Nevertheless, as will be seen with Saxon graves, silhouette burials have advantages.

More permanent settlement, indicated by pits and especially by shallow ditches

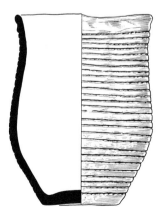

Figure 46   Mucking, Essex: All-over combed Beaker from grave 137 (Scale: 1:4)

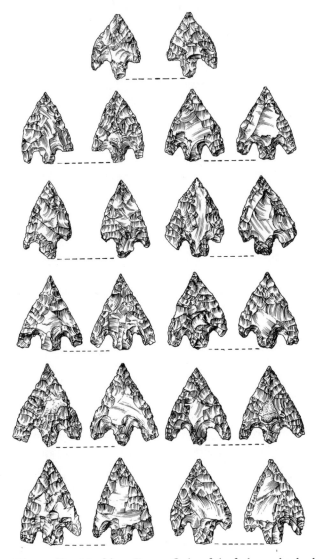

Figure 47 Mucking, Essex: Quiverful of eleven barbed and tanged flint arrow-heads from Beaker grave 137 (Scale: slightly reduced)

(of which one produced the broken tip of a socketed bronze axe, an unusual find from a settlement feature), followed in the later Bronze Age. To this period also may belong a 10 m diameter barrow ditch, another instance of settlement-with-burial associations. However, there was no trace of actual burial, which may have been on the old ground surface, and the ditch contained only scraps of pottery and flint.

A second flat grave, grave 786, of flexed silhouette within an undoubted composite coffin with a cover, contained only two barbed and tanged flint arrowheads.

The partially humified oak of the coffin gave a conventional radiocarbon date of 1630 B.C. (3580 ± 90 years B.P.).

The Bronze Age culminated in a major earthwork, two concentric ditches, of what may be called a bivallate mini-hillfort, only 80 m diameter overall, conventionally assigned to the Iron Age. Its pottery could be as early as the sixth century B.C. and late Bronze Age affinities are suggested by the very sparse metalwork (bronze pin, tweezers and plano-convex ingot fragments), the entire absence of iron, and pottery with applied bands.

Unlike west Britain, especially along the Welsh border, Essex is not hillfort country (less than ten are shown on the Ordnance Survey period map) so this crop-mark feature, proved by excavation not to be a henge, is noteworthy. Its defensive character and its siting, beside the modern road which may perpetuate an ancient river-crossing route, introduces the strategic aspect of the crop-mark sites.

The main entrance of the hillfort, a simple gap in the ditches, faced the river and there was a slight opposed entrance. There was no way of proving that the concentric (V-shaped) ditches, cut nearly 2 m into the gravel, with internal banks, were contemporary. Most of the occupation rubbish had accumulated in the late fill of the inner ditch and it could be argued that this was the earlier. If so, it could hardly have been more than a temporary refuge for a small group, since the diameter of the central space, without allowing for the rampart spread, is only 40 m. A 12 m diameter hut gully, centrally placed, may also belong to the hillfort.

The earliest sizable group of pottery, for which the Mucking site now provides a regional type series spanning one thousand years, came from the hillfort. The very distinctive fabric, generously tempered with flint grit, has been quite easily copied in practical experiments with the brick earth which in places overlies the gravel. Experimental pots were fired in a shallow pit using a bale of straw for fuel. The hillfort pottery was most probably a domestic product and the astonishing variety of rims, finger-impressed, crimped and pinched, may be seen rather like the idiosyncrasies of neighbouring housewives forming the edges of their pastry cases. Pots range from tiny thumbpots, perhaps made by or for children, through thin-walled and burnished jars, sometimes decorated with geometric combing, through occasional widely flaring bowls, to a range of storage type jars, with walls up to 1 cm thick. Jars commonly have angular shoulders (carination) and occasionally the finger-impressed applied bands are reminiscent of earlier cordoned urns. Perforated rectangular slabs of fired clay were also found in the hillfort ditches. Perhaps these were primitive hotplates.

The distribution of this pottery outside the hillfort should help to establish how the hillfort dwellers made their living. Most probably this was, as in the later Iron Age and Saxon periods, geared to sheep rearing. This is supported by finds of loom-weight fragments. Indeed, before the mechanised cereal farming of today, the terrace was mainly a sheep-run.

The hillfort overlay Bronze Age ditches and in turn its own silted ditches were dug into by later people, Iron Age, Romano-British and finally Saxon. This introduces the problem, common to all sites with a long settlement history, of artefacts which survive from earlier features and become associated with finds properly belonging to later features, but in which both are found. An important contribution of the Mucking excavation is that it will provide a yardstick for other pottery found in the region, both chance finds already in local museums and pottery not yet discovered. The problem of residual finds becomes a critical matter at Mucking with the Saxon huts. Because they are still such a rarity in British archaeology, it is a concern of more than local significance. As will be suggested later, such problems are more convincingly solved by area investigation. Here, it need only be mentioned that where hillfort pottery has been found in Saxon huts, it has been in huts built within the hillfort area.

Penannular hut gullies are among features dug through the silted hillfort ditches. This is what most of the circular crop-marks, thought to have been the ring ditches of barrows, have turned out to be, since crop-marks often fail to show their diagnostic entrance. There is now general agreement that these gullies were dug to catch the rainwater which dripped off a conical (thatched) roof, hence the break at the hut entrance. Entrances consistently face south-east. Otherwise the Mucking gullies, over one hundred of which have now been excavated wholly or in part, have little consistency. Their diameters range from 6 m to 20 m and in depth the gullies vary from a few cm to nearly 1 m. The larger gullies have usually been dug out several times, which argues for a longer occupation. The central space usually contains post-holes, in random arrangement, though one cannot be certain that they belong. However, one gully contained a concentric stake-hole setting and two had possible evidence for porches. The most important structural evidence is provided by the occasional survival of a slight concentric slot, less than 10 cm wide and deep, about 1 m inside the gully. This must indicate the base of a wall trench, in which something like close-set poles may have stood.

It is sometimes argued that the larger gullies are of too wide a span to be roofed and that such a hut is anyway too large a living space. The first point is being approached by practical experiment. As for the second, urbanised readers often overlook the habit among herding people of sharing their homes with their stock.

Who lived in these round huts? In nearly every case, people who used a quite different pottery from the hillfort dwellers, consisting of carefully formed, well-burnished, smooth-curved jars, often with a ring-base and usually a dense black colour. Finger-impressions had gone right out of fashion and the sparse decoration consists of scored lines on the shoulder, within the rim and on the base, where it is usually a cross. Scraps of curvilinear design (Fig. 48, no. 10) are reminiscent of

Figure 48 (opposite)   *Mucking, Essex*: 1–7: Hillfort pottery; 8: Perforated clay slab; 9–13: Early Iron Age hut pottery; 14: Bronze handled iron mirror fragment; 15: Socketed bronze axe fragment; 16: Bronze pin; 17–19: Belgic 'bricks'; 20: Triangular clay loomweight (Scale: 14–16, 1 : 2; the rest 1 : 4)

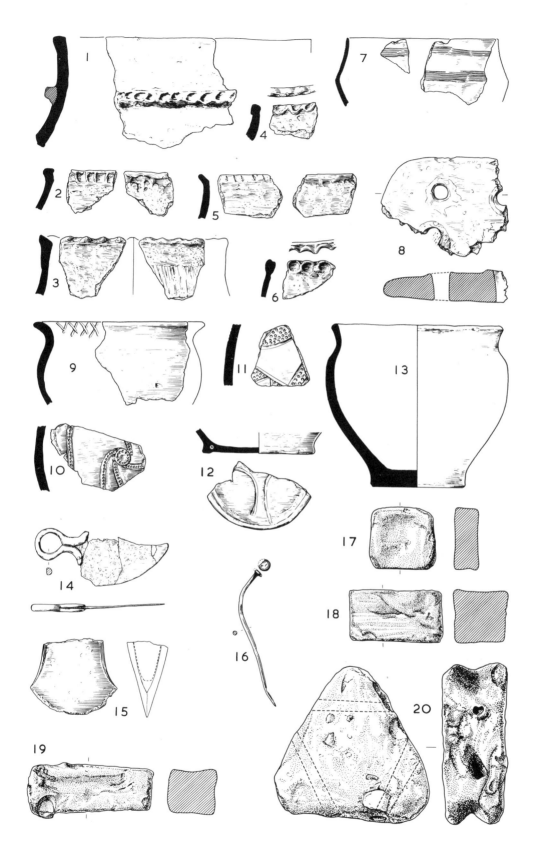

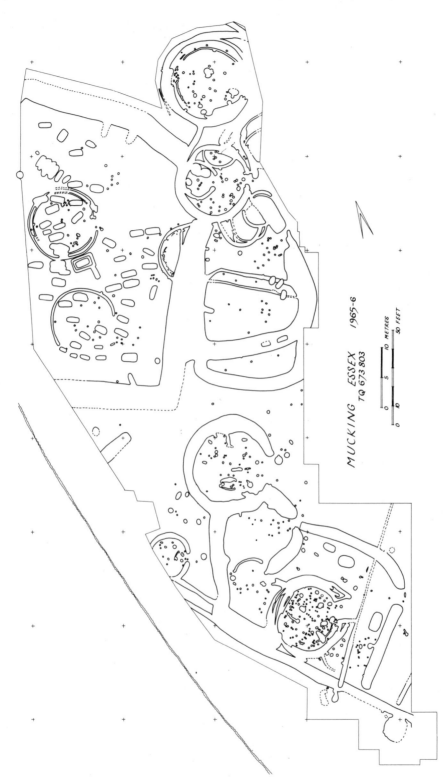

MUCKING ESSEX 1965–6
TQ 673 803

0   5   10 METRES
0   50 FEET

Figure 49 (a) *Mucking, Essex*: Early Iron Age perannular gullies, with attached compounds, one of which has been re-used as a Romano–British cemetery

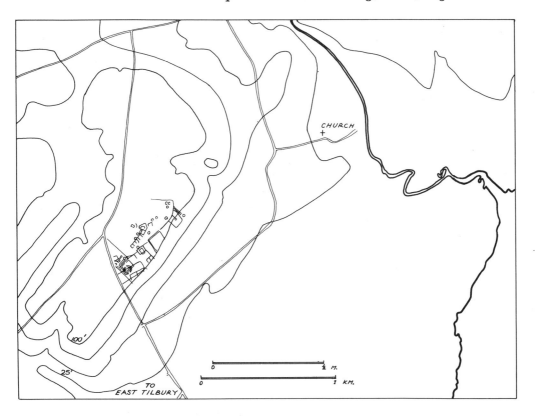

(b) *Mucking, Essex:* The crop-mark sites and their topography

Celtic metalwork of the Iron Age. This tie-up is supported by a rare metal find, a mirror fragment, from a pit within one hut gully. Although difficult to compare with such famous bronze mirrors as those from Desborough and Birdlip with their characteristic geometric curved art style, since this piece is not decorated at all, it is of great interest as it is not a grave find and it has an iron mirror plate, uncommon in Britain and almost unknown abroad (Fig. 48, no. 14).

Now that more than one hundred hut gullies have been investigated, a general picture is emerging. Most huts stand isolated, well back from the terrace edge. Associated with them are pits, probably for cooking and for storage, including a few for water storage. These are pits filled with raw clay in which a large jar has been set upright. Probably a semi-nomadic economy based on sheep can be inferred.

Shepherding in round huts may have been the way of life up to the Roman conquest. The clearest evidence for continuity comes from the first area investigated (Fig. 49a). It is apparent that the most westerly compound was built against a pre-existing boundary ditch which has been traced for about 170 m down the slope and that the ditches of the largest easterly compound must have been visible when it continued in use as an enclosed Romano-British cemetery. But before these burials were made, there was a final Iron Age phase, known as Belgic from the homeland of its many immigrants.

With emerging history comes the archaeologists' biggest challenge. It is no easy task to equate pits and ditches with historic events. It has taken over four years, for instance, to work across the 170 m extent of a ditched complex first seen as cropmarks. Only now is it reasonably clear that this consisted of a broadly contemporary series of mostly open-sided 'enclosures' both curved and rectangular. These are now interpreted as sheepfolds, open to the south and the river view and protected on the north by ditch and external bank from biting winds and perhaps wolves or thieves. It is not certain if round huts were still the common house type, though domestic pits, clay-lined kilns with firebars and post-hole scatters accompany this occupation, which can be dated to the first century A.D.

Wheelthrown traded pottery – platters, butt beakers, cordoned jars and flagons – at times copying imported Gallo-Belgic *terra nigra* and *terra rubra*, now appears. Dating is by comparison with the pottery series from Camulodunum, Britain's first town in east Essex. Metalwork is still sparse but includes potin coins, Britain's first currency, as well as La Tène and penannular brooches. There are triangular loom-weights and Belgic 'bricks', variously sized rectangular blocks, which can be seen as updated versions of the hillfort dwellers' 'hotplates'.

An especially interesting pottery type, which seems to mark the end of the Belgic sheepfolds, is easily recognised by its angular internally rebated rim and its corky (vesicular) fabric, which seems to be due to shell grits having dissolved out. More than sixty of these pots had been scored just beneath the rim, before firing, with recurring symbols, which evidently had a meaning and so can justifiably be called potters' graffiti. Most consist of vertical and horizontal strokes resembling upper case Roman numerals, and diamonds with a vertical dividing line are common. Their evidently narrow dating, about the time of the Claudian invasion, and their local findspots on both sides of the Thames will render their developing distribution map of considerable interest.

Possibly the Belgic shepherds witnessed the building of the accurately surveyed rectangular ditched earthwork, with internal defensive bank, which was sited almost precisely where the hillfort had been, beside the suggested route to the East Tilbury river crossing. It must have looked quite formidable, with its 2 m deep V ditch and its squared butt ends at the single entrance. Was it unfinished, or was there a change of plan to explain why the slight outer ditch was never dug along the fourth side? It has been refused recognition as a military and therefore Roman work because it has only one entrance facing inland and insufficiently rounded corners, though a legionary's sporran pendant was found in its interior.

Nevertheless, one feels bound to remark that after the Medway battle Claudius' troops would have had a much more direct crossing of the Thames by East Tilbury, than the roundabout trip to Camulodunum by London. However, this is only one of three strategically sited enclosures strung out along the terrace edge, so perhaps more decisive evidence may yet come to light.

The emerging picture is of an Iron Age with a warlike opening (the hillfort) and a warlike close (the para-military earthwork on the same site) – dramatic episodes in long centuries of shepherding. To match this period of some six centuries with burials is a far from simple task. Very few burials which can be attributed to the Iron Age have been found and they are mostly late in date, isolated inhumations or cremations often in ditch fills and often without grave goods. A few cremation pots have curvilinear or cordoned decoration. A few unurned cremations contain La Tène brooches. A group of eight inhumation graves, including flexed silhouettes in coffins, lay parallel to a Belgic sheepfold ditch and outside its bank. One of these graves contained a slightly cordoned pot.

Whatever the original purpose of the three strategically sited enclosures referred to above, there seems no doubt that they provided the framework of the Romano-British landscape. Reading partly from crop-marks, they can be seen linked together by lengths of ditch which seem to form the hill boundary of an agricultural settlement. This would be called a villa, except that no romanised buildings have yet been located. Since they lie almost certainly at the foot of the terrace slope, below the spring line, gravel rescue excavations are unlikely to uncover them. There would be difficulties in locating them, not only because of the deep soil but because of the absence of local building stone, which makes the recognition of buildings a much more formidable problem than in, say, the Cotswolds.

The evidence so far is suggestive enough, consisting of two corndriers with flues built from knapped flints, chalk blocks and tiles, six wells, in three of which part of the timber framing survived, and six circular updraught clay-walled pottery kilns, sited on field margins. Ditch fills contained rubbish from romanised buildings, such as roof, floor and flue tiles, the latter for underfloor hypocaust heating, and window glass (though not painted plaster, cement or *tesserae* from mosaic pavements). Many fragments of querns made of imported stone (lava from the Rhineland, millstone grit from the Pennines, puddingstone and sarsen from the south-east) and a sickle, comprise, with the enclosed fields and corndriers, the first direct evidence of arable farming. The coin list suggests this continued throughout the Roman period, with issues from Vespasian, A.D. 69 to Arcadius, A.D. 398, making up the very low total of less than one hundred, including several British coins. This low total need refer merely to the fact that the crop-mark area lies in Roman farmland and also that bronze survives badly in this soil. Other clues hinting at average Romano-British sophistication are seal boxes, iron keys, a perforated bronze key handle (Fig. 50), a silver signet ring with Cupid on its cornelian intaglio, moulded glass bottles and blown glass bowls and fragments of pipe-clay figurines, of which Mars (Fig. 50), of a coarser than usual fabric, seems to be unique in Roman Britain.

The pottery, the archaeologist's alphabet, includes the wide range of types traded within the Province and Empire common to Romanised living. In the

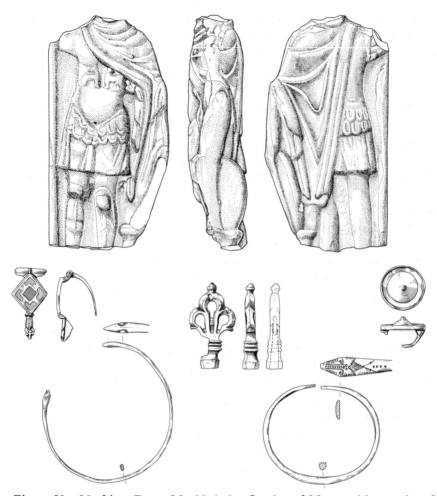

Figure 50   Mucking, Essex: Moulded clay figurine of Mars and bronze key finial from settlement; brooches and snakeshead bangles from graves (Scale: 1 : 2)

mid-Roman period the Mucking kilns themselves no doubt supplied the estate with its jars and pie dishes. The kitchen *mortaria*, the *amphorae* of wine and oil and the flagons for serving at table came from market. Finer wares included red samian wine cups and bowls from Gaul and their British copies in red and brown, sometimes painted and stamped, and colour-coated ware from the Nene valley, Oxford region and elsewhere. Rhenish beakers and roulette stamped Argonne ware are represented, as well as sherds decorated with suggestively Saxon bosses and dimples, the so-called 'Romano-Saxon' pottery.

There is no way of knowing if the Roman cemetery, in its Iron Age compound (Fig. 49), is directly related to the presumed villa. The grave goods suggest no more than a modest economic status. Most of the eighty graves were inhumations in nailed coffins. In some cases the nail positions showed that the coffins had lids. Eight graves were cremations. Inhumation offerings were pots, some deliberately holed in the side, bronze bangles, several with snakeshead terminals (Fig. 50) and one bronze anklet. Two cremations contained a disc brooch and an enamelled plate brooch. In several graves hobnails still in position suggested that the corpse was buried in everyday clothes (Fig. 51a). Not all Roman burials lay within the cemetery. As well as a few just outside, there was a group of three cremations at a field corner, with bones and pots, including samian, placed in large jars.

Cemeteries in the Roman world were commonly sited beside roads, so there may be some significance in the position of this cemetery beside the suggested East Tilbury river-crossing route.

More than any other British excavation carried out in recent years, Mucking is providing an opportunity to demonstrate or disprove settlement continuity. There has been no reason to suppose the gravel terrace was abandoned at any period since the late Neolithic, nor is there any reason to doubt an extensive and reasonably prosperous Romano-British occupation. At no other site have anything like one hundred and twenty-one Saxon huts plus two Saxon cemeteries yet been investigated. Surely here we should expect an answer to one of the major puzzles of British archaeology. What contribution can Mucking make to the Roman-Saxon transition, which is still the Dark Ages to archaeologist and historian alike?

With work expected to continue for several more years, any simple statement, even if one were possible, would be untimely. Excavation does provide answers but more often it poses further questions. It seems better to attempt here a review of the Saxon settlement so far examined.

If one includes the evidence from the 1955 Mucking (Linford Quarry) site, just across the road from Orsett Quarry, where present work continues, and the partly checked evidence of crop-marks, a scatter of some one hundred and fifty Saxon sunken huts (*Grubenhäuser*) has now been established. These lie mostly along the river edge of the terrace and extend at least as far as a small valley which has cut into its eastern slope and is the nearest point to the creek. Enough work has now been done on the north-west limit of the crop-mark sites to establish that although this hut distribution, which extends for more than 1 km, has no obvious boundary, though there are slight straggling ditches, the hut density, in common with settlement traces of all periods, diminishes away from the terrace slope. This widely dispersed hut distribution almost certainly continues down the slope, beyond the crop-mark area.

Apart from the slight ditches referred to, the only other Saxon settlement features so far recognised are small pits, of cooking or storage type. Occasional Saxon finds from the late fills of large Iron Age to Roman features may have come from unrecognised intrusions such as pits. In this category a 'Luton' brooch is notable. In view of the association of sunken huts with ground-level post-hole buildings in the Linford Quarry excavation and also at West Stow, Suffolk — the only other English site where sunken huts have been found in quantity – it should be added that none of the post-hole structures so far found is certainly Saxon. Post-hole structures range from four- and six-post settings attributed to the Iron Age, to buildings as large as 17 by 7 m and 23 by 10 m. These seemed to be Belgic or Romano-British.

No pattern is evident in the hut distribution. After the first few years of excavation, one could say that many huts, about a dozen, seemed to be sited on or near Roman field boundaries. Now that one hundred and twenty-one huts have been excavated, this is no longer a significant proportion. Midway along the hut distribution lie the two Saxon cemeteries, Cemetery One on the landward side of the terrace and Cemetery Two lying towards its edge, at a distance apart of some 150 m (Figs 51b, c). Although there are fewer huts in the central cemetery area, graves and huts are not strictly co-terminous. This is shown most graphically where inhumation grave 566 is dug into the fill of hut 84 (Fig. 52).

Now for the huts themselves. As their name (sunken hut, sunken floored hut, *Grubenhaus*) implies, they are small buildings with floors below ground level. These floors may be dug out as little as 30 cm or as much as 1 m below the gravel surface, to which one must add about 30 cm for subsoil and topsoil. The modern ploughed out surface can be no more than an approximation of the Saxon surface. The huts are not consistent in size. Some are as small as about 3 by $2\frac{1}{2}$ m, some as large as about 6 by 4 m. The larger huts are usually deeper. Two substantial post-holes are invariably dug centrally into the narrow ends of the sunken floors, sited so that the posts would stand against the gravel side. In some huts, these post-holes are duplicated, or may be of hourglass plan, suggesting the original posts had been replaced or buttressed. Sometimes, in the larger huts, there are small additional post-holes or stake-holes in the floor corners or along the floor sides. There are several instances of two, even three, huts overlapping on the same alignment, and possibly to be seen as rebuildings, though the alignment of their long axes is the only consistent feature of the huts at Mucking. This is south-west to north-east and it may have been influenced by the terrace slope, or the prevailing wind, or both.

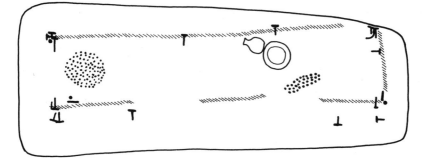

Figure 51 (a) *Mucking, Essex:* Plan of a grave in the Romano-British cemetery showing coffin nails and stain, head stain, hob nails and pots (Scale: 1 : 24)

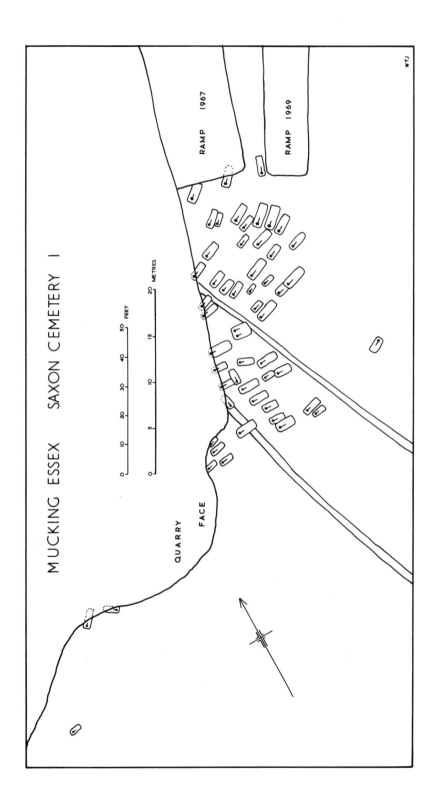

(b) *Mucking, Essex*: Plan of Saxon Cemetery 1

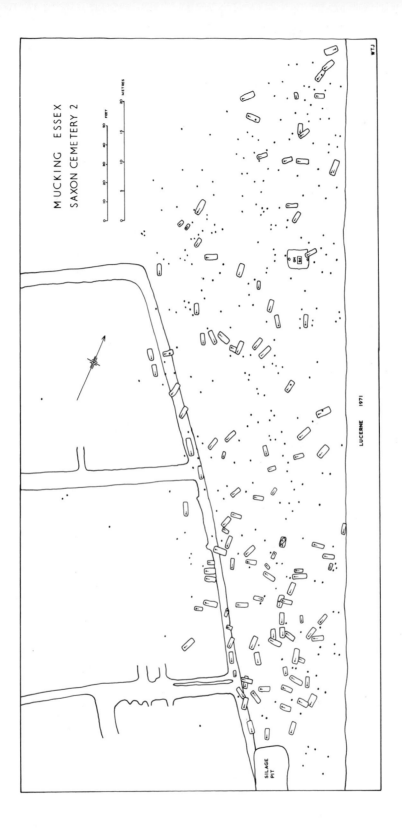

(c) *Mucking, Essex:* Plan of Saxon Cemetery 2

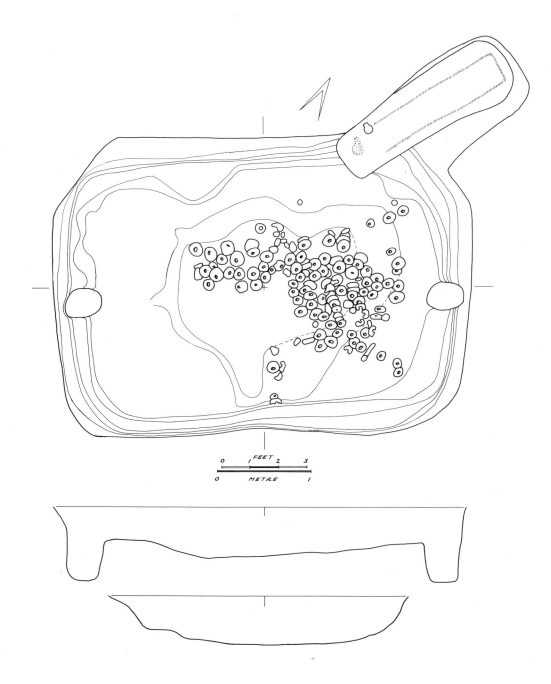

Figure 52   Mucking, Essex: Plan of Saxon hut 84 and grave 566

The gravel sides of the sunken floors are in places vertical but usually slope slightly. Since only immediately backfilled features, such as graves, retain their original upright walls in the uncemented gravel, some slope is to be expected. What seemed to be deliberately raised ledges against the walls, which continued like collars round the post-holes, are now recognised as areas of the original floor level, un-affected by trampling, cleaning and so on. The effect is seen quite well in hut 84 (Fig. 52) where the loomweights lie on the lower, worn, floor level.

The two main post-holes are usually the only certain clues to the hut structure. Evidence for floor covering, walls, roof and entrance must be sought in the hut fill. Since this is not directly informative, one must conclude that the huts were built entirely of organic materials. Where evidence is incomplete, as here, an archaeologist can set up a model and see if his evidence fits. Or he can interpret with the help of parallels.

It is not difficult to imagine a model of a Mucking hut. One can guess that the turf was cut into blocks to make walls for the longer sides, and the subsoil and gravel dug out above the sunk floor could be piled behind them. The two posts would have supported a ridge pole, on which could be tied roof rafters sloping down to the wall tops and covered with some kind of thatch. Because of these low side walls, the entrance cannot have been anywhere but beside one of the gable posts, so the gable infilling was perhaps of split logs or planks. Bearing in mind the rainbearing westerly winds, a sensible Saxon would have put his door in the east gable. Within the hut it seems certain there was some sort of panelling, or perhaps boxed-in benches or beds. It is difficult otherwise to imagine how the gravel sides escaped collapse. For the same reason, one can guess there were boxed-in steps down from the door. A few huts contain evidence of fire on the floor but not of such sophistication as to require a chimney.

Sunken huts from other sites might help. Up to 1968, only twenty-two rural Saxon sites were known in England where sunken huts had been excavated. At the classic site of Sutton Courtenay, Berkshire, information was rescued from gravel quarrying, in days before state finance was available for such work. At West Stow, Suffolk, another rescue excavation, the huts were built in almost pure sand. This has resulted in much clearer stratification than at Mucking and a case has been made for a floor at ground level built over a shallow cellar. Some West Stow huts have three posts, not one, at either end of the sunken floor. Other huts in gravel are recorded from Bourton-on-the-Water, Glos., and Eynsham, Oxon., and in chalk at Puddlehill, Beds., and Keston, Kent. A recently published plan of an exceptionally large sunken hut at Upton, Northants., showed planked walls, for which there is evidence also at West Stow. At both these sites evidence for wattle and daub walls is quoted. Sunken huts from non-rural sites are recorded from Dorchester, Oxon., Canterbury, Kent, Thetford, Suffolk and Portchester, Hants. The continental litera-ture was summarised by Radford in 1957, but a reclassification of sunken huts (*Grubenhaüser*) was published in 1966 (by Ahrens). A photograph of a sunken plank floor refers to a hut at Wijster, Netherlands and the writers have seen a post-Migration sunken hut in the Dutch island of Texel. This has turf walls built inside the sunken areas and a floor of laid clay.

The basic facts which emerge from 'parallels' is that sunken huts are, with rare exceptions, a Saxon introduction to England and that they are the least sophisticated of timber buildings on the continent. The basic hut type at Mucking is what used to be called the two-post type but now belongs to Ahrens' new category, gabled post house. It is also evident that at very few sites indeed have so many huts been found together.

So much for their 'architecture'. What of the hut fills, their contained finds and the picture they suggest of their occupants? The soil fills of the huts at Mucking are as variable as their size and depth. In the first place the nature of the fill is obviously influenced by the actual siting of the hut. Many huts have been dug into earlier features, such as hillfort or Roman ditches. In two cases huts were dug into the backfill of Roman wells. Even when dug into undisturbed gravel, a hut fill may vary from sandy to pebbly and may include naturally silted hollows and their claylike fills. As a rule, a post-occupation fill can be distinguished in the larger, deeper huts but in shallower huts, especially where the fill contains much humus, very little stratification can be discerned, except to say that the upper fill is turning into sub-soil.

There is no evidence that the floors were not the bare gravel, which has indeed in some huts formed a hard thin crust or pan, and there are many instances of a definite dark and greasy occupation layer. Above this one cannot always be sure which finds were strictly contemporary. In hut 84 (Fig. 52) no one would doubt that the 140 or more green clay loomweights lying on the floor belonged to the hut occupation. Hut 80 had been dug beside, and evidently into, the spoil heaps of a Romano-British pottery kiln, so it was not surprising to find an inverted stratification of innumerable Roman sherds lying just above another spread of green loomweights. In some huts, finds seem to lie a few inches up the side. Had they fallen behind a bench? Elsewhere, much of a floor was littered with red deer antlers, of which one tine had been sawn off. It would have been impossible to walk about in the remaining space. Had this hut been used as a bone dump before being abandoned, and if so, can it logically be called a workshop? In hut 17, melted lead, perhaps once the plumbing in a romanised house, lay amid ash, having carbonised an animal bone it covered. Nearby on the side of the floor was a lead ring, presumably a loomweight, though of a shape peculiar to Mucking. Was this workshop rubbish? It is difficult to imagine an occupied hut with the articulated and therefore at least partly fleshed bones of a dog lying about. Reason seems to demand that a hut floor with a canine skull and forelimbs on it was no longer lived in, though canine bones seem to have been used deliberately as post-hole packing in another hut and something similar was observed at Sutton Courtenay. Again, were a pair of shears in one hut post-hole and a coin in another, intentionally placed?

How are we to understand why no less than twenty-two late Roman coins, mostly those of Valentinian I, came to be in a single hut? Even if one accepts that they belonged to the hut's occupants, the opinion of numismatists is that they were kept as curios, not currency, as we might today still have some non-decimal pieces in our possession. If this can be argued for coins, how are we to be sure that a gaily coloured sherd, white-painted red colour coated, or red-painted parchment ware, for example, did not get into a hut in this way?

It is easy to be convinced that Iron Age pottery came into a hut fill simply because it was there in the ground in which the hut was dug. Unless this same argument can be clearly demonstrated for Roman pottery, as with the kiln waste referred to above, it might well be supposed that Roman pottery was used by the hut occupants, especially if such pottery is of known fourth-century type and the Saxon pottery can, through parallels on the continent, be assigned to the fifth century. One might even feel that here, archaeologically expressed, is what Myres terms the phase of over-lap and controlled settlement.

Really it begins to look as if the Saxon hut fills, for all their finds, are more of a problem than the entirely floorless round huts of the Iron Age known, in most cases, only from their surrounding eaves' drip gullies. There can be no simple answer and perhaps complete agreement will never be reached. At any rate, the more huts there are, the more easily can one escape subjective conclusions by expressing statistically the types and positions of Romano-British pottery throughout the Saxon hut fills. This cannot yet be done, since sheer rescue has delayed background work on the finds. It provides yet another illustration of the rewards from landscape rescue: the reduction of the element of chance. Had excavation finished after the first twenty or so huts had been investigated, much Roman pottery, including Romano-Saxon frag-ments, would have been assigned quite logically to the hut occupants. Now that so many more huts have been excavated in areas remote from Roman features, which contain no Roman pottery at all but may on the other hand contain Belgic sherds, there must be some doubt. Obviously much depends on the recognition and dating of the Saxon pottery itself.

The Saxon pottery at Mucking is handmade and can be considered in two groups: the coarse wares which are numerically the more important, and the decorated and fine wares. The latter might be described as likely prototypes of the coarse pots. At its best the fine ware is a hard, polished dense black. Of even greater distinction than its fabric is its sophistication of shape and decoration. This enables very close com-parisons to be made with pottery from continental sites. To quote Dr J. N. L. Myres, writing in 1968 in the *Antiquaries Journal*, the first twenty huts at Mucking

> have already produced between them more pieces to which a date in the decades before and after A.D. 400 must be assigned, than any other domestic site in England. . . .

In particular, Myres refers to two main groups of carinated bowl (Fig. 53). The first

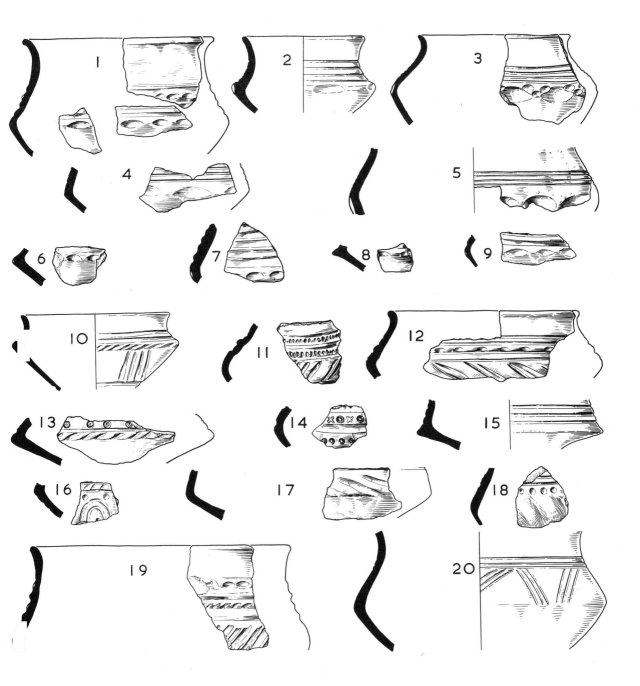

Figure 53 Mucking, Essex: Saxon settlement pottery: Carinated bowls. 1–9: Faceted carination; 10–20: With cabling, slashing, stabbing, linear decoration of standing arches and chevrons, impressed dimples and stamps (Scale: 1:4)

has a pedestal foot which seems to have gone out of use soon after 400. The second, which has a plain base, often almost round-bottomed, he describes as

> exceedingly common on both sides of the lower Elbe in the fourth century and spreads thence SW along the N. German coast into Frisia. . . . It seems to have lasted longer than the [pedestal foot]: it is, for example, well represented in the final phase of the settlement of Feddersen Wierde, near Bremerhaven, which came to an end about 450. The pottery from this final phase at Feddersen Wierde shows many very close parallels to that from Mucking.

Myres further remarks that

> Both types of carinated bowls have been found associated in continental burials with bronze belt-fittings . . . characteristic of the uniform equipment issued to Germanic *laeti* in Roman service at the turn of the fourth and fifth centuries.

On some bowls the actual carination is faceted (Fig. 53, nos 1–9) – 'a practice very common on examples from E. Holstein in the fourth century' – so that in addition to dating by form, comparisons can also be made of decorating motifs. This is fortunate, since so much of the decorated pottery found in the huts is in small fragments.

Such motifs, if they are sufficiently distinctive, can help not only to relate the settlement and cemeteries at Mucking but can serve as a reference collection for other sites, though one can never overlook, when considering handmade pots, that many influences have led to their creation. It is by no means a simple matter of reference as with most postage stamps and coins.

Motifs found on the settlement pottery at Mucking (Fig. 53) include concentric grooves round the neck, faceting, not only of carinations but also of cordons, slashed cordons which give a twisted or cabled effect, simple geometric patterns formed by scored and grooved lines such as chevrons and standing arches, at times punctuated with rounded or straight-sided dimples, and dimples arranged in lines or groups, such as rosettes. Then there are the stamps, not so far as numerous or as elaborate as those from the cemetery or funerary pottery (Fig. 57), which include ring and dot, crosses, cross in circle and rosettes. Finally there are the bosses, which more than anything else epitomise to most people the barbaric character of much pagan Saxon ceramic. These might be applied or pushed out, round or linear or diagonal or whirling.

Since the coarse wares are usually undecorated and often clumsily shaped (Fig. 54), it is fortunate that the fabric itself is as a rule quite distinctive, so that confusion with the other main handmade groups found at Mucking – Iron A (hillfort) (Fig. 48, nos 1–7) and Iron B (hut gullies) (Fig. 48, nos 9–13) – is rare. There is a superficial similarity between some black burnished sherds which occur in both Iron B and in Saxon groups, but Iron B ceramic is so much better potted that most fragments can be attributed by their even thickness and curve. This may be a reflection of a craftsman's skill, in contrast with the homely, rough and ready appearance of most Saxon coarse pots.

Judged visually, two basic fabrics are recognised, both commonly a dense black in section and presumably much reduced, though the surface may be locally oxidised (reddened). These are:

1 A hard sandy fabric, with noticeable burnish lines

2 The so-called 'grass' tempered fabric. This is a ware with a varying but usually high content of organic particles suggestive of grass seeds, stalks and leaves in short lengths, resembling chaff. These show as burnt-out impressions on the surfaces and in the break, which is consequently laminated. The fabric is light in weight, usually dense black and friable.

The 'home-made' impression one obtains from handling the coarse wares is borne out by variations in these two types of ware: sandy but showing some 'grass' tempering; 'grass' tempered sherds which are burnished and so on. The common form seems to be a jar, with slightly everted rim, little or no neck, sagging profile and plain base which is sometimes quite rounded. The size ranges from thumbpots about 10 cm in diameter, to storage jars about 40 cm in diameter, having walls over 1 cm thick. There are a few bowls with vertical or flaring sides and several sherds are reminiscent of Roman forms, such as foot rings, or a straight-sided pie dish. As with all rough handmade pots, there are variations of profile within one pot, which reduces reliability when classifying small sherds.

It has already been mentioned that the local brickearth has proved suitable for potting. In the case of Saxon wares, which are invariably much reduced, pots could have been fired in clamps which need have left no surface trace.

A few pots have small lugs, sometimes with a tiny horizontal perforation, sometimes blind, perhaps indicating a survival like the vestigial sleeve buttons of tailored jackets. Another type of lug is a simple perforation through a raised part of the rim. Several sherds have been found, as at West Stow and Sutton Courtenay, of small pots with all-over perforations about $1\frac{1}{2}$ cm apart (Fig. 54, no. 6).

A most helpful characteristic in the coarse ware group is a variety of surface treatment, which may have been done not so much for its decorative effect as for the practical purpose of compacting the clay. Burnishing is one example, another is rustication, which is quite different from the applied clay blobs on Roman pots but resembles quite closely that found on Beaker and Bronze Age sherds. Saxon rustication consists of a variety of fingernail impressions, or of clay pinched up between thumb and finger, in one case even incorporating applied clay strips, which cover the whole pot. Combing is another all-over treatment, quite different from the parallel scored or grooved lines on the decorated pots. Other sherds have had their outer surface deliberately roughened by smearing a liquid slip containing coarse particles, which produces a result reminiscent of the *schlickung* of some native pottery found on continental sites of the Roman period. This, too, may have had a practical purpose in making a non-slip surface.

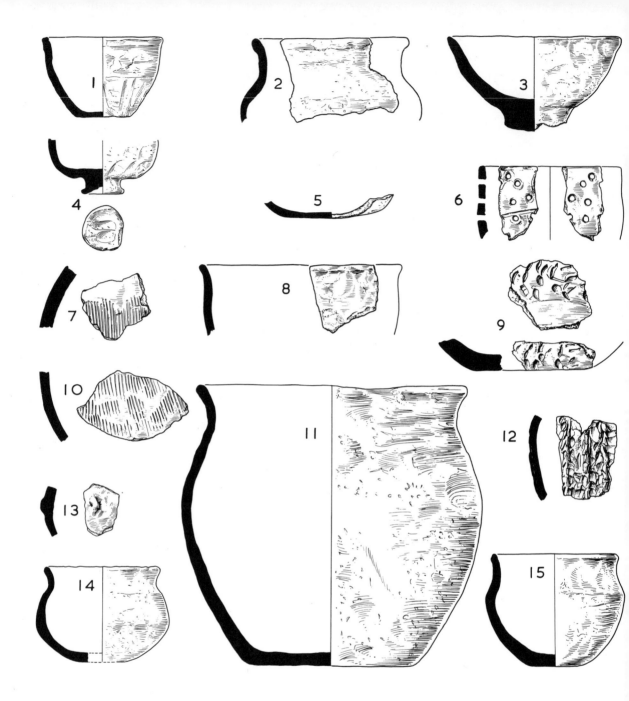

Figure 54 Mucking, Essex: Saxon settlement pottery: Coarse wares. Plain forms: 1–5, 8, 11, 14–15; 6: Perforated vessel; 13: Horizontally perforated lug. Surface treatment: 7 and 10 by combing; 9 and 12 by rustication (Scale: 1:4)

Finds of clay, other than pottery, are spindlewhorls (Fig. 55, no. 10), some purpose-made, some fashioned from sherds of Roman pottery, and loomweights resembling doughnuts (Fig. 55, nos 13, 14). Many of these are found in a green, unfired state and are occasionally marked by hollows perhaps made by poking a finger almost through the clay. Round flat plates may have had some use in cooking like the clay 'bricks' of the Belgic occupation and the perforated slabs used by the hillfort dwellers.

The usual accompaniment to potsherds in settlement sites is animal bones. As with other periods at Mucking a big gap in knowledge results from poor bone

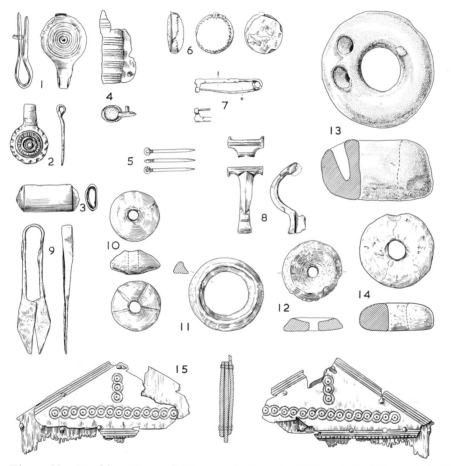

Figure 55   Mucking, Essex: Settlement finds. 1–4: Military belt fittings; 1 and 2: Looped disc attachments; 2: Inverted for re-use as a pendant; 3: Tubular mount; 4: Belt stiffener; 5–8: Dress fittings; 5: Garnet-headed pin; 6: Claw mounted paste pendant; 7: Safety pin brooch; 8: Bow brooch; 9: Iron shears; 10: Clay spindle-whorl; 11–14: Loomweights; 11–12: Lead; 13–14: Clay; 15: Bone comb (Scales: 9–14, 1:4; the rest 1:2)

survival. Many huts contain fills evidently rich in humus and it is usual to find some bone in these. The range of species so far identified includes sheep, pig, ox, horse, deer, dog and possibly wolf, represented in most cases by single bones or teeth, which survive better. At least a quarter of one hut floor was covered by a red deer antler. The articulated skull and forelimbs of a dog lay on another and one hut post-hole also contained the articulated cervical vertebrae of a dog. Bones thus provide further evidence of a mixed farming economy, possibly with hunting, in addition to the sheep farming implied by frequent loomweights.

Bone objects are correspondingly rare, though the sawn tines of the red deer antler mentioned above suggest its common use and fragments of three bone combs have survived (Fig. 55, no. 15). These are triangular three-ply combs, with the central plate, in which the teeth have been cut, sandwiched between decorated covers and joined with iron rivets.

There is no doubt that the fairly ubiquitous pottery and animal bones in hut fills belonged to the Saxon occupation. In the case of finds in the upper fills they may have come from the adjacent ground.

There is a doubt with better surviving materials, especially metals, and it is noticeable that more metal finds come from huts in the area of most intense Roman occupation. Coins are an obvious case. That they were kept as curios is borne out by the finding of pierced coins in graves. This may also be the explanation for a bronze steelyard found in one hut. Joinery nails might be Roman survivals, since so many huts have none at all. Timber buildings do not need nails and no nails have yet been found in Saxon coffins. No practical purpose suggests itself for the scraps of Roman tile found in some huts, though fragments of quern stone might have been picked up by the Saxons to sharpen their tools and weapons. Iron knives were common objects in the Roman period but to judge from their frequent occurrence in Saxon graves, it is reasonable to accept them as Saxon. Other metal objects which occur in both graves and huts are iron shears, bronze tweezers and bronze repair binding from wooden bowls.

The lead rings (loomweights) already mentioned compare with examples from Ezinge *terp* (Netherlands). Twenty had already been found in the Linford Quarry excavation.

Saxon metalwork implies, above all, jewellery and other objects used on dress, of types already long established by comparative studies in England and on the continent. Indeed, the dating of the huts, especially in the fifth century, depends, with the decorated pottery, on a few noteworthy pieces. The bronze components of the wide leather belts used in the late Roman army belong to the fourth and fifth centuries (Fig. 55, nos 1–4). These were made on the continent and worn by Germanic soldiers. One such piece is part of a tubular belt stiffener of a type found in England only, to quote Miss V. I. Evison, 'in the Germanic contexts of a grave at Dorchester and a hut at Mucking'. Two other huts contained disc belt attachments from which knives and weapons could be suspended, though one disc had evidently been adapted

Plate XXVII *Mucking, Essex:* Complete belt-set made of bronze inlaid with silver, from Saxon grave 117. The buckle-plate is 10·1 cm long

for re-use as a pendant. A flattened bronze tube of a type also thought to relate to military belts was another hut find. These military bronzes also help to tie in the settlement with the cemeteries, for the splendid complete belt set from Mucking (Plate XXVII) came from a grave.

Three exceptional pieces of costume jewellery lay on hut floors (Fig. 55, nos 5–7). A fifth century bronze saucer brooch with spiral and beaded decoration, a bronze pin with garnet inlaid head and a pendant of paste set in a bronze claw mount. Other pieces from hut fills include disc, penannular and safety pin type brooches, iron pins and a spiral finger ring. These finds not only strengthen the cemetery connections but confirm that the huts were lived in as long as the cemeteries were in use.

It was to be expected that a sizable Saxon settlement such as this would have a cemetery but crop-marks provided no clue as to its possible location. Cremation pits are too small to produce crop-marks and so are most inhumation graves, especially since these, being immediately backfilled, often have clean gravel in their upper fill. For this reason, graves are sometimes difficult to recognise even as soil-marks in cleared gravel.

Cemetery One (Fig. 51b) came to light in dramatic fashion, after little more than a year of rescue work, in an area abandoned to quarrying at a time of exceptional gravel demand, since it contained no recognisable crop-marks. First an axe head and then a spearhead were picked up by quarry workmen while spreading outsize pebbles on an approach road to the face. The finds had clearly been dug out by the dragline, before being graded at the quarry plant. Once recognised as Saxon, it remained only to watch the quarry face. It was the quarry foreman's vigilance which was eventually rewarded by the sight of two more spearheads projecting from the face itself.

There followed a quick cleaning down of the face, the recognition of a partly destroyed grave and its excavation, the hasty clearing of adjacent ground and the hurried excavation of the half dozen further graves exposed. In these conditions some of the most outstanding finds of the site came to light, notably the claw beaker and equal-armed brooch (Plate XXVIII). Subsequently it was possible to investigate all the adjacent land between farming and quarrying. As with so many other cemetery excavations, it was clear that only part, containing sixty inhumations, had been rescued and one can only guess how large Cemetery One had been.

Cemetery Two, on the other hand, provides a textbook illustration of the rewards of area stripping. Work had reached an area comparatively free from crop-marks but it was agreed to continue with attempted 100 per cent rescue for the sake of the settlement plan, especially of the Romano-British field layout. It was while the box scraper stripping this area was being followed that Saxon cremation pots were exposed (Figs 56, 57). Since then over seven hundred graves, inhumations as well as cremations, have been excavated. There is a good chance of Mucking Cemetery Two becoming the first sizable Saxon cemetery in England to have been excavated in its entirety.

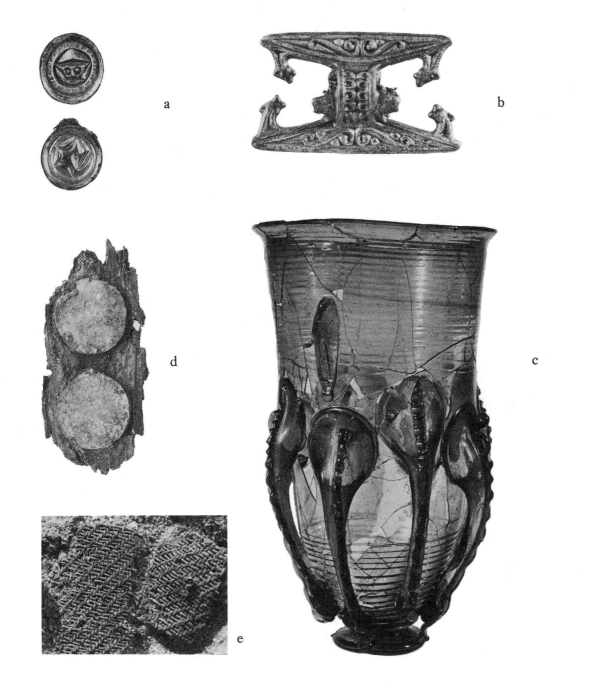

Plate XXVIII *Mucking, Essex:* Finds from Saxon graves. (a) (top left) Two gilt-bronze button brooches; (b) (top right) an equal-armed brooch; (c) (right) a claw beaker; (d) (middle left) rivet-heads, leather and wood from a shield; (e) (bottom left) fragment of textile preserved in the hand grip of a shield

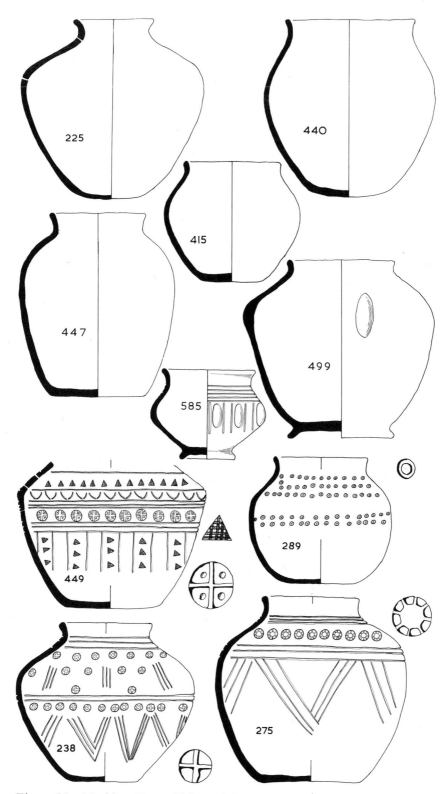

Figure 56 Mucking, Essex: Plain and decorated pots from graves (Scale 1:4; stamps 1:1)

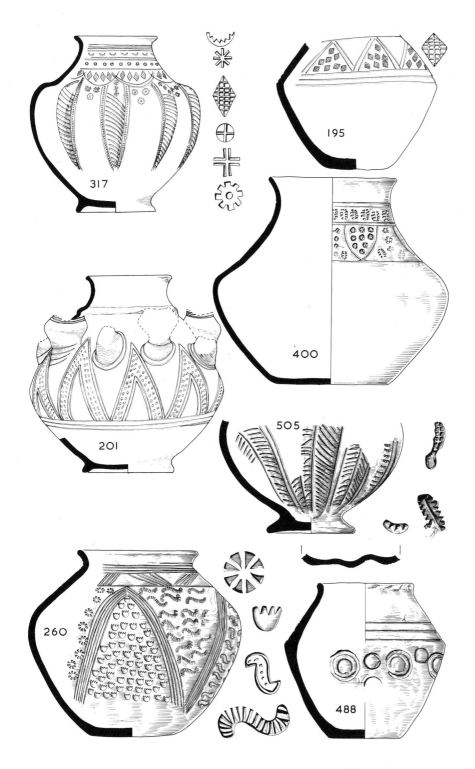

Figure 57   Mucking, Essex: Decorated pots from graves (Scale: 1:4; stamps 1:1)

Both cemeteries lie midway along the known hut distribution. Whereas Cemetery One is on the landward side of the gravel terrace and remote from settlement traces of all periods, in what might be regarded as waste land, Cemetery Two lies towards the terrace edge with commanding views and close to a fairly concentrated settlement area, with one hut actually cut into by a grave, and a second hut cutting graves.

Cemetery finds have long provided archaeologists with one of their main sources of complete objects, occurring in association. At Mucking, with two Saxon cemeteries containing some eight hundred graves and over one hundred huts, plus perhaps fifty more known from crop-marks, there are additional opportunities of forming associations, not just between 'live' and 'dead' Saxons but also between Saxons settled in England and those who remained in their continental homeland. This leads naturally to the complex matter of dating, which must await a final assessment of the finds.

Since excavation of Cemetery Two still continues, any comparison between the two Saxon cemeteries at Mucking must be provisional. It can be stated that no other cemeteries of comparable size lie so close together as at Mucking, while the discovery of Saxon sites in England where both cemetery and settlement are known is very rare.

The cemeteries offer contrasts in the rite of burial, Cemetery One consisting entirely of inhumations, Cemetery Two consisting of mixed cremations and inhumations. There are contrasts in grave orientation as well. In Cemetery One there appears to have been some attempt at 'sideways alignment', new graves being added *alongside* existing graves, and there are two distinct orientations – west–east, that is, head to west, and north–south. In Cemetery Two there is no apparent order, either in the position or in the orientation of graves. Orientations include most points of the compass, though north–south burials are noticeably fewer. Only one adult grave had the head towards the east, though a few children's graves had this orientation. There was no apparent attempt to align individual graves, except for a few dug along and into the fill of a Roman field ditch and others lying parallel to its line. As further evidence of haphazard burial, a number of graves were cut into each other, in some cases at right angles, some graves have disturbed earlier cremations and some cremations have been inserted in the fill of graves. So far, there have been no instances of overlapping cremations. Neither cemetery has produced any direct evidence for grave markers and neither cemetery is enclosed.

The time span of both cemeteries together compares with that of the huts (early fifth to early seventh century), but there are, so far, very few finds of pottery or metalwork from either cemetery which can be assigned to the early fifth century. This is in contrast with the fairly numerous finds of this period derived from huts.

Significant stratigraphic relationships between graves and other features are few. There are the simple hut/grave sequences already mentioned. Two Cemetery One graves were dug through a possible Saxon ditch and there are the Roman ditch graves mentioned above. Do these help with the Roman-Saxon transition? One could

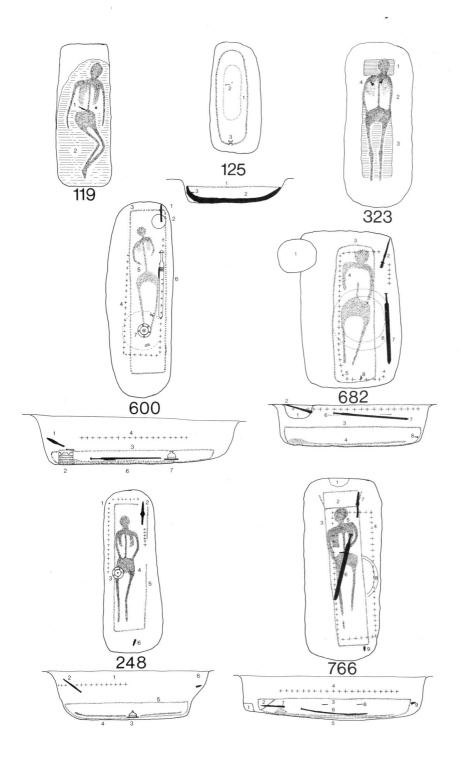

Figure 58   Mucking, Essex: Grave plans (Scale: 1:48)

argue that a faint hollow still survived along the ditch and was visible to the grave-diggers or that it was not the actual ditch but an accompanying hedge which influenced grave sites. Since the English countryside today can show many instances of hedges perpetuating boundaries many centuries old, one must conclude that these graves need not imply close continuity.

Before considering detail, the graves call for general comment. Cremations are simply round holes, rarely more than 50 cm across, into which have been placed either the cremated bone with accompanying ash and charcoal, or more often the bone and ash contained within a pot or urn. Unlike some Roman cremations from Mucking, there have been no accessory pots, while the actual bone fragments are usually smaller. Some cremation pits are so shallow that ploughing, by steam plough in the 1930s and by today's shallow tractor-drawn plough, has already destroyed the rims and shoulders of pots. Cremations contain fewer grave goods than inhumations and these are usually burnt.

Inhumations (Fig. 58) have provided the bulk of the grave finds, other than pots, though the few pots from inhumations include notable examples. Since inhumations are deeper, though as a rule shallower than in Roman times, grave finds are also normally undamaged. As well as pots, metal objects such as spears, brooches and knives are quite common and there are glass vessels and many beads (Figs 59 and 60). Because of the poor bone survival, skeletal information, as with the cremated bones, is scanty.

Cremations

This rite was followed in Cemetery Two only.

Because so many cremation pits are shallow, machine scraping has to be controlled within fine limits. Once the plough soil is removed, about 3 cm levels are stripped off, so that cremations which then appear can be excavated. A control area about 16 m square was stripped entirely by hand but it seemed that in many cases pots had already lost their rim and even their shoulder. In cases where the pot lay undisturbed, deep in the gravel, no evidence could be seen for the pot having been covered. Nor was there any evidence for above-ground markers such as a post.

In cases where the two types of burial overlap, it has not so far been possible to estimate the length of time which elapsed between graves, owing to the lack of closely datable grave goods. There was one notable instance of an inhumation/cremation association where similar objects were found with a cremation and an inhumation only 3 m apart. These were garnet inlaid buckle plates of bronze decorated in Salin's Style I (Fig. 60, 231). In this instance buckle plates and *buckelurne* (from the cremation; Fig. 60, 197) could be assigned to the sixth century.

It is difficult to estimate the proportion between plain and decorated pots (Figs 56, 57, 60), as in many cases the rim and shoulder (which often carries the decora-

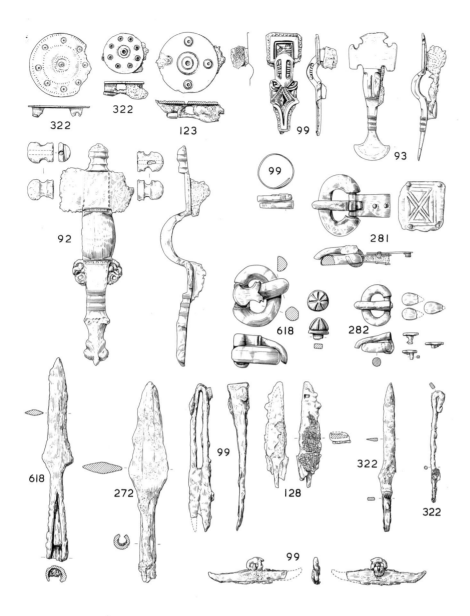

Figure 59   Mucking, Essex: Metalwork from graves. Disc brooches (322, 123); Square headed brooches (99, 93); Cruciform brooch (92); Finger ring (99); Buckle and plate (281); Buckles and rivets (618, 282); Spearheads (618, 272); Shears and purse mount (99); Knives (128) (with textile) (322); Pin (with textile) (322) (Scales: brooches, buckles and ring 1:2; the rest 1:4)

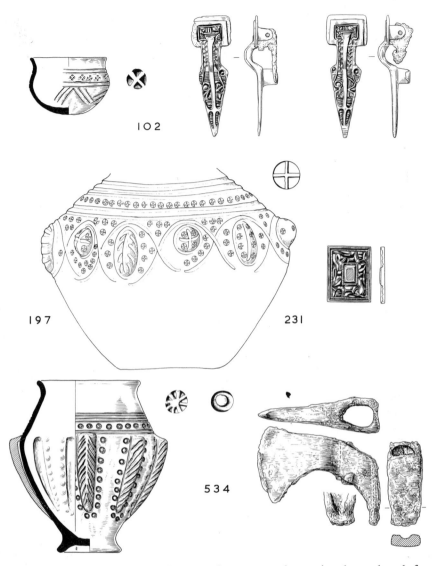

Figure 60   Mucking, Essex: Decorated pottery and associated metalwork from graves
(Scales: pots and francisca 1:4; brooches and buckle plate 1:2; stamps 1:1)

tion) had been destroyed and, of course, many damaged pots have still to be treated. One has the impression that nearly all the cremation pots are of domestic type, plain and decorated being in both 'grass' tempered and sandy and intermediate wares. Some pots have applied lugs and ring bases.

Undoubtedly the highlight of the cremation burials are the decorated and fine wares (Fig. 57). To quote Dr J. N. L. Myres in *Anglo-Saxon Pottery and the Settlement of England*:

There is no other group of primitive hand-made pottery in Europe which displays anything approaching the imagination, variety and spontaneity of the ornamental designs devised by Anglo-Saxon potters during the first two centuries of the settlement in Britain.

It should be noted here that only one sherd of a fifth century carinated bowl has been found in either cemetery. This was in the fill of a cremation pit and so could be residual. Another contrast is that bossed pots (*buckelurnen*), which are rare in settlement rubbish, are quite common in Cemetery Two where both round and long pushed-out bosses have been found. Decoration consists otherwise of linear grooves, sometimes in association with dimples or stamps. Stamps are mostly simple, cross-in-circle, rosette, S-shaped, and reticulated, but a few pots such as 260 and 505 (Fig. 57) show more elaborate stamps.

The first results of detailed examination of the contents of cremations have shown that little skeletal information can be expected. In some cases, where there is a fair quantity of bone, or there are large fragments, it has been possible to determine if the individual was adult and of which sex. The greatest weight so far recorded is 375 g, the longest fragment 8·3 cm.

Cremations have rarely contained grave goods. The burnt buckle plate referred to already lay beside its cremation pot. In one case, clear glass beads had fused onto bone, and partly melted polychrome beads have been found. Buckles of iron and bronze, bronze tweezers and a bronze toilet set on a ring all came from cremation pots. Two unusual finds were a bronze shield rivet and a spearhead with closed socket.

A few identifications have been made of cremation charcoal as follows: oak, ash, poplar, hawthorn, hazel.

Inhumations

Evidence from both Saxon cemeteries is considered under this heading.

An average adult grave (Fig. 58) is 2 m long by 75 cm wide and between 40 and 60 cm deep, measured from the level of the gravel. To this must be added about 30 cm of subsoil and topsoil. The sides are normally vertical with rounded ends and with a level bottom. Where the grave has been cut in gravel, the backfill is mostly clean gravel in which lumps of topsoil can be seen. Where the grave has been dug into an earlier feature such as a Roman ditch, the effect of its more humic fill seems to result in partial preservation of actual bone. The clearest silhouettes occur where the grave has been dug into sandy gravel where there are fewer pebbles to break up the lines of the silhouette and also, of course, where there is no coffin.

The silhouettes (Plate XXIXa, b) are attributed to iron manganese stain replacement in acid gravel. Usually the head is three-dimensional and several centimetres

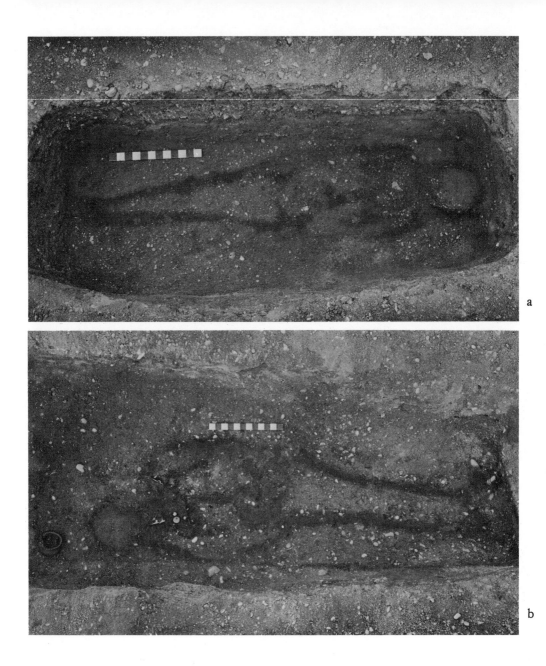

Plate XXIX a, b) *Mucking, Essex:* Silhouettes in Saxon graves. The pot and brooches from grave 102 are illustrated in Fig. 60 (Scales of inches)

deep and the enamel of the teeth usually survives. It seems to consist of a fine silt which has filled the brain cavity and is usually surrounded by a darker brown silt like a halo, which is the characteristic material of the rest of the skeleton, which is often only a few millimetres thick. Although the posture of the body and the positions of the grave goods are easily recovered, silhouettes cannot provide reliable skeletal measurements, so that age, cause of death, disease and so on must remain for the most part unknown, and sex is usually inferred from grave goods.

It seems that the Saxons laid their dead in the grave with some care. Evidence for grave lining has been discovered where it has been in contact with metal objects, which have preserved both the actual material or impressions. One such object was a spear, which rested on a 'pillow' and projected beyond it onto the grave floor. On the projecting part only were there impressions of bracken and grasses. Other evidence came from the backplate of the grave 117 belt set (Plate XXVII). This lay on the grave floor and a sandwich of surviving materials was found to consist of bracken and grasses (grave lining), textile (cloak or shroud), bronze and leather (backplate and belt) and textile (garment).

In six graves there was an irregular-edged stain beneath the body which did not seem to be of wood but gave the impression of something like cloth, which had been either laid on the floor of the grave or used like a sling to lower the body. In one of these cases there was also a 'pillow' beneath the head. There are twelve graves with 'pillows' so far, all graves without coffins. Six are women, two are men and four are of unknown sex. In size the 'pillows' range from 20×35 cm to 30×61 cm and in one case a long narrow 'pillow' measured 15×48 cm.

There is some evidence in the form of textile preserved on top of metal objects, such as a shield boss (Fig. 61) or brooches, for the body having been covered by either a cloak or shroud. Bracken impressions on one shield boss suggested that this material had been strewn over the body before the grave was filled. Coffins were quite common: 24 of 60 graves in Cemetery One and 38 out of 153 inhumations in Cemetery Two. They were shallow (between 15 and 20 cm deep) and their ends, in particular, suggested that they were constructed of planks, since some ends had collapsed inwards, leaving the ends of the long sides projecting. These were unlike the Roman coffins as they had no nails. It seems that the Saxon coffins at Mucking were made of thin planks probably joined with wooden pegs. Part of the side of one coffin, in contact with the bronze of a bucket, had survived to indicate that the plank had been 10–12 mm thick. Evidence from one bronze object in a coffin suggested that the coffin had been lined with bracken and grasses.

The existence of a coffin usually made it difficult to see the silhouette and in some cases only a part of the body could be seen.

Pagan Saxon graves are often recorded as having stones or wood laid over the grave, though it is not clear whether this means that the material was laid directly over the body, or some way above it, in the grave fill. At Mucking there is evidence for wood 'covers', which may have been no more than a framework, placed in the

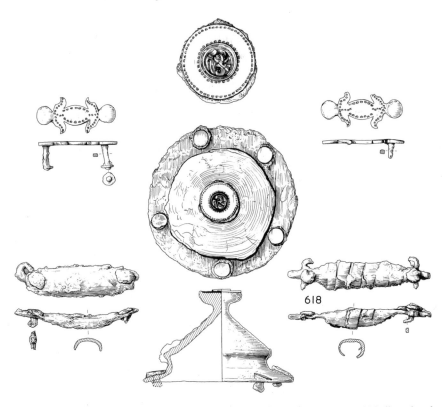

Figure 61   Mucking, Essex: Decorated shield-boss from grave 600 (hand grip from grave 618 added to show binding with strips of leather and textile)

partly backfilled grave. These first become visible as a rectilinear carbonaceous stain in the shape of a coffin. After being traced for 5–7 cm in the grave fill, there was then about 15–20 mm of grave fill without staining before the actual coffin stain appears. On the grave plan the two stains are out of register and it is suggested that the upper stain relates to some form of cover in the grave but not a coffin lid. The evidence from stains is supported by the fact that spears, plus in one case a ferrule, lay high in the grave fill, on some cover. Normally the 'cover' stains are associated with coffins but in one case, where the body had been laid on a bier, the cover must have lain directly on the body. Biers are assumed in a few graves where no coffin sides were discernible.

The gradual settling of decaying flesh and bone has undoubtedly helped the survival, in their original positions, of such objects as brooches and attached bead strings. The soil conditions at Mucking are also favourable to organic traces, such as the carbonaceous stains of wooden coffins and biers and of 'pillows'. There are many instances of actual preservation of organic materials, such as the wood of coffins, shields or buckets, and there are many examples of textiles, sometimes actually preserved but more often surviving in a replaced or 'mineralised' form in the corrosion products of bronze and iron objects (Plate XXVIII).

Fragmentary evidence, compiled from many graves, is providing a picture of varied inhumation rites. Judging from the positions of dress pins and brooches, the body seems to have been clothed and placed in the grave with or without coffin or bier, with some care, usually fully extended but in a few cases with the legs slightly flexed or crossed. Grave offerings are rare and apart from the occasional traces of coffin 'covers' the grave fill is not usually informative. In some cases in Cemetery Two there are scattered bones and sherds from disturbed cremations and there is always a possibility of residual finds of prehistoric pottery and flints.

Grave goods from Saxon inhumations can be considered in three groups:

1 Those without sex distinction such as knives, which are common, buckles and vessels — bronze-bound wooden buckets, wooden vessels with bronze repair binding, glass and pottery
2 Weapons indicating male graves
3 The beads and brooches of women.

Many grave goods are still awaiting laboratory treatment.

Associations with finds from Saxon huts are mostly through pottery and the rare pieces of military belt equipment. Spindlewhorls and shears give a hint of everyday life, while graves contain a few instances of re-used Roman objects such as melon beads, pierced coins and even Roman brooches evidently worn as pendants.

Knives were common in male, female and children's graves and were frequently the only object found. They are usually regarded as personal equipment, used for cutting food. Most knives are single-edged and quite small with the blade often worn down by sharpening. They are between 8 and 18 cm long. Traces of wood and bone handles are often preserved on the tangs and there is evidence for leather sheaths. The position of knives in most graves, usually near the waist and with the point lying towards the head, suggests they were not attached to a belt but were placed on the body.

Buckles are invariably found at the waist. The types range from simple iron buckles to a one-piece bronze military buckle loop and plate and the elaborate and ornate silver inlaid bronze military buckle and belt set seen in Plate XXVII. Their sizes indicate a narrow belt, either of leather, or, in one case, a 'tablet braid belt with reinforced leather ends' discovered from the surviving fragments on the buckles. Iron buckles are mostly plain and may indicate a poor person's dress, though some iron buckles are inlaid with silver. Bronze buckles include many elaborate examples, some being gilt or silvered. They were often attached to the belt by sets of three rivets, named because of their distinctive shapes as 'shoe', or 'tear', rivets. There are two examples of buckles on purse mounts.

There were twenty-five graves where the sex of the body was known, where it was possible to see to which side of the body the buckle pin pointed. Nine men had right-pointing buckles, four left. Five women had right-pointing buckles, seven left.

Belts were used for the suspension of useful articles; purse mounts, bronze toilet sets and iron keys, all coming from women's graves.

There were also instances of re-used fragments of metal objects hanging from belts, presumably serving as dress ornament. Half a bronze sword chape had been pierced for suspension, as had the foot of a Midland type of gilt-bronze great square-headed brooch, a brooch type so far only minimally represented at Mucking. A pierced second century coin, together with a Roman bow brooch, seemed to have been suspended in this way and the ring of another Roman bow brooch, lacking its pin, had evidently served as another curio pendant.

A child's grave contained an exceptional piece of metalwork, which may also have been discarded. This was a silver inlaid iron purse mount, suspended by a strap to which three bronze discs had been attached.

Vessels of pottery, wood and glass, which presumably contained drink and which were placed beside the head, were rare in both cemeteries. The only two examples of glass vessels came from women's graves in Cemetery One. They were a plain bowl and an outstanding claw beaker (Plate XXVIII) assigned to the sixth century.

Evidence for simple wooden vessels, presumably bowls turned on a lathe, survived where they had been repaired. The repair consisted of a thin sheet of bronze folded over the rim and riveted. The metal preserved the wood and in two cases helped to establish the diameter of the bowl. In one grave, the bowl had two repairs on opposite sides, indicating its diameter, which was about 13 cm. In another grave a circular carbonaceous stain continued the line of the repair binding to indicate a similar diameter. Altogether, six bowls are known from graves and one came from a hut.

Six buckets have so far been found, one in Cemetery One and five in Cemetery Two, of which one was incomplete, only about half of one side surviving. Since they are still having laboratory treatment, descriptions are provisional.

The buckets are about 10–15 cm high and about 10 cm in diameter, made of wooden staves held in place with bronze bands, the proximity of the metal resulting in almost complete survival of the wood. The bucket from grave 600 is described below. Another bucket is 11·5 cm high and has three bronze bands and three suspension rings. Its staves are about 2 cm wide. Two of the bronze bands are also about 2 cm wide, the third being slightly narrower. Each band is joined by two rivets and is decorated by punched dots and repoussé arcading. The half bucket is embellished with vandykes.

Spears (Fig. 59) were the main weapon and in many graves are the only object found. The spearheads have open sockets and range in length from 16·5 to 42 cm. Where there was a ferrule the length of the weapon could be measured, examples being 1·85, 2·11, 2·30 and 2·80 m. This was invariably laid to one side of the grave, with the spearhead by the head. In one case only, the ferrule was on the opposite side of the body to the spearhead, and for this reason the shaft may have been broken.

Shields (Fig. 61)   Ten shields were found in the sixty graves of Cemetery One but only six so far in the 153 inhumations of Cemetery Two. In all cases where the grave was complete, a spear accompanied the shield. Shields were recognised not only from their iron shield bosses and their metal components but also in some cases from the round carbonaceous stain surrounding them. The stain indicated the diameter, together with the decorative rivets on the edge of the shield (Plate XXVIII). Eight of the Cemetery One shields were between 60 and 64 cm across. In Cemetery Two, the size range was again between 60 and 64 cm except for one stain which was 53 cm in diameter.

Wood fragments survived on the rivets of bronze and of iron, both the decorative edge rivets and also those fixed on the flanges of the bosses. These indicated both the direction of the grain and also the thickness of the leather-covered wood — 11 to 13 mm. Thin fragments of the leather covering survived beneath and between some of the rivets.

From traces in various graves it is possible to make a tentative reconstruction. Presumably such a wide wooden object was made up of narrow boards joined together with cross bars and wooden pegs, since no metal cross bars were found. At right angles to the boards, the hand grip was fixed. This was a straight iron bar, in some cases of U-section, riveted to the shield across a central hole, which was then covered by the circular iron boss. The boss was carinated, topped by a flat knob or button and rimmed by a flange by which it was attached to the shield. Sometimes the rivets which secured the hand grip continued through the flange, sometimes there were separate rivets. The rivets on the boss flange usually totalled five, though in one case there were ten arranged in five pairs, and in another case three single rivets. On some examples, the hand grips were elongated so that they extended almost to the edge of the shield. They were not connected to the rivets on the edge of the shield, which one must conclude were decorative.

There was no consistent shield position in the grave, such as there was in the case of spears. Invariably the actual boss was uppermost, with the shield covering head, chest or legs. In one grave, the boss stood on its flange, suggesting that the shield lay vertically between the side of the coffin and the side of the grave. In another, the boss rested against the side of the grave. In both these cases the boss was on the right side of the body.

Evidence for shield ornament is so far confined to a single grave, 600, described below and in Fig. 58.

Swords (Fig. 58)   Six swords were found in Cemetery Two. These had double-edged medium broad blades. Four blades were straight, with a width range between 4·8 and 5·2 cm, and two swords had tapered blades, one tapering from 5·9 to 4·2 cm, the other from 5·5 to 5·0 cm. The tangs ranged from 10·3 to 13·0 cm and the overall lengths of the swords ranged from 86·6 to 92·4 cm.

All the blades were plain, none were pattern welded. All except one sword had iron pommels, the exception (in grave 600) having a bronze 'cocked-hat' pommel. Fragments of the scabbard made of leather-covered wood survived on each sword. One scabbard was still attached to a belt or baldric, which lay folded over or round the hilt and top of the scabbard, which had a gilt mouth. None of the scabbards had a chape. The wood of one scabbard has been identified as willow or poplar.

Axes   In addition to the axe which led to the discovery of Cemetery One, two others have been found, in Cemetery Two graves. These are both throwing axes, where the cutting edge lies at an angle to the socket (Fig. 60). These so-called *franciscas* were the preferred throwing weapons of the Franks and are found only occasionally in Britain. They had both been placed in the grave beside the head, with the blade pointing away from the body. The length of one shaft was 56 cm.

Brooches   Nearly a hundred brooches have so far come from the two Mucking cemeteries. They are made of cast bronze, usually with a hinged iron pin, and the face of the brooch is often gilt, silvered or tinned. The typology and consequently the dating of brooches is based primarily on their shapes, which are really no more than decorative covers for a basic safety pin. The most common types in the Mucking cemeteries are disc, small long, saucer, button (Plate XXVIII, Fig. 62) and applied and there are several cruciform and one bow brooch. Quoit and penannular brooches are also represented, but so far no garnet inlaid brooches have been found.

An important type is the equal-armed brooch, of which Cemetery One had one example (Plate XXVIII). This is significant, not only because of its rarity – less than half a dozen have been found in England – but also because it is an import from north Germany and an early one of the fifth century. Its decoration reflects both Germanic and classical art styles, animal forms and scrolls. Two square Frankish brooches are also regarded as early; while a pair of square-headed brooches (Fig. 60) has been described as 'unique in form i.e. square headed with a triangular foot' and possibly from Denmark.

The ornamentation of brooches is an important element in their typology. Stamped and cast decoration are both represented. Stamped motifs are usually simple, for example, ring and dot, crescent and half round impressions. Cast designs include classical motifs such as beading, pellets, spirals, scrolls and Germanic forms such as animals and human masks. Some cast designs employ the so-called chip-carved technique. A typologically early chip-carved style embodying animal forms is often referred to as Salin's Style I.

Anglo-Saxon brooches are as complex as decorated pottery, though unlike pottery they form the subject of a large and increasing literature. When one considers that brooches found in graves may well belong to the category of heirlooms, it will be appreciated that further comment, especially on their contribution to dating, must wait.

Brooches are of interest as costume jewellery. They were invariably worn in pairs, placed high on the chest and near each shoulder. The foot of the brooch, the head being the hinge end, lay toward the shoulder, though it may be remarked that brooches are usually illustrated with the hinge at the top. The function of brooches as bead attachments is described under *Beads*. An alternative position was for the

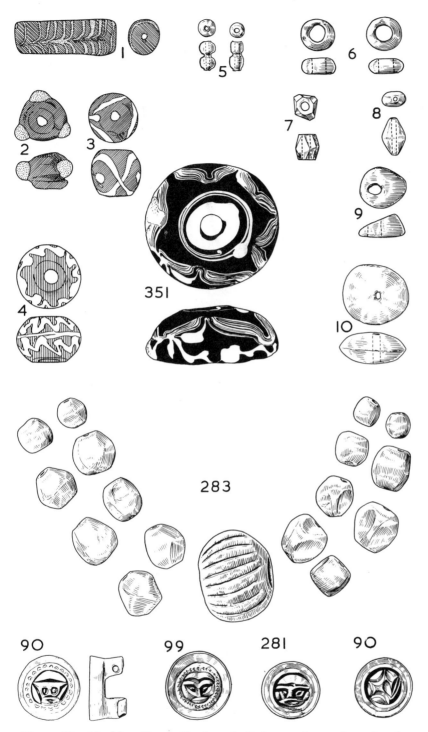

Figure 62 Mucking, Essex: Beads and gilt-bronze button brooches from graves (grave numbers given in the cases of the Roman melon-bead and amber necklace, the glass spindle-whorl and the brooches only). Bead types: 1–4: Polychrome; 5: Clear glass gilt, segmented; 6: Blue glass annular; 7: Faceted jet; 8: Conical amber; 9: Wedge-shaped jet; 10: Annular crystal (Scale: 1:1)

brooches to lie parallel, pointing to either left or right, one above the other on the chest. In some graves which contained a single brooch, it lay in the middle of the chest.

Sometimes women had been buried with two pairs of brooches. One pair lay vertically in the normal shoulder position and the other pair between the chest and waist.

Many of the brooches in the Mucking graves have an additional interest, as fragments of textile are often preserved in the corrosion layers of the metal.

Beads (Fig. 62) as well as brooches are the principal indication of a woman's grave. Since they have in most cases remained in their original positions, it is possible not only to plot and reassemble strings but also to gain direct evidence for the various ways in which beads were worn. In only one case was there clear evidence of a necklace, that is, of a string placed round the neck. Beads were commonly found in strings attached to two brooches, two metal rings, or two perforated bronze discs, placed high up on either side of the chest.

Bead strings contained up to 176 beads and can be described as either single type, where only one type of bead makes up the string, or multiple type. Three examples of single type strings contained 80-plus glass beads, 16, and in another 90, graduated amber beads. Multiple type strings are made up from a variety of bead types, of which some, especially the wedge-shaped amber beads, suggest they may have come from other strings for which they had been specially shaped or selected. The multiple type strings may well have been collected by the wearer over a period of time.

Beads were made of amber, glass (including paste), crystal and jet. Glass beads were by far the most common. They are either translucent or opaque, virtually colourless or coloured, of simple or segmented shape, monochrome or polychrome, or gilt. Shapes include cylindrical, round and globular. Colours are primary. Gilt occurs rarely and so far only on segmented clear-glass beads. Polychrome beads have self-coloured opaque bodies with applied trails, spots or blobs of one or more contrasting colours. Amber beads vary from perforated lumps of irregular shape to wedge-shaped pieces and symmetrically cut beads of cylindrical or biconical shape. Where the entire string of beads is made of amber, there is the impression that the amber has been selected or shaped in regular arrangement, especially the wedge-shaped beads which lie together like voussoirs. Crystal beads are rare and range from simple round beads to a large faceted example 21×30 mm in dimension. Only a few jet beads, some faceted, have been found. There are also three instances of re-used Roman melon beads.

An outstanding example of a single type string contained 90 amber beads suspended from a 16 mm diameter bronze ring and an 11 mm diameter iron ring placed high on each shoulder. The beads were of irregular shapes carefully selected so that the smallest were at the top and the largest at the bottom of the string. The larger beads were wedge-shaped.

Multiple type strings were much more common. They ranged in size from several beads in a child's grave to 176 in a woman's grave.

Examples of the more complex strings are as follows.

1   A string of 96 beads of which 24 were of amber (irregular shaped, wedge-shaped and biconical), two of crystal (of which one had been broken and abraded in antiquity), five of segmented gilt, ten polychrome (for example, red spots on green, green spots and trails on yellow), the rest single-coloured glass – yellow, red, green, white, blue and black. This string was suspended in two loops from two disc brooches. These were set 15 cm apart, near the shoulders. The top loop was nearly straight, but the lower loop was 28 cm deep and extended nearly to the waist. The beads were grouped: four blue glass beads and five amber beads lay together. The more showy polychrome and the crystal beads lay at the centre of the lower loop.

2   A string of 176 beads which hung in a single loop from two gilt bronze saucer brooches and consisted of 22 amber beads, some irregular, some biconical; two round crystal beads; two polychrome; four opaque yellow or green; five translucent blue; the rest translucent purple glass. The crystal and the larger amber beads lay at the centre.

3   A third multiple string with an exceptional component. This was a round flat-bottomed glass spindlewhorl with a 6 mm diameter perforation (Fig. 62). It was of dark blue-black, opaque glass with off-white trails.

Two graves had unusual bead arrangements. The more elaborate example consisted of six silver and two bronze contracting rings about 2 cm in diameter, each threaded with three beads of glass or amber. The rings were arranged in a loop across the chest and may have been spaced out and individually secured on a string.

Finger rings   In comparison with the Roman period, finger rings were rare (Fig. 59, no. 99). So far nine have been found, all in women's graves, six on the left hand, two on the right and one uncertain. The rings were silver or bronze and included spiral rings. Some rings had sparse line decoration.

Textiles   The traces of, and at times the actual preservation of, organic materials has been referred to: the wood of spear shafts in their iron sockets; the wood of shields on their bosses, hand grips and rivets; the wooden staves of buckets; leather fragments on knife sheaths, sword scabbards and shields; plant remains and the stains of wood and bone.

Above all, the graves complement the evidence of weaving in the huts provided by loomweights of raw and fired clay and of lead, by the survival of textiles, both actual and replaced. Since specialist work continues (by Miss Elisabeth Crowfoot), only brief mention can be made here.

Textiles have been identified in men's, women's and children's graves, on metal objects on the body, such as brooches, buckles, knives, and occasionally on weapons – shield boss, francisca and spear. Linen as well as wool has been identified, each fibre occurring in both coarse and fine threads. Plain, twill and tablet weaves are represented.

A few examples may be given: undyed linen, plain weave, with a thread count of 16×16 per cm (on brooch); regular 2×2 twill weave (on tweezers); probable two-hole diagonal tablet weave showing border (on brooch); tablet braid belt (on buckle); plain weave in check pattern in two shades of naturally pigmented wool, light and dark brown, possibly a light woollen cloak (on brooch).

Plans and sections of seven Saxon graves (Fig. 58)

Stains and objects are recorded three-dimensionally as the fill is being removed, in very thin layers, in order to produce the composite sections. These serve to indicate the relative sequence both in the fill and within the coffin. No Saxon coffins appear to have had lids. The section shows the height of their sides. The top of the grave fill is the level of cleared gravel, to which some 30 cm must be added for subsoil and topsoil.

Grave 119   Cemetery One. A good example of a well-developed silhouette in a grave 46 cm deep. The only grave goods were an iron knife and buckle (1). Most of the grave floor was covered by a stain (2) which might be organic material such as matting. Head at west.

Grave 125   Cemetery One. A child's grave (28 to 30 cm deep) which contained five beads (2) and two iron clamps (3), presumably at the foot. A thick carbonaceous stain (1) with rounded outline and hollow profile suggests a dug-out coffin. Head at west.

Grave 323   Cemetery Two. The particular interest of this woman's grave (56 cm deep) with its pair of small long brooches (4) lay in the stains beneath head (1) and body (3). Both 'pillow' and 'mattress' stains were dark brown-black. Head of well-developed silhouette (2) at west end.

Grave 600   Cemetery Two. This is the most richly furnished male grave so far found and the metalwork is still undergoing conservation. The body (5) lay in a coffin (3), with a cover (4) some way above it in the grave fill. The spear (1) rested on the side of the grave and within the coffin lay the sword and knife (6) and bronze-bound bucket (2). The sword had a bronze 'cocked hat' pommel. Bound round the scabbard, near the mouth, were three strips of leather. The bronzework of the bucket was responsible for the good survival of its wooden staves and part of the coffin side which lay against it. The vandykes (beardlike mounts) on the top band of the bucket were of tinned bronze and decorated with human masks and the handle bore stamped decoration. The shield boss is illustrated in Fig. 61. The flange rivets are silvered bronze, the double decorative rivets silvered and gilt bronze, while the knob consists of a flat silver disc, inset with a gilt button, which has been decorated in Salin's Style I. Head at west.

Grave 682   Cemetery Two. The top fill of this grave was disturbed by a later un-urned cremation (1). It appears that the spearhead (2) rested on the side of the grave, with its nail-type ferrule (8) lying inside the coffin. The sword (7) lay above the coffin, yet beneath the 'cover' (5), and at about the same level was an annular stain. This was somewhat larger than shields so far recorded from Mucking. As there was no shield boss, it cannot be assumed that the stain came from a shield and it remains inexplicable. Head at south.

Grave 248 Cemetery One. It seems that both spearhead (2) and ferrule (6) were placed on the 'cover' (1) which lay above the coffin (5). Dispersed round the shield boss (3) were four decorative iron rivets and a fragment of the hand grip extension, not illustrated. Head at west.

Grave 766 Cemetery Two. The spear (7) seems to have been placed within the coffin (3), with the ferrule (9), which has apparently sunk, extending beyond it. The sword (6) was evidently placed directly on the body (5). Conservation, not yet complete, suggests that the baldric or belt had been wrapped round the mouth of the scabbard and hilt. The scabbard itself was of leather-covered wood with fragments of textile above and below it. The mouth appears to have been gilt. Like 682, this grave had part of an annular stain. The head end of the coffin (2) had collapsed inwards, which furnished good evidence for a planked construction. (1) is a patch of cremated bone and charcoal probably from a cremation disturbed in digging this grave and thrown in with the fill.

The final report on Saxon Mucking will doubtless contain many guarded statements and tentative conclusions, but in essence the contribution which this piece of gravel rescue has already made has been suggested from different points of view by two eminent scholars. Remarking on the finds of carinated bowls and Dorchester-type fittings in the huts, Dr J. N. L. Myres suggested that

> the occupation may have begun with a deliberate posting of Germanic *laeti* charged by whatever authority then controlled Roman London with the duty of giving early warning of any suspicious or unauthorised movement of shipping in the lower reaches of the river. Such a service, whether or not it was first established before the breakdown of direct Roman rule, could have remained useful to sub-Roman London throughout the first half of the fifth century . . . After this, the occupation could have gone on unofficially . . .

To quote Miss V. I. Evison:

> with the additional evidence of the Mucking buckle (from grave 117) it looks, therefore, as though the Quoit Brooch belt mounts were made for a privileged and possibly military section of the community, Germanic of taste, but equipped partly after the Roman fashion, and who were active in the period soon after the recorded withdrawal of the Roman army. One might assume that they were *foederati* invited early in the fifth century who became settlers in

due course. In this manner the complete archaeological blank which appears to have descended over this country for a generation after the withdrawal of the Romans is disposed of.

With the last Saxon buried, this terrace gravel with its 'magnificent visual command of the Thames estuary' withdrew from its important role in British history. The land became part of the Essex estates of Barking Abbey and the medieval church and village grew up near the creek. Gun flints, gin traps, ploughshares, clay pipes, scraps of farmyard rubbish, buried sheep and shrapnel from two World Wars are almost the only archaeological traces to bridge the gap from the early Middle Ages to the mechanised cereal growing of today. And so we arrive at the crop-marks, which have served the archaeologist like H. G. Wells's time machine.

Addendum

Since the foregoing chapter was completed Saxon Cemetery Two has been totally excavated. The earliest graves were in the south-east corner of the cemetery, on a commanding spur of the gravel terrace. Unfortunately this was just where the cross-trenches of a medieval post windmill had been dug, and since part of an early equal-armed brooch was in their fill, at least one grave must have been destroyed.

These first graves were of both sexes and between them contained late Roman belt fittings, early Saxon brooches, and a faceted carinated bowl. Grave groups included: *grave 987:* a woman's grave with late Roman buckle and early Saxon (Luton) brooch. Long, flat pieces of partly melted lead lay on the body. *Grave 989:* a woman's grave with early fifth century bronze bow brooches, bronze dolphin buckle, faceted carinated bowl and beads. *Grave 979:* a male grave with military type fixed plate buckle and disc belt attachment (previously found only in huts at Mucking), spear with closed socket and large ferrule with four grooves, an iron penannular brooch, purse mount, knife and bronze tweezers. Several of the graves in this south-east corner had early iron penannular brooches, while one grave contained another, complete, equal-armed brooch.

Three more glass vessels have been found. Two are cone beakers, one of Kempston type; the third is a second claw beaker with four double claws. Its cupped rim, panels outlined in trails, and wide foot indicate a date about A.D. 400. However, the two silver brooches which accompanied it are of a Kentish type datable to the early sixth century and so this glass must have been more than a century old before burial.

Further prehistoric material includes the first saddle quern (of sarsen), more cylindrical Bronze Age loomweights, and sherds, from more than twenty pots, of the so-called grooved ware, with characteristic decoration of grooves, scored lines, applied cordons and twisted cord impressions. These make Mucking the fourth findspot in Essex for this late Neolithic pottery.

Two more small Romano-British cemeteries have been discovered. Each contained thirty graves, both inhumation and cremation. The third cemetery was like the first in lying outside the main villa field-boundary and in having poor grave goods. The second, however, lay in an enclosure within the Roman fields and contained richer objects. These included a bronze socketed finial in the form of an eagle's head, probably a vehicle mount, which had been wrapped in cloth before burial; and three *tazze*, five colour-coated beakers, eight pie-dishes, ten mica-dusted pottery lamps and nine coins, all burnt and lying in a mass of charcoal which included seeds of *Pinus pinea*.

Two certain and at least two probable ground-level post-hole buildings can now be assigned to the Saxon settlement. All are double-square in plan. The most substantial 'hall' is 7 m wide. It has an internal division at the north-east and opposed entrances in the longer sides.

A recent numerical count of excavated features includes nearly 10,000 pits and post-holes and more than 7 km of ditches.

Acknowledgments

The Mucking excavations were initiated and are financed by the Ancient Monuments Directorate of the Department of the Environment, with support from the Thurrock Borough Council, the Essex County Council, The British Museum and the Society of Antiquaries of London.

Bibliography

Barton, K. F., 'Settlements of the Iron Age and pagan Saxon periods at Linford Quarry, Mucking, Essex', *Transactions of the Essex Archaeological Society*, vol. 1, part 2 (third series) (1962), pp. 57–104.

Evison, V. I., *Fifth Century Invasions South of the Thames*, University of London, Athlone Press (1965).

Evison, V. I., 'Anglo-Saxon grave goods from Mucking, Essex', *Antiquaries Journal*, vol. liii (1973), part II, pp. 269–70.

Jones, M. U., 'Saxon pottery from a hut at Mucking, Essex' in *Berichten van de Rijksdienst voor het Oudheidkundig Bodemonderzoek*, 19 (1969), pp. 145–56.

Jones, M. U., 'The Mucking, Essex, Crop-mark Sites', *Essex Journal*, vol. 7, no. 3 (1972), pp. 65–76.

Jones, M. U., 'Potters' graffiti from Mucking, Essex', *Antiquaries Journal*, vol. lii (1972), part II, pp. 335–8.

Jones, M. U., Evison, V. I. and Myres, J. N. L., 'Crop-mark sites at Mucking, Essex', and (V. I. Evison) 'Quoit brooch style buckles', *Antiquaries Journal*, vol. xlviii (1968), part II, pp. 210–46.

Jones, M. U. and Jones, W. T., *Journal of the Thurrock Local History Society*, 11 (1968), pp. 33–45; 13 (1970), pp. 32–44; 14 (1971), pp. 33–7; 15 (1972), pp. 20–9; 16 (1973), pp. 32–8; 17 (1974), pp. 31–9; 18 (1975), pp. 32–41.

Jones, M. U., 'An ancient landscape palimpsest at Mucking', *Transactions of the Essex Archaeological Society*, vol. 5 (1973), pp. 6–12.

Jones, M. U. and Rodwell, W. J., 'The Romano-British pottery kilns at Mucking, with an interim report on two kiln groups', *Transactions of the Essex Archaeological Society*, vol. 5 (1973), pp. 13–47.

Jones, M. U., 'Excavations at Mucking, Essex: a second interim report', *Antiquaries Journal*, vol. liv (1974), pp. 183–99.

Myres, J. N. L., *Anglo-Saxon Pottery and the Settlement of England*, Oxford (1969).

Myres, J. N. L., 'An Anglo-Saxon *Buckelurne* from Mucking, Essex, cemetery', *Antiquaries Journal*, vol. liii (1973), part II, p. 271.

St Joseph, J. K., 'Air reconnaissance: recent results', *Antiquity*, vol. xxxviii, no. 151 (1964), pp. 217–18, Plate XXXVII(b).

Chapter VII

The most important recent archaeological discoveries made in European Russia

A. A. Formazov, E. N. Chernykh,
D. B. Shelov, R. L. Rozenfeldt,
with a foreword by B. A. Rybakov

Summary

Important discoveries have been made in the study of the earliest agriculture of the neolithic and eneolithic periods. Exceptional interest attaches to the results of research in the Tripolye culture in the Ukraine. Villages of the fourth to third millennia B.C., with populations of up to 5,000 inhabitants, have been revealed, and the chronology of the settlements and the evolution of their agriculture worked out. In Central Asia, the oldest settlements are linked to cultivation by irrigation. Palaeobotanists have determined the age of the canals, that is, the fourth millennium B.C. The art of the first farming tribes reveals their outlook on life, resembling that of the ancient Indo-Europeans, who produced the religious books of the Rigveda and Avesta.

The numerous cultures of the Bronze Age have been extensively studied by archaeologists in all the Soviet republics. So detailed has the research been that it is possible to speak not only about the form of economy in this or that area but about specific tribes, their migrations, wars and mergings. A whole series of ethnogenetic problems arises in this period: the origin of the Slavs, of the Baltic tribes, the courses taken by Finno-Ugrian colonisation, the spread of Iranic tribes and much else.

Soviet archaeologists have unveiled for science two impressive civilisations of the ancient world: Urartu in Transcaucasia and Khorezm in Central Asia. A third field of major archaeological discovery (outside the Caucasus and Central Asia) is the Eurasian steppe from the Carpathians to the Altai. The chief peoples here in antiquity were the Scytho-Sarmatian and related tribes. There have been excavations of great scientific interest in both areas flanking the Scythian world. In the south, in the dozens of ancient Greek towns on the Black Sea coast with the slave-operated estates surrounding them, and in the north, where the settled tribes of the forest zone lived in small hillfort settlements.

An important problem that has prompted lively discussion concerns the origin of the Slavs. Significant variations in the standard of living among the ancient Slav tribes of the wooded steppe and forest zone have been demonstrated, corresponding to the Russian chronicle evidence about cultural contrasts within the Slav world. Students have put forward a number of hypotheses about the location of the Slavs 'pre-homeland'. The expansion of Slav culture in the sixth to seventh centuries of our era has also been studied in the last few years.

Foreword

by B. A. Rybakov

Archaeologists in the Soviet Union regard their science as that inseparable part of history which deals with the earliest period of human culture as a means of understanding the deep-rooted formation and development of the multiplicity of peoples of Soviet lands.

Besides work within the territory of the USSR, Soviet archaeologists have undertaken, and are undertaking, research abroad in Afghanistan, Bulgaria, Egypt and Mongolia.

The historically significant results of the archaeological discoveries in different fields have twice been described in publications intended for the general reader. In 1956 and 1958, two volumes of *Outlines of the History of the U.S.S.R.* appeared with an overall size of over one thousand pages (Volume I, *Primitive Society and Slave-Ownership*; Volume II, *The Crisis in Slave-Ownership and the Birth of Feudalism in the third to tenth centuries A.D.*). In 1966, the first volume appeared of a twelve-volume work, by the Institute of Archaeology of the Academy of Sciences of the USSR, entitled *A History of the U.S.S.R. from the Earliest Times to the Present Day*; publication has now reached the early thirteenth century.

The palaeolithic period, almost entirely unrecognised before the Revolution, is now represented by hundreds of sites. In this field, archaeologists are settling questions about the origin of man, his earliest environment and the establishment of human society.

In recent years Soviet archaeologists have been occupied with the study of the mesolithic cultures at the time of the melting of the last ice-sheet. A sharp change in the form of economy has been established, as well as in the type of settlement and the size of community. The mesolithic period was the time when wandering hunters colonised large expanses of plain and bog, still only half-dried-out from the glaciers. Study of the neolithic has defined distinct cultural zones, explained the process of settlement of the north of Eurasia and the emergence from a uniform hunting system of regions of agriculture and pastoralism.

The work of Soviet archaeologists on many kinds of rock drawings (*pisanits*, petroglyphs) in the north, Siberia and the Caucasus, attracts great interest. The drawings reveal a most interesting side of religions, beliefs, and aspects of daily life such as whale-hunting, skiing, spring festivals of herdsmen and so on.

The study of the economy of Kievan Russia through archaeology has been especially significant, since in this matter old, pre-Revolutionary science had turned down a blind alley. Hunting was regarded as the basis of the economy and the towns were considered as mere administrative and trading centres with a culture of Scandinavian, Varangian origin. Extensive systematic excavations of mediaeval Russian towns (Kiev, Chernigov, Novgorod, Pskov, Smolensk, Polotsk, Minsk, Vladimir, Moscow, Galich, Ryazan and a multitude of small towns such as Vshchizh, Drutsk, Gorodsk, Pronsk and the like) have shown that the basis of the economy was highly developed agriculture and that the towns had complicated and wide-ranging crafts at their disposal. The theory of Scandinavian influence has lost relevance because it is no longer tenable.

Archaeologists have brought to light dozens of examples of medieval architecture, so that the history of Russian art has had to be written anew.

The most outstanding success in the study of Russian medieval towns has been the excavation at Novgorod the Great. (An account of these excavations in English is available in M. W. Thompson's *Novgorod the Great*, 1967.) Here the organic remains survived well: log frames of houses, street decking, tools, footwear and the like. The birch-bark documents of the eleventh to fifteenth centuries have earned a world-wide reputation. They dealt with business affairs and personal correspondence of the ancient townspeople.

Archaeological discoveries in the field of study of medieval Russia have caused the problem of the level of its culture and the place of medieval Russia in contemporary Europe to be wholly altered. These conclusions have been discussed in a two-volume work, *A History of the Culture of Medieval Russia*. Analogous successes have been achieved by the archaeologists of Armenia, Georgia, Azerbaijan, Central Asia and the Baltic area in elucidating the cultures on their home ground.

The thirteenth and fourteenth centuries may be regarded as the limit of the study by archaeology of the past. The last major historical subject is the Tartar–Mongol invasion upon which, in old scholarship and among some Soviet historians, very mistaken views had been held. Sometimes they even wrote about the occasional beneficial influence of the Tartars. Archaeological work in Volga, Bolgaria, Khorezm, Transcaucasia and in Russian towns has shown the terribly destructive force of the onslaughts by Chingis and Batu Khans. The irrigation system that had brought water to Central Asia for thousands of years perished and flourishing valleys were turned into deserts (Kara-Kum, Bet-Pakdala and others). Hundreds of towns were burnt and the population annihilated. Archaeologists have shown that this was not a transitory catastrophe but permanently affected the subsequent development of the country.

In certain instances, particularly in the case of rescue archaeology when observation is being kept on constructional excavations, archaeologists pass beyond the fourteenth-century limit and study later layers of the fifteenth to seventeenth centuries. Such has been the case, for example, in very interesting studies on ancient Moscow that have added clear new pages to the history of the Soviet capital.

One of the basic conditions for the development of any science is an overall survey of available material, a sharp and clear systematisation. The Institute of Archaeology of the Academy of Sciences of the USSR in 1960 undertook publication of the great series *A Corpus (Svod) of Archaeological Sources of the U.S.S.R.* The publication of three hundred volumes is contemplated, upon which all the archaeologists of the country are working. Material from thousands of expeditions, from as early as 1710 onwards, will be described systematically, chronologically and cartographically. The latest mathematical methods are being employed in the statistical treatment of the subject.

When the work on the *Corpus of Sources* is complete, science will possess exhaustive archaeological maps of the whole of the Soviet Union for each period. The deserted areas will be distinguishable from the populated ones and the density of population, the grouping of settlements, the distribution patterns of objects and structures will emerge, as will the blank spots where further research expeditions are required. It will constitute a firm canvas upon which the broad historical pictures can be drawn out. Furthermore this full corpus of archaeological sources will bring forward a number of illuminating matters and make clear the course of development in various aspects of material culture: hunting and fishing, agricultural implements, weapons, houses, tools, dress and adornment at all periods.

I Developments in palaeolithic archaeology in the USSR

by A. A. Formazov

During the 1930s to 1950s, traces of early palaeolithic stations had already been recognised in the southern zone of the USSR, the study of which has subsequently intensified. The basic mass of these very old settlements has been washed away in the thousands of years that have elapsed since their abandonment, and the stone implements of Mousterian, Acheulian, and sometimes evidently of the even earlier Chellean type have been transported to marine and river terraces, to gravel beds and so on. But in several cases cave sites are known where cultural layers of the lower palaeolithic that occur as the initial deposit contain bones of the animals hunted in antiquity, hearths and so on.

Especial interest attaches to three caves in the Caucasus, Kudaro I and II in

South Ostia and Azykh in Azerbaijan, which had a great thickness of cultural layers, containing Mousterian tools above and Acheulian below. The excavations of M. M. Guseinov in the cave of Azykh have yielded a fine series of Acheulian hand-axes, a fragment of a Neanderthal mandible and a cache of cave-bear skulls, recalling well-known finds on Mousterian sites in the Alps.

New Mousterian cave sites have been found in the Crimea. Hitherto, such occupation had been found in the western part of the peninsula but now about a dozen sites have been found in its eastern part, in the rocky massif of Ak-Kaya near Belogorsk. Some of the caves had collapsed in antiquity and were more in the nature of buried caves. Y. G. Kolosov's excavations on the site of Zaskalnoe V revealed a sequence of several layers with a good series of flint tools marking different variants of the Mousterian culture. An interesting find was the occipital part of a Neanderthal skull and, collected around a hearth at the cave entry, a heap of large mammoth bones, marking the site of a hut.

Study of the occurrence of lower palaeolithic tools in the various regions of the European part of the USSR is essential for settling the problem of their original colonisation by man. Thus, Acheulian remains in Trans-Carpathia (Rokosovo – V. N. Gladilin's researches) cause one to reflect on the possible penetration of the earliest men into eastern Europe by south-western routes. Recent discoveries by Bulgarian and Soviet archaeologists in the Balkans favour this view. Mousterian tools from Pechora (Krutaya Gora, studied by V. I. Kanivets) reveal a movement far further northward by Neanderthalers than anyone had hitherto supposed.

Late palaeolithic sites have been studied in the last few years in many regions; in the valleys of the Dniester and lower Dnieper and central Don, in the Oka basin, on the Black Sea coast of the Caucasus and in the Ural area. The method of excavating these sites by simultaneous uncovering of large areas, worked out by Soviet archaeologists in pre-war years, has allowed the identification of traces of houses of late palaeolithic time. On the site of Dobranichevka in the Dnieper area, I. D. Shovkoplyas exposed a whole settlement, consisting of four huts arranged in a circle; each hut, covering roughly 12 m², was circular with a diameter of about 4 m (Plate XXXa). Mammoth skulls let into the ground served as a wall foundation, into the rear orifices of which poles had been inserted to support the skin cover. Other large bones were used for the frame. According to the calculations of the Ukrainian palaeontologist, I. D. Pidoplichko, in each house, on an average, up to 125 large bones were used, derived from eighteen individual mammoths. Pidoplichko himself dug a settlement at Mezherich in the Cherkassk oblast of the Ukraine. Here also, remains of a circular hut, 23 m² in area, came to light. Its wall foundation consisted of twenty-five mammoth skulls, supplemented by the mandibles, forming a zig-zag outline. The frame was made up of 385 bones – shoulder blades, tusks and skulls. All the excavated bones were carefully collected, treated, listed and transported to Kiev. There, in the Museum of the Academy of Sciences of the Ukrainian SSR they were used to reconstruct the Mezherich house, the first time such a reconstruction

Plate XXX (a) (above) *European Russia:* Dobranichevka, the palaeolithic hut at the beginning of dismantling
(b) (centre) *European Russia:* Double burial of adolescents at the palaeolithic site of Sungir, Vladimir
(c) (below) *European Russia:* Stone settings: labyrinths on Great Zayatsk Island in the Solovets archipelago in the White Sea

of a palaeolithic house has been attempted. The sites of Dobranichevka and Mezherich belong to the Magdalenian period. In the latter site a number of very interesting objects of art were found: schematic bone statuettes of women, a mammoth skull painted with ochre, a bone plate bearing an engraving and so on.

An unexpected discovery has been made by O. N. Bader in the continued excavations at the site of Sungir on the outskirts of Vladimir, first started ten years ago. The settlement dates from the first half of the upper palaeolithic (characterised by bifacially worked points, recalling the Solutrean style). In 1964 a burial with abundant goods was found and in 1969, 3 m from this one, a second came to light with the bones of two boys, 7–9 and 12–13 years old (Plate XXXb). Close by were parts of the skulls of three other people. Thus we are dealing with a cemetery, the first of its type from the palaeolithic period. The corpses had been laid in a trench in an extended position, with their heads towards each other and thickly sprinkled with ochre. On the bones, thousands of beads of mammoth ivory were recovered, that had evidently been at one time sewn on a garment. The head-dress had been decorated with these beads, as well as with perforated canine teeth of polar fox. On the children's arms there had been bracelets, on their fingers rings and on their chests plaques. One of the latter bore the schematic figure of a large-headed horse, already known to archaeologists from this site. In addition to these objects, there were sixteen ivory spears, darts and daggers in the graves. The spears were surprisingly long, measuring 1·66 m to 2·42 m, testifying to the great skill of the palaeolithic craftsmen, who were capable not only of whittling down and polishing but also of straightening curved tusks. Such weapons had not been encountered previously.

II   Neolithic and Bronze Age developments in the USSR

by E. N. Chernykh

In the last few years archaeologists have recognised many new things in the culture of the neolithic period. In the Dniester and south Bug valleys, settlements have been investigated that give firm evidence of the appearance of a productive economy in the south-west of the USSR, under the influence of the Balkan centres of early agriculture. The most interesting group of sites has been those excavated by V. I. Markevich at the town of Soroki in Moldavia. Some of the sites are multi-layered. In the lower layers are normal late mesolithic flint microlithic types without pottery, and in the upper levels similar stone tools together with potsherds, recalling the Starčevo-Krish ware of the Balkans. Both upper and lower layers belong to settlements occupied by people familiar with stock-breeding and agriculture. Thus at Soroki I in the lower pre-ceramic level, besides bones of red and roe deer, wild boar and wild horse, those of domesticated animals, ox and pig were also found. Amongst the flints was a cache of sickles with the characteristic blade gloss. In the upper ceramic levels there were querns, sherds with impressions of wheat and barley grains and an antler hoe. The following absolute radiocarbon dates have been calculated for Soroki II: layer 1, 4,880 ± 150 B.C.; layer 2, 5,470 ± 100 B.C. The formation of the Bug/Dniester neolithic culture can therefore be placed in the sixth millennium B.C.

In the neolithic period, the northern zone of the European part of the USSR was originally occupied by tribes of hunters and fishers. Russian and Baltic archaeologists have been studying these cultures for about a hundred years, yet every season's work reveals something new in the history of the ancient population of the forest zone. Excavations in peat sites in White Russia (Osovets, by M. M. Chernyavsky), Latvia (Sarnaty, by L. V. Vankina), the Pskov oblast of the RSFSR (Usvyaty, by A. M. Miklyaev), and in the western Ural area (Vis, by G. M. Burov) have yielded a lot of interesting bone and wooden objects that normally do not survive in the sandy subsoil of the general run of sites. Wooden vessels have been found with animal heads on the handles, human figures and those of elk, together with numerous bone tools.

In Latvia, F. A. Zagorskis has worked for several years on the extensive, neolithic cemetery of Zveinieki. About two hundred burials have been uncovered that can be divided into two groups. The oldest graves, sprinkled with ochre, belong to the fifth to fourth millennia B.C., the latest, without ochre, to the third millennium. They contain many tools, pendants of animal teeth and amber. A particularly curious statuette, an idol with a forked head, is closely analogous to one found in the nineteenth century, during the construction of the Ladoga canal.

Besides occupation sites and cemeteries, such characteristically neolithic monuments as flint mines and stone settings in the form of labyrinths on the sea-shore have also been studied. N. N. Gurina identified over five hundred shafts at Krasnoe Selo in the Grodnensk oblast of White Russia, where over a hundred shafts were cleared of soil. On the edge of the flint deposit there are simple pits, but in its centre are true shafts with timber lining, columns, passages and galleries. The depth of the shaft reaches 5 m, the length of the galleries, 12 m. Picks and dagger-shaped tools of elk antler, lamps and axe rough-outs were found in the shafts. Workshops for working flint and a huge quantity of half-finished objects have been studied in close proximity to the pit-heads.

Settings of stones in the form of labyrinths are well known from the coastal areas of northern Europe (Plate XXXc). In the USSR they occur on the shores of the White and Barents Seas. Until recently it was not possible to date these constructions, nor to relate them to any ancient settlement. In the last few years, however, the excavations by A. A. Kuratov on Great Zayatsk Island in the Solovets archipelago revealed traces of cremations and neolithic tools beneath the stone settings. This offers an explanation acceptable with some degree of confidence for these puzzling monuments.

Another major discovery has been made near the White Sea. By the 1930s, two groups of neolithic rock engravings had already been studied on the granite sides of the river Byg near Belomorsk. From excavations conducted near one of them, Zalavruga, Y. A. Savvateeb ascertained that a large number of the figures, pecked out in the granite, had subsequently been covered over by soil and so, having cleared the rock face of soil, he exposed almost a thousand new figures. The petroglyphs concealed by sand were overlapped by an occupation layer of the second millennium B.C., which is very important for precise dating of the drawings. These have been pecked out in the granite with quartzite picks and take the form of silhouetted figures, 20–30 cm long, arranged for the most part in compositions of a narrative character. Amongst the newly discovered petroglyphs there are many very curious scenes, remarkable episodes in the life of the primitive hunters. One scene represents the winter hunting of elk, a herd of which are pursued by skiers with bows in their hands. An elk has already been transfixed by several arrows. The tracks of the elk and skis are indicated as well as the marks of the ski sticks. The curves of the ski tracks are evidently intended to represent the hilly landscape of Karelia. There is a curious composition telling a story about marine hunting; a line of oars-men sit in a great boat (*karbas*); at the bows a harpooner has successfully discharged his weapon at a white whale; the wounded beast plunges in the water, pulling from side to side on the harpoon line, but this is firmly held by the hunter. On other rock faces are scenes of such boats (*lodki*), figures of archer-hunters, elk, deer, waterfowl and so forth.

In recent years, studies of the remains of the period of early metal have been carried out on an extensive scale both in the southern zone of Eastern Europe, comprising the steppes from the Caspian area as far as Moldavia and, in the north, comprising the wooded steppe and the forest regions extending from the Ural area to the western borders of the USSR.

The eneolithic of the south European part of the USSR is traditionally connected with the famous Tripolye culture of the western Ukraine and Moldavia. Some three hundred settlements of the Tripolye culture are known in their regional and chronological variants. Recent research has allowed the inference that the first contacts of the Tripolye population with the pastoral steppe cultures of the Pit-grave or the Dnieper/Donets type, took place earlier and were closer than had formerly been supposed. The barrow excavated at Kainary station in Moldavia deserves attention in this connection. Under it was a skeleton, thickly sprinkled with ochre, while among the grave goods was a pot of a type very characteristic of stage B1 in the chronology of T. S. Passek and also a copper bracelet and torque (*grivna*). Spectrographic analysis has revealed that such copper only occurs in the early stages of Tripolye. Consequently this monument can be considered as bearing marks of both early Pit-grave and mature Tripolye cultures.

Thanks to the extensive excavation of D. Y. Telegin, evidence has appeared of links between the Tripolye population and tribes of a late stage of the Dnieper/Donets culture. For example, copper adornments reached this tribe from the Tripolyans and found their way into Nikolskoe cemetery.

A very important find for reconstructing the houses of the mature phase of the Tripolye culture has been the discovery of a model of a two-storeyed hut from the village of Rossokhovatka on the middle Dnieper. The model stands on four little column-legs. The upper room, which is much larger than the lower chamber, has an extensive clay floor (*ploshchadka*), oversailing the walls of the latter. There is a larger entry and small circular window and the pitched roof is circular.

Significant field discoveries in the last few years are connected with the early Bronze Age monuments of the third and early second millennia B.C. There is a change from the sharp cultural differentiation of the preceding period in the population occupying the area between the Hither Caucasus and the Danube area: processes of cultural integration and levelling of former differences took place. This is most clearly evident in the widespread distribution of similar metal objects: shaft-hole axes, knives, chisels with quadrangular tang and such like. The latter were made predominantly of arsenic-bronze, which had its source of extraction in Transcaucasia. Elements in the culture of this population were barrow burial, sprinkling ochre on the corpse, stone construction of the graves and so on.

In 1968–9 on the outskirts of Nalchik in the north Caucasus, I. M. Chechenov dug a huge barrow of the Maikop culture which reached 11 m in height and had a diameter of not less than 100 m. Under the mound, a tomb was found constructed of massive stone (*tufa*) blocks.

The tomb, oriented north-east to south-west, consisted of a rectangular construction 314 cm long, 234 cm wide and 105–10 cm high. The walls were well formed by thirty-two tufa slabs, set upright with sharp ends embedded in the ground. The dimensions of the slabs were variable: the length ranging from 166 to 223 cm, the width from 36 to 75 cm and the thickness from 15 to 31 cm. The burial chamber was constructed of vertical blocks, covered by six more massive slabs. The largest of these was 422 cm long, 60–64 cm wide and 20–26 cm thick.

The last roof slab had originally been a stele bearing the schematic representation of a little head. This slab, the surface of which was decorated with diagonal linear grooves, had not been the only stele; there were others of smaller size, sometimes ornamented with more intricate geometric patterns. It is surprising that one of them had its head buried in the ground, evidence of secondary use of the stele. The inner face of the tomb walls had been thickly coated with red colouring.

Within the chamber, the remains of two people, crushed by the collapsed slabs, lay in a crouched position with head pointing towards the south-east and freely sprinkled with ochre. One skeleton was probably that of a man, the other of a woman. On the woman's femurs were gold plaques that evidently had been sewn on to the clothing and by the skull lay a very delicate gold spiral reaching 100 cm in length. A knife, the end of the wooden handle of which was gold plated, was found in the chamber. The handles of the awls had been decorated in like fashion. Two spurred shaft-hole axes, a dagger, a gouge and a large copper cauldron completed the inventory of the grave goods.

The erection of the barrow can be dated to the Novosvobodnensk stage of this culture (the last quarter of the third millennium B.C.).

Amongst remains contemporary with this barrow that occur further north, those from the excavations carried out over many years by I. V. Sinitsyn and U. E. Erdniev in the Kalmyk steppes deserve attention. Survey had located more than two thousand barrows here in a multiplicity of groups, in which the mounds counted by dozens up to hundreds are usually strung out in a chain. At the centres of each group are two or three large mounds, 6–8 m high and 60–80 m in diameter.

List of archaeological sites in Fig. 63

1 Kudaro I, II	41 Frontovoe	79 Abidnya
2 Azykh	42 Peschanoe	80 Taimanovo
3 Ak-Kaya	43 Arkhangelskaya Sloboda	81 Sarai-Batu
4 Zaskalnoe V	44 Gaimanova tomb	82 Novotroitskoe
5 Rokosovo	45 'Fat grave'	83 Titchikha
6 Dobranichevka	46 Bashtanski barrow	84 Kiev
7 Mezherich	47 Elisavetovskoe	85 Chernigov
8 Sungir	48 Podazovskoe	86 Novgorod
9 Soroki	49 Tyra	87 Olbia
10 Osovets	50 Niconium (Roksolanskoe hillfort)	88 Smolensk
11 Sarnaty	51 Nikolaevka	89 Polotsk
12 Usvyaty	52 Nadlimannoe	90 Minsk
13 Zveinieki	53 Orlovka	91 Vladimir
14 Krasnoe Selo	54 Berezan	92 Moscow
15 Great Zayatsk Island	55 Old Kabarga, Little Chernomorka	93 Galich
16 Zalavruga	56 Kozyrka	94 Old Ryazan
17 Kainary	57 Chersonesus	95 Vshchizh
18 Nikolskoe	58 Chaika	96 Drutsk
19 Rossokhovatka	59 Donuzlav	97 Gorodsk
20 Nalchik	60 Belyaus	98 Pronsk
21 Lola I, II	61 Panskoe	99 Lyubech
22 Arkhar	62 Mezhvodnoe	100 Brest (Berest'e)
23 Ak-Chokrak	63 Panticapaeum	101 Volkovysk
24 Mayaki	64 Myrmecium	102 Kopys
25 Tli	65 Porphymium	103 Turov
26 Shirokoe	66 Nymphaeum and Kitey	104 Pinsk
27 Lozovsky hoard	67 Ilurat	105 Roslavl (Rostislavl)
28 Shilovskoe	68 Andreevka	106 Gnezdovo
29 Churachkino	69 Mikhailovka	107 Staraya Russa
30 Volosovo-Danilovo	70 Novo-Otradnoe	108 Oreshek
31 Pepkino	71 Zolotoe	109 Staraya Ladoga
32 Urzhumkino	72 Phanagoria	110 Pskov
33 Belsk	73 Kepy	111 Izborsk
34 Nemirov	74 Hermonassa	112 Serensk
35 Trakhtemirovo	75 Tanaïs	113 Trubchevsk
36 Khotovo	76 Gorgippia	114 Pirovy hillforts
37 Alma-Kermen	77 Pirogovo	115 Alexandrova Sloboda
38 Ust-Alma	78 Velemichi II	116 Bolgary
39 Bulganak		117 Bilyar
40 Chervony Yar		

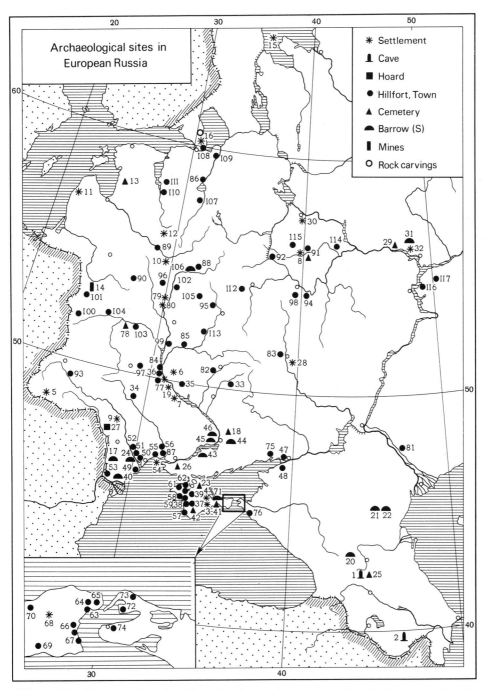

Figure 63 European Russia: Map showing archaeological sites in European Russia mentioned in the text

The general run of barrows measure much less, 1–2 m high and 15–25 m in diameter.

Especially extensive excavations took place in the barrow groups at the sanatorium Lola (Lola I and II, Arkhar) in about eighty barrows, at Elista in about forty barrows and at various other places. In all the cemeteries nearly five hundred burials of the Pit-grave and Catacomb cultures have been revealed.

Pit-graves are as a rule earlier than Catacomb burials. The rectangular shafts average 1·6 m by 1·2 m and are up to 2 m deep. The walls of the shaft were often lined with coarse fabric or matting retained by stakes. The shaft tops were finished with a stone setting, sometimes in the form of a cromlech. In the majority of cases the corpse had been put on its back with legs bent and head towards the east. Extended skeletons are very much rarer. The bottom of the shafts were thickly sprinkled with ochre. A characteristic feature of the burials of the Pit-grave tribes is traces of sacrifice either from the interment or above it (bones of large-horned oxen, censers). As a rule, burials were not associated with numerous grave goods and many of them contain nothing at all. The pottery and metallic objects find their clearest analogies in the north Caucasus.

Graves of the Kalmyk group, assigned by the investigators to the Catacomb culture, are more numerous and sharply defined. The tombs consist of a catacomb proper or the usual rectangular shaft. Here, as with the preceding group, the burial rites included sacrificial offerings. For example, in one barrow at Lola, five ox skulls had been placed over the catacomb grave. All the corpses of this culture lay curled up on the left side, a southern orientation predominating.

Particular interest attaches to the burials with wagons, of which about a score have already come to light. In one such shaft there was a four-wheeled wagon with a body of plaited withies, reminiscent of a marquee (*shater*). A wooden frame of thick quadrangular spars, which formed the base of the body, measured 2·5 × 1·2 m. The wheels, with a diameter of 0·8 m, consisted of two segments held to the central nave by pegs and were fixed on an axle 1·7 m long. The front axle pivoted freely on a thick peg in the frame in order to facilitate steering the vehicle. The wagon had a draught pole and yoke.

The burial in this grave consisted of a middle-aged man and woman lying in the vehicle in crouched position, face to face and head towards the front. Two pots stood by their legs, a richly decorated censer at their heads and a bronze awl rolled to one side. On the man's chest was a bronze hook with tang dislodged from its handle and on the woman's a necklace of agate beads.

Sometimes the wagon was put into the shaft after the corpses had already been laid to rest. The skeletons then have the appearance of being covered by the wooden parts of the wagons. These burials provide us with new and exceptionally valuable material on the history of transport in the east European steppe, evidence, that is, about the means of locomotion of the steppe tribes of the early Bronze Age.

A wealth of grave goods is associated with burials of the Catacomb culture. The pots that occur in large numbers have strongly bellied sides giving them a turnip-shape. There are many censers, earthenware vessels of a special, probably ritual, character. Frequently encountered are the extremely curious bone 'hammer-shaped' maces. Metal finds (knives, hooks, awls, beads) are common, made from an arsenic-bronze alloy imported from the Caucasus. All the materials of the Pit-grave and Catacomb cultures from the Kalmyk barrows testify to the closest links with the Caucasian peoples of the Maikop, Dolmen and north Caucasian cultures.

Another route of Caucasian influence on the steppe peoples has been traced in new materials of the so-called Kemi-Obinsk type in the Crimea. Numerous barrows and also settlements of this culture have been discovered by A. A. Shchepinsky and actively studied in recent years. So far, about two hundred graves of Kemi-Obinsk type are known. The corpses were deposited in stone or wooden cists, the inner faces of which were painted with linear, geometric patterns. Black, red and some-times white colouring was employed. Stone cromlechs were erected around the graves, over which a peculiar stone cupola was sometimes constructed. The base of the tomb was floored with pebbles or snail shells.

Flat stone stelae bearing representations of human beings are one of the character-istic traits of the Kemi-Obinsk culture. A barrow at Ak-Chokrak had such a stele with a stone cist beneath it; the schematically represented head rested directly on straight shoulders and the arms, crossed on the chest, had the fingers interlocking. The figure wore an axe with handle at its belt; below, two struggling human figures were represented.

The metal objects found in these graves are extraordinarily informative. In type, they correspond to those of the Novosvobodnensk stage of the Maikop culture: spurred shaft-hole axes, two-pronged forks, gouges (Kolinka and Kurban-Bairam barrows). Spectrographic analysis has shown that a significant part of them cannot be regarded as imports; they have been cast from pure copper and are clear evidence of local metal-working. Another line of contact of the Kemi-Obinsk tribes extended north-westwards towards the Usatovo folk, who were basically rooted in the Tripolye people.

The Usatovo culture shared a boundary on one side with the western limit of the Pit-grave culturo-historical community and experienced a powerful influence from that direction. The traces of this can be clearly discerned as a result of excavations on barrows in the extreme south-west of the USSR in the lower reaches of the river Dniester and between it and the river Danube. The earliest burials of this area most often can be defined as Usatovo but not uncommonly the grave structure is of Pit-grave style. Out of five hundred excavated burials, more than two hundred showed this feature, amongst which interments with wagons, basically similar to the Kalmyk ones, may be noted. One of the barrows at the village of Mayaki in the Odessa oblast covered a stepped shaft, the upper, wider, part measuring $4 \cdot 2 \times 4 \times 1$ m, and the lower $2 \cdot 5 \times 1 \cdot 8 \times 1 \cdot 3$ m. The lower compartment was roofed with eight logs and its sides lined with rush mats. A four-wheeled wagon had been set on a wooden decking in the upper section.

In about the middle of the second millennium B.C. sharp ethnocultural changes took place in Eastern Europe, processes which were especially marked in the south. The tribes of the Catacomb culturo-historical community, so closely linked with the Caucasus, vanished and in their place came the stock-rearing/agricultural people of the Log-grave (*srubnaya*)[1] culture (or more precisely culturo-historical community). It occupied almost the whole of the steppe zone of the European part of the USSR, from the southern river Ural to the Dnieper area. In the Log-grave community a whole series of distinctions according to locality and chronology have been made by specialists (early Log-grave, Sabatinov, Belozersk and so forth). The Caucasus remained isolated from the steppe peoples and, in the late Bronze Age, independent cultures developed there, best known for their metallurgy and metal-working.

As a demonstration of these differences, attention may be drawn to two large cemeteries dug in the last few years: at Tli in the Caucasus and at the village of Shirokoe on the lower reaches of the Dnieper.

The cemetery of Tli is situated on the southern slopes of the main Caucasian cordillera within the confines of the South Osetian ASSR and has been studied over the last few years by B. V. Tekhov. Three hundred graves have already been uncovered with a time range covering a millennium, from the mid-second millennium to the sixth century B.C. The greater part of the graves belong to the twelfth to ninth centuries B.C. and thus are contemporary with the well-known Koban culture of the North Caucasus.

Interments of this chronological group were made in relatively small graves, lined with stones, sometimes resembling stone cists. The skeletons usually lay flexed on their sides with head towards the north but the earlier graves are distinguished by the extended position of the skeletons.

It is the metal industry of the cemetery that produces the greatest impression: the unusual abundance and variety of forms of weapons, tools and decorations are surprising (Figs 64, 65, 66). Only rarely are graves devoid of bronze objects. Axes of Koban and Colchidian type can be counted by dozens (Figs 64, 65). Their blades are often decorated with geometric engraving or incision and ornamented with figures of horses and fish, while, at their butt-ends, some bear figures of fantastic animals (Fig. 65). A multiplicity of knives and daggers was found, their handles taking a wide variety of shapes. There were massive round maces, also decorated and furnished with spikes. Special place must be given to a broad plated belt bearing engravings representing whole scenes (Fig. 67). There were numerous bronze vessels. Antimony, lead and silver were employed in addition to bronze. The finds from Tli once more emphasise the magnificence of late Bronze Age metal-working in the Caucasus.

[1] Translator's note. A *srub* is the frame of four logs interlocking at the corners used in the Russian log-cabin style of house and for many smaller structures.

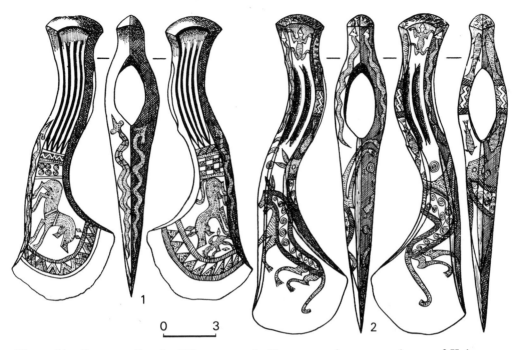

Figure 64 European Russia: Tli cemetery in Transcaucasia; engraved axes of Koban type, *c.* 1000 B.C.

Figure 65 European Russia: Tli cemetery in Transcaucasia; engraved axes of Colchidian type with figures of monstrous animals on the butt, *c.* 1000 B.C.

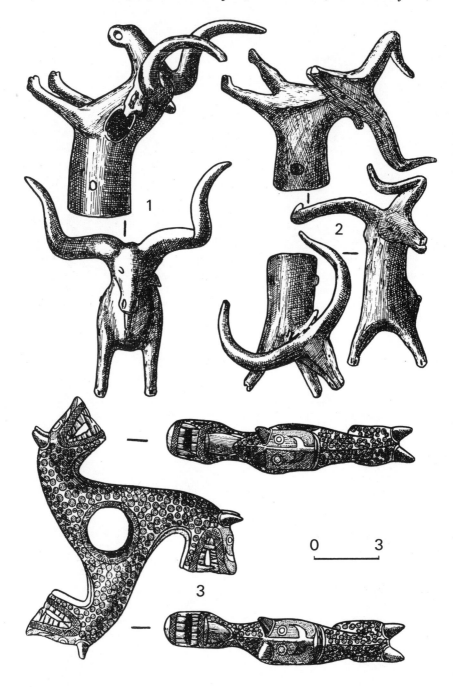

Figure 66   European Russia: Tli cemetery in Transcaucasia; socketed standard tops in the shape of oxen and heads of monsters bearing engraving, *c.* 1000 B.C.

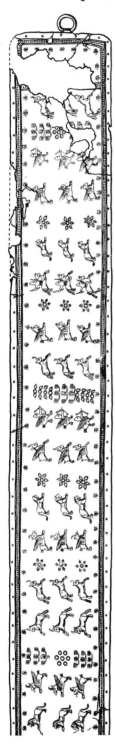

Figure 67   European Russia: Tli cemetery in Transcaucasia;
part of a bronze plated belt with engraving of Urartïan style,
eighth to sixth century B.C.

The cemetery at the village of Shirokoe, near Kherson, is referred by its investigator, A. M. Leskov, to the latest group of the Log-grave community, the so-called Belozersk (eleventh to ninth centuries B.C.). Over an area of more than a hectare about 130 graves have been excavated, which extend in several rows running from east to west. The corpses were buried in rectangular shafts in a crouched position with head towards the west. The graves were covered with a layer of wrack and a wooden roof resting on posts at the corners of the shaft. In contrast to the Tli cemetery, here the poverty of the grave goods — mainly pottery vessels and sometimes bone ornaments — is evident. In the whole cemetery only a few dozen small bronze bracelets and head rings have been recorded. The metal had been obtained basically from the east (Ural and Hither Ural area).

The period of use of the cemetery corresponded with the decline of local metalworking. The *floruit* of this very important ancient centre of production on the north coast of the Black Sea belongs to an earlier period (thirteenth to twelfth centuries B.C.) and is related mainly not to the Ural but to the Balkan–Carpathian area of extractive metallurgy. Traces of these influences are to be found in fairly numerous bronze hoards, which not only reveal the level of the craft of metal-working but also permit deeper study of the culture of the local tribes, their chronology and connections. Among new discoveries the Lozovsky hoard (Dyalul Ursului), from Moldavia, is pre-eminent.

The Lozovsky hoard consisted of about thirty objects, predominantly celts and sickles of shapes well known in Transylvania and the south-west part of the USSR, that are traditionally dated to phases B, D and A1. A large series of daggers with metal handles was found, of the type familiar from moulds at Krasny Mayak and from the implement in the Ingulsky hoard. The socketed standard (*navershiye*) of complicated shape deserves a special place, in some ways recalling a ritual axe-hammer. It has a mushroom-shaped butt, while the front end (the 'blade') is curved under in a spiral manner. It resembles an object from the hoard of Drazhna De Zhos, from near Ploresti in southern Rumania. A still closer analogy to this 'standard' occurred in objects cast from the moulds found in the great hoard of Pobit Kamyk (Dikili-Tash) in northern Bulgaria. This hoard also contained matrices for casting uneared celts, a large sword (reminiscent of the Lozovsky daggers) and shaft-hole axes, precise copies of the shapes of those from the Hungarian multi-layered settlement of Pechka. The latter site is well known for its use, by A. Mozholich, as a chronological yard-stick for the middle and late Bronze Age of the Carpathian basin. The Lozovsky finds can therefore help to create a more precise chronology in these areas.

Moving now to the cultural period of early metal in more northerly (wooded steppe and forest) zones of eastern Europe, we must distinguish between two cultures: the Abashevo and the Fatyanovo–Balanovo groups. In this field surveys and excavations of immense scope have yielded a sharp accumulation of material and consequently led to changes in view about the character of the cultures and more especially their territorial distribution.

The Abashevo culture of the second and third quarters of the second millennium B.C. had previously been pre-eminently localised in the confines of the middle Volga where several barrow groups were known. Recently, the work of P. D. Liberov and A. D. Pryakhin has brought to light settlements and barrows of the culture in the middle Don districts. Furthermore, we may note that stratigraphically Abashevo layers may often occur below deposits of the Log-grave culture, which conflicts with earlier views about the chronological position of Abashevo.

Amongst sites of this culture on the Don, the large and multi-layered settlement of Shilovskoe at the town of Voronezh stands out. A cultural deposit extending over about 3,000 m² has been studied there. It has yielded an immense amount of material: flint knives, spear- and arrowheads; copper knives, bracelets and awls; a bone bit[1] and arrowheads and a large pottery assemblage. Traces were found of a smith's workshop and of sanctuaries, in one of which potsherds were found decorated with incised marks and a very realistic representation of a skier. He holds two sticks in his hands with circular rests on their lower ends. This is the most southerly representation of a skier known from the age of early metal in eastern Europe.

The newly discovered remains in the Don area, as well as the settlements and cemeteries of Abashevo–Balanovo type studied previously in the Hither and Trans-Ural regions, evidently permit us to speak not just about a cultural division but about a great Abashevo culturo-historical community.

Analysis of the vast new materials for the Fatyanovo culture produced by the expedition of D. A. Krainov may bring us to a similar conclusion. These studies have made known the existence of several cemeteries of the Fatyanovo type and dozens have been partially or fully dug. They occur within the limits set by the Hither Ural[2] area on the one side and the upper reaches of the rivers flowing into the Baltic on the other. Here also, archaeologists are dealing with a great culturo-historical community, made up of tribes that sometimes had marked differences of material culture.

In connection with the problems of the Abashevo and Fatyanovo culturo-historical communities, it is necessary to turn to discoveries bearing on the metallurgy and metal-working of these tribes. In spite of the recurrence of significant quantities of metal objects and the relatively late date of the monuments (second millennium B.C.), articles of proper bronze have not so far been found, a fair indication of the isolation of local metal-workers from the production of southern cultures. Furthermore, graves of smiths have been found, a rare thing in ancient burial grounds.

Four pots have been found associated with a male burial of the Fatyanovo–Balanovo type, in a barrow near Churachkino in Chuvashia. In one of them there

---

[1] Translator's note. *Udila* – snaffle bit, but cheek piece is no doubt meant.

[2] Throughout the text Ural refers to the river Ural flowing into the Caspian Sea, not the mountain range; this river is regarded in Russia as the boundary between Europe and Asia.

were two bivalve moulds for casting shaft-hole axes and near the face of the deceased lay a copper axe that had been cast in one of the moulds.

In the huge Volosovo–Danilovo cemetery on the upper Volga, where over a hundred graves were excavated, one of them contained clear smith's accessories: two bivalve moulds for shaft-hole axes and a crucible for casting the liquid copper.

A smith's grave has been discovered in a large barrow of Abashevo type at Pepkino in Mariisk ASSR. There were twenty-eight young men buried in the tomb, amongst whom a smith could be distinguished by the associated grave goods. Beside him lay a mould for a shaft-hole axe and a crucible.

Such finds confirm the view that in this area the smith was a professional craftsman who held a distinct place in the clan community. The grave goods demonstrate that smiths belonged unquestionably to the noble and richer people among the tribesmen.

An important discovery of this kind has been made in the settlement of Urzhumkino. It can be referred to the Volosovo culture, which until recently was regarded as neolithic but is now known to be contemporary with Fatyanovian and Abashevian remains. Several semi-subterranean huts were excavated at this village, in one of which a unique complex was uncovered consisting of over ten casting crucibles. Basically these are broad saucers with a spout for pouring the molten copper, many drops of which had stuck to their sides. The copper had been melted in normal cooking pots, differing only in their thicker sides. The crucibles were remarkable for their size; the largest would have cast up to 6 kg of copper.

As a result of these discoveries a significant number of so-called late neolithic cultures of the late third and early second millennium B.C., in the region of the rivers Ural and Volga, have had to be re-classified by archaeologists as eneolithic.

Such are merely some of the results of recent researches on the cultures and antiquities of the period of early metal in the vast territories of eastern Europe.

III   Scythians, Sarmatians and Greeks: recent work

by D. B. Shelov

Scythians

The antiquities of the Scyths and the tribes bordering on them in the early iron age, all, in varying degrees, of Scythian culture, constitute one of the most remarkable groups of remains of eastern Europe. Excavations on Scythian sites have taken place over the whole extent of the south Russian steppe and wooded steppe from the Danube to the Don, systematic researches on hillforts and settlements being especially important. Amongst the former are such well known early sites as Nemirov and Belsk. The latter lies in Poltavsk oblast and excavations by B. A. Shramko have revealed that, even in the archaic period, it was an impressive economic centre of the wooded steppe with developed bronze-working, jewellery, ceramic and other crafts. Researches at the hillforts of Trakhtemirovo by G. T. Kovpanenko and Khotovo by E. A. Petrovskaya, belonging to the sixth to fifth centuries B.C. and lying on the right bank of the river Dnieper in Kiev oblast, are important in the study of the northern limits of the Scythian cultural zone. A whole group of hillforts has been studied in the basin of the river Vorskla by A. A. Moruzhenko. In the western Crimea, hillforts of late Scythian date, from the second to the third century A.D., have been discovered and studied: Alma-Kermen and Ust-Alma (T. N. Visotskaya), Bulganak and others. Fortified and unfortified settlements of the period have been studied on the lower and middle Dniester and southern Bug (A. I. Melyukova, B. G. Petrenko and others).

Simultaneously with the study of the hillforts, excavation of Scythian barrows of varying periods has been carried out in the Odessa, Nikolaev, Kherson, Zaporozhe, Kirovograd, Crimean, Kharkov, Rostov and other oblasts. The vast construction works for canals and irrigation systems undertaken in the lower reaches of the Dniester, Dnieper and Don and in the Crimea and Hither-Azov areas have required large-scale investigation of the Scythian cemeteries situated in constructional areas scheduled for destruction or flooding. Numerous Scythian barrows of the fourth to third centuries B.C., in particular, have been excavated in various districts of the Kherson and Nikolaev oblasts by E. V. Chernenko, A. M. Leskov, and B. G. Petrenko, in the Dniester estuary by A. I. Melyukov and others. Study of a fifth-century barrow at the village of Chervony Yar, Kiliya district, Odessa oblast (by A. V. Gudkovia) has provided a basis for assuming Scythian penetration into the lower Danube even in this early period.

Many barrows of the fifth to third centuries B.C. have been studied in the eastern and western Crimea by E. V. Yakovenko, S. S. Bessonova, A. A. Konovalov and others, which often contained burials in stone cists or vaults. Flat Scythian cemeteries have been found, for example by V. N. Korpusova, at the village of Frontovoe on the Kerchensk peninsula. Later barrow and flat cemeteries of late Hellenistic times and the early centuries A.D. have been dug at the same place, at the village of Peschanoe in Bakhchisaraisk district (by T. N. Vysotkaya), in the neighbourhood of Sevastopol (by I. I. Gushchina) and in other places.

Amongst the barrows studied, several are distinguished by remarkable finds of objects of Graeco-Scythian art. In 1969 the Kakhovsk expedition, under A. M. Leskov, among other barrows at the village of Arkhangelskaya Sloboda in Kherson oblast, excavated one with two burials from the end of the fifth century B.C. The central burial had been robbed but the side one survived intact. In the wooden coffin with the Scythian warrior, weapons were found: two spears, three quivers with 450 bronze-pointed arrows, two knives with bone handles and an iron warrior's belt. One of the quivers was fitted with gold plates stamped with figures of wild animals. A wooden cup decorated with gold plaques ornamented with fish was found in a hiding place in the wall of the tomb. Over 500 gold plates had covered the cloak enveloping the corpse and on its neck was a massive gold torque with sculptural lion-head terminals and decorated with filigree and cloisonné enamel.

In the same year, the North Rogachik expedition under V. I. Bidziliya excavated a barrow group at the village of Balka, Vasiliev district of Zaporozhe oblast. One of the barrows studied, known locally under the name of 'Gaimanova tomb', belonged to the category of so-called Scythian royal tombs. The original burial under this great mound (8 m high, 70 m in diameter) had been looted, but the remains of wooden coffins and the grave goods confirmed that in the central catacomb, with its two access shafts, two men and two women had been buried. Items that had escaped the robbers were: various gold plaques, including one decorated with winged lions in heraldic posture and another with a splendid representation of fleeing sheep; paste beads and pendants; gold beads and pendants in the shape of little geese; iron spearheads; pieces of a warrior's belt. A horse burial with bridle tags survived intact, as well as two skeletons of adolescents flung into the tomb without grave goods. Two wooden four-wheeled wagons lay on the floor of the access shafts. One of the wall niches and a hiding place in the floor of the catacomb, which had escaped the attention of the robbers, yielded the majority of the objects. In the niche, vessels and other household objects were found: several earthenware *amphorae*, a bronze cauldron containing remains of horse flesh, bronze *oenochoe*, a strainer, a pot (*gorshok*), a situla, a *kylix*, a dish with salver, two iron braziers, iron ladles, tongs and a hook.

In the hiding place there were found: gold casings of three wooden cups, two *rhytons* with silver and gold ferrules, silver *kylikes*, two goblets and finally a silver-gilt cup bearing representations of Scyths. The cut has a spherical base covered with ornament in the form of a rosette and grooving and two horizontal handles decorated with gold plates with relief representations of little rams' heads. The basic frieze on the vessel's body shows six Scythian warriors in various poses, faithfully representing the ethnographic peculiarities of their dress, hair style and weapons. The new cup is not inferior in this respect to the famous goblets from Kul-Oba or the 'frequent barrows' of Voronezh, nor to the silver *amphora* from Chertomlyk. This royal tomb is to be dated to the mid-fourth century B.C.

Another Scythian royal barrow, the 'Fat grave', was excavated in 1971, on the outskirts of the town Ordzhonikidze in Dnepropetrovsk oblast, by B. N. Mozalevsky. The primary burial in this barrow had also been looted in antiquity but since by that time the burial chamber had collapsed in places, some of the offerings had eluded the robbers. In the central chamber, bones of a disintegrated skeleton were found, as well as remains of weapons and tools: iron plate armour, arrow- and spearheads, bronze plates from a warrior's belt, pieces of greaves, a *gorytus*, a mace, vessels and several hundred gold decorations. In the collapsed soil of the passage (*dromos*), there was the skeleton of a servant and remains of a wooden wagon, as well as bronze basins, a lamp, an *amphora*, arrowheads and other things. The most remarkable finds made here were a sword in its gold-plated sheath and a gold breast decoration — a

Plate XXXI (a) (above) *European Russia:* Gold pectoral from 'Fat grave' (detail)
(b) (below) *European Russia:* Relief with dedicatory inscription of a college of corn-
dealers from Olbia

pectoral. On the sheath, scenes of griffins and predators seizing deer and horses were depicted, and the gold mounts of the hilt bore decorations with similar motifs. The pectoral consisted of three openwork zones defined by twisted gold cords (Plate XXXIa). One zone was filled with scenes of struggling animals and griffins, another with plant decoration and the third with Scyths among their flocks. Here, for the first time, the everyday life of the Scyths, such as stitching, clothing and milking sheep, is depicted, not their warrior activities. The gold pectoral weighs 1,150 g.

The corpse buried in the central grave had been accompanied by four servants, a separate burial chamber having been made for one of the maidservants. Six horses with gold and silver bridle fittings had been buried in two special chambers. A silver-gilt frontal plate found among the ornaments bore a figure of a snake-legged goddess, resembling the one from Tsimbalok barrow. Three servants, probably grooms, had been buried with the horses and, in a side tomb, a woman and child. The skeletons of both the latter were covered by a huge quantity of gold plates and discs from their costume. There were also found here: gold ear-rings, finger rings, torques, bracelets, electrum and, silver goblets, a *kylix*, a *rhyton*, a black-glazed bowl and other objects. Remains of two more wooden wagons came to light in the mound, together with a collection of bronze fittings from the wheeled hearse, consisting of openwork standard tops taking the form of stylised deer, little bells, bridle plates and so on. This very rich barrow must be dated to the second half of the fourth century B.C.

In 1970 a second very rich barrow, Khomina Mogila, was dug by B. N. Mozalevsky on the outskirts of the same town of Ordzhonikidze. The central grave, which had been looted in antiquity, yielded scarcely any finds except for the sculptural gold figure of a wild boar, but the horse burials with very rich bridle equipment of the third century B.C. had survived intact. Silver, sometimes gold-curved, frontal plates and cheek plaques and strap fastenings had been executed in the 'animal style', taking the shape of fantastic sea monsters, griffins, eagles and lions, or were covered with stamped geometric ornament. Since all the bridle plates were found in their original position, the form of the bridle head-straps can be fully reconstructed. Their closest analogy is to be found in Thracian graves and the horse decorations undoubtedly derive from there. This very interesting fact indicates mutual cultural and political relations between Scythia and Thracia at that period.

It is desirable to refer to still one further Scythian barrow, in the Bashtan district of the Nikolaev oblast. The Ingul expedition under O. G. Shaposhnikova discovered a burial here in 1971, not distinguished by its richness but by the high degree of survival of objects of wood, textiles and skin. In the first burial of a man and woman, besides the normal grave goods (black-glazed *kantharoi, amphorae*, a bronze cauldron, a mirror, a silver torque, several finger rings and other such goods) there were found in addition a leather quiver, arrows (both the bronze heads and the painted wooden shafts survived), an iron spearhead and its wooden shaft, several wooden vessels and a decorated wooden box, containing two caskets and a collection of spinning instruments – spindles, reel and comb. The wooden caskets are of the greatest interest. On the lid of one squatting women have been painted; the miniature is unquestionably of Greek workmanship. On the other lid several letters of a Greek inscription are discernible. Remains of clothing were identified, embroidered with beads, and leather sandals, that had been secured at the ankles with cords. All the grave goods date this tomb to the fourth century B.C.

The new discoveries in the field of Scythian antiquities, arising from systematic and extensive fieldwork on monuments of all types, make it possible to resolve, with far greater certainty than hitherto, many of the problems of the history of the peoples of Eastern Europe in the early Iron Age. Study of the oldest Scythian remains and comparison with the material culture of the preceding epoch makes it possible to trace in broad outline the ethno-cultural and socio-economic processes that led to the birth in the Black Sea area of the Scythian and parallel cultures. Local variants within the Scythian culture itself, which are even more clearly discernible, were evidently connected with the predominance of this or that tribal group within each region. The new material emphasises the social characteristics of the Scythian society at different stages of its development. It helps to trace the gradual development among the Scyths of the new social institutions peculiar to the transition from the clan-tribe stage to class society and the state. Much light has been thrown on the particular connections between the Scyths and their neighbours and the contemporary tribes and peoples of Europe, the Caucasus, Central Asia and Siberia.

The discoveries of Scythian art shed further light on the origin, character and basic stages of development of many nomadic and semi-nomadic societies of Eurasia, from China to Hungary, in the last millennium B.C.

Sarmatians

To the east of the Scyths in the plains of the Kuban and Azov areas and in the foothills of the Caucasus there lived tribes, the *Meotae*, who were culturally close to them, and, in the steppes of the Volga and Hither-Ural areas, the *Sauromatae*, belonging to the general group of Sarmatian tribes. In the last centuries B.C. and first centuries A.D., the latter subjugated the Scyths and *Meotae* and extended their hegemony throughout the whole length of the Black Sea steppes.

The settlements and cemeteries of the *Meotae* and Meoto-Sarmatians have been the subject of systematic study in the Kuban area and Hither-Caucasus by N. V. Anfimov, V. B. Vinogradov and E. P. Alexeeva, on the Black Sea coast of the north Caucasus in the district of Anapa by Y. C. Krushkol, in the Hither-Azov and lower Don areas. There have been especially important excavations at Elisavetovskoe hillfort, an important economic centre in the Don area in the fifth to third centuries B.C., and at its cemetery, by I. B. Brashinsky, as well as at the later Podazovskoe hillfort, an interesting monument of the Meoto-Sarmatian culture of the last century

B.C. to the second century A.D., by I. S. Kamenetsky. Barrows of the latter culture have been excavated in the Azov area by V. E. Maksimenko.

Basically, Sauromato-Sarmatian culture is represented by funerary remains, since the Sarmatians were nomads and only on the edges of their world, in the Kuban area and in the neighbourhood of Classical cities, did they settle. Study of Sarmatian barrows has been especially intensive in the region between the Don and the Volga and in the lower Volga area. Several archaeological expeditions have worked there studying hundreds of Sarmatian burials, ranging in date between the sixth century B.C. and the fifth century A.D. (V. P. Shilov, A. N. Melentev, I. V. Sinitsin, U. E. Erdiniev, V. I. Manontov, M. G. Moshkova, E. K. Maksimov, L. S. Klein, A. S. Skripkin and others). Sarmartian barrows have been dug in the more eastern area, around the river Ural, in the Orenburg steppes and in western Kazakhstan (by K. F. Smirnov, M. G. Moshkova, G. A. Kushaev, S. A. Popov and others).

The excavated barrows have yielded significant material, not only defining all stages of Sarmatian cultural development but also their connections with the neighbouring civilisations of Asia and Europe. Illustrative of this are the interesting finds made in 1971 in Novo-Kumansk cemetery near Orsk. An ancient Egyptian alabaster vessel of the fifth century B.C. was found bearing the inscription 'Artaxerxes, the great king', repeated in the Egyptian, ancient Persian, Elamite and Babylonian languages. During excavations at the same cemetery by K. F. Smirnov, in one burial a silver *rhyton* was found, taking the shape of a horse protome and a gold torque with terminals in the form of leaping mountain goats. Both these objects derive from Achaemenid Iran and testify, as does the Egyptian vessel with Persian inscription, to the connections between the Sarmatians of the south Ural area and the eastern satrapies of the Achaemenid empire.

Very different connections are revealed by the numerous objects of Graeco-Roman craftsmanship of the last century B.C. and first centuries A.D. encountered in the numerous Sarmatian barrows of the Don and Volga areas: glass and red-glazed ware, bronze and silver vessels and *fibulae* of Italian and Gallic origin, beads and pendants of Egyptian paste, several forms of jewellery and so on. These objects reached the Sarmatians through the medium of the Classical cities of the Bosphorus, notably through Tanaïs. That such western objects were widely used by the Sarmatians is made clear by their discovery in two late Sarmatian burials excavated by G. I. Bagrikov in 1967 at the village of Lebedevok in western Kazakhstan.

Greeks

A number of Classical towns and settlements existed on the north shore of the Black Sea after their foundation at the time of Greek colonisation in the seventh to fifth centuries B.C. Some of the cities maintained over many centuries the status of independent *poleis* but others were drawn into the powerful state formations of either the Bosporan kingdom or the state of Chersonesus. The majority of these towns are being studied by Soviet archaeologists. Excavation, furthermore, has been under-taken not only within the towns themselves but also in the surrounding rural settle-ments, estates and farms and also in the towns' cemeteries. Such complex study of Classical towns with their attendant zones of rural economy (*khory*) and the cemeteries, makes it possible to bring the archaeological material to bear in settling highly important problems of the history of the Black Sea area. Study is directed above all to questions touching the economic and social development of Classical towns, the political and cultural connections between them and the surrounding world of 'barbarian' tribes – Scyths, Sarmatians, *Meotae, Tauri* and others – and the ethno-cultural structure of the cities.

The most western Classical city within the Soviet Union Black Sea area is Tyra, where the last few years have only seen slight work (by A. D. Kryzhitsky and I. B. Kleiman), especially in the excavation of defensive structures of the first centuries A.D. But in the Tyra district excavation of other monuments has taken place. Not long ago, systematic investigation by A. G. Zaginailo identified the site of ancient Niconium (Roksolanskoe hillfort) on the left bank of the Dniester estuary, where urban levels of the sixth to fourth centuries B.C. and first centuries A.D. were excavated. Excavations have been conducted by A. I. Melyukova on local settlements at the villages of Nikolaevka and Nadlimannoe, lying on the bank of the estuary and closely connected both with Niconium and Tyra. Researches recently begun by R. D. Bondar on a hillfort at the village of Orlovka in the lower Danube area have yielded interesting results. The settlement, originally Getic, in the first centuries A.D. became a Roman military station. Beside the earthwork was a Getic cemetery.

Prolonged excavations have continued at ancient Olbia under L. M. Slavin, A. N. Karasev and E. I. Levi. In the last few years, study of the *agora* has been com-pleted, where the surrounding buildings have been uncovered: *gymnasion, dikasterion,* large *stoa*, market stalls and wealthy dwellings of the fifth to fourth centuries B.C. Very interesting finds were made in the gymnasium: a fifth century *kouros* and a dedicatory relief of the second century B.C. with inscription (Plate XXXIb) of corn-dealers. Within the city's citadel, a building was studied that had evidently provided accommodation for the Roman garrison during the first centuries A.D. The lower town, gradually destroyed by the waters of the Bug estuary, was given over to wharves. Besides excavation on the ground, underwater researches have been carried out on the city's remains that lie on the floor of the estuary. West of the city wall an area has been dug where an early settlement (sixth to fifth centuries B.C.) had been subsequently replaced by a cemetery.

In the neighbourhood of Olbia, archaeologists have traced many settlements of the Olbian estate zone (*khora*). On the island of Berezan, excavations by K. S. Gorbunova and V. V. Lapin have found the earliest Greek settlement on the north coast of the Black Sea, dating to the seventh century B.C. Primitive sunken huts, remains of dwellings and service structures of the sixth to fifth centuries B.C., as well as buildings of early Hellenistic, Roman and mediaeval times were uncovered. The settlement's cemetery has also been studied. A very remarkable find, a lead sheet bent over into a tube on which is scratched a fifteen-line private letter, was made in the south-eastern part of the island. Surveys along the shores of the Bug and Berezan—Sosnits estuaries have studied settlements of various periods belonging to the Olbian agricultural hinterland, including settlements of the sixth to fifth centuries B.C. at Old Kabarga and at the villages of Little and Great Chernomorka (S. A. Rusyaeva). In the archaic settlement at Little Chernomorka, among other objects, there were found pointer-coins, dolphin-coins and a whole series of potsherds with dedications to Achilles scratched on them. Excavations under A. V. Burakov have continued at Kozyrska hillfort, lying 12 km north of Olbia and datable to the first centuries A.D.

In Chersonesus several expeditions under G. D. Belov, I. A. Antonova, V. V. Borisova, V. I. Kadeev and others have been at work, studying various parts of the ancient city, where blocks of Hellenistic and Roman times have been investigated. Many industrial complexes of the last centuries B.C. have come to light: fish-salting cisterns, wine presses and remains of glass-makers' workshops. A large building was excavated which had been occupied by a Roman garrison, perhaps the gymnasium, as well as the *thermae* of the third to fourth centuries A.D., already partially un-covered at the beginning of this century. In the course of study of several sections of the city's walls, many gravestones of the fourth century B.C. and later were dis-covered, including one bearing a polychrome painting, re-used in the wall as part of its construction. Excavation of the theatre has continued in order to unravel its history. It was constructed in the third century B.C., abandoned in the second half of the second century B.C., re-founded in the first century A.D., reconstructed in the second to third centuries A.D. and then continued in use until its destruction in the fourth century A.D. Of the various finds from Chersonesus, we may note an interesting marble relief, probably second century A.D., showing a horseman before an altar.

Several monuments have been investigated on the Hercules peninsula very close to Chersonesus. These include the ruins of 'old' Chersonesus, the existence of which was recorded by Strabo, as well as agricultural estates of late Classical times and cemeteries containing vaults of late Roman and early medieval times (A. N. Shcheglov and O. Y. Sablya).

Archaeologists have paid special attention to remains in the coastal zone of the north-west Crimea. Study of the settlements in this district, originally under the control of Chersonesus but then seized by the Scyths and converted into fortified posts, allows a tangible appreciation of the course and conditions of the struggle between Chersonesus and the Scythian kingdom of Skiluros and Palakos, known to us from narrative sources and inscriptions. On the edge of the modern town of Eupatoria the hillfort of Chaika has been excavated by A. N. Karasev and I. V. Yatsenko. The remains indicate a Chersonesan trade factory that arose at the end of the fifth century B.C. and was sacked and destroyed by Scyths in the second century B.C. The Scyths created their own settlement on the site of the Greek factory, by converting one of the earlier buildings into their citadel. It probably also acted as a trading centre and lasted until the second century A.D. A similar assessment has been made in the case of two occupied points situated on the coast north of Eupatoria at Donuzlav and Belyaus (O. D. Dashevskaya). Founded in the fourth century B.C. as Greek colonies (the earthworks at Belyaus belong to a fortified agricultural villa), they were seized by Scyths in the mid-second century and reconstructed. In all these monuments, a difference in building technique is clearly definable between the finely dressed rectangular blocks of the fourth to third centuries B.C., sometimes with cramps, and the later Scythian work, fairly massive but very much less carefully executed. Around the hillfort at Belyaus, a cemetery has been investigated containing Scythian burials in stone vaults and earthen catacombs, and dating from the third century B.C. to the first century A.D.

Still further north of the Tarkhanut peninsula, it has been possible to trace (A. N. Shcheglov) the boundaries of land allotments and rural farms, recalling the subdivisions of the Chersonesan farms in the Hercules peninsula. Aerial photography in conjunction with field-work on the ground has made it possible to distinguish a sequence of several field systems of differing dates overlying each other. Traces of ancient roads, banks and fences around the settlements have also been detected. Several agricultural estates and fortified and unfortified settlements have been studied, the most interesting of which was the settlement of Panskoe I near the bay of Yarylgach. Dwellings and service buildings of the fourth to third centuries B.C. were found there and a sanctuary of Sabazius with a sandstone relief showing this deity. Around the settlement a barrow cemetery was found belonging to the indigenous population of the Chersonesan estate zone (*khora*). At a second settlement in the hamlet of Mezhvodnoe in the same district, a beautiful terracotta head of Dionysus was found by T. N. Vysotskaya and also a Hellenistic sandstone relief showing a resting Hercules.

In the eastern Crimea, in the territory of the European part of the ancient Bosporan kingdom, many Bosporan towns have been excavated, above all the capital of this ancient state, Panticapaeum. Excavations, by I. D. Marchenko, have revealed constructions of various periods. The most interesting consists of remains of buildings of the archaic town and manufacturing complexes, a weapon-smith's workshop, an oven for firing pottery and so on. Of the Bosporan towns lying to the north of Panticapaeum, excavations have taken place at Myrmecium (under V. F. Gaidukevich) and Porphymium (under F. G. Kastanyan) and further south at Nymphaeum (under N. L. Grach), at Ilurat (under I. G. Shurgaya) and at Kitey (under S. S. Bessonova). At Myrmecium, a huge cult complex of the fifth to fourth centuries B.C. was revealed, consisting of a cult room with a thick deposit of burnt material. In Ilurat, investigations in blocks of the second to third centuries A.D., in the south-west part of the earthwork, have continued.

Study of the rural settlements of the European Bosporus have a very great significance, although until recently they went archaeologically unrecognised. Deep in the Kerchensk peninsula, about 13 km west of Panticapaeum, at the village of Andreevka, a rural settlement that started in the sixth century B.C. has been dug by I. T. Krugilikova. In the fourth century B.C. the small isolated houses were replaced by a large country house associated with mixed farming, stock and arable. In the same district, a later fortified settlement, lasting from the second century B.C. to the third century A.D., has been uncovered. A second fortified settlement of the same period has been studied at the village of Novo-Otradnoe on the shores of the Azov sea.

Yet another classical rural settlement that started in the fourth century A.D. has been excavated 20 km west of Panticapaeum, at the village of Mikhailovka (by B. G. Peters). As in the neighbourhood of Chersonesus, so in this area boundaries of numerous ancient fields and properties have been traced. A large Hellenistic wine-making complex, taking the form of stone pressing areas, has been found at the village of Slyusarevo, in the Kerchensk peninsula (E. V. Yakovenko). Finally, we should mention the excavations on the graves of the rural population of the Bosporus, that give a picture of the ethno-cultural peculiarities of this population in early times. Such a cemetery, for example, has been investigated at the village of Zolotoe on the Azov shore of the Kerchensk peninsula (by V. N. Korpusova).

On the Tamansk peninsula, the large towns of the Asiatic side of the Bosporan state have been systematically investigated: Phanagoria (by M. M. Kobylina), Kepy (by N. I. Sokolsky) and Hermonassa (by I. B. Zeest). In the first, layers of various periods have been studied. The archaic and Hellenistic remains are very interesting as well as the industrial buildings of late Classical times: remains from wine-making, glass-blowing and pot-firing. Ceramic manufacture is represented by moulds for casting terracottas (Plate XXXIIa). At Kepy, researches have brought wine-making apparatus of the first to third centuries A.D. to light, as well as the remains of an archaic house with *amphorae* used in the construction, and many finds connected with the cult of Aphrodite, the existence of a shrine being already known from previous excavations. Many objects of art were found in the city, including a little marble head of a youth of the sixth century B.C. and a great painted terracotta relief showing two *sileni* carrying a woman in their arms. Excavations were carried out simultaneously at the city and in its cemetery by N. P. Sorokina.

The discovery and study by the Tamansk expedition under N. I. Sokolsky of a whole system of forts is of especial interest. They were erected in the last century B.C. and destroyed in the beginning of the second century A.D. About a dozen forts were discovered in a circle protecting the north-west part of the peninsula, which in antiquity had been a separate island. They were all built of unburnt brick and had strong walls and towers. Their erection and history is linked to the stormy military events in the Bosporus at the beginning of our era. No less significant an achievement of this expedition was the discovery, during survey work, of special sculptural funerary monuments of the Hellenistic period, that give an insight into

Plate XXXII   (a) *European Russia:* Mould for the manufacture of terracottas from Phanagoria

(b) *European Russia:* Antler facing, from Novgorod the Great

(c) *European Russia:* A Sindian gravestone

(d) *European Russia:* Leaf of a thirteenth century waxed diptych, used for writing, from Novgorod the Great. The back face, seen here, bears an incised alphabet

the local ethnic type of the population. Several dozen of such stelae (Plate XXXIIb), bearing sculptural half-figures, constitute a special category among the monuments of local Sindian sculpture.

In Tanaïs, defensive structures and urban blocks of the early centuries A.D. have been studied by D. B. Shelov and T. M. Arseneva. Finds of recent years that may be mentioned are an inscription of A.D. 229 referring to the erection of the town gates found in the dig on the western fort wall; a series of bronze objects of the early centuries A.D. of Italic or Gallic origin; a cache of light-clay *amphorae* of the third century used for storing oil, as is testified by inscriptions on the throats and shoulders of the vessels themselves.

At modern Anapa buildings and the cultural layers of ancient Gorgippia, lying beneath the present town, have been the object of rescue excavations by I. T. Kruglikova and T. M. Smirnova. Amongst the finds have been pieces of several Greek inscriptions, one referring to Neokles, probably the royal governor in the city, a bronze bust of Aphrodite in the style of the third century A.D. and a little first century marble head of Aphrodite. Surveys and excavations in the vicinity of Novorossiisk and Gelendzik by N. A. Onaiko have identified a series of settlements of Classical time. One of these is of urban character and can presumably be identified with Tauricum (*Torik*), of written sources.

The discoveries referred to above by no means exhaust the list of work of Scythian and Sarmatian students and classicists but they reveal the basic directions and areas of field activity by Soviet archaeologists in their study of Scytho-Sarmatian and Classical antiquities in eastern Europe.

IV   Recent medieval archaeology in the USSR

by R. L. Rosenfeldt

In the last few years, great successes have been achieved in the field of Slavo-Russian archaeology. In the regions of the rivers Dnieper, Pripyat and Desnya, fortified settlements of the Zarubinets culture, of the third century B.C. to second century A.D., have been discovered and investigated, in addition to cremation cemeteries. More than four hundred graves have been dug by E. V. Maksimov in the Pirogovo cemetery south of Kiev and about one hundred graves in the cemetery of Velemichi II on the river Pripyat. Remains of the later phase of this culture have been excavated by L. D. Pobol in White Russia. The settlements and cemeteries at Abidnya and Taimanovo have given especially fruitful results.

The Zarubinets culture is one of the most important for elucidating the problem of Slav ethnogenesis in eastern Europe but, besides these remains, those of the Chernyakhov culture dating from the second to fourth centuries A.D., predominantly cemeteries, have also been investigated. The burial sites of these tribes have been well studied in the cemetery of Nikolaevka, excavated by E. A. Symonovich.

Remains of the early Slav Korchak culture have also been studied, for the most part on the right bank of the Ukraine. Dozens of new villages have been discovered and the fifty or more semi-subterranean huts that have been dug have yielded early wheel-mark pottery of the sixth to eighth centuries A.D. I. P. Rusanova has traced the gradual extension of the remains of the Korchak culture eastwards and northwards on to the left bank of the Dnieper and towards the left banks of the river Pripyat. New Slav hillforts, villages and cemeteries of barrow-covered cremations have come to light, referable to the ninth century A.D. and belonging to the Roman–Borshevo culture. Study of such settlements has taken place in the Kharkov oblast and the Seima and Desnya regions. I. I. Lyapushkin has excavated the medieval Russian hillfort of Novotroitskoe of the ninth to tenth centuries and A. M. Moskalenko the hillfort Titchikha, on the upper Don. Early Slav monuments with similar material culture of the Luka Raikovetsk type have been studied on the right bank of the Ukraine. The area of distribution of the East Slavs in the eighth century A.D. has been more precisely defined; their gradual penetration into the northern forest zone of eastern Europe traced, that is, their colonisation of substantial areas occupied by tribes of Finnish and Balt speech. Study has been made of the process of the gradual formation of the East Slav tribes, the creation of their characteristic ornaments, peculiarities of house construction, costume and burial rites.

Large works have been undertaken on the oldest Russian towns of the pre-Mongol period, with the object of studying their time of foundation, the peculiarities of life, culture and occupations of their citizens, the character of their crafts, their trade connections, the organisation of their buildings and the relationship of the town with the surrounding countryside. Much attention has been devoted to the oldest periods of the history of Kiev, where during construction work, discoveries are constantly made in the urban cultural deposit. In the last few years several thousand finds have been made, including items of jewellery, inscribed objects and articles of high artistic value. In the layers of the pre-Mongol period several dozen huts of ordinary citizens have been uncovered. The sunken houses from the very earliest period of the city's existence are particularly interesting. Remains of craftsmen's workshops and their houses, as well as those of merchants, have been found. P. P. Tolochko, who has excavated a merchant's surface-built house which perished in the Tartar onslaught, found a half-burnt cask of Baltic amber in it. Excavations have taken place in the areas opened up during construction work for substantial buildings. The development of the city's defences, as later and later districts were incorporated into it, has been studied. It has been established that prior to the city's foundation there had been many earlier settlements of the site.

The medieval Russian towns of Galich and Evenigorod the Southern, dug by A. A. Ratich, have been successfully investigated. Remains of permanent, white-stone structures and urban blocks with craftsmen's dwellings have been uncovered. Several major hoards of medieval Russian gold and silver objects hidden at the time of the Tartar invasions have been found in the Ukraine in recent years.

Professor B. A. Rybakov has completed his work in the town of Lyubech (Plate XXXIIIa). A powerful defensive work has been investigated, consisting of a rampart surmounted by an oaken stockade, and traces of wooden mural towers have come to light. Study of the castle (*zamok*) has yielded important results and the remains of a great palace complex were exposed. In Belgorod-Kievsk, several dwellings were found during the excavations and Rybakov has carried out investigations on a twelfth-century church (*khram*). The south Russian towns of Kievan lands, which were protected from the raids of nomads, have attracted the concentrated attention of archaeologists. Almost the whole town has been excavated at Voin, where there had been a medieval river port. Rybakov achieved singular results in his work at the town of Vitachev: a high tower had stood at the centre on top of which a beacon was lit in times of danger.

About a dozen medieval towns have been studied in White Russia. In large-scale works at Polotsk G. B. Stykhov has exposed traces of many wooden structures and collected domestic material consisting mainly of tools and metal items from costume and adornment. Over a hundred barrows have been dug in the vicinity of the towns, both of early cremated burials of a Slav mixed with Slavo-Balt population, and of later typical Slav crouched inhumations of the eleventh to thirteenth centuries A.D. The excavations of these barrows has made it possible to trace the evolution of burial rites in the Polotsk lands.

In the excavations at Brest (medieval Russian *Borest*), P. F. Lysenko has exposed the stratified deposit of the pre-Mongol period, which contained well-preserved timber frames of buildings and remains of street decking together with numerous objects of organic material, bone and metal. A comb with an alphabet scratched on it was found here. F. D. Gurevich has continued with excavations at Novogrudok. In the last few years the citadel has been the major subject of study. Within it, as well as in the suburb (*posad*), rich buildings have been excavated in which master jewellers and merchants lived. In the cultural layer and on the floors of the buildings numerous objects of wood were found and there were many imported objects of high artistic value made of antler and bone, glass and metal. Some of the objects found here had been made in Syria and western Europe. There were numerous finds of leather.

Excavations have also proceeded within the medieval towns of Mstislavl, Volkovysk, Minsk, Kopys, Turov, Pinsk, Rostislavl and many others. The buildings, planning and defences have been studied in these towns.

In the last few years investigations have continued at the Gnezdovo cemetery, the most impressive in the forest zone of eastern Europe and a site of great complexity with a varied ethnic composition in its graves. Several season's work has been devoted to the village of the same name, a settlement contemporary with the cemetery and referable to the ninth to tenth centuries. At the same time, D. A. Avdusin has continued work at Smolensk, where new residential quarters of the town have been uncovered, comprising wooden structures, but where permanent stone

Plate XXXIII · (a) (above) *European Russia:* Hoard found during the excavations of the medieval town of Lyubech in Kievshchina
(b) (below) *European Russia:* Bracelet from a hoard found in 1967 at Old Ryazan

buildings have also been studied. Remains of five churches (*khramy*) of the pre-Mongol period have been studied by D. A. Avdusin, N. N. Voronin, P. A. Rappoport. They had stone bases and the lower parts of the walls retained traces of painted frescoes that imitated Byzantine textiles. These buildings are important for elucidating the stages of development of the Smolensk school of architecture. The late, as well as the early, medieval deposits have been studied at Smolensk. New birch-bark letters and documents have been recovered. In the neighbourhood of the city, E. A. Shmidt has investigated the so-called long barrows left by a pre-Slav people speaking a Balt language.

As in past years, excavations under the direction of A. V. Artsikhovsky and V. I. Yanin have continued at Novgorod, where the cultural deposit in several areas has been investigated. Thousands of ordinary finds have been extracted. Many of the wooden objects were covered by very fine carving (Plates XXXIIc, XXXIId). Remains of wooden structures and buildings and hundreds of metres of wooden street decking have been exposed and the disposition of the yards of the ancient Novgorodians studied. Buildings, decking and structures have all been very precisely dated by dendrochronology. In the last few years, mainly using material from this town, Vikhrov has worked out a new method of preserving wood, thus making it possible to conserve not only small objects but also large structures and buildings over a long period. The excavation of the Gotsky palace (*dvor*) has been successfully concluded. It had been constructed of thick timber posts and during the work, dozens of letters and documents written on birch-bark came to light, among them the first ever found bearing a Latin text. The current total of birch-bark documents yielded by archaeological excavations is 492. They now constitute the most important source for characterising the culture, life and political and economic history of the city and its surroundings.

No less interesting results have come from the excavations conducted by A. F. Medvedev in the town of Staraya Rusa. Dozens of wooden structures were exposed, resting in tiers in the cultural deposit, both numerous street deckings and industrial buildings. The deposit survives in no worse condition than that at Novgorod and has yielded many examples of carved and turned wooden vessels, carved wood and wooden objects bearing painted and incised decoration of varying kinds. Several birch-bark documents with notes of a predominantly economic content have been found in the town. Tools of saltworkers dating from the twelfth to fifteenth centuries have come to light also.

The researches begun by A. N. Kirpichnikov at the Novgorod town of Oreshek, have been fruitful. The site lies on an island in the river Neva at its outflow from Lake Ladoga. The ancient system of urban defences was studied as well as its residential areas and its inner port, the entry to which could be shut off by lowering grilles.

Excavations have continued in Staraya Ladoga, partly connected with the restoration of the fort. At the same time, barrows in the vicinity of the town have been studied, part of which contained typically Varangian burials (in the hamlet of Plakun).

A group of archaeologists carrying out excavations within the town of Pskov has discovered several stone structures within the kremlin (*detinets*), as well as remains of wooden works and street deckings. The defences of the city have been successfully investigated, and the many reconstructions at different periods disentangled. These studies were prompted by a great programme of restoration work.

In the neighbourhood of Pskov, work has begun under V. V. Sedok at Izborsk on the Truvorov hillfort and on other Slav hillforts of this area. Interesting discoveries have also been made at the town of Serensk, the chroniclers' 'Vyatich', situated on the upper Oka. It was destroyed in the Tartar invasion. Traces of the conflagration occur in the cultural layer. It was a notable craft centre, in which traces have been found of the craftsmen's yards where there were tools, including a large series of moulds for making bracelets, ear and finger rings, crucifixes, ear pendants and torques. The system of defensive earthworks has been studied by T. N. Nikolsky. Serensk had been founded on the site of an earlier non-Slav settlement.

At the town of Trubchevsk, P. A. Rappoport has discovered and studied remains of a stone church. Work on a significant scale has been carried out at the capital of the Ryazan lands, the hillfort of Old Ryazan, situated near the town of Spasska on the bank of the river Oka. The remains of the palace of the Ryazan princes have been studied, as well as craft workshops and floors and semi-subterranean dwellings of citizens, with large pits on the sites of their stoves. New material came to hand on the lay-out of the towns. Three impressive silver hoards, hidden in the year of the Tartar invasion, were brought to light, consisting of a variety of ear pendants, chains, bracelets (Plate XXXIIIb), body crucifixes, beads and pendants. The objects were decorated by encrusting, enamel cloisonné, niello and gilding. Several medieval Russian seals and several artistic objects of bone and metal were found in these excavations by A. L. Mongait and V. P. Darkevich. Study of the remains of the brick church in the hillfort has continued, as well as of another, situated hard by in the little town of Olga at the outfall of the river Pron, which was a summer residence of the Ryazan princes. On a northern promontory of the earthwork remains of an eighth-century sanctuary were found, belonging to local Mordvin-Murom tribesmen.

Work has been completed by M. V. Sadovaya on the Pirovy earthworks, which constitute the remains of the chroniclers' 'Yaropolk', situated on the lower reaches of the river Klyazm. Remains of the town of Staroduba near Kovrov have been studied. Minor excavations, mainly related to the restoration of ancient monuments, have taken place at Suzdal, Murom, Vladimir and Kolomen.

The excavations in Moscow have yielded important results. Within the Kremlin, remains of an ancient settlement of the end of the last millennium B.C. and beginning of the first A.D. have been found. Remains of a very ancient flat cemetery that has been exposed at the Uspensky cathedral in the Kremlin belong to the twelfth to fourteenth centuries. In the restoration works at the cathedral, the foundations of the first stone church of the twelfth century have been exposed. During construction work within the town, remains of dozens of pre- and post-Mongol buildings have been revealed, interesting coin hoards found and a huge collection made of everyday things including footwear and clothing and craftsmen's tools. The lay-out of the oldest part of the town has been studied. In Alexandrova Slobada (suburb), excavations directed by B. A. Rybakov revealed the white-stone palaces of 1560–70, lived in by Ivan IV.

Over the last five years several hundred barrows of the Ryatichi, Radimichi and Krivichi, belonging to the eleventh to thirteenth centuries, have been dug, which have yielded not only a profusion of material but also new categories of articles, hitherto not encountered in barrow burials (ear pendants, stone coffins and so on).

Significant work has been carried out in the towns of Volga Bolgaria, Bolgary and Bilyar, by A. P. Smirnov and A. K. Khalikov. At the former, several dozen wood-and-daub surface structures of varying design with complex heating systems have come to light, as well as craft workshops of the twelfth to fourteenth centuries (ceramic and bone-carving). A huge quantity of finds was made, especially frequent amongst which were highly artistic glazed wares from workshops in Iran, Trans-caucasia and Central Asia. There were many such imported glass vessels and tiles. In Bilyar, study has been made of the town's caravanserai and mosque, constructed in the tenth and evidently destroyed in the twelfth century.

On the lower Volga, study has continued of several Golden Horde towns. G. A. Federov-Davydov has excavated the first capital of that state at Sarai-Batu, in which a potter's and a jeweller's workshop were found; dwellings and graves were also investigated. The large number of Russian objects among the finds from this town should be remarked.

Such are the results of research carried out in the last few years in the field of Slavo-Russian archaeology.

Bibliography

A History of the U.S.S.R. from the Earliest Times to the Present Day. Vol. I, Institute of Archaeology of the Academy of Sciences of the U.S.S.R., 1965.

Archaeology in the U.S.S.R., A. L. Mongait, Penguin, Harmondsworth, 1961.

Novgorod the Great, compiled by M. W. Thompson, Praeger, New York, 1967.

Prehistoric Russia: An Outline, T. Sulimirski, Baker, London, 1970.

Chapter VIII

The Celtic oppidum of Entremont, Provence

Fernand Benoît

I   The city of the Saluvii

The primitive population of the coast of southern Gaul at the time of Marseille's foundation, around 600 B.C., was Ligurian. The Ligurian tribes, who were not bound together by any uniting force, occupied the *oppida* which were strung out along the hill-tops, along the routes leading to the Alpine valleys and to the fords of the rivers Rhône and Durance.

The expansion of the Celts, who had dominated northern Gaul and infiltrated south via the Rhône valley and the Alpine passes, did not extend beyond the Durance until the middle of the third century B.C. The Celts had occupied the fertile plain of Lower Provence and, closely mingling with the Ligurian tribes (from whence derives the name Celto-Ligurian which was given to them by Strabo), they had established a powerful military confederation, the Salyes or Saluvii. It extended from the Rhône as far as the Maures mountains, which were held by the independent tribe of the Oxybii who dominated the Argens valley (Fig. 68).

The capital of the Saluvii, Entremont, was situated in a strategic position of foremost importance, in the heart of Provence (Fig. 68). It was at the crossing of the inland route which led to the Alpine passes by way of the fords in the Durance and of the natural route linking Italy and Spain, which followed the Argens and Arc valleys, parallel with the coast.

Saluvian imperialism was bound to come into conflict sooner or later with the Greek republic of Marseille, whose merchants used the hinterland routes. Marseille had complaints about Ligurian piracy harassing her settlements at Antibes and Nice. She appealed to Rome, who shared the same enemies in Liguria and Spain and who

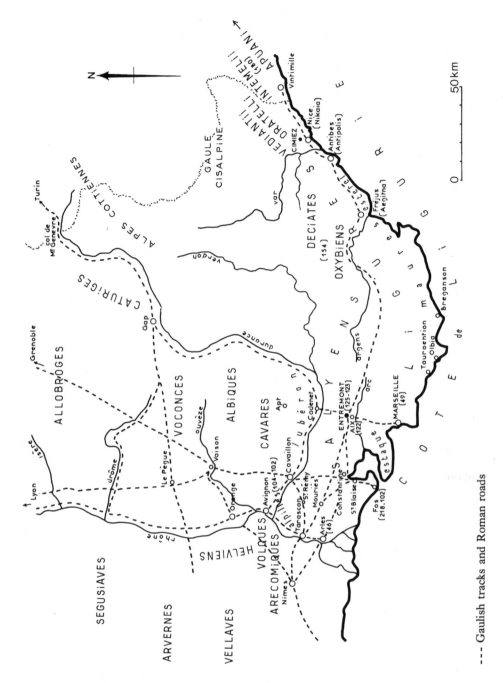

--- Gaulish tracks and Roman roads

Figure 68 Entremont, France: Map showing the position of Entremont and giving the dates of the submission of the Ligurian tribes, from 180 B.C. to the foundation of Aix-en-Provence in 122 and Arles in 46

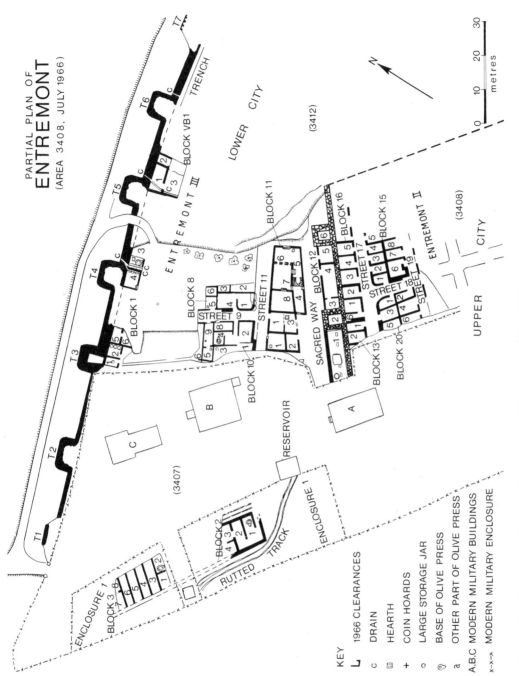

PARTIAL PLAN OF
ENTREMONT
(AREA 3408, JULY 1966)

T7
T6
T5
T4
T3
T2
T1

TRENCH

BLOCK VB1

ENTREMONT III

BLOCK 11

LOWER CITY

(3412)

BLOCK 16

BLOCK 15

BLOCK 12

STREET 17

STREET 18

STREET 19

ENTREMONT II

(3408)

SACRED WAY

BLOCK 13

BLOCK 20

UPPER CITY

BLOCK 8

STREET 11

STREET

BLOCK 1

BLOCK 10

BLOCK B

BLOCK C

(3407)

RESERVOIR

ENCLOSURE 1

BLOCK 2

RUTTED TRACK

ENCLOSURE 1

BLOCK 3

A

N

0   10   20   30
metres

KEY

⌐   1966 CLEARANCES

c   DRAIN

    HEARTH

+   COIN HOARDS

○   LARGE STORAGE JAR

    BASE OF OLIVE PRESS

a   OTHER PART OF OLIVE PRESS

A,B,C MODERN MILITARY BUILDINGS

x—x—x MODERN MILITARY ENCLOSURE

Figure 69 Entremont, France: Partial plan of Entremont II and III

was obliged to ensure the security of the routes from Italy to Spain, by land and by sea, for the movement of supplies for the legions occupying Spain following the Second Punic War.

The Ligurian tribes were progressively subjugated from east to west. Aemilius Paullus overcame the Ligurians of Cisalpine Gaul, who infested the regions of Albinga and Ventimiglia, in 181 B.C. Less than thirty years after, in 154 B.C., Q. Opimius, having crossed the Var, overcame the Deciates and Oxybii, who occupied the Estérel and Maures mountains and who controlled the junction of the Argens valleys. He destroyed the port of the Oxybii, *Aegitna* (Fréjus), which barred the Argens valley and which in turn, led to the plain of Aix-en-Provence occupied by the Saluvii.

Two successive expeditions were necessary to defeat the tribes of western Provence – the Ligurians, Saluvii and Vocontii. The latter, the Vocontii, were settled north of the Durance in the region of Vaison. The first campaign of the consul, M. Fulvius Flaccus, in 125 B.C., was followed two years later by an expedition led by the consul C. Sextius Calvinus.

It appears that the first campaign foundered against the resistance of the fortress of Entremont (Fig. 69), which was not taken by assault until 123 B.C. Several catapult balls have been found under the hurriedly filled-in and re-worked earth of the 'sacred way', at the level of the 'sanctuary of the skulls'; in a street in the area adjacent to the rampart (street 10); and in one of the dwellings leaning against the rampart of Entremont II (Figs 69, 70, block 12, 4). It was during this last period that the 'sacred way' in front of the sanctuary was widened. The raising up of its ground level covered the original soil and concealed traces of hearths and post-holes.

The 'city' of the Saluvii, $3\frac{1}{2}$ km north of Aix-en-Provence (Fig. 68), now known by its medieval name of Entremont (*Intermontes*), was subjugated in 123 B.C. and the name of the tribe was given to the city by the pro-consul Sextius the following year, *Aquas Sextias Saluviorum* (Aix) (on the plain at the thermal spring). The king Teutomalius and the Saluvian princes owed their safety to their flight beyond the territory of the Vocontii, to that of the Allobroges, in the mountains of Dauphiné. The inhabitants of the city were deported, like those of Numance ten years earlier, with the exception of a strong Hellenised party friendly to Rome, whose interpreter, a Saluvian with the Greek name Craton, obtained mercy for these nine hundred inhabitants, whose property was restored to them (Diodorus of Sicily, XXXIV, 23; Appian, *Hist. Rom.*, IV, 12; Livy, *Epitome*, LXI).

The attack had hit the north-eastern angle of the acropolis, where the road entered the city (Fig. 70). On this road, iron *pilum* spearheads have been found. The city was subjected to a violent catapult bombardment, as shown by the presence of basalt or stone balls, similar to those found in *oppida* and sanctuaries destroyed at the same period (such as Baou Roux between Aix-en-Provence and Marseille, and Roquepertuse) and also similar to those used at the siege of Saint-Blaise and Marseille by Caesar in 49 B.C. The concentration of these missiles is notable in the area of the sanctuary and the area adjacent to the ramparts.

Figure 70 Entremont, France: Restoration drawing of the city. A view from the west from the Puy du Roy

The weapons of the defenders consisted of arrows, javelins, iron daggers and especially sling-stones made of baked earth rather than lead, as at the *oppidum* of Piezredon (Fig. 71). A repository and probable place of manufacture for these oval stones was found in one of the small houses adjacent to the rampart. The room contained four *dolia* for water storage and a mass of sling-stones made of clay (see Fig. 69, block 8, 5). The defences appear to have been overcome, as shown by the discovery in street 9 (Fig. 69), which borders this single-roomed building, of about sixty sling-stones and iron spearheads.

The city was pillaged. The *dolia* and earthenware provision jars were smashed in

Figure 71 Entremont, France: Slingstones made of lead and terracotta (Scale: 1:2)

the streets. Hiding places for coins, hollowed out from angles of small houses, were ransacked. However, some of them escaped the pillage and have been found in the upper city and in the artisan quarter. They contained small hoards of drachmas and Massalian obols.

The results of an initial phase of excavation are presented here. It has covered only the rampart and a small sector of the 'upper city'. The military occupy the largest part of this 'acropolis', which consequently cannot be investigated. The excavation here described has been conducted in constant collaboration with M. R. Ambard of the National Centre of Scientific Research, to whom I am indebted for the sections and reconstruction drawings.

The city of Entremont (described as a *polis* by Diodorus of Sicily) occupied a calcareous triangular plateau of gypsum which rises to a height of 365 m. It was defended by steep slopes to the south-east and south-west and a slight slope towards the north. It was divided into two sections which correspond to two successive phases of occupation (Fig. 72).

The Ligurian city (Entremont II), lasted from the fourth to the third century

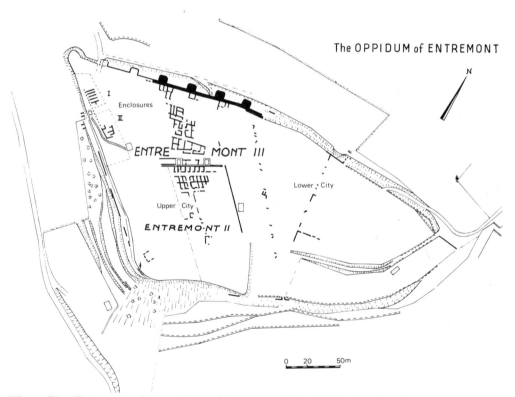

Figure 72   Entremont, France: Plan of Entremont II and III, showing the triangular hill-top enclosure

B.C. and was established in the best defended part of the plateau, surrounded by a rampart. This settlement was to be encompassed by the new city (Entremont III), which extended beyond the old city to the north and east, in the shelter of a new rampart, barring the downward slope for a distance of 380 m. This extension of settlement was undoubtedly contemporary with the Celtic occupation, towards the middle of the third century. Thus, at the time of the Roman siege in 123 B.C., the city appears to have been divided into two sections, consisting of the upper city, extended by an artisan quarter towards the north, and the lower city, which spread eastwards over the entire plateau (Fig. 72). The city was not reoccupied during the Roman period and it reverted to its former rural state. Not a sherd of Arretine ware, nor of *terra sigillata* nor an imperial coin has been found, although in contrast an abundance of them has been recovered from nearby sites.

When the ground was cultivated and the plateau was cleared of stones in 1903, during levelling of the road from Puyricard at the start of this century, it resulted in the disappearance of all trace of the tower which had been noted as a watch-tower in the fourteenth century. In 1233, the peace treaty between the Counts of Provence and Toulouse had been concluded there, at the intervention of the legate of Frederic II, king of the Romans.

Of the first rampart, whose northern and eastern faces are the only ones to have been excavated so far, only the base is preserved. This consists of a course of large squared blocks resting upon a projecting foundation. Its average thickness is $1\frac{1}{2}$ m and it was originally defended by square towers without fill, some 19 m (or 60 ft) apart. In the intervening spaces between the towers, large houses were to be built during the next phase of development. Building material was obtained mainly from natural rock on the plateau but included re-used steles from the sanctuary of Entremont I. The towerless south-eastern and north-eastern corners rest directly on the ground surface, which consists of a layer of earth and ash at the south-eastern corner.

The wall surrounding Entremont III (Figs 69, 72) is about $2\frac{1}{2}$ m wide and bars the plateau, which slopes steeply towards the north, for 380 m. It is $2\frac{1}{2}$ m wide. The masonry consists of small, irregular stones mixed with flat blocks, and is carefully worked especially at the corners of the towers. The towers (see Plate XXXIVb for tower 3), which are equally spaced at 19 m intervals, are filled with a solid mass of rubble and they are principally characterised by their curvilinear profile, destined to withstand the blows of a battering ram. This skilful technique was also used at the *oppidum* of Piezredon at Éguilles.

The ramparts reached a height of 4 m in places but the method of construction was primitive and badly suited for defensive purposes. The base of the rampart was built of projecting, badly cut blocks and it follows the ground surface which had not been levelled in advance of building (Plate XXXIVb). The rampart was pierced at its base with drainage holes, located at the corners of the towers and intended for the channelling of rain water (Plate XXXVb). The irregular openings were placed under

Plate XXXIV (a) (above) *Entremont, France:* The sanctuary of the skulls; constructed between two towers of the rampart of Entremont II (Fig. 69, block 12, 1). A column with twelve mouthless 'severed heads', and a fragment of a lintel with head-shaped sockets, have been re-used in its construction.

(b) (below) *Entremont, France:* The wall of Entremont III, tower 3. The lower foundations form the substructure of the ditch

Plate XXXV   (a) (above left) *Entremont, France:* Crossing of streets 18 and 19. On the left, the buttress of a small house (Fig. 69, block 15, 6)

(b) (above right) *Entremont, France:* Zoomorphic pouring spout of a basin (height 0·07 m)

(c) (centre) *Entremont, France:* A drain in the lower city, entering the rampart (block VB1)

(d) (below) *Entremont, France:* Crescent-shaped ear-ring made of twisted silver wire (diameter 0·032 m)

a slab which formed a lintel. One of the openings was used for the out-flow of two water pipes found in two adjoining houses in the upper city (artisan quarter: buildings 1, 3 and 4). It measures 75 cm high and 50 cm wide. Two other drainage holes in the lower city measure 60 cm by 30 cm and 40 cm by 50 cm; a fourth one in the eastern wall of the upper city measures 40 cm by 45 cm.

The city is about $8\frac{1}{2}$ acres in area and contrasts with the very small area of the typical Ligurian fortresses, which were only used as a refuge and a storehouse for crops in times of danger. At Entremont, the successive walls surrounding the two cities did not enclose all the houses. On the western slope, disposed in tiers along the steep slope of the cliff, rock-cut dwellings have been found with clay hearths, in the style of the simple dwellings observed at Cavaillon, Glanum and Montlaurès. The area which lay between the ramparts in the northern suburban quarter where the potters' ovens had been installed may have been similarly arranged. Taking into account the large number of inhabitants who were Roman collaborators, some nine hundred according to Diodorus of Sicily, one must presuppose that the city did not shelter the entire population. One section of the community must have been semi-nomadic, inhabiting the open plain below the city.

The 'sacred way' (Figs 69, 80), recognisable on the western side, along which statues were found, doubtless entered the upper city by a gateway which is located on the present-day military grounds. Its outline is indicated by ruts grooved in the rock and in the pebble surface. A distance of just under $1\frac{1}{2}$ m separates the axle-grooves. No doubt the sacred way led to a crossroads. It re-appears east of the military grounds along the external face of the rampart surrounding Entremont II, between whose towers the hypostyle room of the 'sanctuary of the skulls' was later placed.

The lower city's principal gate, on the north side, has not yet been located. On the southern side, only a side door, 1·10 m wide, has been found. It gave access via a stairway to the plain and to the water-holes. Soil movement has carried away the rampart along the southern side.

The layout of the upper city has an interesting urban plan, in spite of the different orientation of the two quarters, which were separated by the ramparts of Entremont II. It conforms to a Greek or Etruscan tradition which has been recognised in the Massalian settlement of Olbia (Hyères), but which is apparently lacking at Marseille, though this is nowadays too confused by buildings to be legible.

The small blocks of housing are separated by streets, from $2\frac{1}{2}$ m to just under $3\frac{1}{2}$ m wide, which intersect at right angles (Plate XXXVa, Fig. 69). The same method of construction characterises both quarters of the city, whose last stage appears to have been contemporary. The walls have been rebuilt on several occasions because of their fragility. In fact, the walls of the houses in the Ligurian city are supported by the rampart of Entremont II. The houses are irregular in plan. Most consist only of a single rectangular room, measuring about 5 to 8 m by $2\frac{1}{2}$ to $3\frac{1}{2}$ m. In both quarters, due to the weakness of the wood used as a framework, houses consisting of two and even three rooms have been excavated. One such building (10, 4) has a hall which opens into the street and leads to three rooms. The last of these rooms contains the slab or *area* for an oil-press, installed after the raising of the ground level (Fig. 73). The most spacious of the rooms had a post which can be recognised from the carbonised remains at the centre of the room, to help support the roof.

The doorways are frequently supported by a thick buttress which is generally placed to the right and used as a tower or perhaps as an access route to the flat roof by way of a mobile ladder. The rudimentary thresholds consist of flat slabs, except in the quarter where potters' ovens have been found. There, raising the level of the road involved increasing the original thresholds and doubling their height by a slab with a stop for closing the door and a socket for hinge.

The walls, which were about 50 cm thick, were constructed of stones, placed one on top of another, without mortar. A number of crushed bricks of lightly baked clay (18 cm wide and 7·5 cm thick) in the foundations of the houses demonstrate the use of a technique which was also used at the *oppida* of Caisses at Mouriès, of Pennes at Glanum, and was still current when the Roman docks of Lacydon at Marseille were constructed.

The inner surface of the walls was lined with natural clay tablets of a similar composition, clamped together by iron nails with convex heads. In a large house

Figure 73 Entremont, France: The oil-press in house 10, 4 (Fig. 69). A reconstruction drawing, showing the method of pressing olives

positioned between two towers of the rampart of Entremont II (which was rebuilt after the first century, as shown by the presence of a sling-stone in the fill), the more carefully worked facing of the walls included tablets of stuccoed clay, decorated with fluted or triglyphical relief-work (building 12, 4). The floor was of trampled earth, the hollows in the rocky foundation having been levelled with rubble or flat, irregular flagstones. Roofing tile, which was rare even at Marseille during the Roman period, if Vitruvius' account can be trusted, was not used. The roofs were undoubtedly flat, made of wattle and daub and perhaps of animal skin.

The fragility of the walls and the lack of foundations entailed incessant rebuilding, which is revealed by the differences in the building material and particularly in the substitution of irregular stonework for the original flat, naturally-formed, tablets of calcareous rock (building 15, 6). The walls had been rebuilt in the same position and the ground level slightly raised, as can be seen from the superimposition of several hearths and the presence of fragments of *dolia*, crushed bricks and small fragments of pottery, broken by compression (building 10, 4, 11, 9).

Each house apparently contained a hearth, as evidenced by a mass of cut-up clay. The hearths were sometimes built on a foundation of broken stones or made of fragments of *dolia*. The remains of altar-hearths, of a more compact clay, survive in several small houses in the western quarter. One of these (11, 4) bordering the 'sacred way' was decorated with small circles juxtaposed and incised with a reed. Despite its primitive character, it is perhaps comparable to the altar-hearths, more richly decorated with maeanders and swastikas, which have been discovered in the *oppida* of Roque at Fabrègues, Lattes, le Cayla de Mailhac and, dating from a more recent period, Orgon.

The dwellings all contained one or more *dolia*, for water storage or grain, and contained the débris of wine *amphorae* and Campanian pottery, together with the traditional native Hallstatt earthenware of blackish clay.

In the city the 'arts and crafts' were grouped together. The first ovens to be discovered occupied the quarter between the two ramparts which probably served as the artisan quarter, perhaps before the extension of the city.

The activity of the occupants was above all agricultural. In the same quarter of the city, several slabs, most of them broken counterweights, which served as the *area* of the oil-press, have been discovered. They are rarely found still in their original positions. The poor quality of the local stone necessitated quarrying larger stones for the construction of *areae* and counterweights, at Bibemus and Beauregard, near Aix-en-Provence. The use of stone from the first of these quarries for the pillars of the sanctuary, which were re-used during the periods of Entremont II and III, and the re-use of several sections of the stone presses in the walls of this part of the city, implies that the oil industry was already known in the Ligurian era. The technique was undoubtedly acquired from the Greeks at Marseille and was the same in Provence during the Roman era (Fig. 73). The olives were heaped in flat, two-handled baskets and on round mats of esparto grass, then they were piled on the slab of the *area* and compressed by the action of a wooden lever, which was lowered with the help of a windlass fastened to the ground by a heavy stone counterweight (*torculum*). The oil running from the press ran into the circular groove of the *area* and was directed by the outlet into jars of baked earth serving as receptacles. This method, which was current at the same period as the *oppidum* of la Courtine at Ollioules, did not include purification in basins, which was used in the Roman period.

The milling of flour was done by hand. Two types of quern demonstrate its evolution: first, the rectangular, Greek quern with a grindstone mounted on a wooden framework, which operated by means of a backwards and forwards movement. This type of quern was rare at Entremont but was known to the cities in contact with the Greeks, for example, Saint-Blaise, Arles, Mouriès, les Pennes, Ollioules, Ensérune and Montlaurès. This type of quern was succeeded by the circular grindstone with a rotary movement which was in current use from the La Tène II period, the stone for which came from the lava quarries of Ollioules or Beaulieu near Aix-en-Provence.

Weaving and leather work – whose importance is revealed by the scrupulous reproduction of helmets, cuirasses, doublets and sandals on the statuary – is represented by finds of tools. Small, baked-earth spindle-whorls of the truncated bi-conical type have been found, sometimes ornamented with 'wolf's teeth' decoration, as well as circular discoid-shaped loomweights, bone needles and iron scrapers.

Industrial work was equally well developed, as indicated by the slag-heaps of iron and copper ore which lie scattered in the streets. Iron and lead, derived from mines in the mountains of Maurès and the Alps, had given rise to a small local industry. In the artisan quarter, several ovens with hearths built from fragments of *dolia*, instead of fireproof stone, were uncovered. The workrooms' vaults had caved in. In one of them (building 11, 5), a lead plate weighing about 100 kg was found. Nearby were three ovens (building 11, 6) whose hearths had been destroyed. They may have been used for re-heating the cupels of melted-down lead. The oven had certainly been in current use, if only for repairing pottery and *dolia* and for manufacturing sling-stones.

The cutting-tool industry also produced weapons of war such as javelins, lance- and arrow-heads and swords. It also forged agricultural tools, anvils, goldsmiths' and blacksmiths' tongs, stonecutters' hammers, plough coulters, sickles, gouges and scrapers for leather work.

Excavation has also brought to light bronze ornaments, such as undecorated belt buckles, fibulae with bi-lateral spring bows of La Tène I type (Fig. 74), an appliqué for a belt, decorated with small circles in the Hallstatt tradition, a *phalera* from a harness decorated with a severed head and several *simpula*, similar to those from Glanum and Eygalières, one of which is decorated with an excellently represented head of a canine (fox). Must one suppose that all this ornamental metalwork derived from the local industry?

Figure 74   Entremont, France: (a) Fibula with a pin and interior coil, of La Tène II type
(b) Cross-bow fibula with a bilateral pin, of La Tène I type (Scales: 1 : 2)

Feminine ornaments are rare finds but include blue glass beads and bracelets of polychrome glass inlaid with small zig-zagging threads, which were from Italo-Celtic workshops, and ear-rings of twisted silver threads in the form of closed crescents (Plate XXXVd), similar to those adorning one of the female statue heads. Coral imported from Marseille was worked on the site.

The principal industry was the manufacture of pottery. Each dwelling contained one or more *dolia*, lined up along the inner walls, with the base slightly sunken into the ground. The *dolia* were manufactured locally and were made of clay mixed with quartz, provided with a reinforcing rim like the Greek *pithos*. The carination was striated with a comb and was sometimes also incised before baking with an apotropaic symbol such as a cross, pentangle, or markings in the form of a lyre or an S (a symbol of *Taranis*, also noted at the *oppidum* of Baou-Roux) (Fig. 75).

Pottery for everyday use was made on the spot, and included basins with drainers, small vessels for libations and combed or striated wheelmade black pottery goblets in Hallstatt style, sometimes decorated with a 'wolf's teeth' frieze. Some vessels imitate Italo-Etruscan pottery, such as the handle of a black pottery *oenochoe* in the form of a griffin's *protome* (Fig. 76) and the pouring lip of a pinkish, earthen basin (*pelvis*) in the form of a lion's snout (Plate XXXVc), which was a prototype of the vases from Lezoux.

The local rustic pottery contrasts with the fineness of the Campanian pottery imported from Marseille (Fig. 77). Plates, cups, bowls decorated with a white band, lamps with a keel-shaped reservoir and long-necked balsam containers represent the imports current in the second century. A selection of the types has been provided by the Grand Congloué shipwreck found at Marseille. The imported earthenware was certainly appreciated, as demonstrated by the fact that several vessels had been repaired with lead clamps. The rarity of *graffiti*, Greek letters and crosses, is in contrast with the epigraphic wealth of the Campanian pottery from the Greek coastal settlements of Marseille, Antibes and Olbia. However, one *graffito*, depicting a horse turning his head around backwards, is notable (Fig. 78).

Imports are also represented by a bowl-shaped sigillated pottery of the type known as 'bowl of Megara', which was glazed coral-red and decorated with leaves,

Figure 75 Entremont, France: Restoration drawing of a storage room containing *amphorae* and *dolia*, one of which is marked with an apotropaic pentangle

a zone of maeanders, Cupids and eagles; and also by goblets decorated with a network of 'studding', whose export, along with that of the Campanian pottery, has been noted as far afield as Spain and Africa (from sites on the Balearic Islands, as well as Elche, Ampurias and Lixus on the Spanish mainland).

The most important and highly priced imports were certainly the Italian wine *amphorae*, which were spread through the Rhône hinterland by Marseille's merchants (Fig. 79). A single example from Rhodes has handles bearing the circular engraving mark *ΔΑΜΟΦΙΛΟΥ* and dates from the first half of the second century. Other examples come from Campania and Sicily. Earlier than the Dressel I type, they were in use on the *limes* at the time of Augustus, when they were characterised by an inclined and very short lip and a spindle-shaped conical point, without the massive foot of the *Sestius amphora* from the Grand Congloué shipwreck. Stamps are rare; some examples are *CL.FE., P.I.M.R.* on the neck, and one from Sicily marked *TIBE(ri)* on its handle.

0   2   4 cms

Figure 76   Entremont, France: Zoomorphic handle of an *oenochoe*

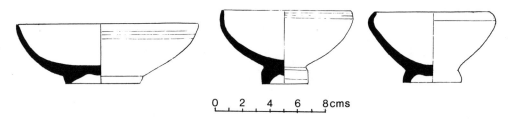

0   2   4   6   8cms

Figure 77   Entremont, France: Campanian cups found in street 17

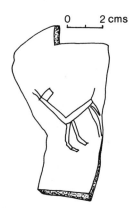

0   2 cms

Figure 78   Entremont, France: Graffito of a horse on a Campanian *patera*

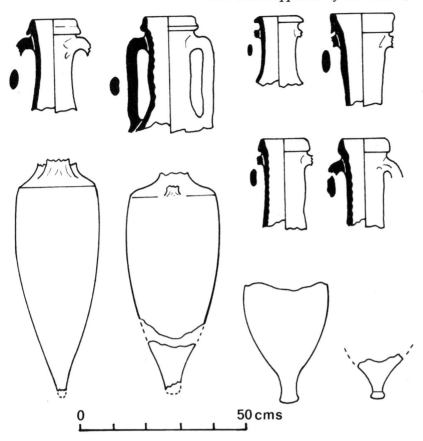

Figure 79   Entremont, France: Graeco-Italic wine *amphorae*

Wine was not the only commodity imported by the Saluvii. Southern Spain supplied salted fish and pickling brine, which was transported in Punico-Roman *amphorae* with flared necks, similar to those from Lixus, Cadiz, Alicante and Ruscino, as well as in cylindrical, wide-mouthed, short-necked vessels, with a downward sloping, projecting rim (*sombrero de copa*), accentuated by painting. From the Catalonian coast came small grey pottery urns with fluted necks, which continued the Phocaean grey pottery tradition.

These imports testify to commercial relations with Marseille, which received in exchange wheat, sheep, animal skins and, no doubt, rare minerals, iron, lead, silver and medicinal herbs from the Alps as well as a major source of revenue, slaves.

Treasures of coins found in hiding places in the houses and the coins scattered in the streets following the pillage consist almost exclusively of Massalian currency, drachmas and, especially, silver obols. One hiding place in the upper city produced 1,435 obols, contained in a pot of split yellowish clay. Another hiding place, 1 m deep, which had been hollowed out in a bank of gypsum and lined with small limestone tablets clamped together with iron nails, contained, beneath iron javelin-heads and arrow-heads, 100 obols and two drachmas. Also found with them were a Roman quinary, with an effigy of the goddess Roma on one side and the Dioscuri on the other, and two Victoriati with a effigy of Jupiter on one side and Victory on the other (240–197) (Fig. 69, block 20, 3). The two other treasures were found in the artisan quarter. One consisted of 27 drachmas found in a wooden money box (block 10, 9) and the other of 110 obols, enclosed in a small clay pot (block 10, 8).

The quantity of Massalian currency is in contrast with the rarity of Allobrogian bronze coins. The wealth of the Saluvian city, derived by importation from Greek lands, seldom extended beyond the commercial sphere, and prior to Romanisation, the civilised world does not appear to have influenced the spiritual life of the Saluvii, who remained in a primitive state.

II   The sanctuary

The religion of the Saluvii

No statues of gods have been found in the *oppidum*, no dedications to the gods, nor even any inscriptions, with the exception of some Greek *graffiti* on the pottery. Graeco-Italic religion had not yet influenced Saluvian beliefs. The Saluvian gods were impersonal and abstract. They did not adopt human form and individuality until after the conquest of Gaul. Caesar, in his *Commentaries*, wrote that the Gauls proclaimed themselves, by Druidical tradition, the descendants of *Dispater*, father of the race, who is identified with *Taranis*, the Gallic Jupiter, god of the heavens and of thunder, master of life and death.

A relief, found with the statues of heroes on the 'sacred way', in the upper city, represents the busts of two people with loose hair, making a gesture of adoration and, with their right arms, holding up an offering of a hare, an animal sacred to the Celts.

The Saluvian religion was essentially animistic and funerary. Their sanctuaries were not built to house the image of the divinity but to house the image of the heroic dead, who were placed under its protection. Nicander of Colophon, an Ionian Greek writing in the second century B.C., informs us in a passage related by Tertullian, that the Celts spent the night beside the ashes of their dead in order to receive oracles from them. Such a cult belongs to the primitive religion of the Mediterranean. It is a feature of the Nasamons in the Great Syrte who lived near the graves of their ancestors and also amongst the Moors and the Sardinians. The Ligurian tribe of the Apuani in Cisalpine Gaul, threatened with deportation by the Romans after Aemilius Paullus' victory at the beginning of the second century B.C., had implored the consul not to drive them from the land of their ancestors, where they had been born (Livy, XL 38).

As in Homeric Greece, the cult of the dead was the federating link which assured the continuation of the tribe, which was thus united by the ashes of its heroes. This religious fact would explain the relentless destruction by the Romans of the Celto-Ligurian sanctuaries of Entremont and Roquepertuse, crushed beneath a hail of sling-stones, as well as the deliberate smashing of Entremont's statues and the deportation of her inhabitants.

The sanctuary went through several phases. The location of the oldest sanctuary (Entremont I) has not yet been determined, due to modern military occupation of part of the area (Fig. 69), but it was no doubt on the summit of the plateau and dates from before the arrival of the Celts to the period of Ligurian fortification. Only the re-used aniconic steles in the walls of the Ligurian rampart of Entremont II are evidence for its existence at all (Plate XXXIVa). The steles of local limestone, roughly squared and with unbevelled angles, are similar to those from Roquepertuse, which were also re-used in the floor-tiling of the final phase of the sanctuary. They are also similar to late Hallstatt steles from Glanum, Saint-Blaise and Mouriès, which were embellished with engravings of horses and horsemen.

This primitive cult place had a portico (Fig. 81), with elements belonging to two periods:

(a) Quadrangular pillars (width 0·35 to 0·45 m) of calcareous stone and stone from Bibemus, several bearing symbolic marks, which were re-used in the foundations of the hypostyle room of the 'sanctuary of the skulls', during the final phase. One pillar was hollowed out with a deep, skull-shaped recess, similar to those from Roquepertuse and Saint-Blaise, for the exhibition of a severed head. Two of the pillars were decorated; one with a serpent in relief, a Mediterranean symbol relating to the afterlife. The other, placed alongside it, the whole length (2·60 m) of which has survived, was decorated with twelve engraved mouthless severed heads, of which the one at the bottom was upside-down as a symbol for loss of speech, which is the symbol of death (Plate XXXIVa). A third fragment of pillar, of Bibemus stone, re-used in the east tower, was inscribed with a double ear of corn. The severed head rite and its mythical representation are contemporary, as demonstrated by a lintel fragment re-used as the base of a post in the same sanctuary and showing the engraving of a mouthless head associated with two skull-shaped sockets.

(b) Three elements consisting of quadrangular pillars (width about 0·40 m) with figural scenes. These were found in 1817, re-used in a modern building. They are carved on three faces with horsemen armed with lances; one of them carries a severed head suspended at the horse's withers, with a standing nude figure making a gesture of supplication before the door of a tomb with groups of severed heads with closed eyes. These reliefs, in spite of their roughness (which, in 1834, led Prosper Mérimée to attribute them to the Saluvii) are contemporary with the statuary, as is demonstrated by the similar clothing and weapons of both. They therefore date to the Celto-Ligurian period (Entremont III).

The 'sanctuary of the skulls' dates from the period of Celtic occupation. Skirted by the 'sacred way' (Figs 69, 80) it was positioned between two towers of the rampart of Entremont II (Fig. 69). It has not yet been possible to excavate it for its entire length. It consisted of one storey, paved with *opus signinum*, which is slightly baked clay inlaid with small dice-shaped pieces of black and white calcareous stone.

The sanctuary contained skulls, which were no doubt nailed onto stakes and placed upon wooden supporting platforms. Crushed skulls have been found inside the sanctuary, but most of them were found scattered on the sacred way near the sanctuary. The skulls were not of great antiquity. They lay in an upper level of the sacred way, perhaps set up after the first siege in 123 B.C., as the presence of a catapult ball in the fill tends to prove. Several skulls bear the puncture marks of nailing, which could only have been made in a recently decapitated skull, un-doubtedly mummified as a preliminary, after the neck had been stripped of its flesh. No cervical vertebrae from the necks have been found.

Of the twenty skulls found, two had been fractured in places by catapult balls. The remaining skulls are in very poor condition and the fragments have been care-fully collected by M. R. Ambard. Ten belonged to men of about thirty years of age, the other eight to men of forty or more. Undoubtedly these represent war trophies. Perhaps they were the severed heads of the Romans who were at war with the Saluvii, whose reputation for atrocities Festus Avienus attests in a passage of the *Ora maritima* (V. 701) concerning Lower Provence.

The practice of decapitating the conquered enemy and exhibiting his head was certainly witnessed among the Celts. At the time of the invasion of Italy in A.D. 295, the Celts hung the heads of vanquished enemies at the withers of their horses – a custom depicted on one of the pillars at Entremont described above. We also know that they had dedicated the head of the consul L. Postumius in their temple, in 216 B.C. (Livy, X, 11; XXIII, 24–6). The barbarous decapitation rite was common to the population of Scythia, Thrace and Decia but it also existed among the Germanic peoples and the Celtiberians.

The practice was noted in Gaul by Posidonius, a Syrian settled at Rhodes, who crossed the Alps at the beginning of the first century B.C. The account of his voyage is related by Diodorus of Sicily (V, 29) and Strabo (IV, 4, 5).

> The Celts, they say, attach the decapitated head of the enemy's leader at the withers of their mount; they nail these lugubrious trophies to the door of their house and embalm the heads of the most illustrious enemies; they keep them with them in a small box, showing them with pride to strangers and refusing to part with them for ransom.

Posidonius wondered at these barbarous customs, to which, however, he said he became accustomed.

Strabo reported, from the same sources as Caesar, various methods of torture practised in Gaul, such as drowning in a cauldron, burning in a small wicker hamper,

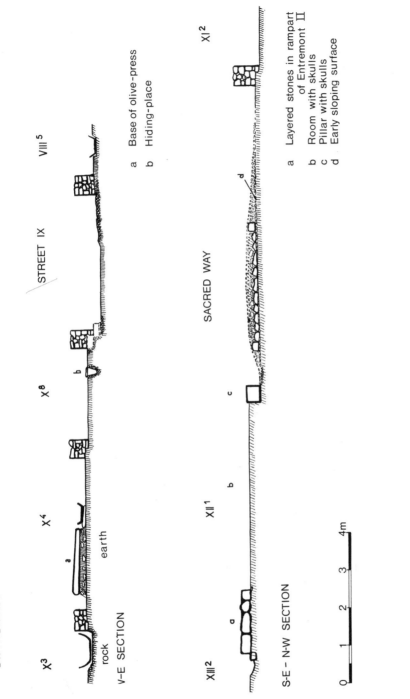

ENTREMONT

X³   X⁴   X⁸   STREET IX   VIII⁵

rock   earth

V-E SECTION

a   Base of olive-press
b   Hiding-place

SACRED WAY

XIII²   XII¹   XI²

S-E – N-W SECTION

0 1 2 3 4m

a   Layered stones in rampart
    of Entremont II
b   Room with skulls
c   Pillar with skulls
d   Early sloping surface

Figure 80   Entremont, France: Transverse cuttings; street 9 and block 10, showing the oil-press room, the sacred way and its two levels, the sanctuary of the skulls and the base of the rampart of Entremont II

hanging and laceration, which are perhaps only literary transpositions of folklore rites. He concluded that the Romans put an end to these customs, characteristic of 'northern peoples', as well as to the practices of sacrifice and divination 'contrary to our customs'.

Posidonius' voyage took place after the campaign of Marius (104–102 B.C.), whose legions occupied an entirely pacified region from the Chaîne des Alpilles to the Étang de Berre for about thirty years after the destruction of Entremont and Roquepertuse. Posidonius' narrative, which does not seem to derive from the accounts of local Marseille inhabitants, appears to be the testimony of a live witness, concerning the still unromanised tribes of the Celtic hinterland.

Were all the skull-bearing pillars war trophies? An exact chronology of the Celtic occupation of Provence and the dating of re-used pillars has thrown some light on a rite which involved the preservation of the heads of ancestors, as much as it did those of enemies.

At Glanum, at the confluence of the Rhône and the Durance, on the ridge of the Chaîne des Alpilles looking out over the route from Italy, where Marius without doubt established his camp to wait for the start of the invasion by the Cimbri and Teutones, the sanctuary of the spring and the cave was a place of pilgrimage from the Ligurian period. The evolution of its architecture makes it possible to trace the succession of styles diffused by Italy at the close of the Republic and the beginning of the Empire. The excavations of H. Rolland have brought to light, along with fragments of a squatting statue, pillars with skull-shaped sockets containing a hook carved inside for suspending a skull and a lintel in a more highly developed state, decorated with a fillet of beads and small coins, unskilfully hollowed out with sockets of the same type. This architectural feature in the Hellenistic style did not appear prior to the second quarter of the first century – the period during which human sacrifice had been outlawed in Narbonnaise.

The cult of the human head in this sanctuary may continue an indigenous tradition subsequently 'humanised' by Roman civilisation. The porch, which was to be filled in during the construction of the twin temples erected during the reign of Agrippa, with all the magnificence of Augustan art, consisted of pillars whose capitals were decorated on all four faces with single heads of men and women, whose modelled features rise up from a corbel of stylised acanthus leaves. The pillars represent aesthetic values entirely different from those of Entremont, nearly a century earlier. The models of these capitals decorated with heads, borrowed from Etruria and Campania, underwent a transformation at Glanum which demonstrates the expansion in Lower Provence of a school of Hellenistic sculpture, of which the Celto-Ligurian sanctuaries represent the archaic period.

There is an evolution in the rite of exalting the head, which can be detected from Entremont to Glanum. The oldest representation from Entremont, a mouthless head whose eyes and nose form the lines of a T (which is an ideogram representing the cessation of life), conforms to a very ancient tradition which appeared in the coastal areas during the Chalcolithic era, on 'owl heads' in the lower Rhône Valley at Avignon, Lauris and Orgon and on the menhir-statues of Languedoc and Cisalpine Liguria. Marking and protecting graves, these mute idols call to mind the ossuaries with mouthless faces noted since 4000 B.C. in Canaan (Tel Aviv), at Troy and at Miskole in Hungary.

Elsewhere the rite of preserving the skull had origins of no less antiquity. The rite was known in the West from the Palaeolithic era onwards but it was in Asia Minor that the rite appeared most explicitly, in connection with artistic practices which sought to restore life. Skulls from Jericho and Tell Ramad, near Damascus, dating from 7000 B.C., had been remodelled in plaster, painted with ochre and the empty eye sockets were either painted (Ramad) or inlaid with cowrie shells to give them sight (Jericho). The paintings in the sanctuary of Çatal Hüyük, Anatolia, represent two vultures stripping the flesh from bodies, whose skulls had first been severed from the trunk.

This custom, common to all peoples, shows the enduring nature of a belief which has lasted up to our own era, in the family charnel houses of Brittany and Poitou. The existence of the rite can be noted during the Bronze Age in the burial cave of Terrevaine (la Ciotat) and in Sicily at the proto-Corinthian necropolis of Gela, where the urns enclose only the skull of an adult or elderly man, without the rest of the bones. Work in La Tène I and II cemeteries at Mount Troté (Ardennes) and at Moeuvres (Nord) have revealed the practice of burying the long bones, after removing the whole or part of the skull. Is it not the same rite which can be observed during the Merovingian period, in the *Life of Saint Arnold*, minister to Dagobert, where the grave of a child is described whose body had been burned *more gentilium* and whose head had been preserved? The skull is in effect the dwelling-place of the soul from whence it cannot escape. The skull was still a cult object during the Middle Ages especially as the 'relic' of a saint, preserved in a gold or silver shrine and attracting pious crowds to the saint's festival.

Were the Celtic skulls those of ancestors or of enemies? Certainly possession of a multiplicity of relics was believed to increase the tribe's strength. Because of the degeneracy of the rite, the two types of skull have been associated in the same superstition. Belief in the magical properties of the severed head has grown up amongst the non-Indo-European peoples in Insulinde (Céleges), in Oceania (New Guinea, Melanesia), in Africa (Congo), etc. Contact with the severed heads collected by the head-hunters of Borneo was supposed to increase the strength of the living and to induce the projection of a supernatural force upon all living things, from animals to harvests.

Entremont's 'sanctuary of the skulls', far from being a primitive sanctuary, was evidently a sacred place where the magical powers of the spirits were harnessed for the protection of the tribe.

III The statues

The emergence of full-relief sculpture in south Gaul, prior to the Roman conquest of Narbonnaise, was an achievement of Mediterranean civilisation whose distribution was limited by the intersection of two routeways — the course of the Rhône and the 'route of Hercules', linking Spain and Italy via the Alpine passes.

The chronology of the centres of sculpture corresponded with the diffusion of Mediterranean civilisation, whose axis gradually moved from east to west, from the sixth century B.C. to the Hellenistic period. Centres grew up along the main trade routes — for goods such as gold, amber, pewter, copper and salt, from as far east as Scythia to the western Celtic areas and southern Spain. Main centres were in Istria at the mouth of the Danube; Nesazio on the Illyrian coast; Capestrano and Numana on the Italian coast; Hirschlanden in Württemberg, not far from the settlement of Heuneburg on the Upper Danube; the princely grave of Asperg, which contained rich imported Ionio-Etruscan objects (an ivory and bone sphinx decorated with amber and gold; a mirror bracket decorated with a 'tree of life'; a bronze stand in the form a lion's claw, which held a cauldron, similar to that from Garenne-Sainte-Colombe in Burgundy); and finally, at the western extremity of the Mediterranean, the mouth of the Guadalquivir in the kingdom of Tartessos, a land which exported copper, silver and tin.

Statuary appeared later on in south Gaul. Based on a Hellenistic *substratum*, it appeared only for the period of Italo-Celtic assimilation which preceded romanisation. This corresponded with Roman imperialist expansion in the Mediterranean between the first two Punic Wars. The statuary was contemporary with substitution of the pottery of Magna Graecia for Ionian and Greek pottery.

The centres of sculpture, not all of which are yet known, influenced and enlivened the sanctuaries of the Celto-Ligurian and Celtiberian tribes in the coastal regions, but statues remained at the *aniconic* stele or statue—menhir stage. There are examples from Ollioules near Toulon, Mont Garou near Sanary, Entremont, Roquepertuse, Pierredon near Éguilles, Glanum and, on the other side of the Rhône, Grézan near Nîmes, Russan, Sainte-Anastasie in the Gardon valley and Substantion on the Lez.

The relative dating of this early form of statuary cannot be established because of its pseudo-archaism and lack of comparative features. One of the statues from Ollioules (a *xoanon*, related to the ex-voto of Heraion of Samos, and the bust of the warrior from Grézan, portrayed with arms adhering to the body) still conforms to an archaic tradition, so the statues from Entremont, Roquepertuse, Glanum, Pierredon and Russan probably fall within a short space of time, from the middle of the third century to the founding of Aix-en-Provence and Narbonne (122–118 B.C.).

This early school of sculpture was short-lived. It did not survive the moral and religious revolution which Romanisation brought to Gaul. It thus represents a unique attempt by the Celts to express their religious imagination, no longer by means of abstract or schematic symbols, but by making use of the repertoire of

Mediterranean sculptural forms, in the development of the technique of full-relief sculpture. Consequently, the school of sculpture follows various aesthetic concepts without any synchronism, a diversity which is proof of the heterogeneity of its plastic models.

In spite of the mutilation and incomplete excavation of the 'sacred way' where the statuary was found, Entremont still represents the richest centre of this art. The largest group consists of 'seated gods', of a type which is also found in other sanctuaries (Plate XXXVIa). Other statues of varying height portray standing figures, mounted on pedestals, one of which, with sandals on the feet, appears to have belonged to a female statue. Also found were a *togatus*, with a detachable head, and an equestrian statue smaller than life-size. Most of the heads are male (Plate XXXVIc) but four heads belonged to female statues (Plate XXXVIb) of which no other fragments have yet been found.

The statues were sculpted in local lacustrine finely grained limestone. They appear to be a related group which makes it possible to place them in the Saluvian Celto-Ligurian period (Entremont III). Most of them portray the heroic dead, in the squatting posture, described as 'Buddhist' (the legs crossed beneath the body), and making the double gesture of placing the left hand on a dead head and holding an iron symbol in the right hand.

This kind of realism is incompatible with the wealth of Graeco-Roman allegory, which shrouds the horrible mystery of Death with ideographs, referring to the last journey or the triumph of death. Nevertheless, the squatting posture, which is essentially funerary, did not completely disappear from Roman Gaul, but continued in use for stone statues and especially for statuettes of bronze or terracotta. At Bourière, close to Limoux, a figure was found depicting a seated person caressing in both hands a 'detached head' with a 'Gorgonian' *rictus*, in his lap, a posture which must also have been used for the figure of a nude hero with missing forearms found at the sanctuary of Hechstheim near Mainz. This is the posture used for squatting gods and goddesses at the altars of Rheims, Vendoeuvres, Saints and Quinssaines (Allier), whose mystical posture is inhibited by horned animals and serpents. It is also the posture of innumerable terracotta and bronze statuettes from Quilly (Loire Atlantique), whose backs are decorated with a constellation of astral symbols, and also from the caves of Jonas at Clermont-Ferrand, from Billom (Puy-de-Dôme), from Bouray, Vésoul, Autun, Amiens and Besançon, whose funerary symbolism is most frequently expressed by zoomorphic symbols, such as a horned serpent or a goat, or simply suggested by the hooves, ears or horns of stags, thus allowing them to partake of the 'divinity' of Cernunnos, the horned god of the sanctuary of Lutetia.

One cannot help but be struck by the contrast between the artistic quality of this statuary, derived from the Greek or Etruscan master schools, and its macabre realism. The statues reveal a knowledge of anatomy in the modelling of the abdomen and the musculature of the arms. The latter, forward-projecting, stand free of the torso and the right hand is supported by a tenon, revealing technical knowledge.

However, even though the arms appear to have been sculpted from a single block of limestone, the statues were probably not monolithic. In a fragment of thigh, a lead tenon is preserved which joined the limb to the torso of the statue.

The male statues are of warriors (Plate XXXVIa). The stomach is usually bare, the loins girded with a *perizoma* or short breeches and the upper torso protected by a leather pectoral, bearing a metal *apotropaïon*, whose double volute sometimes frames a severed head with black painted eyes in the manner of a *gorgoneion* (Plate XXXVIa). From the right side a long La Tène II sword is suspended, attached by a ring to the sword-belt. One of the pommels, decorated with two spheres, is similar to a Hallstatt sword hilt decorated with nodules. The neck is encircled by a torc with two decorated finials, the distinguishing insignia of gods and heroised dead. The wrist is adorned by a large bracelet decorated with Celtic spirals, similar to those found at the *oppidum* of Pennes, near Marseille. One of the male heads wears a leather helmet with cheek-guards and a rear neckguard.

The statues are of a physical type far removed from the Graeco-Italic or Alexandrian ideal. They are related to different prototypes, more representative of the bronze or terracotta technique than of sculpture in stone. The faces, inscribed in a rectangle, are characterised by a visible bone-structure, a jutting, squared chin which abruptly terminates the oval of the face, prominent cheekbones which lack a smooth transition into the line of the nose and compressed expressionless lips. The primitiveness of one head with striated hair and the head from Mont Garou call to mind the heads from Chiusi in Etruria.

The pseudo-archaism of the heads is recognisable in the ears, nose and especially the eyes, the hardest part to model (Plates XXXVIb, c). The ears, asymmetrical and poorly set, are in the form of a concave purse, with an exaggerated lobe, conforming to the design of the heads of Hellenistic Buddhas. They are sometimes divided in two, in 'kidney-bean' style, as on Greek sixth century black-figure vases. The nose is three-sided. The eyes, of regular oval form, are rimmed by the edge of the eyelid. They appear to be exophthalmic to such a degree that the gaze, no doubt originally indicated by a painted pupil, appears sightless. Nevertheless, an element of studied refinement is present, imitated from some Ionic or Etruscan model. The upper eyelid is underlined with a thin, raised ring, a detail also noticeable in the bust of the Lady of Elche.

The hair is stylised in several different ways: curled in fine parallel ridges corresponding to the archaic *kouroi* type, rolled into 'worms' with the aid of a trepan, as in third century Etruscan terracottas; or separated into regular 'snail'-shaped curls, calling to mind the same Hellenistic models as the Buddhas.

The modelling of the female heads is more supple. One of them, the lower part of whose face alone remains, wears an ear-ring in the shape of a closed crescent similar to a piece of silver jewellery found in the excavations (Plate XXXVa). It exhibits the ponderousness of certain Ionic heads. Another, now in a private collection, is notable for the inflection of the lips and the delicacy of the face. The heads

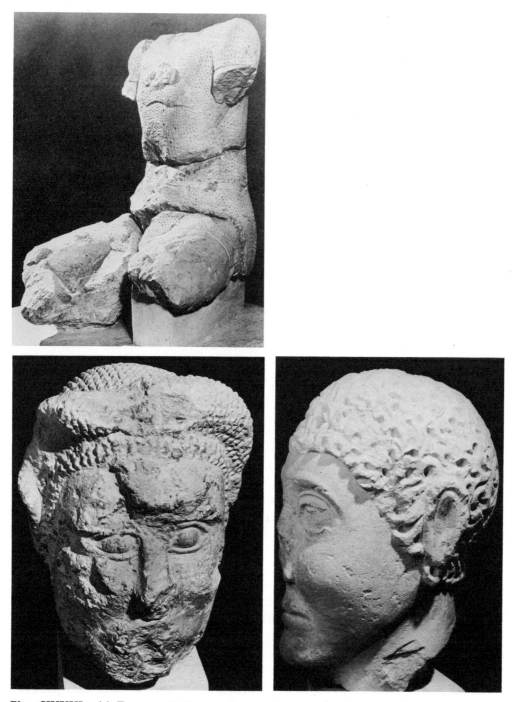

Plate XXXVI (a) *Entremont, France:* Statue of a squatting hero, wearing a leather breastplate and a pectoral ornamented with a *gorgoneion* (height 0·80 m)

(b) (left) *Entremont, France:* Female head with waved hair, forming a crown with traces of red paint adhering (height 0·27 m)

(c) (right) *Entremont, France:* Male head with vermicular ('wormlike') hair (height 0·30 m)

are veiled or their hair dressed in a skilful waving style which coils back over itself onto the forehead to form a diadem (Plate XXXVIb). They are portraits, perhaps rather lifeless but displaying some individuality.

The interest of the statues lies in the fact that they are not simply effigies of the dead. They express religious beliefs which are difficult to interpret, in view of the lack of comparative documentation and the lack of contemporary intermediaries in the Mediterranean world. The statues participate in a scene which takes place in the after-life, as shown by the presence of a cinerary urn, placed to the right of the statue, a style of interment common to the Celts and Ligurians, and by the double gesture of placing the left hand on a severed head with swollen features and eyes entirely or half-closed (Plates XXXVIIa, b), and the holding in the right hand of an iron symbol with divergent rays (Fig. 81), no doubt the thunderbolt of *Jupiter-Taranis* with whom the hero is identified.

The antithesis constituted by the double gesture is intentional and the realism masks an allegory. Even the setting provided by the sanctuary shows the aptitude of the Saluvii for expressing abstract ideas relating to the after-life in sensible forms derived from the stars and the animal world. The image possesses an esoteric value distinct from its esoteric appearance, something characteristic of symbolism.

Everything in the sanctuaries recalls the notion of death and of the survival of the hero in paradise. At Nages, designs of galloping horses alternate with human faces with closed eyes and at Sainte Anastasie, in the Gardon valley, a helmeted bust wears a pectoral engraved with a frieze of horses. At Roquepertuse, the journey to the after-life is suggested by the representation of horses' *protomi* carved in champlevé upon a lintel, or incised in the edge of the 'scapulars' of the statues and also by painted astral symbols, stars and birds. Above the portico rises a bird, sculpted in full relief ready to take flight, with the feet of a palmiped and the beak of a bird of prey. It is the bird of the swamps of the Styx, according to Graeco-Italic symbolism. Perhaps it is the beak of this bird that one recognises in the curved appendage surmounting a double bust, rather than the double diadem derived from the Hellenistic palmette of the Rhenish statue-menhirs (Holzerlingen and Leichlingen). At Entremont, where the mouthless head motif survived during the preponderantly Hellenistic period, the solar disc is inscribed on the door of the tomb, in front of which a ritually naked figure makes a gesture of supplication on one of the pillars with figured scenes, found in 1817. Astral symbolism is also represented by the serpent, the messenger from the after-life. The serpent is carved on one of the re-used pillars in the 'sanctuary of the skulls', beside the pillar carved with twelve severed human heads. Perhaps it must be interpreted not only as a serpent but also as a spiral, a solar symbol, a motif of decreasing diameter which surrounds the severed heads of the pillars with figural scenes and circles round a head with closed eyes. In Greek mythology, the serpent, the son of the earth, reincarnates the spirit of the dead which returns to Mother-Earth. His symbol is known in Provence. It is carved above a severed head on the menhir of Veyssière in Estérel and, during the

Plate XXXVII (a) (above) *Entremont, France:* Laying of the right hand on a severed head with closed eyes (height 0·28 m)
(b) (below) *Entremont, France:* The same gesture applied to a youthful head with half-closed eyes and a plait of decorative hair (height 0·22 m)

Roman era, it is still one of the symbols of the *Jupiter-Taranis* at Seguret, which relates the Celtic wheel, the symbol of thunder, to the thunderbolt and eagle of Zeus.

The symbolism was enriched by the motif of the monster crushing its prey. A severed head, severely defaced, from one of the pillars already mentioned, was surmounted by an animal with arched body (in the position of the 'Tarasque' of Noves) and a leonine mane, placing its claws on a severed head. From the point of view of plastic art, the symbol of the overwhelming and devouring lion, image of the triumph of death and the protector of the tomb, is known from the Etruscan world. The oldest representation is from the necropolis of Vulci, in Etruria, of fourth century B.C. date, which shows a lion imposed on a human head with conventional features. The infernal significance of this scene is confirmed in the necropolis of Genes, which dates from the second century B.C., by the substitution of the triple-headed 'flesh eater', Cerberus, for the lion. The popularity of this symbol was such that it survived throughout the Roman world: in Spain at Alvacète, Osuna and Porcuna; in England at Chester; in Gaul at les Baux, Vaison and Mornas; and in the Rhineland at Metz, Spire and Worms; before being diffused later onto the doorways of Romanesque churches, where the lion is used as the image of Hell devouring the damned. However, in Etruria as in the Roman West during antiquity and the Middle Ages, there was a notable tendency to replace the severed head with animal prey, either a bull or stag, which wild beasts tore to pieces, a substitution which emasculates the symbol, and deprives it of its original meaning. Nevertheless, the laying on of the hand at Entremont, the only sanctuary where it can be restored, is a gesture of gentleness rather than claim. The hand rests lightly upon the hair, sometimes allowing a braided tress to slip through the fingers onto the wrist (Plate XXXVIIa, Fig. 81). This displaying of the braid, comparable to the *crobytos* in the style of hairdressing of children in Greece and Etruria, has a religious meaning: it is suggestive of the 'golden hair' which attaches the mortal to life and which the Fates severed in Virgil's account of Dido's death (*Aeneid*, IV, 690) (Plate XXXVIIb).

The laying on of hands gesture at Entremont expresses a quasi-mystical union between the hero and the severed head (Plate XXXVIIa, b). The only equivalent in Greek plastic art is the touching by the dead of his own funerary *hermes*, or of a siren, on certain steles in Attica, Asia Minor, Thrace and Macedonia. However, the realism of the severed head, considered the seat of life in the animistic beliefs of the Saluvii, may have another meaning. The deified hero would profit from the influx of vitality from the victim, represented by the head, habitation of the soul. In this case, the scene depicts the rite of *devotio*, the sacrifice of a human victim immolated to the infernal gods to ensure the survival of the dedicator in the after-life, corresponding to the Etruscan ritual related by Caesar in his *De Bello Gallico*, VI, 16. The reproduction, eternalised in stone, of a real sacrifice or an allegorical facsimile, would have the same value as the reality. Rite and myth are one and the same thing at Entremont.

The naturalism of the representations owes its macabre expression to the trophy skulls of the sanctuary. They evoke the transcendental notion of Death, expressed

Figure 81 Entremont, France: Squatting hero, on the second level, the doorway of the severed heads without mouths and pillars with skull-shaped recesses

by a sculptor of genius, whose boldness had no equal in any other statuary, until the discovery of the pathos of Death in fifteenth century France.

Entremont's statuary enables us to penetrate the Celtic infernal world for the first time and reveals the magico-religious practices of its funerary cult. It is thus of exceptional importance for our knowledge of Gallic religion on the eve of the Roman conquest. Its barbarous rites, which were not humanised by contact with the Greeks of Marseille, belong to a most primitive stage of civilisation.

The severed human head is the most ancient talisman of mankind. Buried beneath the door-step of a house, enclosed in the rampart, or carved on the rampart of the fortress (as at les Baux, Tarragone, Albarez and Lugo in Celtiberia), it was intended to keep malevolent powers at a distance and terrify the enemy, like the Gorgon head on the shield of Athena.

There is a connection between the human head and that of Medusa. A severed human head with staring eyes protects the pectoral of one of Entremont's carved warriors and another decorates a bronze harness phalera similar to those from Manerbio and Augst. It appears again, on the stock of a lead anchor from a ship-wreck in the Hyères Isles of the second century B.C., in the form of a human head with closed eyes, which performed the role of all the other *apotropaia* currently employed (the Medusa's head, knuckle-bones, dolphins, the column, the principle of stability and even the invocation to *Zeus Soter* – the last resort against shipwreck).

A ferocious-looking front view of the human head appears on a Cretan intaglio from Mallia at the beginning of the second millennium; the tongue is extended like the Gorgon on coins from Eretria, from the treasure of Auriol at Marseille and on certain Gallic coins. Greece, however, had long since gone beyond this barbarian stage. An artist from Sicyon was the first, according to Pliny, to have replaced the skulls of men and animals with apotropaic ornamental summits of pediments constructed at the corners of houses (*NH*, XXXV, 43, 12) and Greek sensitivity had given the body of a monster to the Gorgon decapitated by Perseus, since the Hesiodic period.

Celto-Ligurian 'primitivism' only disappeared during the Roman period, which renewed the out-worn prehistoric rites without affecting the depths of the native soul. It is no doubt to this religion of death, innate to the Gauls, that the dedication of the tomb under the protecting sign *ascia*, opening the door to eternity, owes its popularity in the Rhône valley.

Was it not the Gorgon who, during the Homeric period, served as the intermediary of the dead with Persephone, barring the access of the living to Hades and assuring the dead protection in the after-life (*Odyssey*, XV, 633)?

Bibliography

Benoît, F., 'Chronique archéologique' in *Gallia*, V (1947), pp. 81–97; XII (1954), pp. 285–94; XIV (1956), pp. 218–22; XVI (1958), pp. 412–15; XVIII (1960), pp. 291–4; XX (1962), pp. 689–92; XXII (1964), pp. 573–5.

Benoît, F., 'La estatuaria provenzal en sus relationes con la estatuaria iberica en la epoca preromana', *Archivo español de Arqueologia* (1949).

Benoît, F., 'Le geste d'imposition de la main à Entremont', *Mélanges Charles Picard* (1949).

Benoît, F., *L'art primitif méditerranéen de la vallée du Rhône* (2nd ed.), Aix-en-Provence, 1955.

Benoît, F., 'Le "sanctuaire aux esprits" d'Entremont', *Cahiers de Préhistoire et d'Archéologie*, Bordighera, IV (1955), pp. 38–69.

Benoît, F., 'Les "têtes sans bouche" d'Entremont', *ibid.*, VIII (1964), pp. 68–81.

Benoît, F., 'La statuaire d'Entremont', *VIIIe Congrès international d'Archéologie classique*, Paris; 1963, pp. 654–8.

Benoît, F., *Entremont capitale celto-ligure des Salyens de Provence*, Aix-en-Provence, 1957.

Espérandieu–R. Lantier, *Recueil général des bas reliefs . . . de la Gaule romaine*, XII (1947); XV (1966); XVI (1967).

Chapter IX

Elsloo, a Neolithic farming community in the Netherlands

Pieter Modderman

Since 1900 the village of Elsloo has changed greatly. At the turn of the century the casual visitor would have found only about 120 houses, most of them farmsteads, grouped around the church. In summertime many houses were closed, their windows boarded up, and whole families migrated temporarily to the Rhineland, where they worked for German brick factories. Only those who owned or rented sufficient acres of the rich loess-soils surrounding the village could afford to stay at home. On the whole Elsloo was a poor village in a district where prosperity was rare.

The development of coal mines brought a considerable change to the southernmost part of the Netherlands and to the province of Limburg, where Elsloo is situated. A demand for manpower grew up in the region itself. New possibilities existed for the clay-diggers returning from the brick factories. They were accustomed to heavy work and could easily change to hewing coal.

Flourishing coal production called for improved transport. Railways did not provide an adequate solution and so the waterways to the north had to be radically improved. The river Maas (Meuse), the natural highway to the north, fluctuated greatly in water content. Canalisation of the winding river was badly needed by those who lived downstream from Elsloo and who wished to be saved from the flooding of their fields, which could be expected every year. Many people would thus benefit from a canalised Meuse and the work was undertaken during the 1920s and early 1930s.

Canalising a river when both banks are under the same government does not cause very many difficulties. The Maas, however (Meuse is the name used by the Belgians), happens to be the frontier between Belgium and the Netherlands for some

Plate XXXVIII (a) (above) *Elsloo, Netherlands:* The Juliana canal was dug through the middle terrace of the Maas at Elsloo. In the background the lower terrace is visible
(b) (below) *Elsloo, Netherlands:* How to find the site of the excavations

45 km. The problem was solved by digging a canal on the Dutch side of the frontier, the Juliana canal (Plate XXXVIIIa). To the village of Elsloo, the project meant a thorough change; to **understand this,** one has to know how Elsloo is situated.

The river Maas has **formed the** main features of the landscape. In general terms one can distinguish **three river terraces,** a higher, a middle and a lower (Fig. 82). The latter is the most recent one and the one in which the Maas has meandered for many thousands of years. Remains of the medieval castle of Elsloo can still be discovered in the river, which shows how relatively recent the changes are. The village of Elsloo lies on the middle terrace which is about 20 m above the lower terrace. The river Maas at Elsloo flows for a short distance under the escarpment formed by the middle terrace. These circumstances caused the engineers to plan the canal through this middle terrace and to move one-third of the village. One can understand what this must have meant to the population. Houses had to be destroyed and great building activity resulted. New streets had to be planned along which new houses were built.

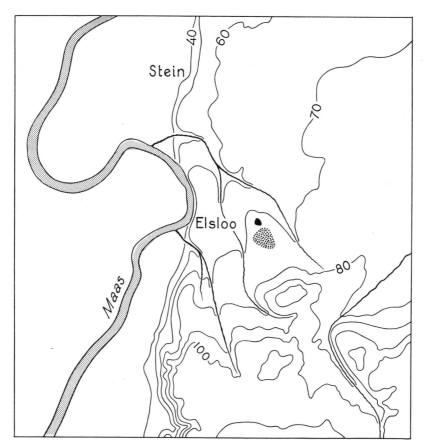

Figure 82   Elsloo, Netherlands: The situation of the settlement-site and cemetery

This introduction would not have been written if it did not have direct archaeological relevance. Archaeology would be nowhere without the interested layman. Near Elsloo, it was the doctor, H. J. Beckers, from the nearby village of Beek, who saved much information for archaeological research. He and his son published the results of all their investigations in 1940, excellently.

Beckers was known not only as a doctor but also as an enthusiastic biologist and archaeologist. His patients took to him everything which looked 'old'. If the find was important the doctor's fee was forgotten. So nearly everything was brought to his attention. When potsherds and dark pit fillings were found during the digging of holes for the cellars of the new houses along one of the new streets in Elsloo called Koolweg, Dr Beckers was informed. This was in 1935 and represented the discovery of the site which forms the subject of this chapter.

Beckers recognised the potsherds as belonging to the *Bandkeramik* culture, the earliest farming culture of western and central Europe. The extensive archaeological excavations at nearby Köln-Lindenthal were well known to him. In the book by Beckers and his son details are given of several different find-spots, all of which belong to one vast site with traces of *Bandkeramik* habitation, which will be discussed below.

Shortly before Dr Beckers' death in 1950 new finds were made, this time by Father A. A. Munsters. In January 1950, during street building activities, he discovered some more pits with dark fill, which from their contents could be attributed to the *Bandkeramik* culture. These finds were sufficient justification for the State Service for Archaeological Investigations in the Netherlands to start a trial excavation in June 1950. This excavation resulted in the discovery of three incomplete house plans which proved that the *Bandkeramik* people did not live in pit-dwellings, as was generally assumed till then.

At this time traces of *Bandkeramik* habitation were also found at Sittard. A choice had to be made as to where further investigations should be carried out. None of the sites had any priority from a scientific point of view but at Sittard most of the plots of land where we wanted to excavate already belonged to the municipality, because a new extension to the town had been planned on the site. This meant that it was not necessary to negotiate with numerous different landowners to obtain permission to excavate. Therefore Sittard was chosen merely for practical considerations. In retrospect this decision proved correct, as it would have been much more difficult to understand what was later found at Elsloo, without prior knowledge of the Sittard site.

After having completed excavations at Sittard we were anxious to know whether it would still be possible to undertake a major excavation at Elsloo. Before visiting the mayor we drove along the site of the 1950 excavation. Many new streets had been built with new houses along them. The post-war industrial development was clearly visible. Elsloo had completely changed from a poor farming society to a prosperous village, many of whose inhabitants were connected with the coal mines and the complex of activities relating to them. An amusing surprise for the archaeologist was to discover that one of the new streets, above the 1950 site, was now named *Bandkeramiekersstraat* (Plate XXXVIIIb). From the mayor, we learned that there were still two hectares at our disposal to investigate. We were just in time, as a church, two schools and several houses were scheduled for building during the following year. This was therefore a rescue dig and work started as soon as possible, at the end of January 1958. By July 1959 digging had been in progress for eleven months; during that period seventy-seven ground plans of houses were recovered and part of a cemetery excavated. In 1960 a further month's excavation took place to demonstrate the *Bandkeramik* culture to an excursion of the Prehistoric Society. An important extension excavation took place in 1963 under the direction of Dr R. S. Hulst from the State Service, who worked for more than two months. He found eighteen house foundations. Eventually, in 1966, it was possible to excavate the cemetery extensively. This research was organised by the Institute of Prehistory of Leiden University. All these excavations were arranged in close co-operation with the local authorities and the inhabitants of Elsloo. The result of this extensive excavation is that Elsloo is the best-known *Bandkeramik* settlement site in western Europe.

The information collected by Dr Beckers, together with that derived from our excavations, makes it clear that at Elsloo traces of *Bandkeramik* habitation extend over some ten hectares. Only about one third of this area could be excavated, so we have to reconstruct what happened from an incomplete record.

The first settlers

We must turn the clock back a very long time before we reach the century in which the first farmers settled at Elsloo. If radio-carbon years are strictly comparable to solar years this was in the forty-fifth century B.C. This date is acceptable until carbon 14 laboratories agree on a new half life. Carbon 14 is the 'absolute' method of dating the arrival of the *Bandkeramik* culture but there is also the archaeological method, which reveals through pottery decoration that the first farmers at Elsloo were not the first generation of *Bandkeramik* people in Europe; although they may have been only second or third generation.

Who were the first settlers and where did they come from? These are questions which are easier to ask than to answer. We do not know anything of the physiology of these farmers and can only speculate as to whether the *Bandkeramik* people originated elsewhere or whether they represented the local Mesolithic population who had adopted the new way of life.

One fact is clear: the *Bandkeramik* economy has its roots in south-eastern Europe. The knowledge of farming must have spread from the Balkans through Hungary, Moravia, Bohemia, Austria and Germany, finally reaching the Netherlands and Belgium. Nothing is known of the manner in which the culture was transmitted. Was it by colonisation or did the Mesolithic hunting groups rapidly change over to the new farming economy because the supply of game was not enough to feed the increasing population? There was probably more than one reason for change.

In the case of Elsloo, the presence of a Mesolithic population nearby cannot be excluded. Only 23 km to the north, near Montfort, many traces of this hunting culture have been found. On the other hand, the great similarity of decorative motifs between Elsloo and the south-eastern find-spots is marked.

Two further points are worth mentioning about the influence of an indigenous Mesolithic population on the *Bandkeramik* culture at its most north-western limits. First, the flourishing flint industry peculiar to this region. In general, flint is not very common on *Bandkeramik* habitation sites. The region under discussion is a clear exception. The Mesolithic flintworkers may well be the source from which this industry arose. Dr R. R. Newell has shown that the *Bandkeramik* flint industry at Elsloo and other neighbouring sites has direct connections with the Mesolithic types in the Maas valley and the Lower Rhine basin.

The second point is that amongst the decorated potsherds is a very small group completely unlike *Bandkeramik*. The whole surface of pot is covered with wide, deep impressed lines (Fig. 83). They very probably belong to an indigenous pottery tradition which can be traced at a site some 40 km north of Elsloo, where a pit containing

Figure 83   Elsloo, Netherlands: Limburger ware pottery with broad bands of deeply incised lines

sherds of this remarkable ware was found. The pottery was christened Limburg Ware, to distinguish its independence from the *Bandkeramik* type. The origins of this pottery are not known but presumably some indigenous culture had a role to play in its development.

A question more easily answered is the kind of site where such a farming community would settle. What attracted them? If we reconstruct the landscape of the time and then consider the site they chose, their skill in choosing it becomes apparent.

The preference of *Bandkeramik* people for the loess-soils, which are among the richest in Europe, is well known. The distribution patterns of the *Bandkeramik* culture and of loess-soils to a great extent coincide. The contemporary climatic conditions were very favourable. It was the Atlantic period, which meant a slightly warmer and wetter climate compared with that of the twentieth century. The primeval vegetation had developed to a maximum. The rich loess-soils must have been covered with forest, in which deciduous trees, such as oak, elm and lime were prominent. Such a forest would be relatively easy to penetrate. Elm and lime which formed, together with oak, the major part of the forest, produce a thick roof of foliage, inhibiting the development of undergrowth.

The greater part of Dutch southern Limburg is covered with loess. Yet, remarkably, the *Bandkeramik* sites are restricted to a small area of only some 15 by 5 km. A study of the differences in the loess-soils makes it clear why only certain areas were preferred. The proximity of water was of great importance. This does not apply only to the direct use of water for man and cattle. The valley would have produced good grazing ground as well. More lime trees grew in the valleys than on the drier parts of the loess. As the leaves and young branches of lime were important as cattle fodder for many centuries, this factor undoubtedly influenced the choice of the site of a new village.

Our site at Elsloo lies between two small valleys (Fig. 82). Nowadays, they do not function as water courses any more; a few decades ago, however, one of them transported large quantities of water when sudden thaws followed a period of heavy snowfall. It is very likely that under natural circumstances the brooks in the valleys were fed all year round from the higher ground of the upper terrace to the south. Nowadays, the valleys have become filled by soil erosion, which has rendered them useless as water courses.

At the very beginning of settlement one would expect a small group of young men and women, with perhaps a few children. The group may have been similar to that of a Mesolithic camp-site, which had a maximum of four or five tents, with four or five persons to each. The group would have formed a true community, in the sense that they would have built up the first hamlet in close collaboration. There are indications that the first houses were of a light construction, as they did not leave any trace in the soil. It is only from the sherds which were found in some of the rubbish pits that we know of these first settlers and of the oldest phase of habitation at all.

Part of the pottery, supposedly the better ware (vessels made to hold liquids) was decorated with simple incised lines. It is a finely polished ware and the vessels are of flat bottomed and bowl-like forms (see Fig. 84). The decoration was carried out with

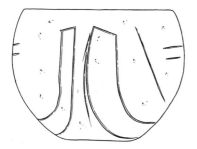

Figure 84   Elsloo, Netherlands: Flat-bottomed pot decorated with simple incised lines, belonging to the oldest phase of *Bandkeramik* habitation (Scale: 1 : 3)

flint flakes. A thicker and coarser ware, rarely decorated, was also encountered. Vessels made from it are bowl-like but they are bigger and generally have lugs and/or handles. The latter type of pottery did not change much in the course of the following four centuries. It is pottery which was made specifically for cooking and for storage (Plate XLa).

Potsherds were not the only objects found. The settlers had their grinding-stones and of course their flint sickle-blades to harvest the crops in the new fields. An implement in use from the first moments of settlement would have been the typical shoe-last celt, known in different sizes. All the sizes were used to work wood (Fig. 97). Shoe-last celts are actually adzes, a fact established beyond doubt during the excavation of the cemetery of Elsloo. This point will be discussed in more detail when describing the results of that part of the investigation.

Flint was worked but the technique employed was of a low standard, compared with the work of later *Bandkeramik* generations. It sufficed for manufacturing scrapers for working bone and wood and for the manufacture of a limited number of arrow-heads and borers.

The first generation of settlers started by constructing the large buildings which are so familiar from our excavations. Their length is never less than 27 m and in exceptional cases over 35 m. There must have been a tradition of timber working of which we have no knowledge. Let us follow the process of erecting such a building, as far as we can reconstruct it.

First of all a large quantity of wood was needed. Twenty-eight trees had to be felled for the support of the roof alone. Half of them would have had a diameter of some 40 cm. For the two long walls, another seventy had to be cut. These would have had a diameter of about 20 m. How such trees were cut is amazing, as the implements used, the shoe-last celts, were only tough stones such as amphibolite and basalt. We have not yet mentioned the wood needed for the roof and other parts of the walls, all of which were of timber. From the excavations at the nearby site at Stein there are several very good examples of split tree trunks, the cross-section of which is either triangular or semi-circular. Thus, a great deal of preparation was necessary before the actual erection of the building could start.

If we look at the plan of such a house, belonging to the earliest phase of the settlement (Fig. 85) we are struck by the great number of posts that once stood inside the rectangle which formed the walls. They are usually seen in lateral rows of three. The centre-post of each three supported the ridge-pole, which means that the roof was gabled. The plan gives the impression that the house was full of vertical beams. A visit to the life-size reconstruction of a *Bandkeramik* building in the garden of the Niederösterreichische Landesmuseum at Klein Asparn shows that this was not so. One can move quite easily in between the posts without feeling cramped.

A further striking feature of many of the house plans of the *Bandkeramik* people is the different way in which the wall shows up on them. Only a small part of the wall is represented by a narrow trench in which piles and beams were set vertically to form a wooden wall. The major part of the wall can only be traced by a number of post-holes. The posts would have been connected by wattlework which was filled in with loam. The loam was dug from just outside the houses, so loam-pits are closely associated with every wattle wall. This building procedure is of great importance to the archaeologist, for the loam-pits were filled in during the occupation of the house with the rubbish of its occupants. The decorated potsherds the loam-pits contain show us what was in fashion at the time when the house was occupied. Houses are dated by the finds from the pits alongside the building.

In studying the house plans of the *Bandkeramik* people in Dutch Limburg, it was possible to reconstruct the internal divisions within the buildings. The houses were divided into three sections. The section which shows up most clearly is that with the timber wall (Fig. 85, left). The cross-row of three posts which connects the two ends of the wall-trench marks the separation between it and the next section. At the other end of the house the plan is characterised by oblong post-holes. This section shows the thickest concentration of posts. It looks impossible to move without knocking into one. A cross-row of normal (not oblong) posts separates this, the south-east end section, from the middle section of the building. This central part is almost certainly where the inhabitants lived, as it is the most spacious, especially in view of the smaller number of posts. It has, as a characteristic feature, a narrow corridor-like room, bordering on the timber-walled part. The remaining area has four post-holes which in plan form the letter Y. This remarkable construction has not yet been explained. The writer would be grateful for any suggestions.

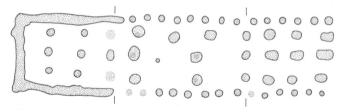

Figure 85   Elsloo, Netherlands: Plan of a house from the first generation of *Bandkeramik* occupation (Scale: 1 : 300)

Unfortunately, no fireplaces or hearths were found. They must have been on the surface, which was subsequently under the plough for many centuries, so that any trace would be obliterated. There are clues to the original presence of hearths in the fillings of the post-holes in the central part of the building. These contained charcoal and bits of baked loam in a high concentration.

There are no indications as to the use of the other parts of the building. It has been suggested that the timber-walled section was a stable and the area with the

Figure 86 Elsloo, Netherlands: Plan of part of the excavated settlement site. The houses are of different periods (Scale: 1 : 800)

oblong post-holes a kind of granary. This suggestion may be right but there is no proof.

There are more difficult questions to pose, such as how was the building covered and where was the entrance? We have no information on these points.

The village of the first and second generation of settlers shows one peculiarity which must be mentioned. It is a feature which lasts as long as the *Bandkeramik* culture itself. A visit to the village would show that all the houses were built more or less parallel to each other (Fig. 86). A comparison with other *Bandkeramik* villages in the neighbourhood would indicate that the direction in which the long axes of the buildings point is between north-west–south-east and west–east. What can have been the reason for this remarkable feature? Probably it was thought wise to catch the strongest wind on the roof rather than on the gable as one might have expected.

Twenty or thirty years after the first settlers had chosen the site at Elsloo as right for their purposes, a small village of five or six big farmhouses occupied it. One of the buildings had a timber wall all around it and it was occupied by the family group which in some way held a leading position in the small community. Perhaps the family included the chieftain or priest or both if both functions were combined in one and the same person.

What happened to the grandchildren in the aftermath of the first settlers? About a century after the first settlers came to Elsloo the village had changed. The houses built by the first generation had long since fallen down and only the sites where they had stood could still be recognised by their descendants. The pits which had been alongside the houses were still partly visible and so were the floors of the buildings which had originally been raised to avoid the penetration of rainwater. Despite these remains there would still have been plenty of fresh ground left for building new houses.

In another respect the village had changed much more. As well as the one original long timber building, there were three or four houses of the same type but there were also three or four smaller houses. A visit to the small type of house would show that the type did not include the south-east section with the closely set posts (Fig. 87). Also, the north-west section with the timber wall did not contribute as much to the length of the building as it had in the first building phase. In one case, the north-west part may have been completely missing. At least every house had a central section.

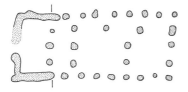

Figure 87   Elsloo, Netherlands: Plan of a medium-sized house from an early phase of *Bandkeramik* occupation (Scale: 1 : 300)

Even the remarkable feature of four construction posts which formed a Y was still recognisable in a modified form. The upright of the Y had been moved to the north-west. A central post was no longer positioned halfway in between the topmost posts (Fig. 88). The original Y-construction must have caused problems or its use

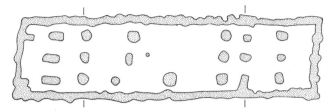

Figure 88   Elsloo, Netherlands: Plan of a big house from an early middle phase of *Bandkeramik* occupation (Scale: 1 : 300)

became obsolete. The builders tried to do without it, as the roof over the living room was the first to sag, as is demonstrated by the secondary supporting posts placed in the open space of the central part of some of the bigger buildings.

In the south-east section, there are no longer as many oblong post-holes but instead, normal round ones. This seems to be a minor change but it is noteworthy as it is of importance for the future development of house building.

If we were able to have a look at the pottery of the century under discussion, we would be confronted with changed shapes. Flat bases were out of date. If pots were placed on a flat surface, they would take a short time to stabilise because of their rounded form.

More striking is the change in fashion for decorating better ware (Fig. 89). More incised lines and dots were used, positioned on the wavy bands and at the end of lines on different pots. The first steps were taken towards decoration covering most of the surface. Just below the rim, a single row of dots or a simple line accentuated this part of the pot. This feature was still a novelty for the fourth and fifth generation

Figure 89   Elsloo, Netherlands:
Decorated pot, typical of a late phase
of the early *Bandkeramik* occupation
(Scale: 1 : 3)

of farmers but by the time of their great-grandchildren it would have been the usual pattern.

The developments both in the plan of the village and in the decoration of the pottery should not be considered localised. The changes in fashion were valid throughout the whole region to which the *Bandkeramik* culture had spread. Connèctions between the villages must have been close. Elsewhere, trade over distances of 40 or 50 km has been proved, which shows that cultural contact may have flourished along with it.

Typical of the villages in Dutch Limburg was the increasing importance of flint working. The technique of working flint was improved, a development which can be followed in the later centuries of the *Bandkeramik* culture even more clearly.

The start of a new period

The halfway stage in the history of the *Bandkeramik* culture meant in many respects a new start. How and where the new impulse began, we do not know. The change is so obvious to the prehistorian that he divides the development of the linear *Bandkeramik* into two main periods, early and late. The term linear is used because the decoration on the pottery is always characterised by incised lines. The ornament differs from the later pointed *Bandkeramik* ware, where the pattern consists only of impressed dots.

The aspect of the village changed again. Only two or three houses were still as long as 27 m, and amongst them was one with an entirely timber wall. Variation in the length of the buildings was much greater than in previous periods. Beside the big houses with a fully developed south-east section (Fig. 90), there are a few with

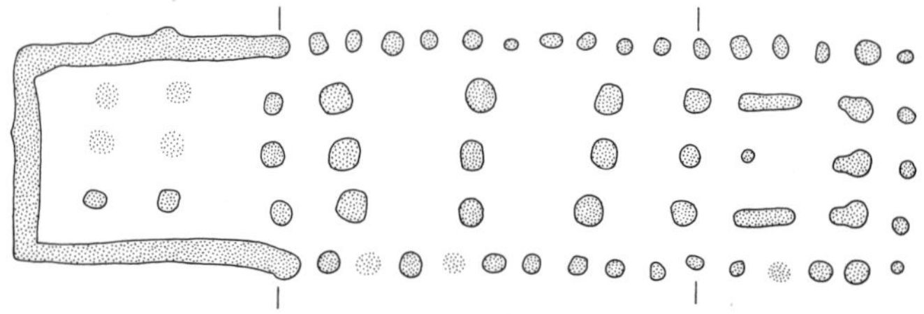

Figure 90 Elsloo, Netherlands: Plan of a large house from the late phase of *Bandkeramik* occupation (Scale: 1:300)

only vestiges of such an annex. Others are lacking the south-east section completely (Fig. 91). The smallest houses consist only of the central section, sometimes with a very small north-west section attached to it, a room which was in some cases only partly surrounded by a timber wall.

The village of Elsloo, in the third century of its existence, would have consisted

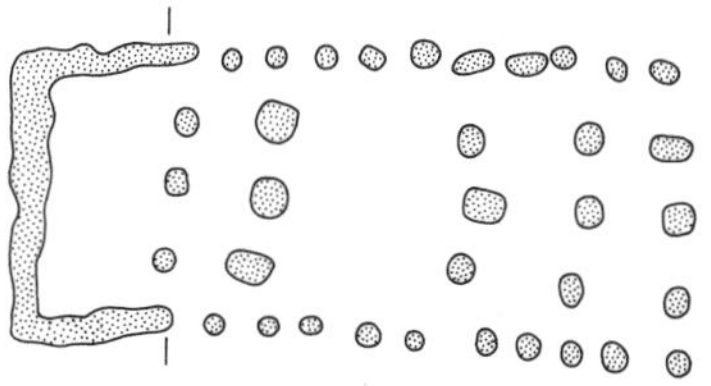

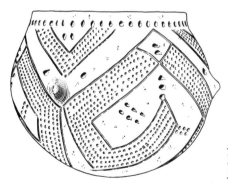

Figure 91   Elsloo, Netherlands: Plan of a medium-sized house from the late phase of *Bandkeramik* occupation (Scale: 1 : 300)

of ten or twelve houses. The increasing number of houses signified a growing population – a development which we are nowadays apt to assume, but which did not always follow.

The differentiation in the size of the houses can only be understood as the result of a social–economical development. What role was played by the inhabitants of the biggest house in the village, with its timber walls, is difficult to ascertain, but almost certainly the importance of the main house was increasing.

In the layout of the houses, the use of the Y-construction of posts came to an end. Instead we find two cross-rows of posts. The central part becomes much more spacious. In the long houses, an open room of 6 m square is realisable without posts. At the beginning of the new period we still find a few examples of south-eastern sections of houses with oblong post-holes (Fig. 90), but soon they have vanished completely.

In the field of decorated pottery, several new patterns were introduced. Under the rim, one or two horizontal rows of dots were always used (Fig. 92). The bands were often filled with numerous dots impressed in regular rows. In other cases the bands were formed by several parallel lines. The trend was to continue to cover the surface of the pots with more and more decoration. For the potters this meant increased labour.

Figure 92   Elsloo, Netherlands: Decorated pot typical of the late *Bandkeramik* phase (Scale: 1 : 2)

To appreciate *Bandkeramik* pottery as it was originally intended to be seen, one has to realise that at least some of the incised lines on the decorated ware were filled in with a white substance. A freshly made pot would have shone, as it would have been polished before firing. The white decoration would have contrasted with the greyish-black metal of the pot.

The newly introduced decorative schemes spread through the western provinces of the *Bandkeramik* culture. This can be explained by diminishing contacts and an upsurge in local feeling, a development which is recurrent in history.

Throughout the whole duration of the linear *Bandkeramik* culture the coarse ware did not change very much. There is, however, one type of lug which is only known from the later period. It consists of a vertical lug positioned from the rim downwards and in several instances protruding over the rim (Fig. 93). Sometimes it has

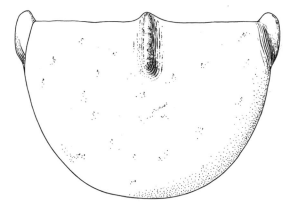

Figure 93   Elsloo, Netherlands: Undecorated pot with vertical lugs, typical of late phase of *Bandkeramik* occupation (Scale: 1:3)

a small finger impression at the top. Vertical lugs are only found on bowls and cups. On rare occasions cups were decorated. It is not known whether these designs had any special use.

The flintworker during this period knew his job far better than his ancestors. We find much better made blades and cores than from previous times. The demand for implements was unchanged.

The swan song

In the forty-first century B.C. the village of Elsloo would have consisted of from ten to fifteen small and medium-sized houses. One large building only was occupied by the most important family in the village. This house was exceptional both in length and in width (Fig. 94). A width of $7\frac{1}{2}$ m was not uncommon for such a building, whereas $5\frac{1}{2}$ to 6 m was the norm. In the central section of the longhouse there was a large room free of posts. The south-east section was now almost as open, which meant that most of the posts no longer had any function. Whether this development was the result of a change in their use in the latest phase, or whether the necessary support was provided by a new technical solution, we do not know. It is worthwhile noticing that only the main building of the village had a south-east section.

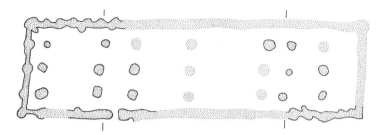

Figure 94 Elsloo, Netherlands: Plan of a large house, from latest phase of the *Bandkeramik* culture (Scale: 1 : 300)

If we accept the hypothesis that the south-east section was a kind of granary, it would explain the fact that the first settlers had a granary each attached to their houses. It is not improbable that after many generations had used the soil for growing wheat and barley, the harvest gradually diminished. Of course the farmers would have moved their fields but in the long run the increasing demands of a growing population would have made it difficult to produce sufficient flour. Corn would have become an economically valuable product, the distribution of which throughout the community would have been an important matter. On such occasions the chieftain or priest was the man who had sufficient power and trust to accomplish this difficult task. Out of the central granary he could distribute the harvest of the village to its inhabitants.

There is one factor which may perhaps support this theory, that is the growing interest of *Bandkeramik* people in husbandry as time went by. This may indicate a gradual development in food production, as the cultivation of wheat and barley diminished.

If we are correct in attempting to find an economic reason for the disappearance of the south-eastern section of the houses during the linear *Bandkeramik*, there is another factor to consider which must have been well known to the inhabitants of Elsloo. Only during the late linear *Bandkeramik* culture were the loess-soils of the province of Liège, in Belgium, occupied. This can be detected from the decorated rimsherds, which all have from one to four rows of dots to emphasise their rims. The relatively late start of Neolithic habitation around Liège could have been the result of colonisation by groups coming from the Limburg provinces and the Rhineland. Such a movement is very often the result of a shortage of food in the existing communities.

The decorated pottery in use during the late *Bandkeramik* period is the result of a clearly defined development. The fashion for filling the bands with decoration at first leads to the making of numerous scratches as if a small brush had been used. The old designs continued alongside the new but the old-fashioned types gradually vanished. One type of decoration took a lot of time to produce. It consisted of long rows of dots impressed into the band. This laborious process became tiresome, so a small bone comb was made for the job, with about five teeth. The latest phase of the linear *Bandkeramik* is characterised by the use of this implement, with which very fine impressions could be made (Plate XXXIXa, b) which sometimes resemble fine wicker-work.

The form of the decorated pots gradually altered as well. The changes which the type underwent can be made most clear by showing what the type was like at the start and what became of it in the end. The bowl form of the first three generations changes into a saggy form during the latest phase; the bottom becomes nearly flat and the rim is separated from the body by an inward bend. The best examples of the late type of pottery came from the cemetery and will be discussed below. Before doing so, however, one remarkable point has to be discussed: the end of the habitation.

Around 4000 B.C. the village at Elsloo came to an abrupt end. At least, there is no continuation of habitation in any form known from the region. In Germany during the next period, that of the pointed *Bandkeramik*, habitation continued at the old sites. There is no factual explanation for the sudden end of the culture in Limburg. Was it a total economic change, for instance to a migrating husbandry? Or was the population severely attacked by some disastrous epidemic?

The cemetery

The great day of the excavation was that on which the first grave was discovered. For months the workmen had been told that the first complete pot found would represent a grave-find. While making some trial trenches in a field, to prove that it ought to lie beyond the settlement area, the find for which we were all silently hoping was made. After two excavation seasons, each lasting about two months, the greater part of a cemetery belonging to the two latest phases of linear *Bandkeramik* was uncovered. The west, north and east limits of the cemetery were reached. It was only to the south that it was not possible to locate the boundary, since houses and gardens were being built on this part of the site by the time the excavations started.

At Elsloo, for the first time in the history of archaeological research into the *Bandkeramik* culture, it has been possible to investigate a cemetery that belonged to a settlement about which much was already known as a result of previous excavation. A number of houses can be seen to have been inhabited by those who lie buried in the cemetery. The characteristic decorated pottery with comb-impression is found

Plate XXXIX (a) (above) *Elsloo, Netherlands:* Pot decorated with toothed spatula, found in a grave.
(b) (below) *Elsloo, Netherlands:* Detail of (a)

associated with a number of houses (for instance Fig. 94) as well as in some graves. Other pots from the cemetery, with a different type of decoration, belong to the same period but one phase earlier. The cemetery can therefore be dated to the last four or five generations of the linear *Bandkeramik*.

Not only were seventy inhumations found in the cemetery but also about forty cremations (Fig. 95). This gave rise to questions about the difference in burial rites. In general the grave-goods accompanying the cremated persons were fewer. To conclude that cremation was a custom of the poor is dangerous, as there were several inhumations without any durable grave-goods at all. Cremations were located haphazardly amongst the inhumations, so no geographical differentiation is possible. In one case a cremation had been placed in the filling of a grave. There is no reason to consider the cremations as a whole later than the inhumations. They are all one complex.

The features of the graves in the cemetery are most diverse. There are only two rules. One is the orientation of the graves, which as in the case of the houses, is north-west–south-east to west–east. There are three exceptions in which graves are orientated north-east–south-west. The other rule (with one exception) is the way in which bodies were positioned in their graves, which is, as far as could be detected, lying on the left side.

It is likely that there was a close relationship between the length and width of the grave-pit and the proportions of the dead. A number of the small graves must have been dug for children. Unfortunately, this cannot be proved, as no bones are preserved in the decalcified loess of this region. Depths of the graves vary. Only the small ones are shallow (about 65 cm). The others vary from 70 to 183 cm.

Once the grave had been dug, the funeral could take place. In twelve instances it could be established from the silhouette of the body that the deceased was laid on his or her left side in a crouched position (Fig. 96). In five cases the head was at the north-west end of the grave and in the other seven cases at the south-east end, which indicates that there was no preference for the direction in which the dead were laid.

The excavation of a silhouette was a thrilling business, as sometimes it was even possible to see the ribs and joints of the long bones. In several cases we found the enamel of the teeth, the only part of the skeleton which withstood the decalcification. It was always a matter of luck whether traces of this kind would be found in a grave, as there was no relationship between the depth or position of a grave in the cemetery and a silhouette. Only the shallow graves never contained traces of the dead.

Gifts were placed around the body. A drinking cup was generally found near the head but the position of other grave-goods did not follow any rule. The number and choice of gifts differed from grave to grave. One of the richest, number 3, contained one decorated pot, three adzes, a flint blade, a millstone covered with red haematite powder and a triangular piece of this blood-coloured stone (Plate XLIa). A further

Figure 95 Elsloo, Netherlands: Map of a major part of the *Bandkeramik* cemetery, showing graves and cremations (Scale: 1 : 900)

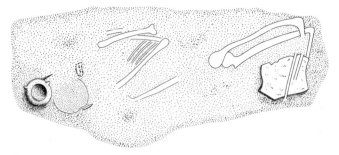

Figure 96   Elsloo, Netherlands: Grave with a silhouette of a body and fragmentary grave-goods (Scale: 1 : 60)

example is grave number 83, which contained two pots, one of which was decorated, an adze, six arrow-heads which, according to their situation, must have been hafted and a millstone with a piece of haematite (Plate XLb). In another grave, a child of about ten or twelve was accompanied by a decorated pot and part of a millstone with a potsherd on it, which apparently served as a small dish.

An interesting feature of some of the graves was the red powder which lay spread all over the bottom. We can tell how the powder was made from the abrasive stones and pieces of haematite with faceted edges which were found. Several examples of abrasive stones, often pieces of worn querns, are known from Elsloo.

Adzes and shoe-last celts were found in quite a number of graves. Sometimes one of each was found in a grave. Interesting observations were made about the method of hafting these stone implements. In three instances the adzes were placed on their cutting edge at an angle of about 75°, with the curved side turned upwards. This shows that adzes were put in graves on hafts of perishable material (Fig. 97).

In graves many of the adzes and shoe-last celts were extremely well preserved. Those found in the settlement were usually rather weathered and the number of undamaged objects was small. This is why the cemetery was a most important source of information concerning adzes. From one adze and two shoe-last celts, information could be obtained about the way they had been hafted. Each of them had been placed with its upper half in a close-fitting hole (Fig. 97). The adze, made of lyddite, shows traces of the protruding section of stem having been cut with a flint knife. The shoe-last celts were loose in their socket, which caused a polished line to develop on the flat side, just where the edge of the shaft would have been. It is too haphazard to calculate the length of the stem. It would have been between 50 and 70 cm.

In one instance six arrow-heads were found close together. The position of the points was such that it is most probable they had been hafted. They had been deposited behind the back of the deceased.

Adzes, shoe-last celts and arrow-heads are known from thirty-one graves. In some of them, a combination of the three types of object was assembled. These gifts may

Plate XL   (a) (above) *Elsloo, Netherlands:* Coarse and undecorated ware from the *Bandkeramik* settlement and cemetery at Elsloo
(b) (below) *Elsloo, Netherlands:* Pottery, an adze, haematite, flint arrow-heads and a blade, all found in a grave

Figure 97   Elsloo, Netherlands: Reconstruction of a hafted adze

indicate that the deceased were men. However, the other graves cannot be dismissed as possibly being those of men. A warning example is a grave which only contained the silhouette of a person some six feet tall. The chance that a woman was buried here is most unlikely.

In some graves, fragments of flint were found. All of them are oblong with a cutting edge but no signs of use. They must have been rejected as blades or they would have been found in pits in the settlement. Still, whatever the flint objects were, they were important enough to be given to the deceased for his or her future life. Discoveries of this kind make the archaeologist think again.

The same goes for the sherds found neatly placed, curved side downwards like a saucer, near the head. In the houses, there may have been many more sherds of this kind which we shall never recognise.

Once the corpse and the gifts had been put at the bottom of the grave-pit, it is possible that a kind of wooden ceiling was constructed over the dead body. In one grave, traces were found of such a construction. Charred beams had been used. A thin layer of charcoal remained, which covered the three pots near the head and could be traced for about two-thirds of the length of the grave. The line of charcoal was parallel to the long side of the grave.

By studying the fill of the graves another interesting feature emerged. There were possible indications that at first grave-pits were intentionally filled with branches and not with soil. This would mean that the space between the branches was gradually penetrated by soil. In several graves, pieces of charred branch have been found. One grave was full of charcoal throughout its filling.

Some graves had a thin layer of very fine clay-like material at the bottom. It was very sticky and shrinks to about two-thirds of its volume if it is dried. This layer can only be washed-out material from the loess. It is familiar from the excavations, especially in summertime when, after a dry period, a heavy shower quickly fills the excavated pits. It may take several days before all the collected water drains away into the subsoil. After the bottom of the pit has dried out, it contains a layer of the same type as the one found at the bottom of the graves. This comparison with present conditions can only mean that the grave was not filled immediately but left open for one, two or even more days.

The dark colour of the fill of the graves is also remarkable. One would expect that at least part of it would be uncontaminated by organic material, which usually causes discoloration of soils. Around an open grave, the fresh colours of the subsoil can be seen. This material is the first to be thrown back onto the pit when it is filled, shortly after the funeral. In this case the amount of organic material in the fill of the graves is much higher than would normally be expected.

Anyone who has been concerned with the excavation of a *Bandkeramik* grave knows how extremely tough the fill of the graves is. It is amazing to observe how the fill is still tougher than the surrounding undisturbed loess even deep down. This can be explained by the fact that the filling of a hole can be made very firm with the help of water. The result is best if the soil is spread evenly with water. This is the reason why sand is thrown in a pit which is then partly filled with water to reduce shrinkage of the soil to a minimum if the hole is to be surmounted by a wall or road. This example is of importance, because it is comparable with the tough filling of a *Bandkeramik* grave-pit. The proportion of water and loess during the filling of the grave must have been such that the soil could precipitate in the water. The branches in the grave-pit would have been of great help in bringing about this action.

In a number of cases, sherds, pieces of flint and other stone material were found in the grave-fill. Small fragments of calcined bone also turned up. They have not yet been identified as human but it seems highly probable they are, because of the nearby cremations. It would be further evidence of the contemporaneity of inhumation and cremation.

Most of the cremations were shallower than the inhumations. The holes dug to bury the cremated varied from 25 to 45 cm below the recent surface, which must be approximately the same as the ground level of some six thousand years ago. There are a few much deeper holes but they are exceptions. One was as much as 90 cm below the ground level.

The cremation pits were only small compared with the inhumations. This fact, together with the small number of grave-goods with the cremations, gives the impression of a funeral rite which was simpler and cheaper than inhumation (Plate XLIb). This impression must not be overstressed, because funeral rites are a very sensitive feature of social life. It might have been merely a matter of changing religious ideas. The practice of cremation is known to the author only from one site near Jena in Thuringia, where they also may be dated to the second half of the linear *Bandkeramik* period. From the early period inhumations only are known.

In the preceding account most of the available facts have been presented. The material has been studied in more detail for the final publication. There is, however, still one point I should like to discuss briefly. It is the major question of how long the cemetery of Elsloo was in use. This would give us a clue as to the density of population in such a *Bandkeramik* village, provided that the deceased were all members of that particular community and did not include the occupants of nearby villages.

Unfortunately, radio-carbon dates are of no use, as they do not give the required precise dating. We need to know for how many decades the cemetery was in use. The only remaining way to acquire such data is to employ the decorated pottery. As stated previously, we consider the pottery to belong to the most recent phase of the linear *Bandkeramik*. From the whole duration of this culture in Dutch Limburg, seven or eight phases can be distinguished, which would mean that each phase lasted on average about fifty years. This is the only possible way to estimate the duration of the cemetery. It may have been used for a century but a shorter period of about eighty years could also be reasonable. The number of bodies in the cemetery implies that the period of its duration covered at least thirty years, as otherwise a very big village, too big in our opinion, has to be reconstructed.

The death rate can be brought into this discussion but again it is only based on assumption. For a comparable community, the death rate would be between thirty and forty dead for every thousand inhabitants each year. Half of them would be children under one year old but this age group can be excluded from our estimate, as there are no clear traces of it in the cemetery.

Let us accept for a moment that the cemetery was in use for eighty years. There are at least 114 inhumations and cremations, out of a possible total of 120, because the cemetery was not completely excavated. To produce this number of deceased in eighty years, a population of one hundred is required, with a death rate of thirty per thousand, or seventy-five, with a death rate of forty per thousand. These figures are only estimates. If the cemetery had remained in use only one or two decades longer, which would have been quite possible, the figure for the number of inhabitants of the village would have decreased. How rapid this decrease would be can be illustrated by a rather extreme example. In one hundred years, with a death rate of forty per thousand, there would only have been 65 persons to fill 120 graves.

The village of Elsloo must have grown to include from ten to fifteen dwellings in the forty-first century B.C. If the cemetery was used for eighty years, this would mean that in every house lived a family or small clan of from five to ten souls. If the cemetery was in use for one hundred years, the number of persons in each house varies between four and eight. What the situation in fact was we shall never know but these figures give a general idea as to the acceptable variations.

All the aforementioned theories have their basis in data collected during the excavations. The conclusions drawn from them are only relative, which we are the

Plate XLI   (a) (above) *Elsloo, Netherlands:* Pot, grinding stone used for rubbing
haematite, three adzes and a flint blade from an inhumation grave
(b) (below) *Elsloo, Netherlands:* Pot and two pieces of haematite, found with cremations

first to acknowledge. However, the spectrum of possibilities is not so wide as to prevent us from forming a picture of an early farming community such as Elsloo. The second and third generation were prosperous, after initial settlers had shown the way. With a gradually growing population, the struggle for existence became more and more onerous. The general aspect of the settlement is consistent throughout its development, with its parallel-built houses, whose number and lengths alone changed as time passed.

Bibliography

Modderman, P. J. R., 'Linearbandkeramik aus Elsloo und Stein', with contributions from R. R. Newell, Elisabeth J. Brinkman and Corrie C. Bakels. *Nederlandse Oudheden III/* Analecta Praehistorica Leidensia III, 's Gravenhage, 1970.

Chapter X

The Lower Palaeolithic site of Vértesszöllös, Hungary

Laszlo Vértes

The discovery in 1963, at Vértesszöllös in Hungary, of one of the earliest settlements in Europe came as a surprise. There was little sign of any possible Hungarian Lower Palaeolithic remains and no one would have predicted a discovery of comparable magnitude from this period.

Hungary is remarkably rich in archaeology. There are thousands of Neolithic, Copper, Bronze and Iron Age sites. The western part of the country, formerly the Roman province of Pannonia, is rich in relics of its occupation, and Migration Period finds are equally numerous. Hungary's great wealth of prehistoric and historic archaeology is due, in part, to its geographical position on the central Danubian plain, between the Western mountains and the great East European Steppe. The country seems always to have been a zone of transition between east and west in terms of politics, climate and animal geography. The Danube divides Hungary into two and forms a barrier to migration. Different groups and peoples have faced one another on opposite banks of the river throughout antiquity.

In contrast to the rich discoveries of later periods, little is known of the Hungarian Palaeolithic. Just over a hundred Palaeolithic sites have been found since 1864 and many of these are of little importance. Until 1963 the oldest Hungarian implements were those of the Mousterian culture found in the mountain caves and believed to have been made by Neanderthal man, approximately fifty to sixty thousand years ago. Szletian and Aurignacian discoveries of a later facies, thirty to forty thousand years old, are also found in the mountains of central Hungary and, in the loess plains of eastern and western Hungary, the oldest finds are those of the East Gravettian peoples, who hunted horse and reindeer on the plains, ten to thirty thousand years ago.

There are also very few Pleistocene human or hominid remains in Hungary. Subalyuk Cave in the Bukk mountains provides one Neanderthal fossil and one cranium and a few fragments represent the makers of the later Palaeolithic stone industries. It appeared, therefore, that Lower Palaeolithic stone implements, of the types thought to be made by *homo erectus* and by Swanscombe man, were entirely missing from the archaeological record in Hungary. However, this shortage is characteristic not only of Hungary but of the whole of central and eastern Europe. Thousands of beautiful Acheulean handaxes are found in France, Spain and England and in south-eastern England there are many Clactonian choppers and flake implements, but the hominids responsible for their manufacture apparently had not ventured far into the interior of the continent. East of the Rhine were a few scattered handaxes and even these were mostly surface finds, of uncertain age. It is true that stone fragments somewhat similar to the Clactonian were supposed to have been found with the five hundred thousand year-old fossil, Heidelberg man (*homo Heidelbergiensis*), at Mauer in Germany, but these were generally thought to be accidental forms and not artefacts.

Different theories have been put forward to explain why there are so few finds for this period in central Europe. It is usually assumed that the continental climate was generally unfavourable to settlement, or that more recent glaciations have destroyed the evidence of occupation. The Vértesszöllös finds, in 1963 and later years, changed the whole context of this argument.

During the summer of 1962 Márton Pécsi and his geographical colleagues from the University of Budapest had carried out a new field survey of glacial river terraces near the village of Vértesszöllös in western Hungary, 50 km from Budapest. The fourth terrace of the Átalér, which is now only a small stream, but was a large river in the Pleistocene period, is partly made up of calcareous tufa or travertine deposits, quarried for centuries to produce quicklime and cement. In one of the workings of the Vértesszöllös quarry were found bones and fragments of quartzite, which were brought for study to my department in the Budapest National Museum.

When I first studied the material in the laboratory, I was struck by the resemblance of the quartzite fragments to those I had previously excavated in 1958, in another travertine quarry at Tata, on a lower terrace of the same Pleistocene river system, not 5 km from Vértesszöllös. The travertine at Tata was in a later river terrace, belonging to the *last* glaciation (that is, from forty to fifty thousand years ago) but the Mousterian industry it contained included many choppers of Lower Palaeolithic typology and was made of quartzite, a material difficult to use for making implements, so that it had an archaic appearance. It seemed likely that at Vértesszöllös we had another Tata Mousterian site. On the other hand, the Vértesszöllös travertine was known to be very old. Fossil animal bones, found in the deposit by previous collectors, showed it to belong to an early glacial stage in the Hungarian succession dating several hundred thousand years before Tata. There seemed to be some conflict of evidence here.

I had visited Vértesszöllös some years previously with a palaeobotanist, collecting leaf and plant impressions from the calcareous travertine, and had looked for stone implements or other traces of human occupation, without success. This supported the view that there were no people living in Hungary at this period.

When I revisited Vértesszöllös to inspect the site of Professor Pécsi's discoveries, what we found seemed to confirm this currently accepted point of view. The animal bones and quartzite fragments were lying in a basin-like hollow in the travertine, under layers of mud and loess. It seemed obvious that the windblown loess had settled on the surface of the travertine towards the end of the Pleistocine, long after tufa formation ceased, and that man had arrived at this time. The Vértesszöllös quartzite implements at first sight bore a close resemblance to the Mousterian of Tata, and burnt bones were found, another fact appearing to reaffirm the Mousterian age of the site. The use of fire by Early Man was known for the period of the Vértesszöllös tufa but only from Choukoutien in northern China. There was no recorded instance of its use in central or western Europe at this time, or for hundreds of thousands of years afterwards. As I also found a few horses' teeth, of which the palaeontologists could only say that the animals had lived in a *cold* climate and thus associated the find with the loess rather than the travertine formation, I felt reassured. The Vértesszöllös discovery could be attributed to the later Würm period, when climatic conditions became more severe, and was a degenerate form of the Tata Mousterian culture found in Hungary, in the milder conditions at the beginning of the same glacial period.

Though superficially attractive, this conclusion was to prove totally incorrect. In the summer of 1963 I made a further visit to the site with a university student in order to excavate and collect this 'Mousterian' industry. Careful excavation showed that the culture stratum was approximately 5 cm thick and that, where it was found in the section, it was enclosed in a rock-hard travertine from above and below, suggesting that it was *in situ* and of the same age as the host rock. From a more or less horizontal horizon about 13 m long, we scooped out as much material as was possible with a knife. On the second or third day, my companion recovered a tooth from the horizon which was identifiable as *Trogontherium*, the giant beaver belonging to the Elster (Mindel) glaciation. The association of the tooth with the cultural horizon confirmed the evidence of stratigraphy. The cultural finds at Vértesszöllös were of the same age as the travertine and belonged to the Lower Palaeolithic. We had found the first undoubted living floor from this period in Europe.

Excavation was carried on for a further week in 1963. Many more quartzite implements were recovered and also a large quantity of animal bones, unfortunately in a poor state of preservation. A few implements were also found in the loess, above the cultural horizon, and with them were found a number of teeth of small rodents. These were identified by Kretzoi as belonging to species confined to the period represented by the Vértesszöllös travertine and therefore confirmed the assessment made of the age of the industry on the basis of the single *Trogontherium* tooth.

A further six months' excavation was undertaken in 1964–6. This enabled us to investigate the conditions under which the Vértesszöllös site was occupied. A complete study of the quarry showed that the quartzite implements were found in four separate layers in the site of the first discovery, later known as Site I. In addition, a number of other sites were found in the same quarry.

At Site I, the two lower layers containing relics of human occupation are in lime mud, the two upper ones are in loess (Fig. 98). To understand the character of these

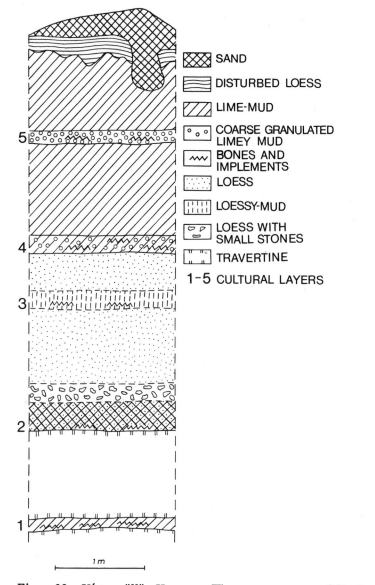

SAND

DISTURBED LOESS

LIME-MUD

COARSE GRANULATED LIMEY MUD

BONES AND IMPLEMENTS

LOESS

LOESSY-MUD

LOESS WITH SMALL STONES

TRAVERTINE

1–5 CULTURAL LAYERS

1 m

Figure 98   Vértesszöllös, Hungary: The strata sequence of Site I, schematised

Plate XLII   (a) (above left) *Vértesszöllös, Hungary:* Excavation at Site I
(b) (above right) *Vértesszöllös, Hungary:* An opened-up area of the first culture-level at Site I
(c) (centre) *Vértesszöllös, Hungary:* Site III before excavation
(d) (left) *Vértesszöllös, Hungary:* Site III during excavation

Vértesszöllös sites, something must first be said on the formation of travertine or tufa, which takes place in the neighbourhood of natural geysers or hot-springs. These springs, over a period of time, deposit their dissolved content of lime, forming a cone of débris, cemented together like a miniature volcano (Plate XLIIa, b). Such cones are numerous and the water flowing down their sides accumulates in a series of natural basins between them, running down in small water-falls from the higher to the lower basins. Small basins of this sort are to be found in every stalactite cave, but in many places, for instance at Yellowstone Park in the United States, or at Plitvica, in Jugoslavia, there are some basins of extremely large size. At the previously investigated site of Tata, these had been used as a camp by Mousterian Man, so that it seemed quite practicable at Vértesszöllös. These basins can only be made use of as a camp site by a prehistoric man when the water from the spring has dried up, or has taken another course. When the water came back it drove the inhabitants away. Thus, at Vértesszöllös, the lowest horizon of Site I, lying on the bottom of the basin, was a typical living floor. When the water returned it deposited a layer of hard limestone, then another cultural horizon was found, sealed by a further layer of limestone. In the two lower cultural strata there were bones of animals of types that live in warm climates. On the uppermost limestone sheet, however, a 1·5–2 m thick layer of windblown loess had been deposited, which was full of the bones of rodents of types insensitive to cold, demonstrating a climatic change from warm to cold between the earlier and the later layers.

In the loess layer in the travertine basin are two further cultural horizons (3 and 4), at the base and at the top of the deposit respectively, and sealing-in the loess is a thin layer of lime-mud, containing further quartzite implements and rodent bones, which is therefore the fifth cultural horizon at Site I. After this, renewed travertine formation takes place and makes the site uninhabitable (Fig. 99).

The fourth terrace of the Átalér, in which our discoveries were made, runs from north to south, and the terrace is covered by travertine for several hundred metres in this direction. The travertine on the surface was excavated during the last century and in some places 15–20 m deep pits were made by explosives. In the sides of these cavities one can see a row of cones, formed by the springs, falling away from the edge of the terrace which is sealed-in under the hill above. At the further side of this sloping terrace are the basins filled with loess, mud and sand. As these materials are worthless from a modern mining point of view, when the travertine was removed in the nineteenth century they were left standing as small mounds with a base of approximately 100–200 m² at a height of 4–5 m. It was fortunate that these travertine basins were preserved, as they contained further sites of the same character as those already described.

The quarry in question is still open, and during exploitation in 1964 Site II was discovered in its northernmost part. This site differed from Site I, not in age but in character. Site II was a natural abyss, or cavity in the rock, with a layer of thick mud on its floor, into which the animals fell and died. The finds from this site are

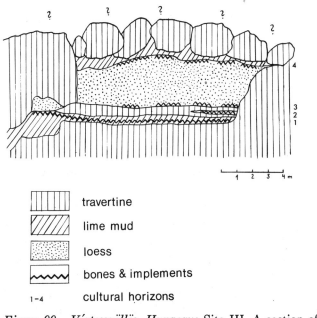

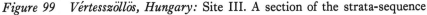

|||| travertine
|||| lime mud
|||| loess
~~~ bones & implements
1–4 cultural horizons

Figure 99 Vértesszöllös, Hungary: Site III. A section of the strata-sequence

being studied by the palaeontologist D. Jánossy. It is interesting to note that while mainly fragments of bones of herbivorous animals were found in the occupation site (Site I), entire bones of animals and beasts of prey were common in Site II, which was a natural trap. Human beings had also visited the neighbourhood of Site II, for we found about a dozen stone implements here. Possibly they came as scavengers, to collect the carcasses of dead animals to eat and this may have been the reason for the absence of herbivorous animals at this site.

Site III (Plate XLIIc, d), which we began to excavate in 1966, is in the southern part of the quarry and also contains five cultural horizons.

The fourth horizon at this site differs from the characteristic living floor of Site I type. At this level there were heaps of bones like those of the so-called butchering sites at Olorgesailie in Africa at the same period. The bones here were not broken into small pieces by man but split open or had their articular ends cut off to extract marrow, and in several cases there were sharp cuts from stone implements near the joints. In this butchering level there are fewer implements than in the living floors and there were no half-finished implements and no chips left over from their manufacture. This is a new activity site, differing from the living floors and from the scavenging area in Site II.

During the Vértesszöllös excavations two types of observation thus had to be undertaken: on the one hand the vertical stratigraphy of the layers was observed, and on the other hand – whenever possible – the horizontal surface was explored carefully and with great delicacy, to uncover the different living sites of early man. Here we find that Vértesszöllös man had walked on the ground; here he had strewn about broken pieces of bone from which he had removed and eaten the marrow and gnawed off the flesh; here he had struck fire. There were even fragments of human bones. Horizontal surfaces such as this were excavated by dividing them into metre squares and these were drawn with a grid divided into squares of 10×10 cm. We made a drawing of every square together with the finds it contained (Fig. 100). Whenever possible we identified the implements and the animal bones on the site and marked them down in the drawings. In many cases there were so many finds on each surface that after drawing and collecting the objects, the square had to be re-excavated and re-drawn several times. The lowest horizon of Site I, for example, was excavated four times.

By the end of 1966 we had collected almost eight thousand finished tools, many chips and a vast number of animal bones from the first three sites at Vértesszöllös. The identification of the animal bones showed that Vértesszöllös man hunted mainly horses, deer, bison and rhinoceros and also, less systematically, giant beaver, a sort of wolf (*canis mosbachensis*) and two bears, *ursus Deningeri* and a smaller form (*ursus stehlini*). In the third horizon the tip of a canine tooth of sabre-tooth tiger was found. Unfortunately, there are no other remains of this characteristic animal, which is understandable when we remember how difficult it was for man to hunt. The hunting methods of Vértesszöllös man must have been reasonably efficient, for neither the giant bison (about a third larger than the American bison), nor the aurochs or the Etruscan rhinoceros were easy prey.

Besides the remains of these large animals, we were able to recover teeth and other bones of small rodents, which illustrated the age and climate of the different floors. While in all the five cultural strata there are approximately the same species of macrofauna, the species of microfauna change from one level to another. Animals such as voles and mice, which are extremely sensitive to climatic conditions, provide a climatic spectrum showing changes in the environment of primitive man. In the lowest two strata we found hundreds of bones of mice and rats of types which were habituated to a mild climate [*mus (Budamys) synanthropus, microtus arvaloides, pitymys arvalidens, plyomys episcopalis*]; in the loess above there were bones of more cold-resistant species (*M. gregaloides, Myodes rutilus* s., *M. coniungens*). Because of the rapid rate of evolution, these small mammals are replaced by more modern species in the next stage of the Pleistocene and are therefore the most reliable indicators of date.

A great many of the bones found in the living floors of Sites I and III had been broken by man into finger-sized pieces. The surface of the breaks have characteristics which Professor Dart took as a basis of his 'osteodontoceratic culture' in South Africa. At Makapansgat in South Africa and in other places where a man-ape, the *Australopithecus*, lived Dart found a large number of bones with a 'torsion break', broken in the same way as those from Vértesszöllös. To judge from their sharp points and shaped edges some of the fragments could have been used as tools.

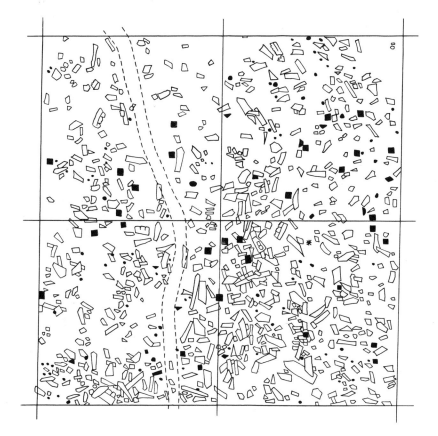

KEY

● CHIPS, PEBBLES

◆ CHOPPING-TOOL

▶ CHOPPER

◭ SIDE SCRAPER

✱ SUBSPHEROID

■ LIMESTONE CHIPS AND IMPLEMENTS

⬭ BONE

⬪ BURNT BONE

⸽⸽ FISSURE

Figure 100 *Vértesszöllös, Hungary:* Site I. Section at the first culture-level

If these were really tools, it must be assumed that the first implements made to 'standard shape' were contrived not by man but by his predecessor *Australopithecus*. But there is one drawback to the recognition of the 'torsion break' type of tool. A carnivorous animal of a higher order, in the course of generations, naturally develops the most expedient method for breaking the bones of the animals it has killed as one of the elements of its specific behaviour-pattern in order to get at the marrow. It is therefore not surprising, for example, that hyenas produce the same type of bone fragments, without wishing to 'make' tools. At Vértesszöllös man did not have any good tools for breaking bones and he, too, used the most efficacious method, so that he too produced fragments similar to those found at Makapansgat. With these fragments, however, we also found at Vértesszöllös pieces whose tips or edges had been shaped with the same technique of chipping as those of the stone choppers. They were unmistakably made to serve as tools. It is significant that while there are only a few dozen of these, there are many thousands of 'osteodonto-ceratic' broken bones: the refuse of the settlement.

There was also another function of the bones found at Vértesszöllös. On the living floors themselves were small but intensive hearths or rather fire-surfaces. These consisted of a 1–5 cm high layer of fragments of burnt bones. Thus it seems that at Vértesszöllös man used both fire and bones for fuel. Both these facts are remarkable.

Previous to our discovery, it was only at Choukoutien in China that traces of the use of fire had been found. Oakley states that the use of fire is first documented in Europe at the Acheulean stations of a much later period at Torralba in Spain and at Swanscombe in England.

The fire-place or hearth of primitive man is usually recognised by piles of charcoal, more rarely by charred bones. Charcoal is imperishable and when any is used on a prehistoric settlement, it generally remains to be found. But at Vértesszöllös we did not find a single piece of charcoal. The use of fire was only proved by the location of charred or entirely burnt fragments of bone. Considering that we found the most extensive hearths in the lowest cultural stratum, the animal remains of which show that the climate was warmer in central Europe than at the present time, we may well wonder why wood was not used as fuel as it must have been plentiful in the surroundings. Of course, the use of bones for fuel was not rare in prehistoric times, nor is it unusual among modern primitive peoples. But, generally, fatty bones are used for this purpose only when there is not enough wood grown in the district because of unfavourable climatic conditions. This was not the case at Vértesszöllös, in the earliest levels. It may be that man in this period knew how to use fire but not how to light it, and that he had to rely on fire kindled by lightning, which he had to preserve carefully. Fire from wood soon turns to ashes. If it was to be kept glowing longer-lasting embers would have to be found. This can be effected with the use of small pieces of broken fatty bones which keep the fire glowing for a long time. As an experiment, I placed a few kilogrammes of fresh bones of cattle upon a heap of burning wood, covering them with a thin layer of sand when they began to glow.

Two days later, I opened the experimental 'hearth' and found the bones still glowing, but the intense heat had reduced all the wood to ashes. Thus my hypothesis would seem to be at least possible.

Thousands of stone implements were found in the different cultural levels at Vértesszöllös. Their common characteristic is that they were made of silica. Approximately half of them are of quartzite, the other half of flint. The most characteristic implements were the choppers and chopping tools. The difference between these tools is that only one side of the first is sharpened, while the edge of the second is sharpened on both sides. These implements are made on rough pebbles from which flakes were removed with blows from a quartzite hammer producing an irregular, often S-shaped cutting edge. Further tools were made from flakes struck from the larger pebbles and with their sharp edges retouched by secondary chipping in order to get the preferred shape. Such tools are generally referred to by archaeologists as scrapers.

The industry in general is so primitive that if the implements were found by anyone without specialist knowledge, they would probably be discarded as unworked. It took us months of study before the different implement types could be recognised. Archaeologists regard implement types as standard products, appearing in large numbers or series in similar shapes and made by the same methods. The Palaeolithic standard types show that their makers had a very definite idea of the instruments required for their life. They are believed to have made them all to standard shapes, from the beginning of the most ancient period of man's existence, nearly two million years ago. Which came first: the idea of the standardised tool for which man then in the course of time acquired the necessary skill; or did he first have the skill and think of the form of these implements afterwards? The tools found at Vértesszöllös suggest the answer to this question. Although they definitely belong to certain types, they are very varied within the limits of these types, both as regards their shape and the retouch on their edges. It is evident that their form was by no means accidental but made according to a precise plan since their measurements – that is, their size and the angle of their working edges or the angle between the butt and the dorsal surface made when a flake was struck off – are always the same. If one measures the standard deviation of these measurements, it is extremely small. This leads one to believe that manual skill came before the exact standardisation of the shape of the tools.

After studying the implements found at Vértesszöllös, it was interesting to see those of the same type coming from Olduvai Gorge in East Africa, excavated by Dr and Mrs Leakey during the last decade. The most ancient Olduvai strata were recently shown to be about two million years old by potassium/argon dating. The latest 'Oldowan' strata are about the same age as those at Vértesszöllös, roughly half a million years old. It is striking, almost startling, to see how similar were the stone implements made at these living sites many thousands of kilometres apart. Their basic types and also their details of manufacture were essentially the same.

The greatest difference is between the size of the tools and the material from which they were made. Those from the Olduvai Gorge are larger, mostly made of basalt, lava and a sort of quartz which outcrops on the surface, close to the living site. The implements at Choukoutien, in China, are also not very different from the Vértesszöllös industry, only here they were mostly made of vein-quartz, which is difficult to split, so that the types of implement are slightly modified. Again, the finds of Locality I at Choukoutien seem to be about the same as those of Vértesszöllös.

In view of these industrial parallels, it may be asked whether it is merely by chance that finds in three different continents far apart resemble one another or whether they were all the products of the same group or related groups of men, who wandered across the ancient world for many generations from some early centre of dispersal. Our present belief is that all the groups of early man did disperse from one centre and this centre must have been somewhere in eastern or southern Africa.

How long do these widespread chopper industries last? In eastern Asia they appear to continue unchanged for a very long time, perhaps until the end of the Pleistocene. In Siberia and Mongolia, for example, it appears that the main tools were still choppers six to eight thousand years ago. But, in general, we cannot trace these cultural traditions later than the Mousterian culture, and the industries most closely related to Vértesszöllös are amongst the earliest cultures in western Europe. The East Anglian Clactonian industry in Britain, which is at least 250–300 thousand years old, is a good example of a chopper industry but it is more developed than those of either Vértesszöllös or Africa, the main reason being that the implements were made from large lumps of very good quality flint obtainable in great quantities from the chalk of southern Britain.

In quite a number of sites of much more recent Middle Palaeolithic industries, some of the tools have a striking resemblance to the products of the chopper industry. This is true of the High Lodge industry in England, or the French 'Charentien', type 'la Quina' and the 'denticulated Mousterian' as well as the tools of the Micropontinian industry in Italy. This would seem to suggest that the primitive chopper-producing human species lived and evolved over a long period of time and preserved its basic ideas of tool-making until the appearance about forty thousand years ago of modern man, *homo sapiens*, and perhaps in eastern Asia for even longer. It has been suggested that the Middle Palaeolithic survivors of the European chopper group of cultures might be called the 'Epi-Chopper-Industries'.

So far, we have described the domestic refuse of the human beings who lived half a million years ago in the settlements of the tufaceous limestone basin of Vértesszöllös. We and our colleagues were, of course, eager to find out more about the type of human beings who had lived and worked here.

Human remains from this period have been found at Swartkrans in South Africa, at Olduvai in East Africa, at Ternifine in North Africa, at three places in Java, and at Choukoutien and more recently at Lantian in China. In Europe, finds from this period were almost non-existent. At the quarry at Mauer near Heidelberg, a human jaw-bone from the same period has been discovered without any other finds. Anthropologically, all these discoveries are regarded as belonging to the species *homo erectus*, although some of them were given other specific names when they were first described, such as *Pithecanthropus, Sinanthropus, Telanthropus*.

In Africa and Asia there are hundreds of find places from which Lower Palaeolithic chopper industries and handaxe industries have been excavated; in contrast there are less than ten Lower Palaeolithic anthropological finds. Therefore there seemed little likelihood of discovering human remains at Vértesszöllös, and when this occurred it took us by surprise.

The first human remains were discovered in January 1965. During the excavations in 1964 part of the mud from the cultural strata was washed through a sieve in the pond of Tata nearby and this was sorted during the winter in the laboratory. As a result, we found many teeth and jaw-bones of small rodents and also many flint and quartzite chips 1–2 mm in length, the débris of implement manufacture, which could not have been recovered in the mud loam by normal excavation methods. While washing the loam, my colleague Dr Viola Dobosi found a human canine milk-tooth. Soon after, fragments of three molars were recovered. A. Thoma states that these may belong to the same jaw-bone as the milk-tooth. Examination of the mud has enabled us to reconstruct part of the left side of the jaw-bone of a child, approximately five years old, from the lowest cultural horizon. Among these specimens the canine milk-tooth of *homo erectus* is the most diagnostic and resembles similar specimens of *Sinanthropus*. Interesting observations have also been made on the fragment of the largest molar, which can also be attributed to *homo erectus* by its measurements and by the so-called Dryopithecus pattern which can be recognised on this specimen. In general, the human remains in the Vértesszöllös site were scarce and because they came from a juvenile, not of great value.

On 21 August 1965 at 1.30 p.m. we blew up a rock which was in our way, on the edge of the living site, and when my colleagues Jenö Futö and Lipót Skoflek wrenched it apart with a crowbar they found part of a human skull upon its interior surface. As a result of his examination of this fossil, Thoma has stated that the occiput found at Vértesszöllös in 1965 can be attributed to *homo erectus*, taking into account all its morphological characteristics. There is only one striking difference between it and the other fossil specimen of this species: the brain of the man from Vértesszöllös appeared to be much larger than that of any previously discovered *homo erectus*. In addition, the impression of the interior of the brain case is very smooth, showing that this human species increased its intelligence, or at least its brain capacity, by increasing the size of its brain and not by multiplying the grooves on its surface. As the fossil is incomplete, Thoma has not been able to give a definite taxonomical place to Vértesszöllös man but has named him *homo (erectus seu sapiens) palaeohungaricus*. Thoma would also say that among the human remains so far discovered, those from Swanscombe are the nearest to those at Vértesszöllös. Probably the two fossils are genetically related.

This statement is interesting from the archaeological point of view, because we know that Swanscombe man – 250,000 years ago – generally made handaxes in preference to choppers. Nevertheless, at a lower level at this site, a Clactonian chopper culture has been excavated and there is also a much younger British chopper industry at High Lodge; so that the tradition of choppers had not died out in English territory at the time of Swanscombe man. However, finds made all over the world show that the smaller diversities in the species of the Lower Palaeolithic Age (*homo erectus*) cannot be directly related to the two important archaeological traditions of that time: the handaxe and the chopper industries.

Another measure of the intelligence of Vértesszöllös man is produced by further study of the stone industry associated with the fossils. I have already mentioned that measurement of the mean and standard deviation of the lengths of these stone tools enables us to investigate the relation between man's manual dexterity and his capacity for conceiving new tool types. However, the standard deviation also seemed suitable for another purpose. It appeared that for each tool type the more developed the technology of toolmaking, the smaller should be the deviation from the standard norm of manufacture, so that its study over long periods might be a suitable means of displaying the progress of technology. If we are dealing not with a single tool type but with all the tools in one industry, this tendency may be counteracted by another. New tools are always being invented as additions to existing tool kits and the number of types made according to ever-changing ideas grows, which would increase the standard deviations. However, the interval (expressed in millimetres) between the largest and smallest tool may be divided by the standard deviation, to obtain a factor which should increase through time, providing one is studying industries belonging to the same industrial tradition. This factor can be plotted along one axis of a graph against the age of the industry so as to obtain a curve illustrating the acceleration of technological development in prehistoric times and a measure of the intelligence of Vértesszöllös man, in relation to the human fossil tool makers of earlier and later times.

Further excavations will be carried out at Vértesszöllös in the future. The work is still far from complete. It is already evident that the site of Vértesszöllös has much of importance to add to our knowledge about our most ancient ancestors.

A note on dating by G. de G. Sieveking

The age of the Vértesszöllös travertines can only be an approximation. They form part of a Pleistocene river terrace system related to that of the Danube itself, whose chronology is established by contained mammalian fossils. The chronological position of microfauna at Vértesszöllös itself is an even better indicator of age, but it is not yet possible to date this part of the Pleistocene with any reasonable degree of certainty, except in a very few cases. Five hundred thousand years would seem to be in the right order of magnitude for the Vértesszöllös industry. A date in terms of years has been published for a sample from

Vértesszöllös on the basis of the thorium/uranium dating method. This is sometimes given as 350,000 years B.P. (Before Present) (Oakley, 1969; Oakley *et al.*, 1971). But, in fact, the Russian scientists dated the site 250,000–475,000 B.P. (Cherdyntsev *et al.*, 1965. See also Oakley *et al.*, 1971, p. 228) and so the central date of 350,000 years could be misleading. Today, thorium/uranium dating, on what is known as the carbonate fraction, is regarded as unreliable, and the Vértesszöllös date, for this reason, has been rejected by a number of scholars (Bishop and Miller, 1972). Samples of bones and teeth from Vértesszöllös have also been dated by another physical method, T/L or thermoluminescence dating, which gave a date approximately 50,000 years ago (Christodoulides and Fremlin, 1971) but this date would seem outside the bounds of possibility, unless the premises on which the present article is based are at fault. It can also be said that the dating of bone by this method has not yet been successfully demonstrated. One would prefer to continue to regard the site of Vértesszöllös as dated by geological means to the Elster Glaciation, for which an age of 500,000 B.P. can reasonably be argued.

Bibliography

Bishop, W. W. and Miller, J. A., *Calibration of Hominoid Evolution*, Scottish Academic Press, Edinburgh, 1972, p. 452.

Cherdyntsev, V. V., Kazachevsky, I. V. and Kuzmina, E. A., 'Age of Pleistocene carbonate formation according to thorium and uranium isotopes', *Geokhimiya*, 9 (1965), pp. 1085–92.

Christoduilides, C. and Fremlin, J. H., 'Thermoluminescence of biological materials', *Nature*, 232, 23 July 1971, pp. 257–8.

Kretzoi, M. and Vértes, L., 'Upper Biharian (intermindel) pebble-industry occupation site in Western Hungary', *Current Anthropology*, 6 (1965), pp. 74–87.

Kretzoi, M. and Vértes, L., 'Typology of the Buda industry', *Quaternaria*, 7 (1965), pp. 185–95.

Oakley, K. P., 'Discovery of part of skull of Homo Erectus with Buda industry at Vértesszöllös, North West Hungary', *Proceedings of the Geological Society, London*, no. 1630 (1966), pp. 31–4.

Oakley, K. P., *Frameworks for Dating Fossil Man*, 3rd ed., London, 1969, p. 302.

Oakley, K. P., Day, M. H. and Powers, R., *Catalogue of Fossil Hominids, vol. iii, Europe*, 1971.

Thoma, A., 'On Vértesszöllös man', *Nature*, 236, 28 April 1972, pp. 464–5.

Vértes, L., 'Bilan des découvertes les plus importantes faites de 1963 à 1966 dans les fouilles du site paléolithique inférieur de Vértesszöllös (Hongrie)', *Revue Anthropologique* (1968), pp. 1–13.

Chapter XI

Ostrów Lednicki (the Isle of Lake Lednica): an early Polish prince's seat on a lake island

Konrad Jażdżewski

A traveller using the great European trunk route, Paris–Berlin–Warsaw–Moscow, after crossing the Oder and the German–Polish frontier, has to travel a little over a hundred miles before he comes, on his road eastwards, to Poznań. Today, it is a city of almost half a million inhabitants, noted for its industry, its university and its trade fair, and is an important communications centre. Some thousand years ago, it was already one of the residence towns of the first, relatively well-attested, Polish princes and kings. Here, too, was the oldest episcopal see in Poland, founded in 968. If one leaves the modern trunk route at Poznań and proceeds in an east–north-east direction, one joins a far older major route, one which, while certainly not so old and celebrated as the famous Celtic Peddars, Icknield and Ridge Ways, which go from Norfolk over the Chiltern Hills to the Berkshire and Marlborough Downs, can none the less look back on a history of at least 1,200 years. It is the road which links together in an almost direct line several places of especial importance in the heartland of early medieval Poland, the territories of the Polani and the Kuyavians: namely Poznań itself, together with Gniezno, the second and probably the most important residence town of Mieszko I (960(?)–992), Bolesław the Brave (Chrobry) (992–1025) and Mieszko II (1025–1034), as well as of the metropolitan church of Poland; and further, in an easterly direction, other towns of rank (in the ecclesiastical or political sphere), such as Trzemeszno and Mogilno and Kruszwica, a town of particular importance, surrounded with ancient legends, whose political significance reaches far into the past as the centre of the once leading tribe of the Goplani; and, finally, Włocławek on the lower Vistula, which was also counted in the first rank of Poland's fortresses at the turn of the tenth and eleventh centuries.

Figure 101 Ostrów Lednicki, Poland: Poland and its neighbours at the end of the tenth and beginning of the eleventh centuries A.D.

On this ancient road, 31 km as the crow flies east of Poznań and 15 km west of Gniezno (Fig. 101), there is another place which once played an extremely important role but which subsequently, in a relatively short time, sank into such insignificance, through the fickleness of fortune, that its lot would have been almost total oblivion had not archaeology revived a great interest in it over the past 125 years. This is Ostrów Lednicki (the Isle of Lake Lednica), a place known in the Middle Ages simply as *Ostrów*, situated on a lake island (*ostrów* in Polish).

The island lies in a fresh-water lake 7 km long and up to 1 km wide. The water flows in a north–south direction and is on average 10 m deep. The main island – for there are four smaller islands as well – is oval, becoming wider at its southern end, measures 460 m from north to south, and has a maximum width of 250 m (Fig. 102). Its total area is approximately 7·8 hectares. Today, the island is uninhabited and its only occasional visitors are teams of archaeologists, anthropologists, historians of art and architecture, tourists and fishermen. But between twelve and eight centuries ago there was lively activity here, and in the year 1000 Ostrów Lednicki was at the centre of political negotiations of European significance. Medieval tradition, set down in writing in the thirteenth century (the *Chronica Polonorum* or the *Chronicon Polono-Silesiacum*)[1] and supplemented by the more or less contemporary *Miracula sancti Adalberti martiris*,[2] as well as by the *Chronicle* of Bishop Thietmar of Merseburg (d. 1018),[3] records that the emperor Otto III, on his pilgrimage from Rome via the episcopal seats of Regensburg, Zeitz (Citiza) and Meissen on the Elbe, to the tomb of his friend St Adalbert (Wojciech) at Gniezno, stayed at Ostrów Lednicki after crossing what was then the Polish frontier at Iława (Ilwa) on the R. Bóbr in Lower Silesia. Here he was received in great style by Bolesław Chrobry, and it was in this very place that the young German emperor is supposed to have crowned the Polish prince with his own crown. From here, the emperor is said to have set out barefoot – but on roads strewn at the command of Bolesław with costly cloths – to walk to Gniezno two miles distant (= nine and a half modern English miles). It was the year 1000. Many prominent personages in western Christendom, in particular those with a marked tendency towards religious mysticism, associated this date in their minds with the imminent onset of earth-shaking happenings. Agreements were already reached here – and especially at that time at Gniezno – between the Empire and the young Polish state that was then rapidly arising, which ought to have guaranteed a common course for both powers for a long time ahead. But with the unexpected death of Otto III soon afterwards (1002), things turned out quite otherwise, and what should have been set in motion at that time was never fully achieved during the course of the next ten centuries. One of the stages where these colourful events, with far-reaching, if for the most part unfulfilled, consequences, were played out, namely Ostrów Lednicki, sank after scarcely more than a few decades into such insignificance that as early as the late Middle Ages the former destinies of this place were known only in a semi-legendary form, and there was puzzled speculation about the nature of its ruins. The 'sleeping

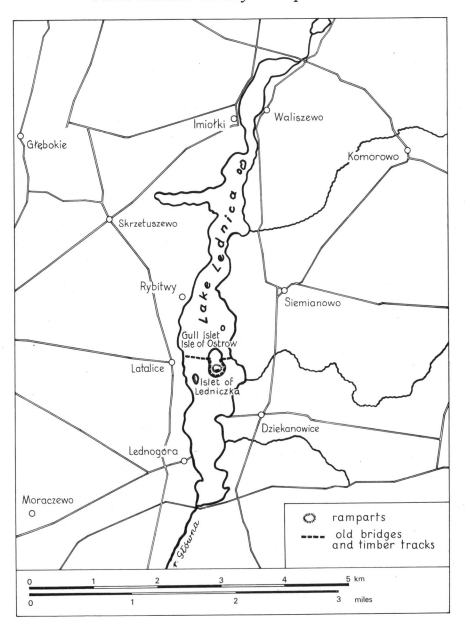

Figure 102   Ostrów Lednicki, Poland: Lake Lednica and its islands, Great Poland

beauty' of Ostrów Lednicki was not awakened from its long slumbers until 1843, when Count Edward Raczyński published the first accurate account of the state of the remains and drew attention to the urgent need for conservation and research. Thus began a whole series of excavations and cataloguing of the material, which, beginning in 1845, have been conducted by successive generations of scientific investigators, with several intervals of greater or lesser length in between. The work of the scholar appointed by the Cracow Academy of Sciences, M. Sokołowski (1875), whose standards of cataloguing were exemplary for the time, must be particularly emphasised. In the past two decades (since 1948), the investigations at Ostrów Lednicki have undergone a great revival, occasioned by the large-scale research programme associated with the celebrations of the thousandth anniversary of the Polish state. The principal contribution has been made by Professor K. Żurowski, Miss Gabriela Mikolajczyk, Mr J. Lomnicki, Mr A. Nowak and Mrs L. Pawlicka-Nowak.

None the less, although an area of nearly half a hectare has so far been carefully examined, we are still a long way from possessing a full and satisfactory picture of the conditions which once obtained here. In parenthesis it may be remarked that, in spite of the application of modern methods of research and the laudable striving for complete accuracy, there are diverging interpretations of the results, in many of the details, among the scholars who have worked at Ostrów Lednicki in recent years. The present writer, although familiar with the site and the finds, partly from personal inspection and partly from study of the relevant publications, has not participated personally in the excavations, and does not feel himself to be in a position to reconcile these divergences in every case. Thus, from time to time, the reader will be offered alternative interpretations.

Now we may let the facts which can be established speak for themselves. First, some remarks about the island itself, especially its topography and its make-up. Its present ground surface has been fairly radically transformed by human occupation, mainly in the early medieval period. Sectioning in various places, mainly in the southern part of the island but to a limited extent in the northern part as well, has shown that the subsoil is clay. Here and there, this is covered by a thin layer of sand. The island is 'hilly'. The highest points of these small 'hills' (some seven in number) reach something over 4 m above the mean level of the water-table. The depressions between them are in places little more than some tens of centimetres above the water-level of the lake, but in many places they are between 1 and 2 m higher. The southern part of the island is the more favoured for settlement, not only thanks to its greater breadth but also because of its larger area of more suitable building land.

Ostrów Lednicki was already fairly densely settled at the beginning of the second phase of the Neolithic period in Poland (first half of the fourth millennium B.C.), as witnessed by several dwelling-houses and rubbish pits that have been uncovered, as well as numerous finds of flint tools and sherds of the Funnel Beaker Culture. Subsequent, perhaps less intensive, occupation of the island is attested at the late

Bronze to early Iron Age transition (first half of the first millennium B.C.), at a time when people of the Lausitz Culture were living here and further, at various stages during the Iron Age, above all during the Roman imperial period and probably during the migration period as well (mainly second to fifth century A.D., finds belonging to the Przeworsk group of the Venedian Culture). The characteristic settlement pattern on the Ostrów Lednicki first became a real development in the ninth century A.D., although the possibility cannot be excluded that its origins go back to the eighth century. The evidence for this depends on completely isolated finds. For example, a pit (probably a habitation pit) 3 × 4 m in size and 3·11 m deep, was found to underlie a timber-framed building of the first half of the tenth century. In it was found primitive hand-made pottery, of early medieval, West Slavonic (Polanic) type, decorated with very clumsy wavy lines and dots.

The results of excavations so far conducted at various points on the island offer a picture – as yet one made up of disconnected fragments – of an unfortified village settlement with different groups of houses on the individual hills. This settlement probably did not significantly differ from the average level of the surrounding villages belonging to the West Slavonic Polani who had been settled here for several centuries. Communication with the mainland was possibly only by skiffs and perhaps by ferry-boat, so far as is known at present. Professor K. Żurowski, who directed excavations here from 1949 to 1960, concluded on the basis of his observations that at about the turn of the ninth and tenth centuries, a small circular fort was built at the southernmost point of the island, with an external diameter of some 70 m and a timber and earth rampart that probably stood more than 10 m high. On the basis of his investigations, he felt able to conclude that in a section cut, as he believed, inside a later wall, he had uncovered a timber-frame construction composed of more than forty layers of oak beams laid alternately across one another (bonded with dark earth), associated with a clay wall on the inside with faint traces of timber constructions. The ground plan of the supposed 'earlier' wall, where sectioned, ran in a northeast direction, while the outer edge of the 'later' wall that covered it went due east (or rather east-north-east). Professor Żurowski encountered the same timber construction again some 55 m north of the south face of his 'earlier' wall. He therefore felt that his interpretation was fully justified. This 'earlier', small wall was dated on the basis of the pottery found within it and immediately beneath it.

However, the scholars (A. Nowak, Ł. Pawlicka-Nowak and J. Łomnicki) who succeeded Professor Żurowski in the direction of excavations at Ostrów Lednicki (1960–5), contested this interpretation in decided fashion. They cut several long sections in the southern part of the island, in a northerly and westerly direction, and they also stripped several areas. On the basis of this work above all, they established that during the second half of the tenth century, levelling had been carried out in the southern part of the island. The main purpose of it had been to make a kind of platform, to create enough space and a sufficiently firm foundation for the construction of what were, for those times and in the conditions then prevailing, grandiose fortifications, as well as impressive official buildings of both religious and secular character. This levelling was achieved by filling up the dips between the various hillocks that were originally here, with timber hurdles and dumped earth and clay. The use of timber beams laid alternately across one another for this purpose was, in the opinion of these scholars, designed to ensure good drainage and to create a dry, level substructure on which to build comfortable houses, in what was, in places, pretty barren countryside. Excavations conducted in the western half of the southern part of the island showed that there were originally two natural eminences here. One of them, some 60 m in diameter and something over 4 m high, lay close to the southern shore of Ostrów Lednicki and had a fairly steep slope down to the lake on the southern and western side. The other one, about a foot lower, lay north of this, separated by a depression 24 m wide and reaching a height of only some tens of centimetres up to a maximum of $1\frac{1}{2}$ m above the level of the lake. The frame construction here, which stretched to the western shore of the island and of which a minimum length of 40 m could be tested by excavation, was constructed of alternating layers of timber beams laid across one another – which frequently changed their orientation (south-east–north-west, north–south, south-west–north-east) – as well as from layers of yellowish–greenish clay. The pottery preserved in this levelling layer consisted of sherds from early periods which, together with the settlement levels taken from various places on the island (above all those of the middle Neolithic, of the Roman Imperial period and from the period *circa* A.D. 800–950), were dumped here at a secondary stage, as well as sherds of completely wheel-made vessels of a kind that in Great Poland may not be dated earlier than the mid-tenth century. These latter, found in fairly large quantity and in various different places on the site, provide conclusive dating evidence. Not less decisive for the dating of this building is the fact that beneath it, on top of the subsoil, three successive layers (X, Y, Z) of a somewhat earlier building on the west side of the island were identified. The lowest (Z) contained, *inter alia*, fragments of totally wheel-made vessels (including pieces of a great storage-vessel with beading running right round the belly). As already mentioned, one may assign the appearance of this type of vessel and this pottery technique in north-west Poland to the mid-tenth century at the earliest.

Immediately above this make-up level (in, or probably at the beginning of, the second half of the tenth century), a timber and earth wall was built with the same frame method of construction. This wall encompassed approximately one-third of the southern, broadest part of the island, and formed an oval shape, of which the long axis (measured from the middle of the wall (in the direction west-south-west–north-north-east)) was some 137 m and the short axis (north-north-west–south-south-east) about 125 m in extent, while the total circumference was something over 400 m. From sections on the south and west, it may be calculated that the width at the base was about 6 or 7 m, while it was probably somewhat thicker on the north side. The prevalence of this type of construction, which is certainly characteristic of an early phase in early Polish fortification-building, should also point to a date in the first decades after A.D. 950. As they now survive, the remains of the wall rise about 6 m above the water-level of the lake and the tumble at its base is between 12 and 15 m in width. One may therefore estimate that the original height may have reached as much as 7 or 8 m. The courtyard of the fortress probably embraced an area of 1·4 hectares. Unfortunately, we do not have exact information about the precise location of the gates and their type of construction. From the sketches left by the scholar who directed the post-war excavations here in 1948 (W. Kieszkowski), which he did not continue owing to his untimely death, it is possible to deduce only that there was a gateway on the south side. Two parallel rows of upright posts flanking the entrance could be detected in the rampart section. In the north-western part of the circuit, where a depression is clearly visible, there must have been a second gateway which linked the fortress with the 'suburbs' in the northern part of the island. Close to the north gateway, on the east, there was probably a watch-tower, to judge from the platform-like extension on top of the rampart-wall. As for the interior of the fortress, that will be described presently.

For the moment, we may turn our attention to the parts of the island that lie out-side the fortress and the means of communication with the outside world. Trial trenches did not reveal traces of a ditch in front of the ramparts to divide the fortress from the 'suburbs'. But, it has been supposed, certain depressions found on the island north of the fortress-wall are the result of earth being dug out to build the ramparts. On the other hand, the greater part of the building-materials for the ramparts, above all the tens of thousands of cubic metres of oak-beams and stones, were transported by water across the lake. The 'suburbs' as a whole have not yet been investigated on a large scale. Only certain isolated sectors are known. Apart from traces of settlement belonging to earlier periods, which intensified in the eighth and ninth centuries and the first half of the tenth century in particular, intensive settlement is attested for the second half of the tenth century and in the eleventh and twelfth centuries, from the content of sections cut at various points through occupation levels. Here and there, traces of small dwelling-houses have been encountered, set some way into the subsoil and measuring $2·5 \times 3$ m in plan. Stone hearths, remains of iron furnaces, iron slag and lumps of melted lead have been met with frequently. Everywhere there is a colossal quantity of pottery sherds (including pieces of a vessel from the late tenth or early eleventh century decorated with the so-called 'chain-link' pattern of Anglo-Irish-Scottish origin),[4] as well as animal bones, carbonised wood and seeds, which have to be recorded. More detailed investigations have been carried out on the western and eastern lake-shores of the 'suburbs' (Fig. 103).

Local people have for a long time, certainly for more than a century, told of the existence of remains of old bridges which once linked Ostrów Lednicki with the mainland on both sides, and the fishermen who operated here used to complain that their nets were frequently fouled up by the numerous underwater piers. Stories were also told of bridges between the adjacent islands, Ostrów Lednicki and Ledniczka,

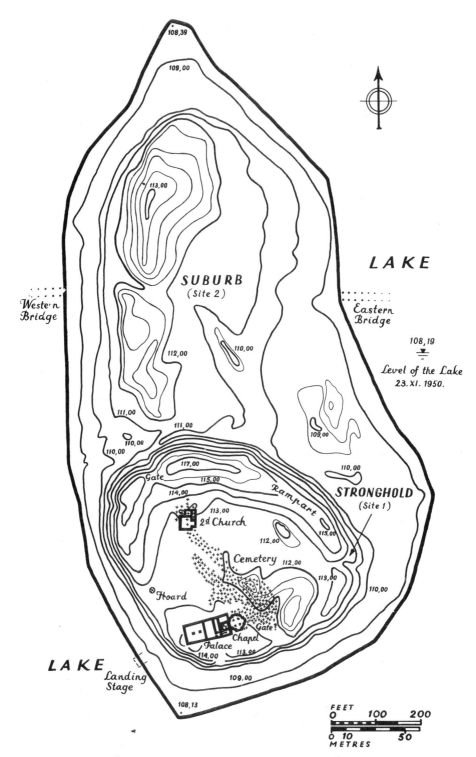

Figure 103   *Ostrów Lednicki, Poland:* The island of Ostrów Lednicki in Lake Lednica, Great Poland

and between Ledniczka and the mainland. These vague reports have now been confirmed to a large extent by modern investigation. To this end, the bed of the lake was
first of all thoroughly combed with a hawser in the places where local legend
indicated that there had been bridges, and also places where wooden piers were
visible in shallow waters near the shore. The sites of these piers were marked by
buoys fixed underwater by amateur skin-divers. A number of measuring instruments
on the shore of the lake then recorded the exact course of the individual elements
of the bridge. Thereafter, detailed work was carried out by skin-divers on the lake
bottom. Using a firmly positioned 100 m² net, with the help of small detachable steel
grids 1 m square they worked along a fixed axis. The details were recorded on
'aquaplans' on the spot. At the same time, stratigraphic observations were carried
out on the lake bed. A trench was dug for the purpose and an 'aquaplan' was driven
vertically into the trench wall. The mud was removed from one side and the visible
layers were traced through. To link up with the research carried out below water
level on either side of Ostrów Lednicki, the bridgeheads on the lake shores of the
island were also investigated. No doubt only limited portions of the whole complex
have so far been examined but on the basis of all these observations one may sum-
marise the bridge-system here at that period as follows. The west bridge, which
joined the western side of Ostrów Lednicki (approximately in the middle of the long
axis of the 'suburbs' – Site 2) with the west shore of the lake by the village of
Latalice, had a length of 438 m. It ran almost exactly east–west with a slight deviation to the north. The east bridge followed this alignment almost exactly, in a west–
east direction on the eastern side of the island and stretched for 187 m due east to
the eastern shore of Lake Lednica, close to the spot where the village of Dziekanowice
now lies, a little to the south-east. To these measurements, calculated on the lake-
bed only, one must add several tens of metres for the parts of the bridges on land,
which carried them over the easily flooded portions of the shore. Two double rows
of piers at a distance of 4·8 to 5·5 from one another indicated the course of the
bridges. The superstructure of the bridges was carried by double piers set on
average 3·5 m apart from each other. These piers stood for the most part in lake
water 10 m deep. They were composed of two pairs of upright posts set close
together (in the direction of the long axis of the bridge), the normal dimensions of
which were 13–14 m long and 25–30 cm thick. They were supported on each side by
the somewhat longer wooden posts set at an angle as buttresses and they were
joined together on top by horizontal cross-beams 6·24 m long (probably about 1 m
above the water level). Above these lay the bridge roadway itself, made of long
battens and cross-planking. The vertical supports for the bridge-parapet were driven
in between the cross-beams at intervals of some 3·50 m and were 6 m apart (Fig.
104). It is reasonable to suppose that there were wooden gates to the bridge at the
bridgeheads, although, as yet, excavation has not provided any unequivocal evidence
for their presence. It is noteworthy that there was no direct communication between
the two bridges, across the island. Excavation has clearly demonstrated that on

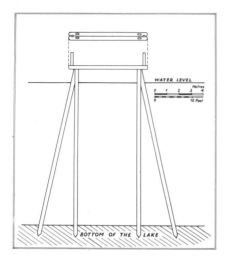

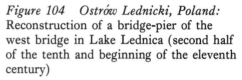

Figure 104   Ostrów Lednicki, Poland:
Reconstruction of a bridge-pier of the
west bridge in Lake Lednica (second half
of the tenth and beginning of the eleventh
century)

leaving the bridge it was necessary to take a right-hand turn to the south, for there
was no direct road going from west to east over the steeply sloping edge of the
island here. There was a good reason for this omission. A prudent assessment of the
demands of security must have made it desirable to cause any stranger, on his
arrival, to pass first along the narrow shore road. On one side, he would have had the
'suburbs' – probably fenced about with wooden palisading at the least – and then
the high timber and earth ramparts of the fortress, the stone walls, several metres
high, of the monumental building flanking it on the south and the massive wooden
south gate-building; on the other side, the lake. Only after rounding a stretch of
road 600 m in length, constantly under watch or indeed even under fire, and after
forcing the eastern bridge-gate, would it have been possible – for one who possessed the necessary superiority – to gain the eastern bridge, whether on foot or
on horseback, and then reach the mainland in the direction of Gniezno. This shore-
road was constructed of oak and birch trunks laid on a foundation of three parallel
beams and was 5 m wide; in other words, more or less the same width as the bridges
themselves. It was found to be in a better state of preservation where the ground
beneath it was wet. Autumn and winter storms and pressure from ice-floes in early
spring must have made such a shore-road very dangerous. Besides this, in the event
of enemy attack over the lake in boats, it could have served in places as an ideal
landing-stage, and to prevent this, two rows of wooden hurdles with stone packing
between them, 2·2 m wide, were set in place, as well as a breakwater in front of this,
made from a row of posts set close together and rammed into the lake bed (Fig. 105).
Stratigraphic observations, both underwater on the lake bottom and on land, at the
bridgeheads, have produced the following picture of the chronological sequence for
the bridge and the shore-road. In the earliest period, on top of the subsoil and on the
lake-bottom, lay a few objects belonging to the time before the mid-tenth century.
Above this was a light-brown layer produced by fallen timber, with a mass of wood

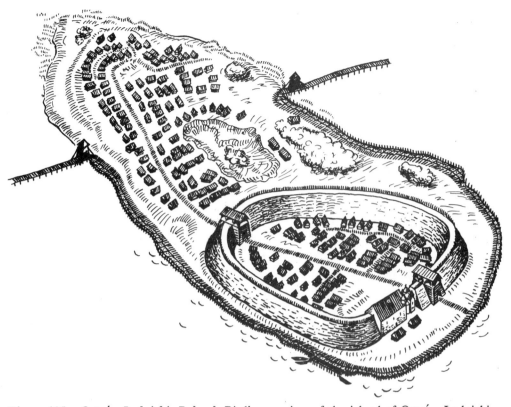

Figure 105   Ostrów Lednicki, Poland: Bird's eye view of the island of Ostrów Lednicki in Lake Lednica, during the second half of the tenth and beginning of the eleventh century

chippings and shavings, various other types of building material and pottery (sherds of completely wheel-made pots) that must be placed in the period around 950 (and perhaps somewhat later). On top of this layer was another thin layer of mud containing a great many animal bones and tools and utensils of wood, bone, iron, stone and pottery. Next above this came a sooty black, sharply defined burnt layer containing carbonised timber, animal skeletons, a lot of iron military equipment and pottery that for the most part was dated to the turn of the tenth and eleventh centuries (Plate XLVIb). This was overlain by a fairly compact layer of mud which included dead organic matter, water-plants and animal remains, and then came the topmost layer of all, a recent deposit of mud containing living organic material.

This evidence permits the following clear conclusions to be drawn: before the mid-tenth century there was no bridge here. Bridge construction was commenced at the beginning of the second half of the tenth century and there followed a relatively short period of peaceful use. Later – in the first half of the eleventh century – the bridge came to a fiery end and at the same moment, in dramatic circumstances,

Figure 106 Ostrów Lednicki, Poland: Stamp on pots of identical type, found on examples from the lake bed, the settlement in the 'suburbs' on the eastern lake shore and in levels from the building period of the west bridge, in Lake Lednica. Second half of the tenth century

weapons, vehicles and beasts of burden sank to the lake bottom. The uniformity of the ceramic material (including identical potters' stamps; Fig. 106) found in various different places confirms the contemporaneity of bridges and shore-road. The bridges were never rebuilt after they were burnt down.

We shall return later, in a wider context, to the interpretation of this set of circumstances. For the moment we may turn our attention to the fortress itself and its immediate vicinity. Let it be noted first of all that – according to Professor Żurowski's interpretation – on the south-west edge of the wall footings there was a landing-place on the lake-shore (Plate XLIIIa; Fig. 107) 20 m in length. It was a timber construction, with clamps fixed across, long beams and planks laid on top of

Figure 107 Ostrów Lednicki, Poland: Timber construction of the landing stage, on the south-west shore of the island of Ostrów Lednicki and an adjacent portion of the shore road. Second half of the tenth and beginning of the eleventh century

Plate XLIII　　(a) (above) *Ostrów Lednicki, Poland:* The clamped construction of the landing-stage on the southern shore of the island. Second half of the tenth century
(b) (below) *Ostrów Lednicki, Poland:* Portion of the south wall of the palace. Second half of the tenth century

it. Of all the antiquities at Ostrów Lednicki, interest has been focused for a long time on the ruins of stone-walled buildings. As early as the fifteenth century, at the time of the outstanding Polish historian of that period, Jan Długosz (1415–80), these remains were already in such a ruined state that their origin was not accurately known. They were variously thought to be the original seat of the metropolitan arch-bishops of Gniezno, the remains of a pagan temple that had later been taken over and transformed into a Christian church and — according to the popular tradition still current in the mid-nineteenth century — the remnants of a palace of King Bolesław Chrobry that once stood here. The nineteenth century, a period so pitiless, with its harsh utilitarian attitude, towards so many of the venerable monuments of continental Europe's most ancient past, was no less unfavourable here too. Thus, for example, the lessee of what was then the Prussian state domain at Dziekanowice, Karl Johannes, before 1837 allowed the ruins of Ostrów Lednicki to be used as a stone quarry. Almost the whole of the extensive quantity of dressed and sculpted limestone that still remained here before that time was broken up and carried away and burned down for lime, to be used for mortar in modern industrial buildings. After the intervention of Count Edward Raczyński, a halt was called to this barbarous destruction, and investigations of the ruins were ordered to be under-taken by the Prussian authorities. But unfortunately, in the course of the very un-professional work carried out by the government architect, Gadow, a stone arch which was still preserved at that time and other pieces of vaulting were seriously damaged (Plate XLIVa). Nor were the subsequent fortunes of the ruins up till the past few decades very much happier and it is only in recent years that one can speak of serious conservation and rational investigation. It is not surprising, therefore, that remains which have been so decimated can be accorded rather varied interpreta-tion.

In the centre of the first natural eminence on the south-west side of Ostrów Lednicki, which was included within the area of the fortress, in a place not reached by the earth and timber wall of the defences, a building complex was erected in the early Middle Ages. It consists in the eastern part of a chapel, a central building con-structed on the plan of a Greek cross and, in the western part, of a rectangular build-ing closely connected with it, the palace (*palatium*) (Fig. 108). Both buildings lie on a line 42·75 m long, on a long axis which (in the east) exhibits a $13\frac{1}{3}°$ curve to the north. The chapel has a semi-circular apse at the east end, where the altar once stood and the interior was divided by four columns (each of them built, on the plan of a quarter-circle, on foundation-rafts which went through the entire room, crossing at right angles). The columns were so arranged as to create a very short nave, $9\frac{3}{4}$ m long, including the apse, and a transept 7·7 m long, each with a width of 2·7 m and entrances 1·4 m wide, shaped like a quarter-circle. The outer walls of the chapel, 1·11 m thick, were constructed of long flat stones (between 30·and 50 cm long) specially cut from drift-blocks of multicoloured granite. These stones were laid in horizontal layers, not always regular, and bonded together with a generously applied

Plate XLIV (a) (above) *Ostrów Lednicki, Poland:* Ruins of the fortress chapel (first chapel), view from the SE. Ruins of the tower in the middle; ruins of the palace on the left. In the background, the fortress courtyard, and behind it the west and north-west sector of the fortress wall (b) (left) *Ostrów Lednicki, Poland:* Structure of the stone wall of the apse of the fortress chapel and construction of the foundations below it, of granite blocks and boulders. Second half of the tenth century

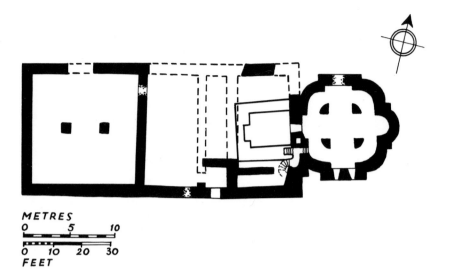

METRES
0   5   10

0   10   20   30
FEET

Figure 108   Ostrów Lednicki, Poland: Plan of the fortress chapel (first chapel), together with the tower added later, and the palace. Second half of the tenth to thirteenth century

and particularly strong and resistant pink mortar containing powdered pottery. In places the walls are still standing to a height of almost 2·5 m (Plate XLIVb). In the entrances, the springers of the vaulting, at a height of 2·05 m, made of a lighter, porous stone, are also to be seen. This, together with the fact that the small window-openings of the chapel are placed very low above the ground (1 metre) and that there are the remains of a circular staircase in a poorly preserved little round tower between the chapel and the palace, shows that the chapel originally had an upper storey with a gallery going round. A dome supported on the four columns must originally have roofed over the whole. Some scholars, observing that the end walls of the chapel have deeper and more massive foundations than the walls of the entrances going round in a quarter-circle, have concluded that only the straight walls (built on the plan of a Greek cross) of the nave and transepts had an upper storey and that the quarter-circles of the entrances were confined to the lower storey only. But on this interpretation there would have been no connection between the individual straight sections of the Greek cross on the upper storey; and in any case this would conflict with the then accepted constructional principles. Excavations in the vicinity of the chapel have demonstrated that its roof was covered with rectangular lead slabs.

Building materials and techniques, particularities of the construction, and analogy, all unequivocally support the view that the chapel and the adjacent palace formed, from their inception, a functional and chronological unity. The walls of the palace – which is rectangular in plan, with a few divergences, measuring 31·5 × 14 m – are preserved to a slightly lower height (something over 1 m) than is the case with the chapel (Plate XLIIIb). Contrary to suggestions that between the chapel and the *aula regia* (12 × 12 m) which lies in the western part of the rectangular walled area, adorned with two square pillars, there lay an inner courtyard, subsequent excavations and analogy show that the palace formed an organic whole. Not only the existence of the pillars but also the presence of circular staircases in the round towers and, besides this, the discovery of an undamaged gable wall on the west, probably 12 m high, guaranteed that there was at least one upper storey in the palace. The function of the individual rooms on the ground floor is relatively clear only in the case of the *aula regia*, with its two pillars. The very narrow rooms, only 1·2 and 2·2 m wide, in the western part of the palace are not easy to explain. The narrowest of them may perhaps have housed a wooden staircase, either going straight up or curving round to the right. A well, 7 m deep, of rectangular plan (0·8 × 0·65 m), is of very great interest. It is 'hollowed out' in the wall between the palace and the chapel and is accessible from the chapel and earlier could probably have been reached from the first storey of the palace as well. It goes down to the water-level of the lake and is constructed at the top of flat granite slabs, with the usual pink mortar used both for bonding and to plaster the face, while at the bottom it is built of closely compacted dressed stones packed with sand but unmortared and it ends in a watertight clay cistern, dug out underground. Excavations have demonstrated the existence of a lime-kiln, mortar-containers and post-holes for the scaffolding necessary for the construction, in the immediate vicinity of the well. Exact measurements have revealed that the master-builders of that time were using the architectural rod (*canna architectonica*), which was made up of ten spans (*palmi maiores*), each of 22·3 cm, and was 2·2319 m long, in the construction of the chapel and the palace. In places it can be established, on the foundations of the two linked buildings, that they were once plastered on the outside and inside. As already mentioned earlier, this building complex originally possessed carved architectural decoration in limestone and stucco. Of all this, there remains only the drawing on the upper part of a single fairly rich, horizontally profiled capital and the reports of ornamental sculptures which have long since disappeared. Investigations carried out in the interior of the *aula* have revealed that immediately on top of the clay subsoil, which shows signs of burning, there lay carbonised timber beams, the ends of which fitted into openings in the side-walls of the *aula*. These must be joists for a wooden floor. On top of them was a layer of limestone rubble and pottery from the eleventh and twelfth centuries as well as later material here and there. Two successive plaster floors have been identified in the chapel of which the earlier, some 40 to 70 cm lower, corresponds to the wooden floor of the *aula* in the palace. As far as my personal observation can tell, the timber-framed constructions mentioned earlier stretch from the east to a point close to the outer wall of the chapel, but no trace of them has been discovered beneath it (Plate XLVb). The pottery from the levels sectioned immediately south of the palace, which antedate the building of the palace, belongs to completely wheel-made vessels and cannot be assigned to a period *earlier* than the mid-tenth century. It is also important that the remains of a rectangular pit-dwelling, with the same east—west long axis as the palace, has been uncovered here, in other words on the outermost southern edge of the first (southern) natural rise, on which the palace and chapel were erected, right on the slope which drops down to the lake shore and 1·2 m from the southern wall of the palace. This building, 7 m long and 5 m wide, was sunk 1·4 m into the subsoil and cuts through a further 20 cm of humus above that. A passage-way, like a *dromos*, flanked by vertical stakes on either side, led up to it from the west, measuring 4·1 m long by 2·4 m wide. The side-walls of the building were in all probability built in block-construction and the interior was divided into two rooms of unequal size, one measuring 5 × 4 m and the other 5 × 3 m. The pottery from here indicates that this building, probably a watch-tower near the south gateway of the fortress, belongs to the period after 950 and is approximately contemporary with the building of the eastern bridge and earlier than the palace and chapel. There are signs that it was then abandoned, owing to the excessive dampness of its underground floor level — thick layers of accumulated material on its wooden floor and a hearth outside the building.

East of this but still in front of the southern face of the palace, remains of a wooden storehouse have been uncovered. It had been destroyed by fire and its contents were revealed by pieces of carbonised sacks and a mass of burnt corn (wheat and barley) and peas, found in great heaps presumably deriving from these sacks.

How then is one to assess this set of facts in its wider context? The archaeological evidence and the scanty literary sources, based on long-lived oral traditions, give a fairly united verdict in favour of the view that the great building programme which fundamentally altered the existing character of Ostrów Lednicki belongs to the second half of the tenth century. That is, roughly speaking, the reigns of the two most important rulers of the Piast dynasty, during the early period of the Polish state, Mieszko I and Bolesław the Brave (Chrobry). The rapidly rising monarchy was, precisely in the first decades of the second half of the tenth century, engaged in a process of unification that was suddenly gathering momentum. Its assumption of Christianity in its western, Roman form in the year 966 involved it in thoroughgoing changes in many spheres. Everything supports the view that it was Mieszko I on whose orders, perhaps as early as the late fifties or, more probably, the sixties of the tenth century, a start was made with the development of a large-scale building programme at Lake Lednica, on the island Ostrów Lednicki. Ostrów Lednicki was destined for the role of an official residence of the Polish rulers, situated as it was between two alternately used residence towns of which one, Poznań, was the first episcopal see, as early as 968, and was the place where, after their deaths, the two aforementioned princes of the Piasts were laid to rest, while the other, Gniezno, was promoted in the year 1000 to become the permanent ecclesiastical metropolis of all Poland. Ostrów Lednicki was protected on the west by what was then, no doubt, the strongest fortress in all Poland, Poznań on the Warta, and further by a chain of lakes on the road that led here from Poznań (north of the river Główna).

Plate XLV   (a) (left) *Ostrów Lednicki, Poland:* Oak dug-out, 10·2 m in length, from the lake bottom near the west bridge. Probably from the year 1038
(b) (right) *Ostrów Lednicki, Poland:* Lower beams of the frame construction of the wall, immediately north-east of the fortress chapel (the first chapel). Beginning of the second half of the tenth century A.D.

Likewise on the east it was protected by the markedly closer Gniezno, with the double defensive system of the fortress there and its strongly walled outer works. The site for this projected princely residence had good security itself, both from its natural defences and from the extra man-made additions to its defensive capability. In view of the necessity of providing heavy building-materials, especially for the stone buildings (granite blocks, quarried limestone, significant quantities of lead and so forth), a start was probably made with the construction of solid bridges. Calculations have shown that to build the palace and chapel must have required 1,300 m³ of granite. It would probably have taken some 7,000 double-spanned wagons to transport such a mass of stone at that time. The tens of thousands of cubic metres of oak, birch and pine beams and planks to build the bridge gates, the landing-stage, roads, fortress wall and gates, ordinary dwelling houses and farm buildings, probably reached the island for the most part by water (on rafts and perhaps on ferries). It is not certain whether the supply of timber in the surrounding forest sufficed for the colossal requirements and it is reasonable to suppose that part of the lighter building materials (but also a great deal of earth and stones to make up the ramparts) was transported here overland and came over the bridges to Ostrów Lednicki.

Mieszko I, who frequently (especially in the 970s) stayed at the Imperial Court and who also had active contacts from the start and throughout his reign with Bohemia and Moravia, certainly had sufficient opportunity to familiarise himself with the ideas then current among the leading circles, both in his neighbours further to the west and those closer to him in the south-west. Carolingian and Ottonian practices, with considerable Byzantine elements too, were of decisive influence on the building programme launched at Ostrów Lednicki. It was, naturally, adapted to the conditions there prevalent and to the capabilities of the young state. If the tradition, first written down in the late Middle Ages but probably stretching back several centuries earlier, is correct, that the chapel at Ostrów Lednicki was dedicated by Mieszko's first wife, the Bohemian princess Dobrava (Dobravka, Dąbrówka), in honour of Mary the Holy Mother of God, then its foundation must have taken place not later than the year 977, the year of this princess's death. When the Emperor Otto III was received here, according to tradition, with such pomp and ceremony in the year 1000, the palace together with the chapel must already have been built. Although one cannot rule out Bolesław Chrobry (after his accession in 992) as the builder of the monumental stone buildings at Ostrów Lednicki, one is nonetheless more inclined to regard Mieszko and Dobrava as the founders of the palace and chapel, if one wishes to remain in tune with the tradition and if one regards a period of some eight or nine years as much too short for the completion of what must have been, for the prevailing conditions and the possibilities of the place, a very lengthy and expensive building programme.

It is very interesting to note that in recent times, at two other places within the territories of Mieszko I and Bolesław Chrobry, remains have been discovered of remarkably similar palaces with chapels. One of these is 24 km south of Ostrów Lednicki, within an enormous fortress wall, at Giecz (in the district of Środa), in central Great Poland. There, foundations had been marked out with boulders of a building that was never completed, which in plan and size could almost serve as a copy of Ostrów Lednicki. Here, too, there were clear indications that the building of a palace with an upper storey was planned. The only difference is that the chapel, which, in the same way as that at Ostrów Lednicki, was to have been linked with the secular building, was designed here as a simple rotunda without apse or internal divisions. The death of Bolesław Chrobry in 1025, or at latest the disturbances in Poland in the years 1034–8, probably caused work on this building complex at Giecz to be brought to an end. This discovery is of particular importance for the history of the palace and chapel at Ostrów Lednicki in so far as it decisively demonstrates the contemporaneity of the two buildings, the absence of an inner courtyard, the uniformity of the building principles and so much else besides. The second case is at the fortress at Przemyśl on the San, in the south-eastern corner of Poland, in an area which at that time fluctuated between Poland and the empire of Kiev. Foundations are preserved here of buildings erected either before 981, or, more probably, between 1018 and 1031. Here, too, the plan and the scale are unusually similar to that of Ostrów Lednicki, only here one knows virtually nothing of the internal arrangements of the secular building, while the chapel (a rotunda) here has three-quarters of a circle apse. But, in spite of the modifications, one can see here that one and the same principle was decisive in the building of these structures. At Ostrów Lednicki, the plan reached its greatest development (as one sees above all in the elaboration of the chapel) and it was probably – with certain simplification – the model for the later building at Giecz and Przemyśl, very likely as early as the time of Bolesław Chrobry in the 1020s (Fig. 109).

The fortress, together with the palace, the chapel and the other adjacent buildings and storehouses on Ostrów Lednicki and the great bridges leading to the island, were not to have a long life. They probably lasted somewhat more than half a century but certainly less than a hundred years. After decades of continuously growing prosperity and increasing power, to which the Polish Chronicle of the so-called Gallus Anonymus, concluded in 1113, bears eloquent testimony, came a severe crisis, which threatened almost the very existence of the young Polish state. The first serious symptoms of this crisis were already marked in 1031, when Poland was simultaneously attacked from the west, by the German Empire, and from the east, by the empire of Kiev, and had to suffer heavy losses of territory. Bolesław Chrobry's son and successor, Mieszko II, was compelled to seek refuge abroad. The troubles which followed – internal struggles, the death or expulsion of several candidates for the throne, the collapse of the central government and of the unity of the state and the outbreak of a popular rising – reached their conclusion in the year 1038, or rather 1039, in a large-scale invasion by the Bohemian prince Břetislav, whose army overran Silesia and entered the heartland of the state, Great Poland, without meeting serious

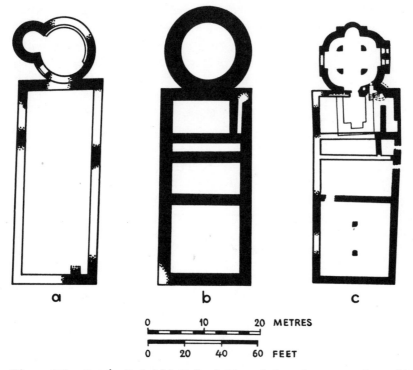

Figure 109   Ostrów Lednicki, Poland: Plan of the palaces, together with the associated fortress chapels: (a) at Przemyśl (S.E. Poland); (b) at Giecz (Great Poland); (c) at Ostrów Lednicki (Great Poland). End of the tenth and beginning of the eleventh century

resistance. The principal fortresses and towns of this part of the country – Giecz, Gniezno and Poznań – fell into the hands of the invader and were plundered and sacked. As a result of the murder of a large part of the clergy, including several bishops, and the destruction of the most important episcopal residences (including the metropolitan archbishopric of Gniezno), the ecclesiastical organisation of Poland was badly shattered for several years. Only after the passing of a few years was it possible, with great effort and for the most part on a sharply reduced scale, to re-build the organisation of state and church. The centre of gravity of the state had, however, decisively shifted to Little Poland, with its capital at Cracow. The former residence-towns of Gniezno and Poznań and principal fortresses, such as Giecz, never again (except for periods of short duration) regained their original political or social and economic importance. Even the status of Gniezno as the metropolitan church of Poland was for a time seriously in doubt but it did manage to retain it for later centuries.

In this general collapse, fate did not spare Ostrów Lednicki either. It appears that the residence of the first completely historic representatives of the Piast dynasty, defended both by nature and by the arts of fortification, remained intact throughout the period of disturbances. But the indirect testimony of the historical sources and the direct evidence of archaeology show that when the political leadership of the state had been crippled, it could not resist the superior power of the foreign foe. From everything that is known, we must suppose that the war bands of Břetislav took the fortress and the outer works and destroyed the palace. Only the chapel probably remained relatively unharmed. But all this did not take place without any resistance. It is above all the excavations on the bottom of Lake Lednica which have provided observations and finds which give eloquent testimony to the dramatic events of that time. Thus, for example, close to the west bridge, some tens of metres out from the western shore of the island, a number of iron battle axes were found on the lake bottom, within a layer of burning, including some with carbonised hafts still in the socket, also several iron spearheads, an iron spur, the skeletons of three or four horses and three boats (dug-outs hewn from single tree-trunks) which lay partly damaged under the carbonised remains of the bridge (Plate XLVa). In one of the boats (which was made of oak, with two cross-planks) was found a dog's skeleton, with two buttons, morello cherry and plum stones, a complete wheel-made pot and several sherds of pottery. At the bridgehead of the west bridge was found, at the bottom of the destruction and burning layer, a sword of the X-type, with a lentiform pommel and straight cross-piece (a style belonging to the second half, or end, of the tenth century). Further, in the lake by the east bridge, which also displayed everywhere signs of burning on the piers and planking, was found a cone-shaped iron helmet, made in one piece, with a rectangular nose-guard, provided with a little hook underneath (Plate XLVIb). The best parallels for this helmet are in Bohemia and Moravia (the parade helmet of St Vaclav [Wenceslas] from Prague and, in particular, the helmet from Olomouc) with forms which can be dated to the eleventh century and interpreted as Bohemian, although they were also in use outside the Czech lands somewhat earlier than this and after this date too. From the finds as a whole, one may deduce that a battle took place on the bridge between cavalry and infantry, as a result of which many items of arms and armour, dead beasts and probably men too were thrown into the water, and the bridges themselves, set on fire by the attackers, went up in flames and buried in their fall men in boats who were perhaps taking part in the battle. At the same time, too, the entire fortress with its timber fortifications, the palace and the wooden farm and other dwelling houses were burned down.

After this total destruction, a completely new chapter in the history of Ostrów Lednicki began. From now on, it was a prince's seat no longer. The subsequent period could not lend the great island its former glory. The great fortress with the earth and timber fortifications in the southern part of the island was certainly never re-built. Only its sacked ruins remained, in the shape of the wall-circuit, today 6 m high. The two bridges were never again re-built and the shore-road which encircled the fortress from the south was in time abandoned. Only the fortress chapel on the southern edge of the fortress remained standing next to the ruins of the burned-out palace and probably continued – although somewhat damaged – in use for divine service. It seems that the grandson of Bolesław Chroby, Prince Casimir the Renovator, when he launched the reconstruction of the badly shattered Polish state, attempted once more to resume his links with the old tradition of the famous family home of the Piasts (Plate XLVIc). There are vague notices about this preserved in the Silesian Chronicles of the thirteenth and fourteenth centuries (*Chronica Polonorum vel Chronicon Polono-Silesiacum, Chronica Principum Poloniae cum eorum gestis*), to the effect that this prince, before a decisive battle, sought and found spiritual sustenance precisely in the fortress chapel founded by his grandmother, Dobravka (Dąbrówka), at Ostrów Lednicki. However, he later transferred his seat to the south of the country, to Cracow, and the rulers of Poland never more returned to Ostrów Lednicki. The whole place then played a narrowly restricted local role in the following few centuries, and by the turn of the fourteenth and fifteenth centuries it had completely disappeared from the view of history. In 1136 Ostrów Lednicki was included among the places of which the tithes (*decimationes*) belonged to the archbishop at Gniezno. In 1234 a prince of the principality of Great Poland was prepared eventually to relinquish the *castrum Ostrów* to the archbishop at Gniezno and in 1235, 1257, 1284, 1352, 1397 and for the last time in 1404, the office of the castellan, or the castellan himself, is mentioned in the written sources; while the historian Jan Długosz, already mentioned above, who composed his twelve-volume *Historia Polonica* or *Annales seu cronicae incliti Regni Poloniae* between 1455 and 1480, could report only on the shattered ruins of the chapel and the palace but of nothing else remaining at Ostrów Lednicki.

Archaeological finds provide evidence that life on the islands of Lake Lednica moved on normal plain and simple lines from the mid-eleventh century onwards. A hoard of sixteen silver coins (denars and pfennigs) found in the fortress courtyard, at the foot of the western inner side of the ruined wall-circuit, some 30 m from the north-west corner of the palace ruins, between 20 and 50 cm below the modern ground surface, shows that in the sixties or seventies of the eleventh century a moderately prosperous person had to conceal his wealth below the ground in what were, no doubt, dangerous circumstances and that he was never in a position to retrieve his hidden property. Among the silver pfennigs, of which the earliest belongs to the years 1027–54 and the latest to the period 1064–74, are two German (including one of Bishop Bernold from the Netherlands mint of Deventer), twelve so-called *Wendenpfennige* (Cross pfennigs) and one Bohemian (of Břetislav I) as well as a Hungarian one.

In the northern part of the fortress courtyard, on the second natural eminence, which was originally included in the building area of the fortress in the second half of the tenth century, at the foot of the inner side of the original wall and 75 m north of the palace ruins, the remains of a second sacred building, probably a funerary chapel or church, or a mausoleum, were discovered in the course of recent excavations. All that survived were the ghost-walls of the foundations (foundation-trenches 90 cm wide) with, in places, pieces of the granite drift-blocks and the clay

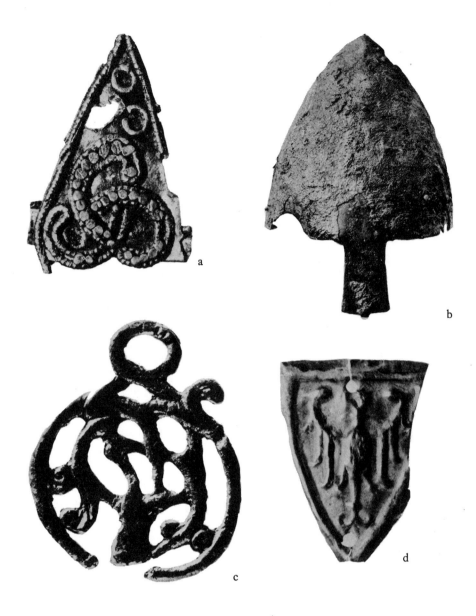

Plate XLVI   (a) *Ostrów Lednicki, Poland:* Golden plate with filigree decoration, found close to the palace (1·5 cm long). Probably from the fortress courtyard. Eleventh or twelfth century (Scale : 4 : 1)

(b) *Ostrów Lednicki, Poland:* Iron helmet with nose-guard from the lake bottom, probably A.D. 1038 (Scale : approx. 2 : 7)

(c) *Ostrów Lednicki, Poland:* Decorated pendant of lead and tin (engraved) found near the burial chapel (second chapel). Probably second half of the twelfth century

(d) *Ostrów Lednicki, Poland:* Small bronze foil shield with the arms (white eagle) of the Polish (Piasten) state (2·5 cm in length). Found in the fortress courtyard. Probably thirteenth century (Scale : approx. 2 : 1)

bonding and bedding within the foundation-trenches. This second chapel was orientated on a strict east–west bearing and was 13·5 m long. The almost square nave (9·5 × 10 m on the outside) was joined on the east end by a rectangular apse 3 × 6·5 m on the outside (Fig. 110). It is certain that this building was erected after the destruction by fire in 1038 (and not before, as supposed by A. Nowak and J. Łomnicki), because its foundations cut through the burning layer. Although it cannot be excluded that the upper storey of this church was of timber construction on stone foundations, one may likewise reckon with the possibility that a stone church existed here. Similar ground plans are known in several places in Poland (for example, Cracow – the earliest church of St Adalbert and Konin-Stare Miasto

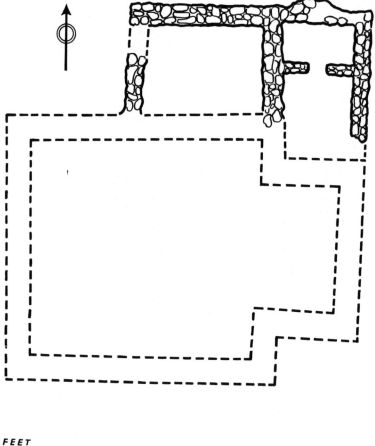

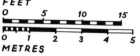

Figure 110   Ostrów Lednicki, Poland: Plan of the burial chapel (second chapel). Second half of the eleventh to thirteenth century

[the old town] — the church of St Peter and St Paul) and are characteristic of Romanesque parish churches in both town and country in the period from the eleventh to the first half of the thirteenth centuries. Beneath the clay spread of the second chapel were found two stone-built graves, set on an east–west alignment on either side of the square nave. They probably belonged to two particularly prominent persons, the first to be buried here. A gold ring from one of these graves (of a child) is another possible clue in this direction. Later, deceased members of the same family or their kinsfolk (in many cases children) for whom the chapel was built as a family sepulchre, found their last resting place in small cell-like subsidiary structures lying on the north side, made of limestone, bog-iron ore and fragments of granite (in *opus emplectum* technique), and also outside it, close to the northern chapel wall, in many cases beneath plaster-slabs. The date at which the second chapel and the associated graves came into being can be indirectly calculated on the basis of the following additional observations. Parallel to the north side of the chapel, at its north-west corner and west of the cell-like constructions, and beneath the graves here (outside the chapel), were found the remains of two timber dwelling houses of almost square ground plan. On the floor of one of the houses (measuring $4 \times 5 \cdot 6$ m), overlain by the graves, was uncovered a fine liturgical horn comb as well as a small bronze cross with arms of equal length. This comb is particularly noteworthy, for it is an import from western Europe, which, derived from a Syrian original and developed in an Irish–Scottish milieu, finally reached Poland via France, Germany and Bohemia. It is decorated on the neck with the silhouette of a couchant lion, on one side with a rosette and on the other side with a simple plant-design. Combs like this served a ritual purpose in the church. Fairly close parallels are known from the old city of Lübeck, Lund in southern Sweden (mid-eleventh century) and Prague in Bohemia.[5] The bronze cross has three arms branching out (one of them is broken off) and shows traces of a figure of Christ that was originally attached to it. Probably these houses were inhabited by a priest (probably the chaplain of the *first* fortress chapel) and were destroyed in the fire which encompassed the whole fortress. Thus it seems they existed between ca. 970 and 1038. The second chapel, the clay spread from which overlies this burning level, fills the interior of the houses and covers them over and cannot, therefore, have come into existence before the second half of the twelfth century. It is possible that it was in use during the twelfth century and beyond. Evidence for this is provided both by the material from the occupation level above the clay spread (mainly sherds of strongly turned vessels with cylindrical necks), and by various small finds of bronze and lead, and further by the decorated horn inlay of a casket from the adjacent grave cell on the north and by a gilded, portable bronze reliquary (pectoral), in the shape of a Greek cross, uncovered in the destruction layer outside the chapel among the graves to the north of it, with the remains of its leather case still adhering to it. This pectoral cross is certainly of Byzantine origin, as is shown by the double arms of the cross and by the Christ monogram on it composed of two Greek letters. The chapel, which probably had a wooden roof, is unlikely to have survived beyond the middle of the thirteenth century.

It was probably in the course of the twelfth century but at the latest at the beginning of the thirteenth century that an addition was made to the earlier, first (fortress) chapel. It consisted of a tower several storeys high and over 6 m in width, abutting directly into the west side of the old fortress chapel and connected with it through the west entrance on the ground floor. A straight, narrow stone stair was also built, leading from the chapel to the upper part of the tower. The window-sill was raised and the amount of light provided for the chapel was thereby reduced, its floor-level was raised by some 40–70 cm and its walls were reinforced on the outside. The tower was built of re-used stone from the old palace ruins, in which it stood. Its long axis was aligned at a rather sharp angle to the long axis of the former palace and its foundations (of *opus spicatum*) rested in places on earlier palace walls. The walls of the tower were faced on the outside with squared granite (*opus quadratum*) and on the inside with broken granite (*opus emplectum*), bonded with lime mortar and here and there strengthened with timber through-beams, in spaces left free for the purpose. The whole thing was covered on the ground floor by a barrel-vaulted roof, while on the upper storey was a gallery opening into the chapel and linked with the chapel galleries (Figs 111, 112, 113). The building technique adopted here is typical of the late Romanesque buildings of Poland and, likewise, the relationship

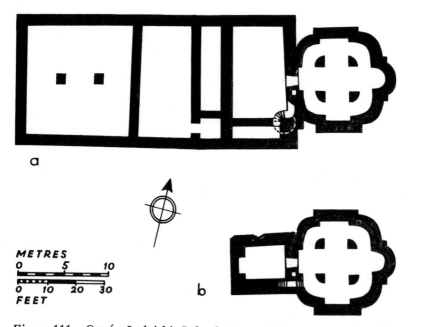

Figure 111   Ostrów Lednicki, Poland: Plan of the monumental buildings: (a) first phase: plan of the fortress chapel (first chapel) with the palace of A.D. 1038; (b) second phase: plan of the fortress chapel with tower. Late twelfth and thirteenth centuries A.D.

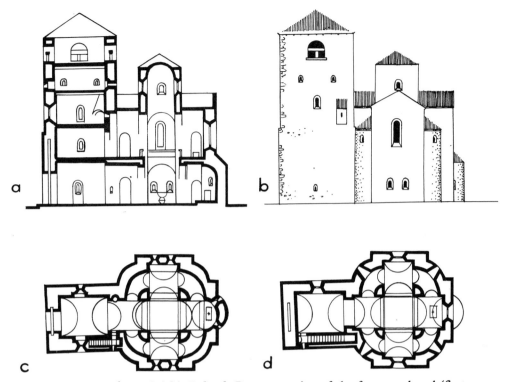

Figure 112 Ostrów Lednicki, Poland: Reconstruction of the fortress chapel (first chapel) with tower, during the second phase. Late twelfth and thirteenth centuries A.D. (a) elevation; (b) exterior, from the south side; (c) plan of the ground floor; (d) plan of the first storey

between tower and nave found here is met with in several private and fortress chapels and churches founded by members of the leading aristocratic families and by representatives of the state (castellans) in various places in Poland (for example, Prandocin, Żarnów, Inow Łódz and Strzelno) during the entire twelfth century.

The cause of the final destruction of this second phase of the fortress chapel and the tower belonging to it is not known in detail. It has been suggested that these buildings came to an end during a destructive raid by the Teutonic Knights in the year 1331. Perhaps even the second chapel lasted until this time.

What then is the historical significance of all this? As mentioned earlier, at least from 1235 to 1404 castellans, representatives of the princely or royal power, were active at this place. The destruction of the great fortress on the main island in the lake, new principles of fortification and changes in social and political conditions which made themselves felt in Poland during the first half of the thirteenth century (and to some extent even earlier), resulted in a much more modest seat of the princely administrator of the stewardship of Ostrów Lednicki, a tower on a hill, like a motte, being erected on the neighbouring, far smaller island of Ledniczka. The little island

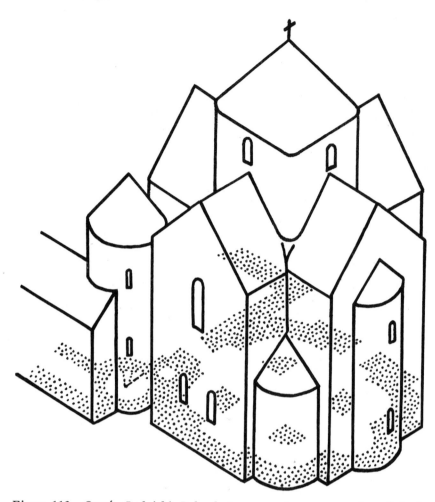

Figure 113   Ostrów Lednicki, Poland: Axonometric reconstruction of the fortress chapel (first chapel) with the small round tower at the crossing from the chapel to the palace; during the first phase, before A.D. 1038

lies between Ostrów Lednicki and the western shore of the lake, not quite 200 m south-west of Ostrów Lednicki. Here, on a level part of the island, measuring 150 × 110 m, rises a motte (that is, a stumpy earth mound) now 6 m high, with a flat, slightly indented, top 20 m across. It is surrounded by a ditch twelve paces wide. In the middle of the flat top was found a great rectangular hearth of stone and clay, surrounded by a great deal of iron military equipment and pottery typical of the late Middle Ages (second half of the thirteenth century to the fifteenth). There were also limited quantities of early medieval (tenth century to first half of the thirteenth century) and neolithic sherds. One may postulate, on the basis of better-known contemporary parallels, that a single large tower-like wooden building, or several smaller ones solidly fortified, stood here. The castellans who lived and carried out their duties here, members of a prominent noble family from the immediate vicinity, used the old fortress area on Ostrów Lednicki in the late, last phase when there was still activity here, mainly for religious purposes. The old fortress chapel was made use of by the castellans and members of their families and probably by the people still living in the 'suburbs' and by the serfs and retainers of the castellans, for normal religious services. It is highly likely that one may associate traces of occupation in the abandoned old fortress, near the first fortress chapel, which belong to the period after 1038 and reach into the late Middle Ages (and also probably the coin-hoard from the last quarter of the eleventh century) with the existence of dwelling-houses of the castellan, his helpers and servants, who lived in the immediate vicinity of the fortress chapel. It is extremely probable that the renovation of the fortress chapel, intended for normal religious services, and the building of a new tower to the chapel (perhaps for dwelling purposes) on Ostrów Lednicki, took place on the initiative of the castellans here and of their aristocratic kinsfolk. The same members of aristocratic families here, from whose ranks the castellans came, are probably to be regarded as the builders of the burial chapel (mausoleum) in the northern part of the fortress courtyard. Their dead, interred here, within and in close proximity to the burial chapel, were laid out in exact accordance with the east–west orientation of the chapel, on their back and with the head at the west.

It cannot be determined exactly when burial of the dead began on Ostrów Lednicki. The possibility cannot be excluded that some prominent persons were buried near the fortress chapel while the great old fortress and the palace were still in unimpaired existence, in other words before 1038, for similar customs are known at other great Slavonic fortresses of this period. But the official nature of the palace and the fortress courtyard, affording little space for the purpose and being intensively used, would probably have to a large extent hindered any interment within the fortress before its destruction. Isolated graves in which silver pfennigs from the turn of the tenth and eleventh centuries (for example, of Otto III, 983–1002) and other objects from the first decades of the eleventh century were found, can perfectly well belong to the period after 1038. Stratigraphical observations and the nature of the grave-goods demonstrate in very general terms that the courtyard of the Ostrów Lednicki fortress served as a graveyard for the entire 'ordinary' population settled on the islands of Ostrów Lednicki and Ledniczka and on both lake-shores, from the twelfth century up to the fifteenth century. It seems that the dead were buried on either side of a road that linked the old north gateway of the fortress ruins with the second chapel, the fortress chapel and the former south gateway of the fortress. The reason for this view is that a narrow strip free of graves can be observed running straight through the courtyard across an area thickly studded with burials. The layout of the dead took place south of the burial chapel, parallel to the long axis of the fortress chapel, in other words orientated west-south-west to east-south-east. When, in time, the fortress chapel together with the tower built on to it finally became a ruin, some bodies were even buried in the floor of the chapel tower. So far over 1,500 graves have been identified within the fortress walls.

It is not yet possible to determine precisely how long the 'suburbs' were inhabited. In general terms, one may say that the settlement probably did not last beyond the thirteenth century (with the possible exception of one or two farm-houses).

A few brief remarks may be added about some of the major small finds from Ostrów Lednicki. They include, from the area of the fortress, mainly in the immediate vicinity of the palace, a gold head-band, a piece of a golden three-cornered ornamental plate, with an interlaced motif in filigree (Plate XLVIa), a trapezoidal bronze *Kaptorge* with the representation of a stag, and a gilded bronze stud, with plant pattern decoration and with the leather remains of a liturgical book. These finds, taken together, because of their pronounced rarity in the context of material found anywhere in Poland, underline still further the significant role of Ostrów Lednicki at the turn of the tenth and eleventh centuries. Apart from these items, a fine decorated bone stave from a miniature cask, found in the 'suburbs', also deserves attention as an extremely rare object.

In conclusion the following must be said. One is still a long way from possessing a complete picture of medieval Ostrów Lednicki. More than half the fortress court-yard, the greater part of the ramparts, together with the north gate, almost the whole of the 'suburbs', more than nine-tenths of the bridge system and the adjacent lake-bottom, still await professional investigation. Nonetheless, on the basis of more than a century of research, it can already be stated that a place which was the scene – for a brief span to be sure but full of significance for all that – where central European history was played out, has finally been rescued from complete oblivion.

Notes

1   St Smolka, 'Über eine bisher unbenutzte Königsberger Handschrift des Chronicon Polono-Silesiacum', *Zeitschrift des Vereins für die Geschichte and Alterthümer Schlesiens*, XII, H. 1875, p. 454. *Scriptores rerum Silesiacarum*, ed. Sommersberg, 1724–32, ed. Stenzel, 1835.

2   Pertz, *Monum. Germ. SS.*, IV, p. 615.

3   Thietmar, *Chronicon*, L., III, p. 28.

4   J. Żak, *Importy skandynawskie na ziemiach zachodniosłowiańskich od IX do XI wieku (część analityczna)* Poznań, 1967), p. 336; A. Abramowicz, *Studia nad geneza polskiej kultury artystycznej (Studies on the Origin of Polish Artistic Culture)*, Łódź, 1962, pp. 89–90, notes 14–19.

5   R. Blomquist and A. W. Mårtensson, 'Thulegrävningen 1961', *Archaeologia Lundensia*, 2 (1963), p. 216, fig. 244; J. Żak, loc. cit., p. 333, n. 21, p. 336, n. 36. In the treasury of the cathedral at Prague is the so-called comb of St Adalbert, which provides an analogy for the example from Ostrów Lednicki and has received much attention in Czech publications, together with associated forms.

Bibliography

Łomnicki, J., *Ostrów Lednicki – Pomnik historii kultury narodu polskiego (Ostrów Lednicki – A monument of the cultural history of the Polish nation)*, Poznań, 1968 (with a summary in French), 46 pp., 47 figs.

Łomnicki, J. and Wasilewski, T., 'Ostrów Lednicki', *Słownik Starożytności Słowiańskich. (Dictionary of Slavonic Antiquities)*, Wrocław–Warsaw–Cracow, III, L-O, part 2, N-O, pp. 551–4, figs 253–5, Wrocław, 1968.

Mikołajczyk, C., 'Une résidence des Piastes sur l'île de Lednica (Ostrów Lednicki), distr. de Gniezno', *Archaeologica Polona VI* Wrocław–Warsaw–Cracow, 1964, pp. 219–31.

Nadolski, A., 'Wczesnośredniowieczne militaria zjezioi Lednickiego' ('The medieval military finds from Lake Lednica') (with a summary in English), *Poznańskie Studia Muzealne*, Poznań, 1966, pp. 7–18, 20 figs.

Sokołowski, M., 'Ruiny na Ostrowie jeziora Lednicy' ('The ruins on the Ostrów island of Lake Lednica'), *Pamiętnik Akademii Umiejętności, Wydziały Filologiczny i Historyczno-Filozoficzny*, III Cracow, 1876, pp. 116–277.

Acknowledgments

I would like to thank above all Professor Kazimierz Żurowski, Miss Gabriela Mikołajczyk, Mr Andrzej Nowak and Mrs Łucja Pawlicka-Nowak for the help which they have given me. Without their co-operation it would have been impossible to produce this article.